WARS I

WARS IN PEACE
British Military Operations since 1991

Edited by Adrian L Johnson

Contributions by
Malcolm Chalmers
Michael Clarke
Michael Codner
Robert Fry
David Omand
Joel Faulkner Rogers & Jonathan Eyal
Trevor Taylor, John Louth & Henrik Heidenkamp

Foreword by Lord Richards of Herstmonceux

Published in 2014 by Royal United Services Institute
for Defence and Security Studies (RUSI)
Whitehall, London SW1A 2ET, UK
www.rusi.org

Copyright © 2014 the authors

The moral right of each contributor to be identified as the author of his or her work has been asserted by the author in accordance with the Copyright Designs and Patent Act 1988.

All rights reserved. Except for brief quotations in a review, this book, or any part thereof, may not be reproduced, stored in or introduced into a retrieval system, or transmitted, in any form or by any means, electronic, mechanical, photocopying, recording or otherwise, without the prior written permission of the publisher.

ISBN 978-0-85516-193-4

ISBN (e-book) 978-0-85516-198-9

Printed and bound in Great Britain by Stephen Austin and Sons Ltd.

CONTENTS

Foreword *Lord Richards of Herstmonceux*	ix
Editor's Preface	xiii
List of Tables and Figures	xv
Acronyms and Abbreviations	xvii
Introduction Adrian L Johnson	1
I. Fighting for Peace, 1991–2001 Michael Codner	13
II. The Two Towers, 2001–2013 Michael Codner	49
III. The Strategic Scorecard: Six Out of Ten Malcolm Chalmers	89
IV. The Domestic Balance David Omand	137
V. Of Tails and Dogs: Public Support and Elite Opinion Joel Faulkner Rogers and Jonathan Eyal	161
VI. On the Offensive Malcolm Chalmers	191
VII. Strategy and Operations Robert Fry	215
VIII. Brothers in Arms: The British–American Alignment Michael Clarke	237

IX. The Sinews of War *Malcolm Chalmers*	267
X. Industry and the Military Instrument *Trevor Taylor, John Louth and Henrik Heidenkamp*	291
Conclusion *Michael Clarke*	321
Notes and References	335
Appendix	373
About the Authors	381

FOREWORD

ANYONE who has studied war, and better still had some experience of it as well, will vouchsafe the need to avoid it in the first place. But history is clear: there will sometimes be no alternative to standing up for oneself, for one's friends or for what is right. Too many people, the intelligentsia to the fore, are in denial of this inevitability. To explain weakness and cover fragility, forcing them shamefully to talk big but act small, so-called statesmen will repeat the mantra that there is no military solution to a given crisis. That this is errant rubbish is self-servingly ignored. It takes a lot of willpower, organisation, skill, money and, yes, passion, but a strategy with military power at its heart, whether to deter or to fight, may be the only answer and can work if that strategy is right. This does not necessarily require the massive use of force, but rather a calibrated employment of the military instrument combined with steadfast political commitment. History repeatedly shows that those who get this calculus wrong dangerously risk their bluff being called and the law of unintended consequences kicking in. In times of crisis, military strength is comfortingly reassuring.

So it is important to reflect on the full record of UK intervention, which began well before the 9/11 attacks. If the campaigns of Afghanistan and Iraq left their mark on how the British public and politicians view and use the military, then so did the interventions of Kosovo and Sierra Leone. This volume rightly judges that the most important step change in where and how the UK used force was not in 2001, but in 1991 – even if it is the wars of 9/11 that dominate current thinking.

There are of course vital lessons to be drawn from the campaigns of the last decade. Yet by stretching back to this earlier time, I would suggest that this volume does a service to the debate by highlighting some crucial campaigns where we got it right. The war against Iraq in 1991 successfully defended the international rule of non-aggression as one state sought to snuff out another. We didn't get it right in Bosnia at first, but in 1995 NATO action imposed a peace that, while not perfect, at least ensured that the country's political differences would not be settled by violence. In Kosovo, we acted in concert with our allies quickly to prevent a repeat of Bosnia. And in Sierra Leone I found myself in a unique position to make a decisive military intervention, with the requisite backing from Whitehall, to provide space and time for a renewed international and local effort to consolidate peace.

It is important also to be balanced. This may seem an obvious point, but with the benefit of hindsight it's easy to say the things we shouldn't have done, the choices that shouldn't have been made. In the field or in a ministry at the time, however, it's often less clear-cut. It is right, then, that this book unpicks the tough choices commanders and politicians had to make in difficult circumstances of uncertainty, pressure and risk. And I would add to this that it's important not to be overly self-critical. I have never shied away from pointing out what we were doing badly; but even in Afghanistan, where we did have to make some pretty fundamental changes to how we went about things, the armed forces have learnt a lot and our conduct of counter-insurgency has improved – and we leave the country in a lot better state than we found it.

Finally, it is important to be comprehensive. As ISAF commander in 2006, I experienced firsthand the particular constraints of operating in a multinational context where we – and I stress 'we', as this was a coalition endeavour – were ultimately at the mercy of the local political process and decisions made in other national capitals.

We may lament that in Whitehall, politicians may have failed to understand what strategy is about – some think that just working at a strategic level, the top level, is being strategic in itself. But strategy is about how the whole machinery of government performs, at home and abroad. We may also lament the mistakes the military made on the ground and the time it took us to adapt our approach most effectively. These are all fair points, but the UK was not alone in these interventions. It worked with allies – and was in most cases a junior partner to the US – and was embedded in an international environment it could not control. The value of this book is in tying together all these various strands – local, strategic and operational – that are all absolutely critical to understanding how better to go about military operations in the future, as much as they are in delivering a historical verdict on interventions of the past.

Looking ahead to the sorts of operations the military might be called upon to make in the future, they are unlikely to be much different from the sorts of wars of the last quarter-century. Events in Ukraine at the time of going to press do remind us of the risk of war between states, even today: the threat of conventional war has not disappeared. But most wars, I would wager, are likely to be 'small wars' between ill-defined, often non-state opponents. And these wars may not be over territory, but over ideas and symbols, and among rather than between peoples. Moreover, our wars will be fought with others and not by ourselves. The UK has had it as policy for many years now that, though we may conduct some operations independently, we will not go to war on our own – even if we still have yet to fully come to terms with what this means for us in terms of institutional constraints. One of the key lessons – or charges, rather – may be to work out how we ensure unity of effort in future multinational operations, even if unity of multinational command may be beyond us.

We may not be able to pick our battlefields in the future. But even so, we will need a careful approach to intervention and commit sufficient resources to realistic tasks. If we are going to intervene, do it properly; otherwise we risk only aggravating the situation. This goes beyond just the military. Over a decade of recent operations countering insurgency have taught us that considerable advances in technology and military firepower are, by themselves, not enough. The military cannot win the war by itself, but only hold the ring enabling the locals to make the right decisions about their own future. At the same time, the civilian effort is primary. The military effort in Afghanistan in 2001 was not matched by a civilian one in 2002 and 2003, and we paid the price later. And in 2006, while many countries were focusing on military efforts, there was no reliable system to cohere the civilian and diplomatic engagement. I, a military commander, found myself having to devise one. This kind of failure could be the signal lesson of the last quarter-century.

Whatever the mistakes that have been made, we must not over-learn from our experiences. The international community took from Somalia in 1993 a phobia of intervention that would come at a terrible cost to the people of Rwanda a year later. Conversely, the success of Kosovo perhaps suggested to some leaders too optimistic a notion of what military force could achieve in transforming societies. We have to be realistic. While the military may have less than it would wish, it will still be required to protect this nation's broad interests through the projection of military force. When lethal force is genuinely required, nothing else will do. The world today is not a safer place and the distinction between home and abroad is strategically obsolete. The lessons contained within this volume will therefore be of continuing importance: they should be learnt.

I commend this book for its perceptive analysis of British military operations over a remarkable period. It avoids both undue pessimism and triumphalism to give a comprehensive and balanced verdict on intervention. Let us hope that its reasoning and findings will be digested by the political and military leaders of tomorrow in a dangerous world.

Lord Richards of Herstmonceux
Chief of the Defence Staff, 2010–13
March 2014

EDITOR'S PREFACE

The idea for this book emerged from a RUSI investigation, published in 2011, into the UK's decision to commit to military operations in Helmand Province in 2006. In his contribution to that edited monograph (*The Afghan Papers*), Sir Robert Fry suggested that a fuller audit of British military operations in the region was necessary.

The scope of the project grew into a wider and deeper analysis of British military intervention since the end of the Cold War. It began in January 2012 with a series of workshops and roundtables at RUSI that built up to the conference 'Wars in Peace: Twenty Years of British Military Intervention', held on 9 October 2013. This presented the findings of the various contributors and hosted an informed and lively debate on British operations since 1991. This book is the culmination of that process. We intend it to be a defining contribution in a vital national – and international – debate.

A think tank such as RUSI derives its value from being a hub of thinkers and practitioners, and as such there are innumerable people to thank for the insights they provided to the volume's authors during the research process. In particular, however, the editor would like to thank the workshop and conference participants and the others who provided assistance along the way: Nick Beadle, Desmond Bowen, Sir Brian Burridge, Lord Richards, Charlie Edwards, Beatrice Heuser, Saqeb Mueen, Peter Quentin, Paul Schulte, Daniel Sherman, Ron Smith, James de Waal and Chris Wilson. And, of course, huge appreciation is due to all the authors of this volume for the time and care they have given in the writing and revision of their chapters.

Most of all, the editor pays the greatest thanks to his editorial team at RUSI – Ashlee Godwin, Cathy Haenlein and Dr Emma de Angelis – who, despite their Sisyphean workloads, lent their extensive talents to the shaping and sharpening of the text with their usual good cheer and superlative ability.

LIST OF TABLES AND FIGURES

British Ground-Troop Commitments to Major Interventions, 1991–2001. 48

British Ground-Troop Commitments to Iraq/Operation *Telic*, 2003–10 (Approximate Annual Peak Figures). 62

British Ground-Troop Commitments to Afghanistan, 2001–13 (Approximate Annual Peak Figures). 68

Scorecard for Intervention. 90

Opium Cultivation in Helmand Province (hectares). 116

'Could you tell me for each of the following whether you support the use of British forces or not?' 163

'Do you approve or disapprove of the use of British troops in Bosnia to protect humanitarian convoys?' 165

'If an international force were trying to enforce a peace settlement in Bosnia, would you personally like to see British troops forming part of that force or not?' 165

'On balance, do you believe that Britain is right or wrong to have joined in the NATO bombing of Yugoslavia?' 168

'Should British troops be brought back home from Afghanistan?' 172

'Do you think the US/Britain are/were right or wrong to take military action against Iraq?' 174

Attitudes to Intervention in Iraq (2003) and Libya (2011) Compared. 177

'Thinking about the conflict in Syria, here are some things Britain could do. Would you support sending...' 179

YouGov/RUSI Study on Support for Action [in Syria] with/without the UN. 181

Answer Options for Survey 1 on Parliamentary Oversight. 183

Answer Options for Survey 2 on Parliamentary Oversight. 184

'How do you think the following type of action should be decided?' 185

'In your view, how important or unimportant are the following activities in serving the United Kingdom's national interests?' 188

Significant Military Interventions by the US and UK, 1989–2014. 245

Summary of Net Additional Costs of Military Operations (2012/13 prices). 268

Alliance Contributions Compared, Iraq and Afghanistan (Peak Levels of Military Personnel). 283

Alliance Contributions Compared, Iraq and Afghanistan (Total Fatalities). 283

Comparing the Financial Costs of Military Operations, UK and US. 284

Estimating the Financial Costs of Caring for Veterans of Iraq and Afghanistan, UK and US. 285

Net Additional Costs of Military Operations in Cash and Real Terms, 1990/91–2012/13. 289

Examples of Modifications to UOR Equipment. 306

Estimates of the Additional Costs of the Kosovo Operation 1998/99–2002/03. 311

British Military Fatalities by Service on Selected Operations, 1991–2012. 374

Net Additional Cost of Military Operations, 1991–2013, £ millions, 2012/13 prices. 375

ACRONYMS AND ABBREVIATIONS

ACE	Allied Command Europe
AFISMA	International Support Mission to Mali
AFRICOM	US Africa Command
APT(N)	Atlantic Patrol Task (North)
AQAP	Al-Qa'ida in the Arabian Peninsula
ARRC	Allied Rapid Reaction Corps
ASTOR	Airborne stand-off radar
AU	African Union
AWACS	Airborne warning and control system
C2	Command and control
C4ISTAR	Command, control, communications, computers, intelligence, surveillance, target acquisition and reconnaissance
CBRN	Chemical, biological, radiological and nuclear
CCRF	Civil Contingency Reaction Forces
CIA	Central Intelligence Agency
CIS	Communication and Information Systems
CJO	Chief of Joint Operations
COBR	Cabinet Office Briefing Room
COIN	Counter-insurgency
CONDO	Contractors on deployed operations
CSO	Contractor support to operations
DCDC	Development, Concepts and Doctrine Centre
DDR	Disarmament, demobilisation and reintegration
DE&S	Defence Equipment and Support Organisation
DfID	Department for International Development
DoD	Department of Defense
DRC	Democratic Republic of the Congo
DSG	Defence Support Group
DVA	Department of Veterans Affairs
EBAO	Effects-based approach to operations

EBO	Effects-based operations
EC	European Community
ECOMOG	ECOWAS Monitoring Group
ECOWAS	Economic Community of West African States
ESS	Equipment Sustainability System
EU	European Union
FATA	Federally Administered Tribal Areas
FBI	Federal Bureau of Investigation
FOFA	Follow-on forces attack
G8	Group of Eight
GCHQ	Government Communications Headquarters
GDP	Gross Domestic Product
GNI	Gross National Income
IED	Improvised explosive device
IFF	Identification, friend or foe
IFOR	Implementation Force
IMS	Integrated Military Structure
INTERFET	International Force for East Timor
IRA	Irish Republican Army
ISAF	International Security Assistance Force
ISI	Inter-Services Intelligence
ISP	Infrastructure Support Provider
JAM	Jaish Al-Madhi
JIC	Joint Intelligence Committee
JRDF	Joint Rapid Deployment Force
JRRF	Joint Rapid Reaction Force
KFOR	Kosovo Force
KLA	Kosovo Liberation Army
LRA	Lord's Resistance Army
MACC	Military aid to the civil community
MACP	Military aid to the civil power
MAGD	Military aid to government departments
MI5	Security Service
MI6	Secret Intelligence Service
MINUSMA	UN Multidimensional Integrated Stabilization Mission in Mali
MoD	Ministry of Defence
NACMO	Net Additional Cost of Military Operations
NAO	National Audit Office
NATO	North Atlantic Treaty Organization
NCW	Network-centric warfare
NEC	Network-enabled warfare
NGO	Non-governmental organisation
NHS	National Health Service

NSA	National Security Agency
OECD	Organisation for Economic Co-operation and Development
OEF	Operation *Enduring Freedom*
OIF	Operation *Iraqi Freedom*
PJHQ	Permanent Joint Headquarters
PRT	Provincial Reconstruction Team
QRA	Quick Reaction Alert
RAF	Royal Air Force
RFA	Royal Fleet Auxiliary
RFTG	Response Force Task Group
RMA	Revolution in military affairs
RRF	Rapid Reaction Force
RUF	Revolutionary United Front
SACEUR	Supreme Allied Commander Europe
SAS	Special Air Service
SBS	Special Boat Service
SDR	Strategic Defence Review
SDSR	Strategic Defence and Security Review
SFOR	Stabilization Force
TIALD	Thermal Imaging Airborne Laser Designator
UKMCC	UK Maritime Component Commander
UNAMET	UN Mission in East Timor
UNAMSIL	UN Mission in Sierra Leone
UNHCR	UN High Commissioner for Refugees
UNOMSIL	UN Observer Mission in Sierra Leone
UNPROFOR	UN Protection Force
UOR	Urgent Operational Requirement
USAF	US Air Force
WMD	Weapons of mass destruction

INTRODUCTION

Adrian L Johnson

SINCE 1990, the UK has undertaken a series of significant foreign military interventions of varying success in Iraq, Bosnia, Kosovo, Sierra Leone, Afghanistan and Libya. Alongside these were operations in Northern Ireland and various other smaller missions abroad. At the time of writing, 782 British servicemen and women had died on these operations.

Every unhappy era is unhappy in its own way. It is commonly said that while the Cold War was a time of great threat, there was at least an element of predictability and certainty to it. By contrast, the following quarter-century has been characterised by a fluid and unpredictable security environment, albeit one absent any major and direct threat to the UK. With its armed forces no longer necessary as a bulwark against Warsaw Pact aggression in Europe, they were increasingly used in a series of more-or-less discretionary commitments.

This period may be a unique one in British history, categorically different from its days as either a concert power or a Cold War superpower's ally. The UK's continuing global influence and wealth offered it an opportunity to help mould, though not determine, the shape of the post-Cold War world order as a partner to the sole remaining superpower. At the same time, a second 'Belle Époque' marked by the further breaking down of barriers to trade and capital, and the inexorable spread of modern communications technologies, seemed to confirm the dominance of a liberal order. Yet challenges to this new order swiftly emerged. First, the attempted annexation of Kuwait by Iraq; then the collapse of Yugoslavia and spike in the number of civil wars worldwide; and then, perhaps most traumatically for the US, the rise of globalised terrorism showcased by the 9/11 attacks.

Throughout this period, the UK has been willing to threaten and use force in pursuit of a broad conception of the national interest. Few other states – perhaps only the US and France – have taken such a role since 1991. As the UK takes pause after years of costly and bloody campaigning in Iraq and Afghanistan, it must consider the lessons of over twenty years of a robust interventionist posture.

An Era of British Exceptionalism
While the problems the UK faced in this environment of uncertainty were not unique to it, its responses were. Its military was the second-most capable in the West after that of the US, and one of only three, with the French, able to undertake major expeditionary operations. While both the UK and France have been militarily active powers – the latter having intervened with regularity in African conflicts, for example – the UK has undertaken the larger operations in the period, and has done so in close concert with the US. France and the UK are themselves different to other rich and globally influential countries – like Germany, Canada and Sweden – whose resort to the military instrument is far more modest, or absent altogether. Likewise, France and the UK are in a different category to other regional powers such as Japan, Brazil or South Africa, which cannot or choose not to develop global power-projection capabilities.

Since the Second World War, even as it shed its imperial ambitions, the UK has endeavoured to 'punch above its weight'. Post 1991, this has manifested itself in an attempt to retain full-spectrum military capabilities – the ability to fight at all levels of intensity, against a range of foes, with top-tier technology and training – linked closely to extensive diplomatic influence and developmental aid and expertise. Underlying these capabilities has also been a heightened sense of responsibility: the *willingness* to play an active role in international affairs beyond a narrow definition of 'the national interest'.

Britain's wealth has underpinned this ambition. The UK remained a rich economy during this period: in terms of real GDP at purchasing power parity, it entered the period as the world's sixth-largest economy and finished it – in the aftermath of the global economic crisis of the late 2000s – as the eighth-largest, one of only nine larger than $2 trillion in size.[1] And, as an indication of the internationalist posture of successive governments in this period, the country has spent substantial sums on diplomacy and development. In particular, since 1997 the UK's spending on overseas development assistance, as measured by OECD criteria, has overtaken that of Germany and France, making it the biggest donor state after the US, due to an increase from $4.56 billion in 1991 to $13.76 billion in 2012 (in 2011 dollars), a proportion of just under 0.6 per cent of GNI.[2] Added to this is the diplomatic clout provided by a permanent seat on the UN Security Council.

And, with this wealth, the UK has chosen to invest in military capability. Even with the post-Cold War peace dividend, the UK remained in the top tier of defence spending. According to SIPRI figures,[3] in 1991, the UK had the fourth-largest defence budget ($49.9 billion), behind only the US ($397 billion), France ($61.5 billion) and Germany ($60.2 billion) (all in 2012 dollars). In 2012, the UK was still fourth globally, with a defence budget of $60 billion. While this figure was lower than that of the US ($682.4 billion), China ($166.1 billion) and Russia ($90.8 billion), it had now surpassed its continental peers France ($58.9 billion) and Germany ($45.8 billion). It has retained this position despite relative economic decline.

But defence spending itself is no guarantee of capability, as quips about certain European militaries being little more than 'unusually well-armed pension funds' cruelly highlight.[4] In this regard, the UK has excelled, unlike most of its European peers, investing heavily in the platforms and enablers vital to a global reach and to retaining a military capable of activity across a relatively wide (though not full) spectrum.

Indeed, the UK has maintained one of the largest equipment budgets in European NATO, both in absolute and relative terms.[5]

So, in one sense, the UK's position as the second military power in the West is more secure now in 2014 than it was in 1990, to a degree but not simply because of the continuing reluctance of Germany to be as militarily active as the UK and France.

Set against this inherent, robust internationalism and the UK's natural strengths, however, are the revealed limits of military intervention.

Much of the UK's global influence has been sought through a close, grand-strategic alignment with the US: a longstanding assumption that, by being relevant to American decision-makers, the UK could in some way steer American policy. This may have invited British politicians and generals to overextend their commitment to discretionary interventions beyond what domestic political will would support or, indeed, what the British military instrument could achieve. This was most starkly shown during the Iraq 'surge' of 2007: while the US piled in troops to arrest the civil war, the UK was withdrawing from Basra (albeit in part to focus on revived operations in Afghanistan).

The seduction of technique – the idea that superior military equipment, training and conduct would suffice in generating *political* victory – was cruelly exposed as stunning 'victories' in Afghanistan and Iraq unravelled (and by growing signs that Libya still might). These examples therefore highlight the limits of transformation: in the UK's wars from 1991, those in support of agendas seeking to remake societies have been the least successful. Rory Stewart notes in *Can Intervention Work?* that this may be an inherent limit of 'over-intervention' in which failure to appreciate local context and political reality is the 'product of an entire culture.'[6] Even the relatively successful examples of Bosnia, Kosovo and Sierra Leone demonstrate how transformation and peace-building are difficult, long-term endeavours; security, which can be provided by the military, is a vital ingredient – but so is economic and political development, which cannot.⁷ And these limits do not just apply to the military agenda; what the developmental and diplomatic levers of state power can achieve is also questionable in remaking societies.

It may be that certain ends are simply too ambitious, too improbable to achieve. This may become even more pertinent in the future; for a great deal of UK action has taken place in coalitions in which the US was a vital player, providing high-end capability, essential logistics and political backing. But as Michael Clarke argues in this book, British-American strategic divergence since 2003 may indicate 'trends that are not cyclical and which, if anything, will have a cumulative effect on the relationship for both military and political reasons'. The UK may find it more difficult to rely on the US as a key partner in the future. And without the means that the US provides, the UK's and other allies' political objectives may in a future crisis be even more difficult to achieve.

Nevertheless, the UK has been the most effective in interventions where it has been able to combine its unique advantages of military power with its diplomatic and developmental tools, and in mobilising a multinational coalition or international attention more generally. The 'Strategic Scorecard' chapter by Malcolm Chalmers (Chapter III) bears this out; the more clearly focused interventions – in terms of aims – with the broadest multilateral backing have achieved the greatest degree of success.

Looking at the record in this book, the interventions in Iraq in 1991 and Sierra Leone in 2000 may be the exemplars of success, each in a different way. In the Gulf War (an inter-state conflict), a broad UN-authorised coalition with strong US military leadership generated a preponderance of force for a focused, militarily achievable goal in defence of the universally ascribed norm of non-aggression. Hindsight may also reveal the wisdom of *not* pushing onto Baghdad and instead retaining the limited goals of the intervention. In Sierra Leone (an intra-state conflict), a judicious use of force in support of a legitimate government and a UN peace operation halted the rebel advance; but alongside this, the UK thereafter also focused international attention on the Sierra Leonean disarmament, demobilisation and reintegration programme for former combatants, as well as addressing the regional sources of support for the Revolutionary United Front rebels.

The question over the appropriate use of the military instrument in foreign policy and grand strategy remains important even as the armed forces shrink to their smallest size since the nineteenth century; and although the interventionist urge may have been tempered, it has not been eliminated. As such, the lessons of this book, drawn from the wider post-Cold War interventionist period, will remain enduring.

A Wider Debate
There has been a recent flowering of analysis on the use of British military power and its outcomes, particularly with a growing perception of defeat in Iraq and Afghanistan.

At the level of troops-on-the-ground, the UK's wars post 9/11 have severely tested assumptions of its competence in counter-insurgency and the ability of its institutions to adapt to unconventional conflicts. Journalistic works, giving a worm's-eye view of combat, have shed important light on the conduct of British campaigns. *A Million Bullets*, for example, highlights an overambitious plan for Helmand accompanied by a disconnect between military and civilian efforts in a campaign marked by little unity of effort, particularly in its vital early stages.[8] In *Six Months Without Sundays*, one officer quips to the author about the continuing gap: 'It would be wrong to say we have a bad relationship with the PRT, because we don't have a relationship with the PRT.'[9]

Frank Ledwidge in *Losing Small Wars* takes a broader perspective, yet also concludes that 'The form of "expeditionary warfare" on which Britain's armed forces staked their future has proved to be beyond their commanders' capabilities.'[10] David H Ucko and Robert Egnell, in an authoritative analysis of British counter-insurgency in Iraq and Afghanistan, show how the roots of failure of these campaigns lay not only in the performance of the military, but also in their resourcing and strategic direction.[11] A failure of adaptation from Cold War military structures has, in their view, also undermined British performance.[12] Ledwidge's critique is perhaps most damning of all: it was not just the politicians that erred; it was also the senior command of the military, none of whom ever resigned.[13]

The question of strategic coherence – the matching of ends, ways and means from the highest-level of decision-making downwards – has dominated much of the literature.[14] Some works, like that of Rory Stewart and Gerald Knaus, focus on the fundamental limitations of open-ended nation-building – where the ends outstrip both the means and the ability to understand a local context. They argue that the chief lesson of international intervention is therefore the need to adopt a policy of 'principled incrementalism'.[15] Others offer a more focused examination of the British experience. In his memoirs of his time in Afghanistan, former ambassador Sherard Cowper-Coles criticises the lack of a comprehensive political settlement in Afghanistan, which made irrelevant many of the tactical successes of the campaign; he also notes the limits of counter-insurgency technique in actually delivering peace.[16] Sandy Gall, meanwhile, argues that what went wrong in Afghanistan can be summed up simply as 'Iraq': specifically, the diversion of effort and inability of the UK to fight effectively in two theatres.[17] In *British Generals in Blair's Wars*, Jonathan Bailey argues that the problem was much deeper; that 'a chasm grew between emerging foreign policy goals, the size and focus of the defence budget, and actual military planning.'[18] Hew Strachan notes that, after 9/11, the UK subordinated itself to an American strategy that, itself, was deeply flawed.[19] Both the US and the UK have fought limited wars with the rhetoric of major war since 2001; yet they 'have not willed the means to wage them.'[20]

In the widely discussed *War from the Ground Up*, Emile Simpson suggests that the strategic mismatch emerges from the very nature of contemporary warfare. Drawing on the Afghan experience, he posits a distinction between operations intended to establish military conditions for a political solution and those that directly seek political outcomes.[21] Simpson argues that the trend in the modern world is away from the former; fewer operations will provide a decisive result for a sequenced transition from war to peace. This will present Western forces with an uncomfortable dilemma: limit engagement to conflicts where the conventional use of force offers a decisive outcome, or engage in more messy conflicts that depart from a 'traditional' conception of war, being in essence 'armed politics'.

Recent works have also shed light on the personal and institutional processes that may have complicated the generation of coherent strategy and operational designs in these messy conflicts. RUSI's *The Afghan Papers* concludes that the army's move into Helmand in 2006 revealed that the British political system was simply unable to cope with two major deployments at once; 'the system as a whole seemed to have no strategic brain.'[22] Patrick Porter identifies an 'intellectual vacuum' in British statecraft in which 'little ranking or prioritisation' is done; tough choices, therefore, are avoided.[23] Paul Newton, Paul Colley and Andrew Sharpe argue that the UK has 'let slip both the mechanisms and more importantly the grammar with which to conduct the relevant strategic discourse within and around defence'.[24] James de Waal's work on British civil–military relations challenges the notion that individual personalities were the drivers of strategic failure: in his analysis, due to the design of the British political system, 'tensions in the political-military relationship are a perennial part of defence policy-making'.[25] The remedy, therefore, may lie in institutional reform and commonly understood frameworks, rather than hoping for the right kind of people in positions of power and command.

In sum, the tenor of these and other works is negative. The UK failed strategically and operationally in two of the most important interventions of the decade; worse, some argue that the roots of failure were in fact sown in a moment of success; the Kosovo War encouraging hubris at the highest levels.

The Purpose and Structure of the Book

This narrative may obscure some of the important successes of British military operations in the post-Cold War period. To contribute to this debate, *Wars in Peace* goes further than these recent works to consider not just the wars of 9/11 since 2001, or 'Blair's wars' since 1999, but the longer trajectory of intervention and the operational, domestic and international context in which it took place. The Iraq and Afghanistan campaigns are not discrete data points: they were the result of a particular configuration of international power and norms, as well as political and military currents at home. While it may be easy to see these campaigns as aberrations, born of a particular US administration's response to 9/11, this volume suggests that they are best analysed in a wider post-Cold War context.

In this spirit, *Wars in Peace* comprehensively audits the UK's use of the military instrument over this period: what it cost, what it achieved, and how it was conducted. Some of the themes in the book are cross-cutting and are tied together in the book's conclusion, which presents an overall verdict on the period. It spans political, economic, operational and strategic analysis to present a full appraisal of almost a quarter-century of British military operations.

Michael Codner provides a concise historical narrative of the era to set the scene in his chapters 'Fighting for Peace' and 'The Two Towers' (Chapters I and II). He also considers the evolution of British military thought and practice: what the military was for; how it went about its tasks; and, more broadly, how it attempted to keep up with a US military whose capabilities continued to further outstrip those of its European allies.

In 'The Strategic Scorecard' (Chapter III), Malcolm Chalmers develops a framework to judge the impact of the UK's wars abroad. Ten major interventions since 1991 are grouped under three main headings, reflecting the country's ambitions to be, respectively, a 'force for order', a 'force for good', and a 'force for change'. All ten are then analysed using several different criteria and are ultimately judged by whether they generated a positive strategic outcome for the UK, in terms of these three objectives.

David Omand assesses the contribution to security at home in 'The Domestic Balance' (Chapter IV). A broad-ranging analysis begins with the military experience in Northern Ireland since 1991, before discussing the panoply of tasks the military is charged with *vis-à-vis* the homeland. His chapter considers the overlap between domestic security and operations abroad, concluding that, on balance, the UK may be considered safer today than on the eve of 9/11.

Also on the domestic theme, in 'Of Tails and Dogs' (Chapter V), Joel Faulkner Rogers and Jonathan Eyal measure, through historical data and recent polling, British public support for intervention and how this has interacted – sometimes uneasily – with elite opinion. They also consider what current polling may indicate about the future use of British military power, including the appropriate role of Parliament in its authorisation, in the aftermath of the Syria vote.

In 'On the Offensive' (Chapter VI), Malcolm Chalmers discusses the confluence of factors that permitted the UK to go on what he terms a 'strategic offensive' since 1991. He suggests that this was a marked switch from the predominantly defensive character of the military's role during the Cold War, and discusses the degree to which the abatement of great-power competition helped to create the conditions that made this possible.

Within this context, Robert Fry in 'Strategy and Operations' (Chapter VII) dissects the broad sweep of British strategy over the era and its interface with operations on the ground. The wars of 9/11 revealed the limits of British power and strategy-making. Ends, ways and means were not suitably balanced, with predictable results on the ground. But more fundamentally, the UK has been unable to exert a strategic effect in theatre, heavily subordinate in both Iraq and Afghanistan to the leadership and commitment of the US.

Sharpening the focus of the strategic analysis is Michael Clarke's chapter, 'Brothers in Arms' (Chapter VIII), which places the British–American relationship of the last quarter-century in its fuller historical context before analysing the strategic and operational 'special relationship' between the US and the UK in the wars since 1991. It further considers what the latter-day campaigns in Iraq and Afghanistan – if not the wars before them – may tell us about the next evolution of this defining alliance.

Material questions of cost and industry are raised in the next two chapters. In 'The Sinews of War' (Chapter IX), Malcolm Chalmers calculates the financial cost to the UK of its ten major military operations since 1991, and also the impact of its wider defence posture on its level of spending. He finds the net additional cost (above the defence budget) of the country's military operations to have been £34.77 billion from 1991, with a possible £6–7 billion of additional medical and welfare costs. However, the overall cost of the UK's activist military posture, and associated expeditionary capabilities well above the European norm, may have added another £100 billion to the baseline over the period.

Finally, Trevor Taylor, John Louth and Henrik Heidenkamp audit the industrial contribution to intervention in 'Industry and the Military Instrument' (Chapter X). The private sector has played an increasingly important role in sustaining British expeditionary operations in the period characterised by a need for assured access to key capabilities in wars not fought on a 'come as you are' basis – a notable difference from the Cold War, and likely to remain the case for some time.

Wars in a Time of Peace

The irony of the period may be that while the UK faced no direct military threat to the homeland in an era free of great-power conflict, it engaged in a string of major military actions. In a very real sense, these have been wars in peace.

In a fully comprehensive audit, this book ties together the martial, political, economic and industrial facets of the military instrument. And while it considers the strategic success of each intervention for the UK – in particular, whether its people and interests were safer as a result – it also analyses the outcomes for the countries in which the UK has intervened to determine whether a reasonable course of action was taken, and if there were better alternatives at the time. In doing so, it highlights the difficult choices of intervention, where outcomes are not assured and inaction also carries risks. But difficult choices do not necessarily lead to failure, and where the UK has matched ambition and resources with effective use of the military instrument, strategic success has been achieved.

Decisions over whether or how to intervene may arise again sooner rather than later. While the rationale of the book is to examine the lessons of intervention for the UK as it looks beyond Afghanistan and the next defence review of 2015, its findings will also be of interest to those who study activist powers and the context of intervention more generally.

Intervention is an inherently difficult and risky undertaking. Policy-makers, analysts and the public should not be glib: it is difficult to tell *a priori* whether a conflict is amenable to the use of force and whether a political solution is feasible. Excessive caution can mean inaction – which also has consequences.

Fundamentally, the question over the appropriate use of the military instrument in foreign policy and grand strategy remains important even as the armed forces, and the perhaps the interventionist urge too, shrink. We hope the lessons of *Wars in Peace* will provide a useful handrail for current and future decision-makers as they consider the tough choices and dilemmas to come.

I. FIGHTING FOR PEACE, 1991–2001

Michael Codner

FOLLOWING the fall of the Berlin Wall in 1989, the disintegration of the Soviet Union in 1991 is considered to be the formal end of the Cold War. Over the decade prior to this, the 1981 defence White Paper known as the Nott Review had formed the basis of defence policy in the UK. Its conclusions – which were to increase the focus of government spending and military capabilities on the defence of Northern Europe at the expense of 'out-of-area' operations beyond those detailed in Article VI of the Washington Treaty – were challenged by the demands of the 1982 Falklands War. Yet while some adjustments to capabilities were made as a result of this war, the priorities remained the strategic nuclear deterrent (including confirmation of the decision to purchase the Trident system from the US); defence of UK home territory (including Northern Ireland); and contribution to the defence of the North Atlantic and Northern Europe at the expense of out-of-area operations. Specifically, British military strategy was to remain aligned with the robust NATO strategic concept of flexible response and forward defence, with the emphasis on NATO reflecting a Soviet military build-up in the early 1980s. (It bears mention that, in 1984, the Doomsday Clock of the Bulletin of Atomic Scientists reached three minutes to midnight. This was the most threatening level since 1953, and it reflected the 'competitive strategies' of the Reagan administration in the US and the Soviet response.)

While the Falklands War was neither catalytic in changing the direction of British defence policy nor in prompting further expeditionary operations over the course of the 1980s, it was a turning point in terms of both national self-esteem and respect for the armed forces and their role in supporting the UK's interests and world influence. It heralded the rebirth of an expeditionary disposition and redressed the public perception, since the process of withdrawal from east of Suez in the late 1960s, of the British military as composed of an army engaged in gendarmerie operations in Northern Ireland and sitting on its backside in Germany; a navy hosting cocktail parties and basking in the West Indies as principal instruments of the UK's global presence; and an air force whose dominant purpose was the defence of domestic and northern German airspace.

Northern Ireland did indeed place great demands on the army, and came at the expense of training and exercising for defensive, high-intensity land operations in Germany. British Army troop numbers in Northern Ireland increased from 17,430 in 1989 to 19,500 in 1994, reducing after the 1998 Good Friday Agreement to 13,500 in 2000.[1] In the 1990s, the British mainland also became more of a target for Provisional IRA terrorist attacks. After very occasional high-profile attacks in the previous decade (such as the Brighton bombing of 1984), there were some forty attacks and known failed bombings between 1991 and late 1997, after which the ceasefires in advance of the Good Friday Agreement were generally honoured. Yet while the needs of Northern Ireland and domestic security in relation to Irish forms of terrorism and insurgency continued through much of the 1990s – reinforcing the British Army's reputation for expertise in dealing with complex emergencies born of imperial policing – these assumed competences were to be severely tested in the following decades.

In the NATO context, the US Maritime Strategy that reached its zenith in the 1980s and the land-air concept of Follow-on forces attack (FOFA) led to an increasing emphasis on operational planning.[2]

There was a US-led rebirth in the 'manoeuvrist approach' in Western land doctrine and the British Army was a leading advocate. Needless to say, the Soviet Union had perpetuated its own interpretation since its experience of the Second World War. Manoeuvrism had a strong literal and physical element in the latter stages of the Cold War and, come the 1990s, the demands of complex emergencies and, in particular, the absence of defined front lines and uncertainties about who had been, was and might yet become the 'enemy' led to a more figurative interpretation of the concept.

As the Cold War ended, the British government conducted the 1990 'Options for Change' defence review. This took place very much behind closed doors, without the government-initiated discussion in the public domain that characterised the later 1998 Strategic Defence Review (SDR). The priority was to cut defence spending to apply the so-called peace dividend. As officials acknowledged, at the time and subsequently, the UK had entered a period of great uncertainty with regard to both the emerging security environment and future strategic priorities. In particular, a peaceful transition in Eastern Europe following the break-up of the Soviet Union and Warsaw Pact was not a given, as events in the Balkans subsequently showed. Europe remained a priority and 'Options for Change' retained the UK's contribution to NATO as the driver for force development and planning. However, British defence policy also evolved incrementally during the 1990s in favour of an expeditionary focus, as an 'arc of instability' on the perimeter of Europe, running from North Africa through the Middle East and the Gulf to Iran and Pakistan, featured increasingly in NATO and national government papers.[3]

A particular concern of the UK at the beginning of the 1990s was to maintain the US's military presence and engagement in the security of Europe. The UK had begun withdrawing forces from Germany and one factor constraining the process was to encourage the retention of US forces there. The UK was also very active in the reform of NATO's command and force structures. In 1992, the UK assumed command of, and 'framework nation' status for, the new Allied Command Europe Rapid Reaction Corps (ARRC). A new Allied Command North West was also established at High Wycombe in 1994.

The First Gulf War, 1990–91

The invasion of Kuwait by Iraqi forces on 2 August 1990 was widely condemned internationally, and by Arab governments in particular.[4] The US administration under George H W Bush insisted on a complete withdrawal of Iraqi forces from Kuwait, without preconditions. Significantly, the Soviet Union under Mikhail Gorbachev backed the subsequent string of UN Security Council resolutions, demanding withdrawal (Resolution 660), and imposing and enforcing extremely robust economic sanctions (Resolutions 661 and 665, respectively), including the termination of international sales of Iraq's and Kuwait's oil.

An immediate concern – fuelled by his own rhetoric – that Saddam Hussein might invade Saudi Arabia provoked the deployment of the first US ground and air forces to Saudi Arabia – the beginning of Operation *Desert Shield* – in addition to naval and air forces for sanctions enforcement and blockade. On 8 November, Bush announced a doubling of the numbers of US troops on the ground in preparation for a potential military offensive to liberate Kuwait. On 29 November, the Security Council adopted Resolution 678, requiring Iraq to withdraw from Kuwait by 15 January 1991 and authorising the use of 'all necessary means' to enforce withdrawal subsequently. The following day, Bush offered direct talks with Iraq to go 'an extra mile for peace'. In the event, a 9 January meeting held in Geneva between US Secretary of State James Baker and Iraqi Foreign Minister Tariq Aziz achieved nothing. The US-led air campaign began at 0300 (Kuwait time) on 17 January with a series of air attacks against Iraq, followed on 1 February by a ground attack to liberate Kuwait from Iraqi occupation.

By chance, British Prime Minister Margaret Thatcher had been due to meet Bush in Aspen, Colorado on 2 August 1990, the day of the invasion. Up to this point their relationship had not been particularly strong, partly because of differences over the unification of Germany, but also because the Bush administration had sought to distance itself from the particular style of the Reagan administration, its very close relationship with Thatcher included. In the event, however, mutually supporting views during the Gulf War developed the Bush–Thatcher relationship profoundly while the latter remained in office. Thatcher had already instructed two warships in Southeast Asia and the Indian Ocean to join the British destroyer on Operation *Armilla* – the longstanding Royal Naval presence in the Gulf and Gulf of Oman. In this, Thatcher noted that her own experience of the Falklands War was valuable in recommending a robust stance.[5]

Thatcher's only significant difference with the US administration was over the need for further Security Council resolutions to permit military deployment and action. Her concerns were twofold and to some extent, again, based on her experience of the UN during the Falklands War. First, she feared that a Security Council resolution may have tied 'our hands unacceptably ... [If] one could achieve an objective without UN authority there was no point in running the risks attached to seeking it.' Secondly, she believed that specific UN approval was not necessary when there was a clear moral case. The UN was 'hardly the nucleus of a new world order. And there was still no substitute for the leadership of the United States.'[6] Thatcher met Bush again on 30 September and presented her view that economic sanctions were unlikely to force a withdrawal by Iraq.

This pattern of pressing for firmer military action continued. British policy was supported by fairly broad and sustained consensus among the political parties and there was strong popular backing. In this respect, Thatcher – and subsequently John Major – did not have the same concerns over popular support as Bush, nor did they share his need to be seen to be taking a considered, measured and UN-authorised approach.

Shortly before the invasion, the defence cuts as set out by 'Options for Change' had been announced. Participation with substantial combat capability in a major crisis outside the NATO area was not one of the overarching missions identified for the UK's armed forces in this review, which continued to focus on the British contribution to NATO as the principal force driver. The government did not want an out-of-area crisis to compromise this focus, with the premise underlying the British contribution therefore being that of attaining maximum profile and influence, but with minimum risk. In addition to the three warships that had already been committed, another destroyer, three minesweepers and support vessels were sent. The government did not respond to pressure from the Royal Navy to send an aircraft carrier because the US already had a considerable battle force. The number of attack aircraft was increased in late August from the original thirty-six to fifty-four, including Tornado GR3 ground-attack aircraft.

In terms of ground forces, Baker had asked NATO for armoured assets on 10 September.[7] It was important that there be broad international support for intervention undertaken by Western powers, and backed by Arab states. Thatcher was cautious about the political implications of, and risk of embroilment entailed in, a large-scale commitment on the ground, but she was also aware that political commitment to the US was important. The then-Chief of the General Staff, Sir John Chapple, recommended a tank contribution on the scale of an armoured brigade. A desert war was an exemplary scenario for the need for heavy armour, bearing in mind that Cold War scenarios had all but vanished by 1990; sustainment of heavy-armour capability after the Cold War was clearly a concern for the army. As such, Thatcher required reassurance that British tanks could operate effectively in desert conditions and could be fully supported logistically. The decision to send the 7th Armoured Brigade (the Desert Rats) was confirmed on 14 September.

The British government was surprised by the US decision to double force levels in early November and was concerned that the time required to do so would delay the expected military operation. On 9 November, Baker met Thatcher in London and asked for a comparable increase in British forces to the level of an armoured division with tank transporters, as well as more minesweepers and surface combatants, which she confirmed shortly before leaving office.[8]

Some key factors affecting the British decision to commit forces to what became known as Operation *Granby* were as follows. First, Iraq's aggression had violated international law and norms, and Margaret Thatcher in particular was committed to reversing the invasion. Her role in leading the reversal of an occupation during the Falklands War had strengthened her personal stance in this respect.[9] Second, Kuwait was a friend of the UK.[10] It bears mention that the UK had intervened militarily in Kuwait in 1961 when Iraq, under Abdel Karim Kassem, threatened attack at the time of Kuwait's independence from Britain. Third, the economic importance of the Gulf to the UK was of relevance (albeit less so than for the US). Finally, the UK government was very conscious of the importance of strong US leadership in the period of uncertainty following the Cold War, particularly in building a 'new world order'. A strong relationship with the US, expressed through close personal relationships between leaders, needed to be sustained and enhanced to permit effective British influence in US decision-making. The Bush administration, for its part, was measured and coherent in its policies and initiatives, and this made co-operation easier.

John Major became prime minister on 28 November 1990, having been chancellor of the Exchequer in the preceding months of the crisis. By this time, British policy had been formed and forces committed. The challenge facing Major was therefore very much one of managing subsequent events, as Bush and his administration made the decision to initiate the offensive campaign. The UK government expected that there would be a combat phase and, at the political and military strategic and operational levels, worked closely with the US in planning for this phase.

It was important for the UK – for reasons of influence, profile and respect for its relationship with the US – that British forces should take part actively alongside US forces and at the highest levels of integration achievable. The close political relationship had ensured that objectives were broadly common. In the event, British naval forces operated alongside the US in the maritime combat zone rather than participating in the more distanced Western European Union naval force with France. The Tornado aircraft made a substantial and specific contribution to the air campaign, providing low-level attack capability at considerable risk. Meanwhile, the core of the British land contribution was made by the 1st Armoured Division to the US VII Corps 'left hook' envelopment operation from the west.

The military capacity and utility of the British commitment in a US-led coalition was important to its influence in the conduct of the war. Indeed, strategic influence required an operational level (divisional) ground commitment.[11] The UK division was capable of operating as one division in a US-commanded corps. Both armies shared a basis of NATO standards for tactics, techniques and procedures, their doctrines having evolved similarly because of the close relationship. This ability to participate directly in the western flanking operation – that the US commander General Norman Schwarzkopf saw as key to a manoeuvrist ground campaign – reinforced UK influence.[12]

Certainly, the high level of multinational military interoperability was essential. Interoperability has a behavioural as well as a technical dimension; forces must have broadly similar doctrines, tactics, techniques and procedures if they are to fight together at an integrated – as opposed to merely a co-ordinated and co-operative level – and, in the absence of this, some separation of roles is required. The British Army was able to take part in a complex manoeuvre operation alongside the US through integration at the divisional level, made possible by the two countries' long history of association within the Integrated Military Structure (IMS) of NATO and regular joint training and exercises. The regular use of exchange postings was also important. This degree of operational interdependence had to be based on a shared understanding of and assent to both the objectives at the strategic level and the concept of operations, as well as on a sense of trust and confidence in the partner's competence. French forces could not achieve this level of interoperability because France had withdrawn from the IMS in 1966.

Similarly, the Royal Air Force (RAF) had doctrine, tactics, techniques and procedures that were coherent with those of the US. The two air forces were practised at operating together as a result of their NATO experience and had the necessary technical interoperability to take part in combined air operations. In particular, they used a common identification, friend or foe (IFF) system to distinguish between friendly and enemy or neutral aircraft. Tornado aircraft were also able and prepared to conduct low-level, relatively high-risk attack missions using their JP233 airfield-denial munitions. This anti-runway weapon was uniquely capable and was an essential contributor to air supremacy, adding a specific capability to the coalition campaign.

Overall, the First Gulf War had an important effect on the subsequent development of British defence policy and military capabilities. The Gulf scenario was later used as a template for major, high-intensity military engagement, and as evidence for the range to which large-scale expeditionary capability should be deployable with the necessary supporting logistics. A deployable combined-arms division would be the core of the Joint Rapid Deployment Force (JRDF) – later the Joint Rapid Reaction Force (JRRF) – at its largest scale and with the expectation that it would be deployed in a US-led coalition force in which divisional scale would be important to ensure strategic influence. These considerations of scale and reach were premises for the 1998 SDR. (British ground-troop numbers for this and other operations of the period are listed in Table 1.)

The Bosnian War, 1992–95

The Bosnia and Herzegovinian crisis followed the collapse of Tito's federalist system of government for Yugoslavia and the declarations of independence by (and wars in) Slovenia and Croatia in 1991.[13] On 25 September of that year, following UN Security Council Resolution 713, the UN imposed an arms embargo on the whole of Yugoslavia. The UN (through the secretary-general's special envoy, Cyrus Vance) and the European Community's (EC) Conference on Yugoslavia (through its chairman, Lord Carrington) conducted negotiations with all parties to the conflict. On 21 February 1992, the Security Council passed Resolution 743, establishing the UN Protection Force (UNPROFOR) to create peaceful conditions for a settlement of the Yugoslav crisis. It was formed, for an initial period of twelve months, as 'an interim arrangement to create the conditions of peace and security required for the negotiation of an overall settlement of the Yugoslav crisis within the framework of the European Community's Conference on Yugoslavia'.[14] France committed battalion-level ground forces to UNPROFOR in Croatia. The UK provided a medical unit.

Meanwhile, however, violence broke out in Bosnia after its declaration of independence in March 1992, the result of a referendum boycotted by Bosnian Serbs. Here, France committed a battalion for the protection of Sarajevo airport in July 1992, with numbers of French ground forces in UNPROFOR subsequently increasing to 6,000 or so by the summer of 1995. The UK committed a battalion in the autumn of 1992, with UK ground-force numbers also increasing incrementally thereafter, to more than 8,000 by mid-1995.[15]

For both France and the UK, the rationale for intervention was to end the humanitarian crisis, concern about wider European instability in a period of great uncertainty and a sense of responsibility – as leading military powers in Europe – to act, particularly given the absence of US participation on the ground. It is also relevant that the UK had assumed the Presidency of the EC in 1992 and that John Major had chaired the August 1992 London Conference on the former Socialist Republic of Yugoslavia and subsequent conferences and meetings. Lord Carrington was the EC envoy in 1991 and was replaced by Lord Owen the following year. Both were former UK government ministers and were instrumental in negotiating peace plans, unsuccessful though they were. Meanwhile, both the UK and France had similar views about the need for an impartial, UN-led approach. Major and Foreign Secretary Douglas Hurd were disposed towards contributing to UNPROFOR, but there was a considerable internal difference of opinion, within government and the Conservative Party, concerning the tension between the humanitarian argument for intervention and the perceived lack of national interest in the Balkans. This difference in views cut across the traditional left–right divide. Indeed, Major's principal opponents hailed from within his own party, while he typically received some sympathy and support from the leadership of the opposition parties over the course of the war.

There was also an initial reluctance to commit forces within the UK Ministry of Defence (MoD). The secretary of state for defence for most of the war (and subsequently foreign secretary), Malcolm Rifkind, was 'dubious' and his successor as defence secretary, Michael Portillo, was 'uneasy' about the prospect.[16] The MoD itself was not well structured to cope with the challenge of expeditionary operations while the armed forces were still very much configured according to the command-and-control arrangements of the Cold War.[17] Furthermore, the UK had not been a regular contributor to UN peacekeeping operations. Indeed, the army had a wealth of experience of counter-insurgency in Northern Ireland and the related aspects of complex emergencies, but was not predisposed to traditional, impartial peacekeeping.

As such, the military advice was largely against a significant British contribution on the ground. At a meeting on 18 August 1992, the chiefs of staff told Major that the requirement on the ground would be a full-scale NATO deployment of 400,000 troops with the prospect of the operation becoming very long-term. This was similar to the advice of the NATO military staff.[18]

The evolution of UNPROFOR's mission in Bosnia was incremental but haphazard. It began as an impartial intervention for humanitarian reasons, but without the agreed truce that would normally presage a traditional UN peacekeeping operation. The intervening powers did not commit the scale of combat forces necessary for peace-enforcement;[19] the US would not commit forces and add the necessary coercive power until late in the campaign. In addition, UNPROFOR's approach was skewed disproportionately against the Serbs,[20] who were not the only party committing atrocities.

The peace operation had four phases. The first was the protection of Sarajevo airport in July 1992. The second, the escort of humanitarian convoys, became an enduring mission for UNPROFOR throughout the war. It followed the London Conference of August 1992, at which the Serbs agreed to lift sieges, close detention camps, co-operate with relief operations and turn over heavy weapons (although they subsequently reneged on this undertaking). The third phase, the protection of 'safe areas', began in April 1993 after Resolution 819 demanded the withdrawal of Serb paramilitary units from around the Srebrenica safe area. This resolution invoked Chapter VII of the UN Charter, and therefore a measure of enforcement, but did not give UNPROFOR responsibility for defending the areas. In May 1993, the Sarajevo, Bihac, Zepa and Gorazde safe areas were established. Resolution 836 of 4 June 1993 required UNPROFOR to deter attacks, promote withdrawal of all but government forces and occupy some key points. These resolutions and the invocation of Chapter VII required a strengthening of UNPROFOR rules of engagement and a UN role that was progressing significantly beyond traditional peacekeeping to the developing concept of 'wider peacekeeping'. The fourth phase entailed the establishment of heavy-weapons exclusion zones, with implications for the use of NATO air power in their enforcement. For France, the UK and the Netherlands, the final phase involved the creation of a Rapid Reaction Force (RRF) following a French proposal of June 1995 to enhance the security of UNPROFOR with national combat capability.

The UK also committed naval and maritime air forces to the NATO maritime sanctions-monitoring operations *Maritime Monitor*, *Maritime Guard* and *Sharp Guard*. The British contribution here had begun with an initial national deployment of a naval escort to the Adriatic in the autumn of 1991, before any other forces had been despatched to the region, in response to the Yugoslav shelling of Dubrovnik.[21] An aircraft carrier was subsequently deployed in support of no-fly-zone enforcement. HMS *Invincible*, *Illustrious* and *Ark Royal* all individually contributed to this task.

Air operations began with the passing, on 9 October 1992, of Resolution 781 prohibiting unauthorised military flights in Bosnian airspace. NATO Operation *Sky Monitor* merely monitored violations, of which there were subsequently some 500. On 31 March 1993, Resolution 816 authorised measures 'to ensure compliance' with the no-fly zone and NATO initiated Operation *Deny Flight* to enforce the no-fly zone by attacking violators. Subsequently, as a result of Serb ground attacks on UN safe areas, Resolution 836 was passed, expanding UNPROFOR's mandate to use force to protect specially designated safe zones. The RAF contributed six Tornado F3s and two VC10 tankers.[22] After the first Sarajevo marketplace massacre on 5 February 1994, the UN formally requested that NATO carry out air strikes against Serb artillery and mortar positions assumed to be related to the attacks around Sarajevo. The Security Council also demanded that the Serbs remove their heavy weapons around Sarajevo or face air strikes. On 28 February 1994, NATO fighters shot down four Bosnian Serb aircraft near Banja Luka for violating the no-fly zone. On 10 and 11 April, UNPROFOR called in US

F-16 air strikes to protect the Gorazde safe area. These were the first combat operations in NATO's history, and were followed by sporadic NATO air attacks during the rest of the year. One Royal Navy Harrier FA2 was shot down by a Serb surface-to-air missile on 16 April 1994 while attacking Serb tanks; the pilot escaped unhurt to Bosniak-held territory. The level of air attacks increased in the summer of 1995 in response to further Bosnian Serb aggression. In response to these early air strikes, the Serbs seized UN hostages and used these as human shields in 1994 and 1995.

The Bosnian Serb leadership reached a decision in March 1995 that the war had to be concluded before the onset of the next winter. The strategy was to seize enclaves in Serb-controlled territory and finally turn on Sarajevo.[23] Events came to a climax in July 1995 when the Serbs slaughtered over 8,000 Muslims in Srebrenica. Following the second Sarajevo marketplace massacre by a Serb mortar bomb on 28 August, a major, systematic NATO air campaign – Operation *Deliberate Force* – began against the Serbs in co-ordination with UNPROFOR artillery provided by the newly created French, British and Netherlands Rapid Reaction Force.[24] During the air campaign, 3,515 sorties were flown against 338 targets. The UK provided twenty-eight aircraft to the operation, including twelve Harrier GR7s and six Royal Navy Harrier FA2s. The Harriers dropped forty-eight laser-guided bombs and thirty-two 1,000-lb bombs. They were supported by Jaguars providing laser guidance and Tornado F3s for air defence, TriStars for in-air refuelling and E-3D Sentry aircraft for surveillance, target acquisition and reconnaissance. British aircraft flew 9.3 per cent (326) of the operational sorties.

Whether or not the air operation significantly reduced Serb combat power, it was effective coercively as a defining event. On 20 September 1995, the air operation was finally terminated when an agreement was struck with the Serbs that opened the way to the Dayton Accords of 21 November. In parallel, Serb-held territory was reduced from 70 per cent of Bosnia to 50 per cent by the

Muslim-Croat Federation ground offensive. The air campaign was also instrumental in part in persuading Serbian President Slobodan Milosevic to distance himself from supporting the Bosnian Serbs.

In December 1995, following the formal signature of the Dayton Accords, UNPROFOR troops were replaced by the NATO Implementation Force (IFOR), consisting of 60,000 US and NATO troops. In most cases, UNPROFOR forces merely changed helmets. The UK contributed 13,000 troops to IFOR, which had at its core the newly established ARRC under the command of British General Sir Michael Walker. IFOR was effective in stopping violence in Bosnia, but issues concerning stability and governance persist to the present day, even after a huge investment of external resources. IFOR was replaced in 1996 by the Stabilisation Force (SFOR) and eventually in 2004 by the European Union Force Althea.

For much of the war, the US administration was reluctant to become involved, except at the policy level where the US line had been of partiality, on the one hand, and of 'lift and strike', on the other. It favoured lifting the UN embargoes – which applied to all entities in the former Yugoslavia – and using air strikes against Serb capabilities from an early stage. This partiality and the preference for a lift-and-strike approach were at variance with French and UK policy. Yet, although the UN arms embargoes were never lifted, the US did facilitate arms flow to the Bosnian Muslims. The eventual US commitment to a clear strategy, leadership and, in the end, a substantial ground presence came as a result of the concern of a small number of key figures in the administration about the nation's reputation both internationally and, crucially, domestically, with a presidential election in the offing and a record of indecisiveness in foreign affairs.

'Front Line First', 1994
In 1994, then-Defence Secretary Malcolm Rifkind initiated another defence review – the Defence Costs Studies, also known as 'Front

Line First', which followed a mini-review conducted in the wake of the 1993 Public Expenditure Survey, which required cost savings from all government departments. Unlike this review and 'Options for Change', 'Front Line First' was intended to protect the fighting capabilities of the armed forces by achieving savings in MoD and service-support costs. The review comprised thirty-three studies conducted over a period of four months. The result was the closure of a number of depots, military hospitals and bases, including Rosyth naval base; the reduction of armed forces personnel by 11,600 and of the civil service by 7,100; and the subsequent establishment in 1996 of the Permanent Joint Headquarters (PJHQ) at Northwood under a chief of joint operations to command overseas engagements. The establishment of this new command, along with the creation of the JRDF the same year, marked a key stage in the progressive shift to an expeditionary national military strategy. It is also indicative of an incremental process of greater integration of the single services, or 'jointery'. As part of this process, in 1997 the Joint Services Command and Staff College was formed out of the single-services colleges, and based first in Bracknell and later in Watchfield (Shrivenham). As part of the same process, the Joint Doctrine and Concepts Centre was established at Shrivenham in 1998, later becoming the Development, Concepts and Doctrine Centre (DCDC).

The Strategic Defence Review, 1998
The Labour Party, in its manifesto for the 1997 general election, declared that it would hold a comprehensive defence review if it came to power. Shortly after the Blair government took office, work began on the review, under the firm direction of new Secretary of State for Defence George Robertson. The White Paper of July 1998 did not present any real change in direction for the UK's defence policy and military strategy.[25] It rather confirmed the shift – underway since 'Options for Change' – from the UK's contribution to NATO being the force driver to, instead, an expeditionary

strategy, in particular through the creation of PJHQ and the JRDF in 1996. The JRRF – as the latter became known in 1998 – was designed to be capable of undertaking a large-scale military operation similar to the First Gulf War, or a more modest overseas deployment of smaller size but longer timescale whilst maintaining the capability to undertake a second substantial deployment. At its largest, it was established that the JRRF would include a division-sized land formation with supporting naval and air forces. Implicit in the concept (but not expressed in the White Paper) was the assumption that the UK could deliver major operational-level capability to a coalition operation led by the US, which would be sufficient to ensure strategic influence in shaping the operation. Another presumption was that the Gulf would represent, for force-planning purposes, the maximum range from the UK at which such an operation would be conducted and for which logisticial capabilities, such as sea- and airlift, would be needed.

The importance to government of the UK's influence, both at the grand- and military-strategic levels, was confirmed in Tony Blair's Chicago speech of April 1999, when he launched a grand strategy relating national interest to globalisation and humanitarian intervention.[26] The subtext was one of maintaining global influence through shrewd use of the military instrument, with a new military mission of 'defence diplomacy' identified. When George Robertson first launched the concept in the consultation period before the publication of the White Paper, he seemed to be addressing the use of the military instrument in support of diplomacy in the widest sense, including coercive, supportive and preventive inducement operations.[27] Yet the actual definition in the White Paper was limited to peaceful uses such as arms control, outreach, training and defence attaché activities.[28]

Meanwhile, the premise of the SDR was that nuclear deterrence in the form of Trident would not be discussed. Nor would the acquisition of the Eurofighter Typhoon attack aircraft; these decisions had already been taken. On the other hand, it did confirm that the UK would acquire two aircraft carriers to replace HMS *Invincible*, *Illustrious* and *Ark Royal*.

While the SDR process was widely praised, there were immediate concerns about the affordability, in the medium term, of a number of these new acquisitions and many other major programmes. The review had been joined up with the ongoing Smart Procurement reform initiative, which resulted in the creation of the Defence Procurement Agency in April 1999. There was a presumption that cost savings through more efficient procurement would address the affordability issue.[29]

Kosovo, 1999
Kosovar Albanian leader Ibrahim Rugova had pursued a policy of peaceful resistance to the Serbian government following the rescinding of the province's autonomy in 1989. Some Kosovar Albanians, inspired by events in Bosnia and provoked by repression from Belgrade, adopted a more aggressive stance. It is relevant that the Dayton Accords neglected the Kosovo question entirely; five months after its signing, the Kosovo Liberation Army (KLA) began a series of attacks on Serbs in Kosovo.[30] Following these attacks and Serbian reprisals throughout the winter of 1998–99, NATO announced on 30 January 1999 that it would initiate air strikes on Serbia if required to compel compliance with the demands of the international community and to achieve a political settlement. Javier Solana, as NATO secretary general, chaired the Rambouillet peace conference that began on 6 February 1999. The outcome was the Rambouillet Accords, which called for NATO administration of Kosovo as an autonomous province within Yugoslavia; a force of 30,000 NATO troops to maintain order in Kosovo; unhindered right of passage for NATO troops in Yugoslav territory, including Kosovo; and immunity for NATO and its agents from legal action under Yugoslav law. While the Kosovar Albanians signed the agreement,

Serbia rejected it. Tony Blair was strongly in favour of intervention,[31] and put pressure on the US administration to that end.

NATO's bombing campaign, Operation *Allied Force*, began on 24 March 1999. The plan, which had received NATO consensus with some difficulty, envisaged a seventy-two-hour bombing campaign that would bring Milosevic to the table within a week. There was concern at the time that NATO unity would not survive a protracted air campaign. Furthermore, neither was there consensus on any ground intervention force unless the Serbs first acceded to the peace accords. In the event, the Serbs responded by stepping up the ethnic cleansing of Kosovo. Of the bombs dropped in these first seventy-two hours, many were not delivered to target. It was essentially a symbolic act of coercion which failed to achieve effect. Bombing by aircraft and cruise missiles continued and increased incrementally in severity throughout the campaign. There were three phased components to the campaign: air control by attacking airfields, air-defence sites and command-and-control centres; the isolation of Serb forces in Kosovo through the destruction of their communications, resupply routes, and fuel and ammunition supplies; and the assault on the Serbian army and police units in Kosovo itself.

The effects of the bombing were hindered by constraints on targeting and the prohibition of the use of aircraft for low-level, high-risk missions. Bearing in mind the humanitarian purpose of the war, the constraints on targeting were eminently reasonable. Targeting comprised both strategic targets in Belgrade and elsewhere, as well as tactical targeting to destroy elements of the Serb army in Kosovo, with an increasing shift towards tactical targets as strategic options dwindled. Countering Serbian air defences was a priority. Meanwhile, the Serb army avoided destruction through concealment and the movement of forces out of known bases. When the army eventually did withdraw from Kosovo, the observed levels of NATO attrition were unimpressive.

The British contribution to Operation *Allied Force* was Operation *Engadine*. Over the sixty-eight days of the air campaign, the numbers of RAF Harrier GR7s rose to sixteen, Tornado GR1s to twelve and TriStar tankers to seven. Other RAF aircraft included E3-D Sentry aircraft and a Nimrod R1 for surveillance, while HMS *Invincible* provided seven Harrier FA2s for close air support. Tomahawk cruise missiles were used by the UK for the first time, launched by the submarine HMS *Splendid*. Targets included Serbian fuel depots, ammunition stores, bridges, airfields, command bunkers, surface-to-air missile sites, and field-force artillery, armour and armoured personnel carriers. Altogether, NATO flew more than 30,000 sorties, including 9,000 attacks. British aircraft contributed roughly 10 per cent of the sorties.[32]

During the NATO campaign, there were a number of incidents involving errors of targeting which were strategically unproductive. These included the bombing and destruction of the Embassy of the People's Republic of China in Belgrade in May and the mistaken killing of seventy-three Albanian refugees near Djakovica shortly beforehand, in April. The campaign also revealed significant NATO inadequacies in terms of co-ordination of air attacks, the detection and destruction of appropriate targets, and precision and avoidance of collateral damage. On 3 June 1999, after a Russo–Finnish delegation began negotiations with Milosevic regarding a peace deal, the latter capitulated after a vote in the parliament in Belgrade, accepting the peace conditions of the G8, which included an end to fighting in Kosovo; the withdrawal of all Serb forces; the return of refugees; the deployment of a UN-sanctioned, NATO-led peacekeeping force; the establishment of an interim administration for the province under a UN mandate, with eventual autonomy for Kosovo; and the promotion of economic redevelopment and stabilisation.

The formal end of NATO's bombing campaign in Kosovo came on 10 June 1999. NATO's peacekeeping force – the Kosovo Force (KFOR), under the command of British Lieutenant General Sir Mike

Jackson – entered the country on 12 June. Comprised of British, French, US, German and Italian brigades, and with a command structure evoking the NATO ARRC framework-nation concept, the entry of KFOR marked the end of the combat phase of the Kosovo War.

Yet, just prior to this, Russian forces had entered Kosovo from Bosnia and seized Pristina's Slatina airport. This move was likely pre-planned and designed to give Russia a strong hand in negotiations with NATO over the subsequent occupation of Kosovo under the so-called Military-Technical Agreement.[33] However, the brigade-sized core of the NATO force, under Lieutenant General Jackson, arrived in time from Macedonia to have a showdown with the Russians over Slatina. While this confrontation was against the wishes of the Supreme Allied Commander Europe (SACEUR) General Wesley Clark, the Russians withdrew and, under the agreed occupation pattern for Kosovo, did not gain control of the (predominantly Serb) northern part of Kosovo, their contribution instead being spread across the sectors.

The operation is now widely considered to have been a success, though not in the way planned at the outset. The war was a definitive event in a way that Bosnia was not. NATO members agreed to military action without a UN mandate for urgent humanitarian reasons – and, indeed, with some Security Council members actively opposed to the action. This set an important precedent for liberal intervention and the duty to protect.

The broad conclusions drawn for subsequent Western interventions were, first, that liberal intervention for morally justified humanitarian purposes could be successful in the new strategic environment, although the basis for judging and evaluating humanitarian outcomes raised difficult ethical questions over enduring principles and norms on the one hand and short-term measurements of consequences on the other. Second, that there was a role for NATO in the post-Cold War environment and that Article V of the Washington Treaty was no longer a widely accepted constraint.[34] Third, that 'compellence'[35] from the air could be effective, and could be much more so if applied scientifically with adequate information, drawing on the disciplines of anthropology, social psychology and complexity theory, as well as on military capability.

East Timor, 1999
The International Force for East Timor (INTERFET) – a UN-authorised force under Australian command of some 11,000 ground troops, with naval and air support – entered East Timor on 20 September 1999 to halt state-backed ethnic violence, following a referendum in which 78 per cent of the electorate voted in favour of independence from Indonesia.[36] Australia contributed the bulk of the troops – some 4,000 – to the mission. With a strong regional interest, and in a period of rapid change following the 1997 Asian economic crisis and the fall of the autocratic Suharto regime in Indonesia, Australia felt driven to respond to unpredictable decisions by the new Indonesian president, Bacharuddin Jusuf Habibie, over self-determination; most notably, Habibie's sudden announcement that a referendum on sovereignty would be held in East Timor. A UN monitoring group, the United Nations Mission in East Timor (UNAMET), was established. Levels of violence soared after the referendum and then-Australian Prime Minister John Howard decided to take the initiative, with UN Security Council endorsement – alongside a vital diplomatic effort by Secretary-General Kofi Annan – to establish and lead an intervention force.

The UK provided a small force to the mission, based on a 300-strong Gurkha infantry unit. While it had no direct national interest in East Timor, the moral motivation for action had recently been institutionalised in the government's grand strategy. Indeed, there was no direct geostrategic argument for involvement, although the timing was good, coming in the context of a wider UK strategy relating to global influence. For Tony Blair and his Foreign Secretary

Robin Cook – himself strongly committed to a British 'force for good' – East Timor was a timely and low-risk opportunity (at least, in the UK government's perception) to reinforce this strategy. And while in terms of distance from the UK it vastly exceeded the assumptions of the 1998 SDR, the core British forces happened to be to hand.

In spite of the country's Kosovo commitments, there were, conveniently, Gurkha infantry based in Brunei and a destroyer, HMS *Glasgow*, in East Asia, resulting in the decision to contribute the small but significant force of 300 troops, including a detachment of the Special Boat Service (SBS), in support of Australia – a long-term ally with whom military interoperability did not pose a challenge. Two C-130 Hercules transport aircraft and a VC20 tanker were also deployed, and the British contribution was sufficiently modest – and without predefined area or other discrete responsibilities – that there would be a low risk of embroilment and a clear exit strategy, while at the same time constituting more than a mere token force.

The SBS were among the first ashore in East Timor and the Gurkhas were in the first wave of ground forces. Brigadier David Richards was the overall national commander of the force and, according to a convincing account by a British officer involved in civil-military affairs during the intervention, took a leading role in advising Major General Peter Cosgrove, the Australian force commander.[37] (Cosgrove disputes this in his own memoir, saying that the 'brigadier from London' was too senior in rank and would have unbalanced the team.[38] He is nonetheless very complimentary about the quality of the Gurkha soldiers deployed.) In the event, INTERFET was effective, with British forces withdrawing at the end of 1999.

Sierra Leone, 2000
The British military intervention in Sierra Leone in 2000 was instrumental in bringing to an end a decade of bloody civil war that had caused tens of thousands of casualties.[39] The civil war had

been punctuated by two peace accords, the Abidjan Peace Accord of November 1996 and the Lomé Peace Agreement of July 1999. The Revolutionary United Front (RUF) was the backbone of the violent opposition to the elected government. It was aided in its formation, and subsequently, by then-Liberian President Charles Taylor, as part of his wider agenda. A major factor in the war was the exploitation of Sierra Leone's diamond mining for the benefit of both Taylor and the RUF.

In both cases, the agreements were intended to bring the RUF into the fold with a general amnesty. Indeed, one of the conditions of the Abidjan Peace Accord had been that the government would no longer employ the South African private military company Executive Outcomes to fight the RUF and train the Sierra Leone Army. Yet without this asset, the elected government of Ahmad Tejan Kabbah fell to a 1997 military coup led by army Major Johnny Paul Koroma in alliance with the RUF. Nigeria attempted to intervene with Economic Community of West African States (ECOWAS) Monitoring Group (ECOMOG) forces, but was repelled by the combined force of the army loyal to Koroma and the RUF.

While in exile, Kabbah began negotiations with another private military company, Sandline International, to support a counter-coup through the provision of weaponry and the arming of loyal tribesmen. The British government was aware of this deal, even though it was in contravention of a UN arms embargo on all warring parties in Sierra Leone.[40] ECOWAS, led by Nigeria, subsequently deployed ECOMOG forces to reinstate Kabbah in March 1998, and UN Security Council Resolution 1181 established a UN Observer Mission in Sierra Leone (UNOMSIL) in July. However, even with the backing of ECOMOG, it did not have the clout to prevent the resurgence of attacks by the RUF. In December 1998, the UK was forced to evacuate High Commission staff and dependants by Hercules C-130 aircraft in Operation *Spartic*. The RUF attacked Freetown in January 1999 but were repelled by Nigerian-led forces.

The Lomé Peace Agreement between Kabbah's government and the RUF, led by Foday Sankoh, was signed in July 1999 with broad international support, including from the UK government. The agreement gave the RUF the status of a legitimate political party, and instated Sankoh as vice president, also granting him a post that had direct control over the country's gold and diamond mines. Meanwhile, a new mission, the UN Mission in Sierra Leone (UNAMSIL), with a force of 6,000, was to oversee a disarmament, demobilisation and reintegration (DDR) process for ex-combatants. As Dorman notes, the Lomé Peace Agreement was very much a compromise, but there was no alternative for the international community because major powers such as the UK were, at that time, not prepared to intervene. Yet the risk of failure of the agreement was heightened by the unanticipated withdrawal of ECOMOG forces in April 2000, meaning UNAMSIL had to readjust to be more proactive in enforcement. There was thus a window of opportunity that the RUF could seize before being subjected to disarmament.

Indeed, RUF violence, triggered by the beginning of the disarmament process, began again and escalated to attacks on UN compounds and hostage taking, including in one instance of approximately 500 Zambian troops and a British UN military observer. The British government, whose military priorities were in the Balkans, was surprised by this turn of events. Through the Foreign Office and DfID, it had already given considerable support to the UN in Sierra Leone and thus did not want UNAMSIL to fail. There was also the urgent need to ensure the safety of some 1,000 British nationals and other entitled personnel in the country, as well as pressure from the UN secretary-general and French and US ambassadors for the UK to take action, evoking the country's global status and responsibilities and, in particular, Tony Blair's moral doctrine, as set out in the Chicago speech of the previous year. In the event, appropriate forces were to hand and Andrew Dorman notes that the British military, in particular the Royal Marines and Parachute Regiment, was 'keen to conduct an operation'.[41]

The UK's military intervention began with the order, on 5 May 2000, for the deployment of an Operational Reconnaissance and Liaison Team from PJHQ, led by Brigadier David Richards, to Freetown. Richards recommended an operation that began with non-combatant evacuation of entitled personnel,[42] which was seen by the MoD as the priority and a discrete operation that would avoid long-term embroilment. While the foreign secretary, Robin Cook, had pressed for a more substantial response to support UNAMSIL, in the event, Operation *Palliser* was directed and structured initially for the evacuation of entitled personnel. The requirements were, most immediately, for air transport, with special-forces support to Lungi airport; as well as the deployment of troops from 1 Parachute Regiment to secure the airport, and the 'self ferry' deployment of four Chinook helicopters from the UK. These would be available to transfer the evacuees from an evacuation centre in a hotel in Freetown across the wide estuary of the Sierra Leone River to the airport. Finally, the alternative, if the airport could not be held, would be the deployment of amphibious forces to conduct the evacuation by sea.[43]

Within thirty-six hours, British forces had been deployed on the ground. In addition to these forces, a forward mounting base with Hercules aircraft was set up in Dakar, Senegal; a Nimrod reconnaissance aircraft and VC10 transport aircraft were deployed to Ascension Island; and frigates HMS *Argyll* and *Chatham* operated close in-shore and on the river, within view. The Amphibious Ready Group had the amphibious assault ship HMS *Ocean* as its sea base, supported by two landing ship logistics and two Royal Fleet Auxiliaries.[44] The carrier HMS *Illustrious* was off-shore carrying thirteen Harriers.[45] The number of deployed forces grew to some 4,500 at the height of the operation from May 2000, including 1,500 on the ground.

With these capabilities in place, Richards decided that British military forces could indeed do much more to stabilise the situation than non-combatant evacuation alone. Lungi airport had been secured as planned and control extended to much of the Freetown Peninsula, including UNAMSIL's headquarters. With UNAMSIL remaining reluctant to fulfil its UN Chapter VII enforcement mandate to repel the RUF from the vicinity of Freetown, British forces therefore focused on building the effectiveness of the various groupings of Sierra Leonean military forces loyal to President Kabbah, with military advisers placed at every level. British military dominance over the RUF – albeit without much actual combat[46] – reinforced by its amphibious and naval presence, turned the tide against the rebel group and, along with a revitalised UNAMSIL and a more forceful regional response, led to the capture of many of its leaders, including Sankoh on 17 May.[47] British forces were also engaged with UNAMSIL in relieving besieged peacekeepers during the summer of 2000. In September, British special forces, in Operation *Barras*, freed six Royal Irish Regiment soldiers who had been taken hostage by a renegade militia, the 'West Side Boys'. One British soldier was killed in this operation.

The situation deteriorated somewhat in October 2000, following the departure of the main British force. Richards and his team were therefore sent back to the country in an advisory capacity and an integrated plan with more effective UNAMSIL action led to the signing a ceasefire by the RUF in Abuja, Nigeria on 10 November 2000.[48]

Sierra Leone was, at the time, considered a success for British government policy and, in particular, for the British armed forces, and David Richards drew some immediate lessons.[49] He considered the operation to have demonstrated an effective use of the JRRF concept defined in the 1998 SDR, noting the remarkable speed of the response time from government decision to the deployment of forces on the ground. He also pointed out the importance of the 'operational level' of command and planning much discussed in the 1980s in the context of manoeuvre warfare, but now institutionalised in the PJHQ and Joint Force Headquarters structure. Here, needless to say, he emphasised the importance of 'mission command', which allowed himself, as the joint task force commander, freedom of action, including, in this case, to expand the mission to take advantage of circumstances and opportunities. He also mentions the importance of 'clout' – that is, the possession of sufficient combat power to dominate events in the cognitive domain and to prevent escalation. Richards notes the effective rapid logistic support, but also mentions that there were problems with short-notice medical preparations including preventive medication. Finally, he addresses the difficulties experienced in reconciling the different views of the MoD, Foreign Office and DfID to achieve an integrated approach at the grand-strategic level.

In the subsequent decade, the success of Sierra Leone has been somewhat marginalised as a result of the fact that operations in Iraq and Afghanistan have emphasised the failure of the presumptions of the 'early in, early out' expeditionary strategy of 1998. However, it is as naive to ignore the achievements of an autonomous (in terms of command and force structure) British operation in Sierra Leone and the insights to be drawn from it as it is to presume that this operation will be a model for British interventions in the future. Later, in 2008, Richards drew a broader set of insights from the operation including the essential but limited role of the military in establishing the necessary level of security; the need for 'greater intra-government and agency coherence' and tempo (albeit a military concept) in delivering solutions; the problems of institutional rivalry and bureaucratic inefficiency; and the need for highly motivated and able leadership working to a comprehensive recovery plan.[50]

Other Military Operations
During this decade, British armed forces were committed to a number of other operations, undertaken alongside those mentioned thus far. Until 1994, strategic nuclear deterrence was provided by the Polaris missile system in the four *Resolution*-class submarines providing continuous at-sea deterrence. This class was replaced from 1994 by

the *Vanguard* class and the Trident II missile system and the security of the nuclear deterrent, particularly while deploying, was and still is dependent in part on fleet submarines and maritime patrol aircraft. Protection of shore bases has thus been a mission for the armed forces and civilian security services more widely.

Meanwhile, on 22 August 2001, the UK committed a brigade headquarters and a battlegroup[51] to NATO's Operation *Essential Harvest* in Macedonia, alongside ten other nations, to disarm co-operating ethnic Albanian groups and destroy their weapons. The operation was conducted in response to a request for NATO assistance made by President Boris Trajkovski of Macedonia on 15 June and was under Danish overall command. It was successful in collecting 3,300 weapons and ended a month later.

Another significant commitment for British forces, and the army in particular, throughout most of the decade was to Military Aid to the Civil Power counter-insurgency operations in Northern Ireland (discussed more in Chapter IV). The Good Friday Agreement signed on 10 April 1998 allowed for an incremental withdrawal – a process that had begun in the middle of the decade. It was not completed, however, until Operation *Banner* formally came to an end in 2007. There were also a significant number of related terrorist bombings throughout the UK during the decade.

Other demands on the military, in terms of domestic security under the 1998 SDR mission heading 'peacetime security', included the outbreak of foot-and-mouth disease in 2001. Meanwhile, although the 1999 Admiral Duncan pub bombing – part of the London nail-bombing campaign – was carried out by a lone terrorist, it was significant because of the pressure it placed on the National Health Service for trauma response and the resulting reliance on the expertise of military medical experts in this field. At the same time, Royal Navy warships contributed to coastal maritime security around the shores of the UK and farther afield, and the RAF maintained its enduring role in rapid response for air defence of the UK.

Finally, the defence of the UK's Overseas Territories required garrisons in the Falkland Islands, Hong Kong until 1997, and Gibraltar, as well as a presence in the Cyprus Sovereign Base Areas. There was also a continuing naval presence in the South Atlantic, Hong Kong until 1997 and in the Caribbean for the defence of Overseas Territories, with routine engagement, in the Caribbean, in counter-narcotics, disaster response and other maritime security operations.

Conclusion

A common feature of the UK's overseas interventions in this decade was that not one, either in fact or in government rhetoric, was undertaken for reasons of direct national interest. The First Gulf War was principally a matter of restoring and supporting international legal norms. In the cases of Bosnia, Kosovo, East Timor and Sierra Leone, there was the overriding moral purpose of relieving human suffering. Although the mantra of a 'force for good' and the script of Blair's Chicago speech were Labour government creations, Conservative leaders were also strongly supportive of the need to enforce international norms.

The difference, in this respect, between the Conservative government from Margaret Thatcher onwards and the Blair doctrine was, perhaps, that for Thatcher and Major and their key ministers, the issue was principally a pragmatic one of maintaining global stability in the post-Cold War era, in the face of the huge uncertainties confronting both Eastern Europe and the world at large. For Tony Blair, with the 1998 SDR, the main issue became that of the UK's global influence and moral reputation.

The prime instrument of power that had to be controlled in support of the country's interests was, of course, the US. While an eager, effective and otherwise competent military is one contributor to influence, the other, one might say, is moral wisdom, with shades here of Harold Macmillan's references to Britain as the 'Greece' to America's 'Rome'.

The relationship between the US and the UK during this period was more balanced than in the subsequent decade. While the US clearly led the First Gulf War, Margaret Thatcher had her say through her close relationship with Bush, born of the Aspen meeting. US administrations were reluctant to be drawn into the former Yugoslavia, although a balanced process of negotiation reflecting events on the ground led to eventual effective US leadership. Meanwhile, the US did not commit forces to East Timor or Sierra Leone, but put pressure in a positive way on Australia and the UK to take on appropriate leadership roles.

It was helpful to the UK that US administrations were essentially internationalist throughout the period, and were not unsupportive of the UN at last coming to the fore following the end of the Cold War. Kosovo was an exception to this, in that there was not a UN mandate for military action, although it contributed to the subsequent debate over the Responsibility to Protect and the evolution of the UN's role in this respect.

The experiences of Bosnia and Kosovo also resulted in a strengthening of the military and political relationship between the UK and France. Although the 1998 SDR did not dwell on Europe and the EU, almost immediately after its publication the British and French governments signed the Saint-Malo Declaration, with a view to strengthening the EU's military utility. The concept was sound, focusing on a bottom-up, capability-based approach, although the initiative was very much hindered by differences between the stances of the US and the UK, on the one hand, and those of France and Germany, on the other, with regard to the 2003 Iraq War.

The British armed forces and those of the UK's allies faced the challenge of complex emergencies in a new multinational context. While the UK had its legacy of counter-insurgency and stabilisation operations from Northern Ireland and empire, Bosnia in particular had also presented the multinational challenge of 'wider peacekeeping', requiring the balancing of traditional peacekeeping

– where the consent of previously warring parties is a requirement – with peace-enforcement – where there is a need to dominate escalation through the capacity for, threat of, and engagement in full-scale combat against one or more of the antagonists.

The experience of the 1990s, in this respect, could have been valuable in influencing decisions by major Western powers to commit to interventions in the following decade and, in particular, in assessing the consequent challenge of stabilisation. There were, however, two important impediments to this. First, US forces had not gained the on-the-ground experience of Bosnia in the critical period up to the Dayton Accords, and US Army doctrine remained essentially combat-focused. The US Marine Corps had, in the past, been more subtle in this respect, but it had suffered a blow in Somalia in 1993 in terms of its claims to be the nation's '911 Force'. Second, interventions to effect regime change, rather than peace operations, generate particular problems of 'counter-insurgency', relating specifically to the moral commitment to governance following the removal of a government;[52] partiality in having to support a new and fragile government; and the fact that any resort to violence through full-scale combat is likely to jeopardise the trust needed to build acceptance, if not assent or full consent.

One issue, in particular, that was seriously ignored in the subsequent wars of the 2000s was the fact that peace-enforcement operations require a specific minimum proportion of troops on the ground in relation to population and territory. This proportion is not the winning factor in complex emergencies, but it is a *sine qua non* which must be considered before intervening in a country and removing its government.

The IFOR and KFOR ratios of troops to local population offer some guidance in this regard, while the concept of 'wider peacekeeping' addressed this need in terms of capacity for peace-enforcement.[53] This concept was initially developed by the UK military during the war in Bosnia, and accepted that the traditional roles of UN peacekeeping and rules-of-engagement restrictions were inadequate for dealing with complex emergencies in which the military capacity for escalation dominance was a requirement. Impartiality and the consent of warring parties were still important aspirations, and the challenge was to be able to return to impartiality after combat had been initiated. (The equivalent French concept was known as *maitriser la violence*.)

At the same time, the Kosovo War gave a great boost to the Western military theology of 'effects-based operations' (EBO) and the 'effects-based approach to operations' (EBAO) – concepts which have, in the more recent past, been disputed by senior, and particularly US and UK, army commanders. The criticism concerns the presumption that, on the one hand, military actions such as air targeting can confidently generate intended military effects and, on the other hand, that military effects can be related predictably to non-military (political) outcomes, despite the uncertainties of the cognitive domain and catalytic effects of violence.

During the course of the decade, there was also a strong focus among Western militaries on exploiting information technology. The Revolution in Military Affairs spawned the US concept of network-centric warfare (NCW), which was purported to bring about a fundamental change in the effective use of the military instrument. Networking would maximise the effects of sensors and weapons, and would allow both the de-layering of command structures and the minimisation of logistics footprints in theatres of operations. As a result, military doctrine would be very different. The British version – network-enabled capability (NEC) – was more modest and incremental in its aspirations, and it was this concept that was adopted by NATO.

Yet, although information technology continues to drive huge changes in military systems and behaviours, there is now some cynicism about NCW and NEC. On the one hand, the rhetoric can be seen as a device to cut costs in terms of sensor and weapon capabilities. On the other, networking establishes large-scale dependencies, which may be vulnerable to cyber-attack or accidents, and there are costs involved in building the necessary redundancies and fallback systems.

As noted, a major criticism of the 1998 SDR that emerged powerfully in the 2000s as a result of the counter-insurgency and stabilisation experiences in Iraq and Afghanistan concerns the expectations of an 'early in, early out' expeditionary strategy. In terms of achieving influence, the SDR exploited the UK's ability to provide forces early to overseas interventions, given the few limitations placed on government by the British constitutional war-powers process. The UK also possessed experienced elite infantry in the form of air assault and amphibious forces, and special forces with distinct capabilities that allowed for this agility to be developed. For the UK, early commitment, alongside the US in particular, would enable it to assist in shaping operations and allow it grand-strategic influence. The pattern of commitment in Bosnia (and subsequently in Kosovo) was that the predominant roles in longer-term peacekeeping and stabilisation would then be taken on by other major European powers with more deliberated war-powers processes and with less expertise in early intervention. Yet the long-term commitments on the ground in Iraq and Afghanistan following regime-change campaigns have seriously undermined this presumption.

The dominance of 'manoeuvre warfare' or the 'manouevrist approach' in Western doctrines also faced a challenge in the 1990s. In its classical sense, in which dominance on the battlefield relates to surprise, envelopment, and an elegant focus on key physical and cognitive vulnerabilities, it evidently triumphed in the First Gulf War under Schwarzkopf. Yet here there were front lines, military control of the battlespace and a clearly defined – and much less competent – military opponent.

Throughout the remainder of the decade, the US and British militaries – and their armies in particular – clung to the concept as the philosopher's stone for victory. Yet the concept acquired a more figurative meaning over this period. Indeed, in 'wars amongst the people' there are no front lines; it is not clear who is the enemy or from where that enemy might emerge. Asymmetric actions by irregulars are themselves 'manouevrist' in the more figurative sense of the term.

This raises the question of whether one can use manoeuvre against an enemy that is cleverer and more imaginative, and has a better understanding of the social and cognitive environment. Moreover, one cannot abandon the advantage of scale on the presumption that manoeuvre will compensate, for the fundamental reason that the cognitive domain is inherently unpredictable: there needs to be a fallback, attrition-based plan should a force fail to 'dominate the will' of the enemy. Finally, in complex emergencies, 'hybrid' enemies have the advantage against democracies of being able to escalate through prolongation, in the belief that if they keep the war going for long enough, Western democracies will become war-weary and withdraw.

The irony of the 1990s is that Western intervention in complex emergencies proved to be more or less successful with the benefit of hindsight. This meant that the paradoxes of 'wider peacekeeping' were never explored to a satisfactory conclusion. In particular, the question remains whether, if peace-enforcing powers (or indeed counter-insurgent powers) are required to use combat violence to dominate escalation, there can ever be a return to broad acceptance, assent and, indeed, consent – and whether the conquering powers will ever again be perceived as a 'force for good' by the communities that matter.

Table 1: British Ground-Troop Commitments to Major Interventions, 1991–2001.

	Year	Operation/Mission	Ground Troops	Fatalities
Iraq	1991	*Granby*	53,462	47
Bosnia	1992	UNPROFOR	1,200	0
	1993	UNPROFOR	2,626	2
	1994	UNPROFOR	3,400	12
	1995	UNPROFOR	8,000+	4
	1996	IFOR	13,000	0
Kosovo	1999	KFOR	10,500	0
East Timor	1999	INTERFET	300	0
Sierra Leone	2000	*Palliser*	1,500	1
Macedonia	2001	*Essential Harvest*	1,500	1

Source: *Ministry of Defence,* Statement on the Defence Estimates *(London: The Stationery Office, 1991–2001).*

II. THE TWO TOWERS, 2001–13

Michael Codner

BRITISH foreign and defence policy in the first decade of the twenty-first century was dominated by the two wars initiated by the US in Afghanistan and Iraq, and by the consequences of occupation and attempts at stabilisation. While British forces conducted a number of other significant operations around the world in this period – which are discussed later in this chapter, as are significant events in the evolution of the UK's defence policy and military strategy – it was Iraq and Afghanistan in particular that fed an apprehension in the British defence community about strategic competence and adequate doctrine.

George W Bush became US president on 20 January 2001, after a closely contested and controversial election. During the election, Bush presented himself to the electorate as a 'compassionate conservative', one interpretation of which might have been of a form of tolerant Republicanism, which would have had some appeal to ethnic minorities and the poor. While this certainly did not imply a powerful ideology,[1] the Bush administration was populated by neoconservatives whose policies included the promotion of democracy, defence of the national interest, an emphasis on the importance of the military instrument in asserting policy, and unilateralism. However, it was after the terrorist attacks of September 2001 that US policy took a particular turn towards neoconservatism. 9/11 was the defining example, in subsequent UK Ministry of Defence (MoD) parlance, of a 'strategic shock', with the catastrophic and catalytic effects of 'a discontinuity or an abrupt alteration in the strategic context'. The Bush Doctrine of 2002,[2] which emphasised pre-emptive military action, was very different to the policies of Bush's father and to those of Bill Clinton in the previous decade. For the UK, under the premiership of Tony Blair, the relationship with the US also changed substantially, from one of partnership, as in the previous decade, to one of eager support.

9/11

On the morning of 11 September 2001, nineteen terrorists organised by Al-Qa'ida took control of four civil aircraft, two of which were crashed into the north and south towers of the World Trade Center in New York.[3] Shortly afterwards, both towers collapsed. A third aircraft struck the west side of the Pentagon, the headquarters of the US Department of Defense (DoD) and armed services, across the Potomac River from Washington, DC. A fourth, targeting the capital itself, crashed in the Pennsylvania countryside after passengers tried to overcome the hijackers. Sixty-seven of the almost 3,000 people killed were British. It was the deadliest terrorist attack in terms of British casualties in recent history, exceeding the Lockerbie Pan Am Flight 103 attack of 1988 (resulting in forty-three British dead), the London Underground bombings of 2005 (causing fifty-two deaths in total) and Provisional IRA bombings on British soil. It was, of course, the television images of the two towers – being struck, burning and then collapsing – that conveyed Al-Qa'ida's 'propaganda of the deed' to the world.

In response to the attacks, Bush launched a 'global war on terrorism' in his War on Terror speech on 20 September.[4] In Security Council Resolution 1368, the UN condemned the attacks and acknowledged the right of nations to individual and collective self-defence. For the first time in its history, NATO's North Atlantic Council agreed to invoke Article V of its charter, stating that members 'will assist the Party or Parties so attacked by taking forthwith, individually and in concert with the other Parties, such action as it deems necessary, including the use of armed force'.⁵ The EU expressed solidarity with the US and Blair affirmed that the UK would 'stand shoulder to shoulder with our American friends' and that 'we, like them, will not rest until this evil is driven from the world.'⁶ Blair spoke directly with the leaders of Russia, Germany, France and Italy, as well as President Bush, the following day. He notes that 'The collective sense of solidarity was absolute'.⁷

The Overthrow of the Taliban and Beyond, 2001–05
Afghanistan was identified as the country in which Al-Qa'ida had developed its main bases, with the acquiescence of the Taliban government. Blair remained in close contact with Bush in the weeks following the attacks, and travelled to Russia, Pakistan and the Middle East to build support for a military campaign to eliminate these bases. US-led coalition military operations began on 7 October with the aim of uprooting Al-Qa'ida's foothold in the country, principally using air power, while the Northern Alliance – a military coalition of opposition forces in Afghanistan – advanced to overthrow the Taliban government judged to have been sheltering Al-Qa'ida.⁸ Following the Northern Alliance's capture of the capital, Kabul, in December 2001, Afghan tribal leaders met in Bonn under the auspices of the UN and came to an agreement over the governance of Afghanistan. The Bonn Agreement established an Afghan Interim Authority, with a mandate of six months, and an Afghan Constitution Commission. The Afghan Interim Authority was later replaced by the Afghan Transitional Administration, with a mandate of two years within which elections would take place.

UK forces were involved from the start in the US Operation *Enduring Freedom* (OEF). The Royal Navy submarines HMS *Trafalgar* and *Triumph* were used in Tomahawk cruise-missile attacks against the Taliban and Al-Qa'ida, while the RAF's Sentry, Nimrod and Canberra aircraft provided reconnaissance. TriStar and VC10 aircraft refuelled US strike aircraft, some of which flew from the British Indian Ocean Territory of Diego Garcia, used by the US as a permanent base.⁹ Hercules aircraft and Chinook helicopters were used for lift, and Special Boat Service and Special Air Service forces were also deployed.

Coincidentally, the UK was conducting Exercise *Saif Sareea II* in Oman at the time, meaning that ground forces, a large naval task group, led by the carrier HMS *Illustrious*, and Royal Air Force (RAF) attack and surveillance aircraft were already in the Gulf. In November 2001, Royal Marines from 40 Commando took part in securing Bagram airfield in Parwan Province, which was to become the largest US base in Afghanistan. Subsequently, from April to July 2002, following the US Operation *Anaconda* against the Taliban and Al-Qa'ida, 45 Commando led a 1,700-strong battlegroup, including US, Australian and Norwegian forces, to sweep through eastern Afghanistan in Operation *Jacana*. The purpose of this operation was to destroy Al-Qa'ida's remaining infrastructure and prevent its movement. Troops found a number of caves and bunkers housing ammunition and supplies, which were destroyed.

In December 2001, as part of the Bonn Agreement, the International Security Assistance Force (ISAF) was formed with UN authorisation to assist the Afghan Transitional Administration in securing Kabul. The UK led the first ISAF mission with a brigade headquarters and infantry battalion totalling 2,100 troops. Meanwhile, the Taliban had dispersed amongst the Pashtun population in southern Afghanistan.

In his autobiography, Tony Blair maintains that the UK's mission, in participating in these coalition operations, was clear and fourfold – 'to exorcise Al Qaeda ... to prevent Taliban re-emergence ... to build democracy ... [and] to ensure there is a proper, not a narco, economy' – and that these elements had to be conjoined. He also admits, or rather posits, that this would require 'a complete and sustained engagement, backed by the resources and the will over a very long period'.[10] In fact, after a brigade-sized commitment to the initial intervention and the first command of ISAF, the UK's subsequent military contribution to Afghanistan from 2002 until 2005 was rather modest. The pattern was one, clearly emphasised in the 1998 Strategic Defence Review (SDR), of 'early in' alongside the US, followed by a handover to less expeditionary nations, allowing the UK an 'early out'. Turkey assumed command of ISAF in the summer of 2002 and the British military contribution was reduced to 300 troops.

Subsequently, until 2006, the British contribution to operations in Afghanistan was principally one of nation-building. In March 2003, the UK began to train junior non-commissioned officers for the Afghan National Army and, later that year, established Provincial Reconstruction Teams (PRT) in Mazar-e-Sharif,[11] as well as in Meymaneh, in the north of Afghanistan.[12] In 2004, the UK contributed an additional 700 troops to a new Quick Reaction Force based in Mazar-e-Sharif, which would provide a theatre reserve for supporting stability in the north. There were five deaths of British soldiers before 2006; two were blue-on-blue killings by colleagues, one was a suicide following one of these incidents, one was the result of a suicide bomb in Kabul, and the other was the outcome of an attack on a convoy in the Mazar-e-Sharif region.

In August 2003, NATO assumed leadership of ISAF with UN authorisation,[13] replacing the six-monthly rotations of national command that had occurred prior to this.[14] By this time, the US and the UK, and some other coalition partners, were heavily engaged in Iraq. In October 2003, the ISAF mandate expanded from its original, very limited focus on security in Kabul and its environs, to incorporate the whole of Afghanistan. Stage one of the expansion was in the north, where the PRTs – including those led by the UK – came under ISAF command. German and Dutch PRTs were also established. This first phase of ISAF's expansion was completed in October 2004.

In September 2004, the UK deployed six Harrier GR7 attack aircraft to Kandahar, in the south, to support OEF operations. OEF remained a US national operation, independent of ISAF and focused on the elimination of Al-Qa'ida.

Stage two of the ISAF expansion, in an anti-clockwise direction to the west, was announced in February 2005 and undertaken in 2006 with Italian, Spanish and Lithuanian PRTs. ISAF also provided security for the presidential elections in 2004 and parliamentary elections in 2005 that concluded the Bonn process.

The 'New Chapter' to the Strategic Defence Review, 2002
In July 2002, the 'New Chapter' to the 1998 SDR was published, taking account of the events of 9/11.[15] The paper addressed the military contribution to dealing with the causes and symptoms of terrorism. Although it accepted that threats of the nature of 9/11 had not been considered in the 1998 SDR, there was a continuity with the expeditionary focus of the SDR and the concept of the Joint Rapid Reaction Force (JRRF) it introduced. Indeed, the New Chapter stressed the need to counter terrorism at range, 'to stabilise, coerce or find-and-strike', and it pointed 'towards the use of rapidly deployable light forces rather than armoured or mechanised forces and artillery'[16] and the likelihood of participation in several, more frequent and smaller-scale operations, which would be 'potentially more demanding than one or two more substantial operations'.[17] Crucially, it also indicated that operations would be further afield than the Gulf scenario that was the range benchmark for the 1998 SDR. Special forces, intelligence aided by 'network-centric capability', precision and unmanned aerial vehicles were all capabilities to be enhanced. A lighter and more agile land component might have been the outcome of the New Chapter had subsequent events not served to impede this.[18]

The New Chapter also considered the military contribution to domestic security, but not at the expense of expeditionary capability. A domestic reaction force of 5,000 was to be formed of army reserves,[19] spread over a number of regional units, and the role of headquarters land command in domestic security was to be enhanced. The New Chapter also emphasised that 'we have made clear that we are not going to allow threats at home to tie up significant numbers of our high readiness Armed Forces and prevent us from acting abroad' and that 'tackling the problem where possible at a distance is preferable to waiting for problems to come to us: in that sense operations overseas are often the best form of home defence'.[20] Although the New Chapter made little mention of naval roles, it seemed to confirm the classical British role of discrete, rapid and elegant use of the military at range in a new 'Columbian Era' – a maritime century predicted by General Robert Fry[21] and discussed in the 1998 SDR. This was not to be; at least, not in the immediate years ahead.

The 2003 White Paper
In December 2003, the UK MoD published another defence White Paper, *Delivering Security in a Changing World*, following the New Chapter of the previous year.[22] This pattern of occasional papers, begun by the Labour government with the 1998 SDR, replaced the annual defence White Paper – the Statement on the Defence Estimates – published by previous governments. The 2003 White Paper continued to confirm the conclusions of the SDR but, in this case, focused on the importance of 'effects-based operations'[23] (EBO) and 'network-enabled capability' (NEC). It was, however, criticised as 'bland' and lacking in detail by the House of Commons Defence Committee,[24] which was concerned that expectations on the armed forces continued to expand, while network-enabled capability would provide the necessary economies rather than enhance the capabilities of existing numbers of systems. In particular, it was argued, the issue of personnel overstretch during recent operations had not been properly addressed. Indeed, in retrospect, the document offered little that was new and its conclusions were overtaken by the real challenges of Afghanistan and Iraq that were to emerge. One might argue that those challenges were the result of deviations from a sound military

strategy for the UK that evolved in the 1990s, that was presented in the 1998 SDR and confirmed by the two subsequent White Papers, although Robert Fry gives another view in Chapter VII.

The Iraq War, 2003
The joint declaration by George W Bush and Tony Blair at Crawford, Texas, in April 2002 was forceful in insisting that Saddam Hussein should allow UN inspections of WMD to take place in Iraq or face removal from office. The meeting followed Bush's State of the Nation address in January, in which he declared the War on Terror. In his autobiography, Blair asserts that the purpose of and justification for the invasion – Iraq's regular defiance of previous UN resolutions from 1991 – was legal.[25] However, in his speech to the Scottish Trades Union Congress of February 2003, he added a moral consequentialist argument that there would be fewer killings in Iraq if a war took place than if Saddam Hussein remained in power.[26] Blair had persuaded Bush to follow legal process and await a UN Resolution to insist on weapons inspections before invading – a choice that some members of Bush's own administration did not favour. UN Security Council Resolution 1441 was passed on 8 November 2002 and, with the threat of military action looming, Saddam Hussein gave inspectors conditional access, but was not fully compliant with the demands of the resolution.

Blair then pressed for a second UN resolution before military action was taken, and this might have garnered greater international support for such action; Canada, for instance, would not commit without a second resolution. By February, Europe in particular had become increasingly divided, with France and Germany opposed to war but with NATO's new Central and Eastern European members in favour of supporting US action. On the day of Blair's Scottish Trades Union Congress speech, there was a demonstration by more than a million people against war in London. In the event, French President Jacques Chirac pledged to veto a second resolution, making it clear that this was not to happen. Blair took the issue of going to war alongside the US to Parliament on 18 March 2003 and won the debate handsomely, despite the opposition of key Cabinet members Clare Short and Robin Cook. The amendment authorising the invasion was passed by 412 to 149 votes. A quarter of Labour Party MPs voted against the motion alongside the Liberal Democrats. Cook resigned after the result, although Short did not. It bears mention that British forces were, by this time, in the advanced stages of preparation for war, and this commitment would have put pressure on MPs to support the nation's troops, despite any reservations they might have held.

There had been three broad 'packages' for the UK's possible military commitment to support the US.[27] The first was a very modest contribution of intelligence support, access to UK bases (in Diego Garcia and Cyprus) and British special forces. The second included a maritime naval and air commitment of around '90 front-line aircraft, 20 warships, with 13,000 personnel all told'.[28] The third added a divisional-level ground force of 'over 300 tanks/armoured vehicles and 28,000 personnel'.[29] It was expected that these invasion forces would enter Iraq alongside US ground forces across the Turkish border. Blair mentions that the Chief of the Defence Staff, Admiral Sir Michael Boyce, had said that 'he would have a real problem with the army if they were not fully involved, and such involvement alone gave us far greater influence in shaping US thinking', adding that this was also his 'own instinct'.[30] James De Waal, a former Foreign Office and MoD insider, explores the problems of this decision-making process and the relationship between senior military officers and the government. He notes the concerns of senior civilian policy advisers about the third option. The deployment of British land forces to Kuwait for preparatory training was finally announced on 20 January. Some 9,500 members of the reserves were, in due course, deployed. One problem with late decisions was that there was insufficient time for all reservists to be properly prepared.[31]

The matter of influence over US decision-making had been an important, albeit unstated, premise of the 1998 SDR, as it would be for the 2010 Strategic Defence and Security Review (SDSR). It would be fair to say that troops-on-the-ground indicate a far greater commitment to an ally than the contribution of other military capabilities. In this case, however, the greatest influence the UK actually had over the US was in pressing for a UN resolution, as while these negotiations were underway, the ground commitment had not yet been made. Subsequent influence in the conduct of the war was decidedly lacking, notably in ensuring that full preparations had been made for 'Phase IV' – the occupation that would follow the overthrow of Saddam Hussein. The British government would have been well aware of the demands of occupation, in particular the scale of the forces that would be needed.[32] (Indeed, the US State Department had conducted a detailed study, but this was ignored when responsibility was handed over to the DoD). In any case, US Secretary of Defense Donald Rumsfeld had been dismissive of the importance of the UK's contribution in this regard in a press statement of 11 March 2003.[33]

An unexpected turn of events just before the invasion may have rendered the British experience of Phase IV operations more difficult than it otherwise might have been. On 1 March 2003, the Turkish Parliament voted by a small majority not to allow US and British troops to invade Iraq through Turkey.[34] This decision, which followed months of negotiation and promises of large amounts of money, was unexpected and it greatly complicated the invasion operation. Indeed, Turkey would have provided a land route from Europe for a substantial portion of the forces, from the territory of a NATO ally with its own robust forces for protection of lines of support. It would also have allowed entry into the Kurdish-dominated regions of northern Iraq. In retrospect, had UK forces been assigned these regions – rather than the south – for the subsequent occupation, it is likely that a more coherent Kurdish regional government would have eased the burden on the UK of nation-building and counter-insurgency.

On 18 March, Bush broadcast a message to Saddam Hussein to flee the country within forty-eight hours. Naval movements into theatre included the pre-positioning of carrier-borne aviation and Tomahawk cruise-missile-armed submarines and ships. Combat operations began on 20 March with air attacks on Baghdad. During the night of 21 March, the 'shock and awe'[35] bombardment of Baghdad was carried out largely by Tomahawk missiles. One might have drawn from the literature of 'shock and awe' and 'rapid dominance' that this sort of initial coercive operation would achieve a near-bloodless war.[36] The problem, in this context, was that only one part of the population needed to be coerced into submission or acquiescence – in this case, the outer circle of the regime, since the inner circle would have nothing to gain from compliance. But the other, far greater part of the population needed to be wooed and reassured if this was truly to be a 'liberation', as the operation's title – *Iraqi Freedom* – implied. However precise the Tomahawk attacks were intended to be, the terror caused that night would hardly be the first step in winning the 'hearts and minds' of the Iraqi people when the coalition needed to meet its responsibilities for occupation. Indeed, General William S Wallace, commander of US V Corps, later commented that the resistance of the Iraqi military was much higher than had been war-gamed.[37]

Only the US, UK and Australia fielded substantial numbers of troops during the invasion. British operations in the war were commanded by the joint commander, Air Chief Marshal Sir Brian Burridge, from his headquarters in Qatar. On 20 March, British Royal Marines of 40 and 42 Commando began an amphibious assault to secure access to the south through Umm Qasr and its waterway. An extensive naval operation proceeded to clear the waterway of mines. Umm Qasr was finally secured on 25 March, with RFA *Sir Galahad* following with supplies of humanitarian aid. An important objective for the Royal Marines was to secure the southern oilfields from sabotage. Some thirty oil installations were set alight, but this was a small proportion of the total number. Meanwhile, the British 7th Armoured Brigade, the Desert Rats, marched on Basra from the Kuwaiti border, investing the city, alongside US forces, with heavy fighting. For the US, V Corps continued its rapid transit to Baghdad along two lines of operation. The 3rd Infantry Division approached from the southwest, while the 1st Marine Expeditionary Force approached from the southeast. Progress was delayed by a large sandstorm on 25 March, though the 'operational pause' at this stage may have been useful in allowing logistic support to catch up with so rapid an advance. US forces besieged Baghdad on 3 April, the occupation of which followed on 9 April, with some 120 US servicemen killed in the operation. US forces benefited hugely from advances in network-centric warfare (NCW) in integrating effects, in particular the co-ordination of ground and air actions. It would not have been practical for British land and air forces to have taken part in scale in the advance to Baghdad as they had not developed the necessary integration. However, British special forces conducted operations elsewhere in Iraq and contributed particular skills. At the height of the invasion, the British force level was 46,000 personnel.

When raiding and reconnaissance missions into Basra indicated that the moment was right, British forces finally occupied the city on 6 April. Kurdish forces, supported by US Special Forces, occupied the northern city of Kirkuk on 10 April and moved to Mosul the following day. Occupation of the principal cities was accompanied by scenes of elation amongst residents, closely followed by periods of lawlessness and extensive looting. Targets included hospitals, museums and banks, and local populations expressed their dissatisfaction with the lack of local security, blaming the occupying forces. Meanwhile, coalition forces continued to seek out and eliminate pockets of resistance and to search for senior members of the Ba'athist regime. On 14 April, US forces occupied the town of Tikrit, 140 km northwest of Baghdad. On 1 May, aboard the aircraft carrier USS *Abraham Lincoln*, Bush announced that 'the battle of Iraq is one victory in a war on terror'.[38] Blair also used the word 'victory' in a speech in the House of Commons, but warned that the conflict was not yet over.

Military commanders could rightly claim complete success in this invasion operation. Coalition forces achieved military control of the territory of Iraq and removed political control from the regime of Saddam Hussein. In spite of precarious lines of support, a shortage of reinforcements and an appalling sandstorm, Baghdad was besieged for fourteen days and was occupied within three weeks. Phase IV, the occupation, was to be another matter.

The Occupation of Iraq, 2003–09

Following the combat phase, Multinational Division (South East) – the force responsible for security in the southeast of the country – remained under British command, with initial responsibility for the southern governorates of Al-Muthanna, Maysan, Dhi Qar and Basra. Its headquarters were at Basra airport and, in the first year, UK forces were able to concentrate on reconstruction and the development of governance through tribal leaders. The region was predominantly Shia, and Basra looked forward to the prospect of rebuilding its wealth through trade and oil. Iranian influence was strong, and smuggling and organised crime were rife, but the British approach was to facilitate local Iraqi authority, rather than to impose governance onto this complex social environment. As subsequent events showed, British planning did not take into account the range of likely outcomes following invasion and regime change in this region. In particular, in spite of the experience of operations in the former Yugoslavia, there was a lack of awareness of the need for adequate numbers of troops and other capabilities for peace-enforcement. This might be seen as the behaviour of a liberating rather than an occupying force. It has also been characterised as a typically British 'soft' approach to complex emergencies.[39]

On 18 April 2004, the Mahdi Army, a Shia paramilitary force formed by the cleric, Muqtada Al-Sadr, began an uprising in central and southern Iraq. British forces, with the help of local leaders, were able to cope with attacks in Basra, giving justification to the British approach when compared with the higher levels of violence further north. In November 2004, a battalion of the Black Watch was deployed to Camp Dogwood, some 40 km southwest of Baghdad, to assist US forces in the recapture of Fallujah, a combat operation characteristic of peace-enforcement rather than reconstruction.

Security in Basra and its environs deteriorated as the situation worsened in Baghdad and elsewhere during 2004 and 2005. Soft hats were exchanged for armoured vehicles. British forces did not have the numbers to cope with this shift to counter-insurgency; nor was there the political will in the UK to increase the British presence following an unpopular invasion. There has been much criticism of the inability of British troops and their commanders in theatre to adapt to the particular demands of counter-insurgency in this environment. US forces are perceived as having come from a poorer understanding of counter-insurgency to adapt their doctrine and practices much more quickly and effectively. However, the political situation in the UK and the strategic direction from government were huge constraining factors. Furthermore, the focus of US military efforts and the target of the 2007 'surge' were principally Al-Qa'ida and Sunni insurgents. There was no overarching strategic direction to cope with the Shia insurgency. There was also the issue of 'boots on the ground'. In any complex emergency, if violent escalation is to be dominated, there is an adequate ratio of intervening troops to population and territory, which, while not guaranteeing success, remains a *sine qua non* for planning. (Although the circumstances were very different, the ratio of troops to population in IFOR in Bosnia and KFOR in Kosovo give an indication of the planning scale.) One study based on historical examples of counter-insurgency suggests a ratio of twenty to twenty-five counter-insurgents (police and military) to every 1,000 residents.⁴⁰ This ratio accords with force numbers for KFOR and IFOR, as well as with those deployed in the Malayan Emergency (1948–60).

In July 2006, the Al-Muthanna Governorate was transferred to Iraqi control; Dhi Qa was similarly transferred in September. Later that month, Iraqi and British forces conducted a robust military operation in Basra codenamed *Sinbad*, with the objective of rooting out police corruption to enable the transfer of responsibility for the city to the Iraqi government. The aim was to target the police and seize police stations. Traditional counter-insurgency methods were used to dominate areas of the city for forty-eight hours or so, in order to build control. The operation was initially successful but there were insufficient forces to impose enduring control.⁴¹ By January 2007, British patrols in Basra were routinely being attacked, with bases regularly targeted by rockets.⁴² Maysan Governorate was handed over in April 2007, as finally was Basra that December. Muqtada Al-Sadr had ordered a six-month cease fire for the Mahdi Army in August of that year and had reached an 'accommodation' with the British command.⁴³

The issue of the necessary ratio of troop numbers to population for effective peace-enforcement and counter-insurgency in a troubled environment is again of relevance: by any calculation based on historical evidence, and given that the population of Basra Governorate was over 2 million at the time, UK troop numbers were far too low, from 2004, to dominate the escalation of violence. Numbers were further reduced in 2008 from 7,000 to 5,500 – camped at Basra airport rather than in the city itself. The objective was one of overwatch: to have forces available to respond and to assist Iraqi security forces if the situation deteriorated beyond their means, but not to engage directly on the ground routinely. David Kilcullen, the Australian adviser on counter-insurgency to the then-US commander General David Petraeus, saw the withdrawal as a British defeat.⁴⁴

Table 1: British Ground-Troop Commitments to Iraq/Operation *Telic*, 2003–10 (Approximate Annual Peak Figures).

Year	Ground Troops	Fatalities
2003[46]	45,000	53
2004	18,000	22
2005	8,600	23
2006	8,500	29
2007	7,200	47
2008	5,500	4
2009	4,100	1
2010	150	0

Source: *The approximate figure for each year is the total number of forces of all three services deployed on the ground in the combat phase. See House of Commons Defence Committee,* Lessons of Iraq Volume 1 *(London: The Stationery Office, 4 March 2014), pp. 39, 52. Thirty-two thousand were deployed through Kuwait; see National Audit Office, 'Operation TELIC' – United Kingdom Military Operations in Iraq', Report by the Comptroller and Auditor General, HC 60, Session 2003–2004, 11 December 2003. Fatality data is from* BBC News, *'Iraq War in Figures', 14 December 2011.*

Widespread violence continued in Basra. In March 2008, with the consent of Iraqi Prime Minister Nouri Al-Maliki, the Iraqi Army conducted a major operation to drive the Mahdi Army from Basra known as *Charge of the Knights*. Opening the Battle of Basra, the army achieved control in some areas, but the operation did not establish the intended levels of security throughout the city. While the US provided air support, there was minimal involvement by British forces. British combat troops ended operations in southern Iraq on 30 April 2009, handing over their base in Basra to US forces – though the UK's Operation *Telic* only finally came to an end when the Royal Navy completed its training mission, the UK-Iraq Training and Maritime Support Agreement, two years later, on 22 May 2011. Table 1 presents approximate British troop levels on the ground in each year of the campaign, as well as British fatalities. The numbers include Royal Marines, RAF and Royal Navy personnel on the ground, while other Royal Navy and Royal Fleet Auxiliary (RFA) personnel and RAF aircrew also took part in the operation, and British government civilian staff and contractors were also in theatre.

The British Commitment to Afghanistan from 2006

In the spring of 2006, the UK's modest contribution of forces operating in Kabul and northern Afghanistan was replaced by 3,300 troops in Helmand Province,[45] as part of the third stage of NATO's anti-clockwise expansion to the south.

In evidence to the House of Commons Foreign Affairs Committee, former British Ambassador to Kabul Sir Sherard Cowper-Coles stated that General Sir Richard (now Lord) Dannatt, Chief of the General Staff from 2006, had told him in 2007 that if the UK did not redeploy the battlegroups becoming free from Iraq, the army would lose them in a future defence review.[46] Dannatt denied this and has since stated that Cowper-Coles has apologised.[47] To quote General Sir Robert Fry and Desmond Bowen, 'The apparent, but illusory, success in the Multinational Division (South East) in 2003–4 encouraged the UK chiefs of staff to conclude that operations could be successfully maintained and concluded in Iraq, while, concurrently, a plan could be scoped in conjunction with close allies for the execution of the later phases of the NATO Afghan campaign'.[48] For the purposes of this chapter, this authoritative statement by the Deputy Chief of Defence Staff (Commitments) and director general for security policy in the MoD at the time can put to rest the dispute between Cowper-Coles and Dannatt.

Michael Clarke has examined the process of decision-making and, in particular, the relationship between the senior military in the MoD and the then-Secretary of State for Defence John Reid.[49] The evidence is that Reid's concerns about the Helmand commitment and the scale of forces required were assuaged by the then-Chief of the Defence Staff, General Sir Michael Walker. Government had capped force levels at 3,150 and these troops were expected to operate in a 'permissive environment'.[50] These presumptions were contradicted by reports from pre-deployment planners from 16 Air Assault Brigade on reconnaissance in Helmand and a study carried out by the MoD's own Directorate of Operational Capability, but such concerns were dismissed.[51] In the event, it was necessary to increase British force numbers progressively to 6,300 by the autumn, and to almost 7,600 by the following summer, rising eventually to 9,500 by 2009.

The decision to commit British forces to Helmand instead of Kandahar Province appears to have been made through an agreement in 2004 between the US, British, Canadian and Dutch militaries. Canadian forces had been in Kandahar in 2002 and it was agreed that they should go back. The Dutch took Uruzgan Province to the north and the British took the large and mostly rural province of Helmand to the south.[52]

With the UK's commitment to Helmand, the Allied Command Europe Rapid Reaction Corps (ARRC) assumed command of ISAF. The UK had command of the ARRC and had provided the command framework since its creation in the early 1990s. This was its first operational employment, reinforcing NATO's 'out-of-area' role. General Sir David Richards assumed command of ISAF as ARRC commander.

The role of British troops in Helmand quickly shifted from one of nation-building to one of counter-insurgency. They first operated in the area between Camp Bastion – where they were based – Lashkar Gah and Gereshk in central Helmand. The 'ink spot' plan presented by General Richards was to establish discrete areas with acceptable levels of security and then to join these up. If this plan was to be effective in Helmand, British forces would sooner or later need to deploy to areas in the north of Helmand. The new governor of Helmand, Mohammad Daoud, pressed for this to happen quickly, and the 'platoon houses' plan was put into effect from April 2006. This plan saw small units of British troops spread across settlements further north in Helmand, including Musa Qala, Sangin, Garmsir, Now Zad and Kajaki. These decisions were taken in theatre without specific UK government approval or, indeed, awareness at secretary-of-state level. Even with the increases in force levels later that year, troop numbers were not sufficient to dominate escalation and impose military control. As a result, British troops ended up fighting small but full-scale battles very much at the high end of the counter-insurgency spectrum in these pockets. Sangin was besieged by the Taliban in July 2006 and UK paratroopers required US and Canadian assistance to retake the town. In August, Musa Qala was besieged and relieved by paratroopers.

In spring 2007, the British led Operation *Achilles* to clear the Taliban from key locations in northern Helmand. Taliban fighters were expelled from Sangin and Gereshk. A follow-up operation temporarily cleared the Taliban from around Kajaki in the lower Sangin Valley. Subsequently, in December 2007, Musa Qala was occupied by the Taliban, before Operation *Snakebite*, led by Afghan forces, retook the town on 10 December. In August 2008, a British-led formation of NATO and Afghan forces was able to convoy sections of a large electricity turbine to the Kajaki Dam to develop supplies of electricity to the region. Through Operation *Panther's Claw*, in the summer of 2009, British-led forces drove the Taliban out of areas in central Helmand in order to secure canal and river crossings, with this operation carried out alongside a US advance further south. Notwithstanding these specific successes, British forces did not have the numbers – even alongside the Afghan National Army and with the support of NATO partners – to prevent the Taliban from returning to relieved areas and from establishing a presence elsewhere. A force of 20,000 in 2006 would have been the minimum requirement for such a task, based on the population of Helmand, and bearing in mind that this province was likely to have been one of the areas of retreat of the overthrown Taliban government (and noting, further, that this figure does not take into account the size of the province and its geography).

Table 2: British Ground-Troop Commitments to Afghanistan, 2001–13 (Approximate Annual Peak Figures).

Year	Ground Troops	Fatalities
2001	4,000+	0
2002	300	3
2003	300	0
2004	1,000	1
2005	1,000	1
2006	3,600	39
2007	7,600	42
2008	8,030	51
2009	9,500	108
2010	9,500	103
2011	9,500	46
2012	9,500	44
2013	7,900	9

Note: *The numbers include Royal Marines, RAF and Royal Navy personnel on the ground. In addition, Royal Navy and Royal Fleet Auxiliary personnel at sea and RAF and Royal Navy aircrew took part in the operation and British government civilian staff and contractors were in theatre.*

Source: *Fatality figures to 23 December 2013 from* BBC News, 'UK Military Deaths in Afghanistan', <http://www.bbc.co.uk/news/uk-10629358>, accessed 4 March 2014.

The ability to disperse counter-insurgent capability is also a factor in such operations, and adequate capabilities for the necessary mobility are essential. In Helmand, helicopter lift had the potential to provide the agility both to respond to the security situation and to remove the threat of improvised explosive devices (IEDs) to troops using ground vehicles. Although numbers of such helicopters were subsequently increased, the demand was neither foreseen nor provided for in the initial intervention in Helmand.

Of course, neither troop nor helicopter numbers are, in themselves, a recipe for success. Even with helicopters present, ground patrols are still necessary. But adequate quantities of both are vital. It was not until President Obama ordered 30,000 more troops into Afghanistan in the 'surge' enacted after December 2009 that allied force levels in relation to population and territory became realistic.

General Sir David Richards, by this time commander-in-chief, Land Forces, acknowledged the need for the army to be on a 'war footing'. A 'war footing' can be interpreted to mean that government and higher command understand the need for properly resourced combat capability that can see the intervention through to the intended end-state of peace and stability. At the same time, war footing implies that the British people must be ready to accept casualties, while another aspect is the need to move away from a garrison mentality, characterised by short-term troop rotations and commanders with little time to build experience until they are relieved. Another interpretation could be the need to establish a sequential military campaign, progressing through decisive events to the intended conclusion: insurgencies are typically 'cumulative' in their effects and the responses to them.[53]

From July 2010, US Marines took responsibility for Sangin and northern Helmand, reducing the UK's responsibilities for territory to a level that was reasonable for the number of troops it had in theatre. The necessary levels of security for the development of governance, law and order and the economy started to become achievable in Helmand. There was a progressive transfer of responsibility for security to Afghan military and police forces. In 2013, British force levels had been reduced from 9,000 at the beginning of the year to

5,200 in December. That month, Prime Minister David Cameron also confirmed that by the end of 2014 there would be no British troops in combat roles in Afghanistan.[54] Table 2 presents approximate British troop levels on the ground in each year of the campaign and British fatalities.

The Trident-Replacement Decision, 2006

During the course of these two wars, there were other important events in the evolution of British defence policy. In December 2006, the Labour government under Tony Blair took the decision to replace the *Vanguard*-class submarines, which carry the Trident strategic nuclear deterrent, in the early 2020s. The 2006 White Paper, *The Future of the United Kingdom's Nuclear Deterrent,* concluded that the UK needed to maintain a minimum strategic deterrent and that a replacement class of four submarines with ballistic missiles would provide continuous at-sea deterrence.[55] The US government offered to participate in the Trident D5 life-extension programme to 2040, if this were to go ahead. Initial Gate – the first formal stage in allocating funding and initiating an assessment phase – was passed in May 2011. In the 2010 SDSR, continuity of the nuclear deterrent was confirmed, but the government took the decision to delay Main Gate – when the majority of funding would be allocated – until after the next general election. This offered the opportunity to consider alternatives to like-for-like replacement. As part of the coalition agreement between the Conservatives and the Liberal Democrats, the latter conducted a study of the available options, which was published in July 2013.[56]

Piracy

While the security of trade routes has been an enduring international concern, in this decade piracy off the east coast of Africa was a particular worry for the UK and other European powers. Three multinational task forces have operated off the Horn of Africa since

2009 in response to the surge of piracy linked to internal instability and a lack of governance within Somalia. The role of the task forces in these operations was first to deter pirate attacks and then to respond to them if they occurred.

The Royal Navy has participated in all three operations but does not have a permanent commitment, in terms of vessels, to any of them. The first, Operation *Atalanta*, is an EU anti-piracy operation launched in 2008 to protect shipping bound for Somalia, and particularly ships of the World Food Programme. It is the EU's first maritime operation and considered to be an effective example of EU military engagement in security. It is commanded from Northwood Headquarters in the UK by a Royal Navy rear admiral. The second, Operation *Ocean Shield*, is a NATO operation that evolved from Operation *Allied Protector*, launched in 2009. The last British sea command of *Ocean Shield* was in 2010. The third, Combined Task Force 151 (CTF-151) is a multinational task force for counter-piracy operations operating in the same area. It is under the command, ultimately, of the US Fifth Fleet in Bahrain, and is part of the Combined Maritime Forces – a twenty-five-nation naval partnership promoting security and stability in the region's maritime environment. The UK Maritime Component Commander (UKMCC), a Royal Navy commodore who commands Royal Navy vessels in Middle Eastern waters, is deputy commander, Combined Maritime Forces. The last British sea command of CTF-151 began in September 2013. Finally, a number of nations – known as 'independent deployers', and including China, India, Iran, Japan and Russia – also conduct counter-piracy operations in the area. These are co-ordinated with those undertaken by the aforementioned formations through various arrangements and processes.

Counter-piracy operations off the Horn of Africa have been effective. The number of attacks in the Gulf of Aden and off Somalia's coast has fallen from 197 in 2009 to just thirteen in 2013. The rate of pirate attacks has not, however, decreased significantly off the coast of West

Africa; neither have rates of attacks declined in parts of South and East Asian waters. Counter-piracy operations are expensive for governments which typically have to commit major warships (including frigates and destroyers) to constabulary operations.

Maritime Humanitarian Operations
While British forces were engaged, over this period, in two wars and conducted standing tasks at home and overseas, they also responded to humanitarian crises caused by natural disasters. While these may not be direct security obligations of the British government or be immediately relevant to national interests, they can be understood as a contribution to the UK's moral status in the world, and therefore to the country's soft power and global influence. One might also expect armed forces to be used for good if they are available to do so.

On 26 December 2004, a tsunami struck the coasts of South and Southeast Asia, killing over 280,000 people, according to the World Health Organization. HMS *Chatham* and RFA *Diligence* were despatched to the Sri Lankan capital of Colombo and the Indian city of Cochin, respectively: *Chatham* provided helicopter lift and a communications centre, while *Diligence* provided workshops, emergency electrical and fresh-water supplies, and transport stores. Trams from both ships repaired fishing boats and made water wells safe. A twenty-strong Forward Support Unit of Royal Navy engineers was flown from Portsmouth to *Diligence*, with engineers also flown to the Maldives to repair generators and a water desalination plant. RAF C-17 heavy lift aircraft also delivered equipment and stores to Banda Aceh, in Indonesia.[57]

In July 2006, five major British warships – the carrier HMS *Illustrious*, the new amphibious ship HMS *Bulwark*, the Type 42 destroyers HMS *York* and *Gloucester*, the Type 23 frigate HMS *St Albans*, and the oiler RFA *Fort Victoria* – were sent to Lebanon to evacuate British and other civilians from the war between Hizbullah and Israel (Beirut airport had been closed and Israeli warships were blockading the coast).

On 12 January 2010, a severe earthquake struck Haiti. Many tens of thousands of people were killed, and many hundreds of thousands injured and made homeless. The Royal Navy did not have an Atlantic Patrol Task (North) (APT(N)) vessel on patrol in the Caribbean at the time, but RFA *Largs Bay*, a stores ship, was despatched on 20 January to transport essential supplies. The UK's contribution to relief funding, civilian response teams and supplies was sizeable. However, had this catastrophe occurred in one of the UK's Caribbean Overseas Territories,[58] an APT(N) Royal Navy ship would have been expected to be on hand at an early stage, showing at least some symbolic support. In relation to Haiti, the Royal Navy had insufficient vessels to maintain a permanent APT(N) Caribbean roulement because the numbers of destroyers and frigates customarily providing this precautionary presence had been vastly reduced since the end of the Cold War.

In November 2013, Typhoon Haiyan struck the Philippines – one of the most powerful storms on record to make landfall. The destroyer HMS *Daring* was sent to help victims followed by the aircraft carrier HMS *Illustrious*. The efforts of her ship's company included rebuilding a school.

The Strategic Defence and Security Review, 2010
Prior to the 2010 general election, all of the main political parties had confirmed that they would conduct a defence review if they came to power. The Labour government set in train a Green Paper discussion process, with cross-party participation, with the Green Paper published in February 2010.[59] The debate before the general election was dominated by the economic crisis and defence had a low profile. The main parties subscribed to the need for the UK to sustain its global influence – despite the recession and austerity – and there was not a wide divergence in their policies. When the Conservative-Liberal Democrat coalition came to power, there were two main

issues of contention: one over options for the nuclear deterrent, as discussed earlier, and the other over the UK's place in Europe.

The coalition established a National Security Council bringing together those government departments with security in their portfolios. This new entity did not have the authority of its US equivalent, nor indeed the directive powers in some key security areas, such as maritime security. Nor did it have the staff numbers to provide the support that would be needed by a directing rather than a co-ordinating authority. But it has had a useful function in educating the various departments and their ministers on security matters.

The SDSR planned for October of that year followed a Comprehensive Spending Review and the publication of a new National Security Strategy. There was very little time for the new government to consult widely and to ensure that the final document had the necessary broad ownership. The Conservative Party did not seem to have a clear vision for defence in the future. The prime minister acknowledged that the result would be short term, and based on the premise that the war in Afghanistan was a priority.

The publication of the White Paper itself followed on the heels of the National Security Strategy.[60] The decisions it contained, particularly in relation to equipment cuts, were inconsistent with any clear policy, notably the abandonment of maritime air surveillance capability and the Harrier GR10 force in favour of the Tornado aircraft. The decision was taken to continue the build of the two large *Queen Elizabeth*-class aircraft carriers, despite the possibility that one might be mothballed. Meanwhile, it was established that all army units would return from Germany to 'super garrisons' in the UK. The Royal Navy and RAF suffered personnel cuts. Army cuts were deferred, but were imposed subsequently as part of the plan to reduce the size of the regular army to 82,000 personnel by 2020.

A series of studies was initiated to consider some of the major questions left unaddressed, including reform of the army; the future role of the reserves, in particular, in substituting for a smaller regular army; the organisation of defence and, particularly, of acquisition structures and processes on the basis of the Levene Report; and reform of the procurement system. Bernard Gray, who had conducted a study of acquisition for the Labour government in 2009, was appointed chief of defence materiel. His study had recommended that the defence-procurement organisation, Defence Equipment and Support, be managed as a government-owned, contractor-operated (GOCO) organisation.

The 2010 Lancaster House Treaty
The 2010 SDSR made much of the establishment of partnerships with other nations in the future, accepting the reality of dwindling clout and rising defence costs. Unsurprisingly, it made little of Europe, focusing instead on new partners, in addition to the US, despite the uncertainties that might be associated with that relationship in the longer term. The 1998 SDR had spoken little of Europe but was followed, that autumn, by the Saint-Malo Declaration between the UK and France, in pursuit of greater coherence in European defence and security policy. In November 2010, there was *déjà vu* when Britain and France once again attempted to establish a common vision for the future: the Lancaster House UK–France Defence Co-operation Treaty.[61] This treaty, signed by David Cameron and French President Nicolas Sarkozy, was distinctly bilateral, to the chagrin of Germany, Poland and others. Yet the relationship was intended to be 'exceptional but not exclusive' – a catchphrase that has since been bandied around in both countries.

The immediate intention of the treaty was for both countries to come together where possible to develop capabilities, such as remotely piloted vehicles and services in the nuclear sector, in hard financial times – an *entente frugale*. Yet the real significance of the treaty, over the longer term, lay in its role in developing interoperability between the two militaries to create the scale that could serve the two nations' common strategic interests. A combined exercise programme was established, as well as a programme to build a Combined Joint Expeditionary Force with high levels of behavioural and technical integration. In 2009, Sarkozy had brought France into the Integrated Military Structure (IMS) of NATO and British-French forces would become valuable hubs of interoperability, particularly for expeditionary operations. For the US, meanwhile, a Europe with greater military clout would enable it to look after its own backyard should America have to turn its attention to priorities elsewhere.

At the political level, after François Hollande came to office in France in May 2012, the relationship became more difficult: Hollande had a more Europeanist focus than his predecessor. However, the treaty opened the door to high levels of military co-operation and the armed services of both nations have embraced the opportunity enthusiastically.

The Libyan Revolution and Civil War, 2011
The Arab uprisings that began in December 2010 started in Tunisia following the death of Mohammed Bouazizi, a market trader who self-immolated in protest at official corruption.[62] After major protests, Tunisian President Ben Ali fled the country on 14 January 2011. The Egyptian government of Hosni Mubarak was subsequently overthrown on 11 February, and President Saleh of Yemen was later replaced, on 25 February 2012, after an election. There were also uprisings and large-scale protests in Bahrain, Syria, Algeria, Iraq, Jordan, Kuwait, Morocco and Sudan.

In Libya, 15 February 2011 is celebrated as the beginning of the revolution against the regime of Colonel Muammar Qadhafi. On that day, security forces killed fourteen protesters in Benghazi. By 24 February, government forces had been forced out of the city; there was an uprising in the city of Misrata; the city of Zawiya, west of Tripoli, had fallen to rebels; and the UK government had begun an evacuation of nationals, with an RAF C-130 Hercules aircraft and chartered civilian planes airlifting civilians from Tripoli airport. The

Type 22 frigate HMS *Cumberland* and Type 42 destroyer HMS *York* secured the port of Benghazi and took evacuees to Valletta, Malta, while C-130s, manned by special forces, airlifted UK civilians from remote oil installations. On 26 February, the UN passed Security Council Resolution 1970, imposing an arms embargo on Libya.

Loyalist forces began a counter-offensive on 6 March. NATO deployed airborne warning and control system (AWACS) surveillance aircraft to monitor troop movements. On 17 March, the UN authorised a no-fly zone over Libya and permitted 'all necessary measures' to protect civilians through Resolution 1973, which would become a key test-case for the Responsibility to Protect.[63] Two days later, Operation *Odyssey Dawn*, commanded by US Africa Command (AFRICOM), began. The British contribution, via Operation *Ellamy*, included the deployment of Tornado and Typhoon aircraft to the Gioia del Colle Air Base in Italy. On 31 March, NATO took command of the no-fly-zone operation under Operation *Unified Protector*, with the UK and France as the leading contributors of forces. Sarkozy and Cameron were instrumental in establishing NATO command and the US took a backseat but continued to provide enabling capabilities. In April, the UK – along with France and Italy – sent military advisers to assist the rebels in defending against the government's counterattacks. The NATO air operation extended to fixed-wing and helicopter ground attacks on government forces. Qadhafi's youngest son was killed in an air attack on Tripoli on 30 April. On 27 July, the UK recognised the rebel National Transitional Council as the 'sole government authority' in Libya. The rebels regained the upper hand as a result of what was effectively NATO close air support and air interdiction, and naval gunfire and cruise-missile support. By 23 August, Tripoli had fallen to the rebels. Fierce fighting continued as loyalists defended Qadhafi's home town of Sirte. On 20 October, Qadhafi was captured and killed, bringing the civil war to an end.

The submarine HMS *Triumph* conducted the first British attack in the war using Tomahawk missiles. HMS *Turbulent* was also used.[64] The UK also deployed sixteen Tornado GR4s and six Typhoon aircraft as major contributors to the air attack operations supported by TriStars and VC10 tankers, as well as four RAF surveillance aircraft drawn from the Nimrod, Sentry and Sentinel fleets. Army Apache attack helicopters and Royal Navy Lynx and Sea King helicopters were also deployed from the amphibious helicopter carrier HMS *Ocean*, which was in theatre from May. Altogether, seven Royal Navy destroyers and frigates were used for enforcement of the arms embargo, sea access, naval gunfire support, and inducement (coercion and reassurance) operations. It was also the first use of the newly formed Response Force Task Group (RFTG) – fusing the old Carrier Strike Task Group and Amphibious Task Group – which was due to have deployed through the Suez Canal for Exercise *Cougar 11* with the French navy, but was instead retained in the Mediterranean for the purpose. During the course of the campaign, the RFTG was usefully split. The aviation support ship RFA *Argus* took elements of 40 Commando Royal Marines off the coast of Yemen, the amphibious ship HMS *Albion* deployed east of Suez for regional engagement and counter-piracy operations, and HMS *Ocean* remained off the coast of Libya.

The Libya campaign exposed problems of co-ordination and execution within the NATO command structure. As France was a relatively new member of the IMS, interoperability between France and other NATO partners had not developed, and French air operations, in particular, were conducted on a co-ordinated rather than a fully integrated basis. It bears mention, however, that without the NATO command structure and organisations, it would have been extremely difficult for European nations to take a lead in the campaign as the US wished.

Mali, 2013

On 11 January 2013, the French military began operations to assist the Malian government in retaking the north of the country after it had been overrun by the National Movement for the Liberation of Azawad, a Tuareg group, supported by the Islamist group Ansar Dine. The French government requested assistance from the UK, which was provided in the form of airlift and air surveillance. There was concern in the UK at the time that a commitment of troops on the ground could lead to embroilment in long-term, counter-insurgency operations. Yet the forty UK personnel who were deployed to Mali itself were a contribution to the EU Training Mission and were not there to support French forces. British troops from The Royal Irish Regiment, 45 Commando Royal Marines and 29 Commando Regiment Royal Artillery arrived in Mali in March 2013.[65]

A further 200 troops were sent to Commonwealth members of the Economic Community of West African States (ECOWAS) to assist in developing the African-led International Support Mission to Mali (AFISMA). AFISMA was expected to provide the force that would take over responsibilities in Mali once France had enabled the government to repossess territory and had embarked on an initial path to stabilisation. On 1 July 2013, AFISMA handed over its responsibilities to the UN Multidimensional Integrated Stabilization Mission in Mali (MINUSMA).

The Mali operation was an early manifestation of the Lancaster House Treaty. While the UK clearly has an interest in the stability of the Sahel region, France took the lead, as would be expected in a nation that is part of the African *Francophonie*. The British commitment was very modest but nonetheless symbolic, particularly at a time when, at the political level, the British–French relationship had become somewhat fraught.

The Syrian Civil War

The Syrian uprising began with protests against the regime of President Bashar Al-Assad in March 2011. In July 2012, the International Red Cross formally declared the situation in the country a civil war. At the time of writing, the death toll exceeded 100,000 and millions had been displaced or had fled overseas. The international community has been hampered in its attempts to resolve the crisis in part by Russian and Iranian support for the Assad regime. Western military intervention has not occurred, with Western powers not wishing to carry out military action to bring about regime change because of the subsequent long-term problems of governance and stabilisation this would entail. Indeed, Western electorates may be unwilling to support an intervention following the experiences of over a decade on the ground in Afghanistan and Iraq. And, in any event, a full-scale invasion and occupation would require over 500,000 competent troops on the ground with a destructive preliminary air campaign threatening highly urbanised communities.[66] The political, social and cultural environments are hugely complex with no obvious replacement government that could command majority support amongst Syrians. There is also the spectre of an Islamist takeover. Meanwhile, the implications of a continued crisis are sombre for Lebanon, Iraq, the Israel–Palestine relationship and the wider Middle East – and all this on the doorstep of Europe, with a NATO ally – Turkey – on Syria's northern border.

After several major instances of the use of chemical weapons against civilians by the Syrian regime, Western pressure to take military action grew. But on 27 August 2013, the British House of Commons voted against military intervention of any kind to eliminate Syria's chemical weapons capability. David Cameron's government was widely criticised for mismanaging the vote and the French government, in particular, was appalled. However, the vote gave President Obama – not enthusiastic about military action himself – some breathing space. No military action was taken and the eventual outcome was an agreement with the Syrian regime for chemical weapons to be removed from Syria under UN supervision.

At the time of writing, the options for any future military intervention are difficult to categorise. If the aim were to be the, at least temporary, federalisation of Syria, overseen by the international community, there might be options for UN or UN-sanctioned peacekeeping operations along internal borders, alongside arms-reduction agreements and processes. However, such an arrangement would require the agreement of all warring parties, as well as external state and non-state supporters. If it were to be effective in such a complex environment, there would be a requirement for the military capacity and combat capabilities for 'overwatch' to dominate any escalation on the ground and to enforce peace. Such a force (or forces) would require strong and effective leadership, probably provided by an experienced framework nation or nations. Would the US, France or the UK – as a triarchy, or two of these countries as a pair – be prepared to take on this burden for at least a decade? And if not, then it must be asked who would.

Conclusion

At the end of 2013, the British coalition government was committed to the withdrawal of British combat forces from Afghanistan over the subsequent twelve months. It faced a general election in the spring of 2015 and another SDSR after that. From the military perspective, the previous twelve years had been dominated by long-term campaigns in Afghanistan and Iraq. Indeed, in MoD language, the word 'campaign' had been adopted to mean enduring commitments on the ground overseas – ironically, perhaps, since the expression has traditionally been used to mean a conclusive, sequential phase in a specific theatre as part of a larger war.

Meanwhile, the doctrinal concept of 'counter-insurgency', which has been at the forefront of military thinking since 2005, has customarily been associated with enduring garrison commitments to support a government to which the forces owe allegiance. And it is here that the issue lies. In both Afghanistan and Iraq, British forces were initially used to aid in removing a government for reasons avowedly to remove threats, enforce international norms and honour a longstanding commitment to a dominant partner nation. Once the regimes had been removed, the purposes, in reality, became moral ones: to repair two nations that had been wounded by the earlier actions. British forces were left on the ground, in the case of Iraq, and reinserted into Afghanistan, in both cases in rather modest numbers, to contribute to nation-building – accepting the prospect of the need for some stabilisation. As such, a partial actor tries to become impartial with the expectation that this will be a short and non-violent process.

At the grand-strategic level of government and the most senior military leadership, the debate of the 1990s about the paradox of 'wider peacekeeping' had been ignored or forgotten. This paradox is that, if there is no formal truce or acceptance of a settlement among all of the parties in a conflict, one must be prepared to engage in peace-enforcement. This requires the ability to dominate the escalation of violence with the capabilities for full-scale combat, and to use combat as necessary against one or more of the parties. If combat is used, however, can the intervening forces ever return to impartiality?

In theatre and in the assigned territories of that theatre – for the UK, in Basra and the south in Iraq, and in Helmand in Afghanistan – troop levels must be adequate to engage in peace-enforcement and the expectation must be that of dominating violence for as long as it takes to establish or re-establish a general truce. The next problem is that an adequate truce will probably be born of exhaustion. One of the key asymmetries of irregular warfare is escalation through protraction – particularly against Western democracies. So, as David Kilcullen preaches in article 27 of his 'twenty-eight articles of counter-insurgency', it is important to 'keep your extraction plans secret'.[67] But this presents yet another paradox for democracies. Electorates expect to know how and why the armed forces they fund and put in harm's way are being used, and for how long. The challenge for militaries is to present a sequential solution to an enemy's cumulative campaign of protraction.

In short, British ground troops have been much criticised for poor counter-insurgency in the struggle for the other 'two towers' of this period, Basra and Helmand. In his damning book, Frank Ledwidge gives many reasons for their poor performance, which include – among others – a failure to adapt, outdated structures and intelligence systems, cavalier post-entry planning, archaic traditions, inadequate equipment, and inflated command structures – ergo lack of accountability.[68] As mentioned earlier, Kilcullen took the view that the British had failed in Basra, while, at the time of writing, the war in Afghanistan is not over.

Yet ultimately the broader failure lay in the grand-strategic choices made. First, there was failure to face the range of possible outcomes following regime change. Second, by any informed judgement, insufficient forces were assigned and without a long-term commitment. Scholars' precise ratios of troops to population can be challenged, but by any measure based on history and experience, in both cases there were far too few. In the case of Iraq, withdrawal to overwatch was inevitable because numbers were not to increase. The US policy of 'epuration'[69] or de-Ba'athification of the instruments of government at every level, including the Iraqi military, left few security instruments and no experienced management in Iraq's regional and central government to relieve occupying forces of their responsibilities early. In the case of Afghanistan, British forces surged somewhat, but it was the contribution of the US Marines to Helmand that turned the tide. Equipment may have been inadequate for the types of operation and the environments, but this was a second-order shortcoming to those of mission, scale and endurance.

There is no question that British forces fought gallantly in the many battles of the two wars. The evolution of British doctrine to counter irregular warfare may have lagged behind that of the US from a sounder original baseline derived from the experience of Bosnia, but things have progressed.[70] As Bosnia showed, the British (and French) have been prepared to take risk and, where the mission is to save lives or make one's own nation safer, that is a military virtue. Yet this exposes the third fault at the grand-strategic level – a failure to define the mission in a clear and convincing way and to accept and adapt to inevitable changes. If the purposes of both interventions were obvious to the British people and were to stop tragedies, or clearly served national security, the British public might have been more accepting of the levels of casualties involved, as they typically have been in the past.

Kilcullen's writing and Ledwidge's criticisms and recommendations about counter-insurgency are invaluable, if open to debate. However, it is important to look more widely at the challenge for the future: that of countering irregular warfare in complex emergencies. Every operation of this type is *sui generis* – accepting that doctrine, if it is good enough, is a resource of experience and resort when uncertainty is overwhelming. Yes, the societal, cultural, informational and geostrategic context must be understood; but irregular warfare evolves, drawing on the fusion of earlier models and adapting, consciously or unconsciously, to immediate events.

An important issue in both wars was that of interoperability. In Afghanistan, multinational military interoperability in Helmand achieved very effective levels between the British, the Danes and the Estonians, and there has been much mutual respect. The US Marine Corps has traditionally worked well with British forces and this continued after the US surge. The problem in Afghanistan was one of interoperability among the many civil and military actors. A NATO command structure with regions assigned to specific lead nations with their own national command chains was not conducive to integrated military effects. Nor was the US counter-terrorist Operation *Enduring Freedom* while it was separated from NATO operations. There was also the hugely complex problem of co-ordinating military activity with civil reconstruction and nation-building efforts. While the need for a 'comprehensive approach' across these boundaries and in co-ordination with local government, NGOs and contractors was well understood and much debated in this period, there will always be differences in mission and objective among entities. For instance, militaries assisting in reconstruction are likely to have an immediate security priority and may not necessarily devote resources to long-term development ends. In Afghanistan, there was no senior civilian official with multinational authority who could co-ordinate all of the instruments of security and development and had the authority to influence the Afghan government until the US administration appointed Richard Holbrooke as special representative for Afghanistan and Pakistan in 2009.[71] Although the term 'comprehensive approach' was originally coined by a UK government agency,[72] it is now shunned by UK officials in favour of an 'integrated approach'.

In Iraq, the US was the framework nation. During the invasion, in some phases, US and UK forces were able to work closely together, during the amphibious landings and the entry from Kuwait, for example. The UK subsequently had responsibility for the south. This geographical separation reflected the fact that it would have been difficult for UK forces to integrate to the required level with US forces in the progression on to Baghdad and the subsequent assault. US forces had achieved a high level of internal integration through the wholesale adoption of the concept of network-centric warfare with a transformative vision. For the UK, network-enabled capability was more of an evolutionary concept which would permit incremental integration as systems developed and were replaced. In the First Gulf War, US and British forces achieved high levels of integration at the divisional level for the campaign of ground manoeuvre to liberate Kuwait. It is unlikely that the necessary integration would have been achievable in a combined US–UK ground-air manoeuvre operation to Baghdad in 2003. The issue of differences in counter-insurgency doctrine and the British retreat from Basra have raised questions about the level of mutual respect between the two armed forces and the implications for a future in which military partnering will become increasingly necessary to achieve advantage through scale. This may be a short-term matter. A more crucial issue for British grand strategy in the future is that of the degree of influence over US decisions that military partnership can provide.

A final issue for British grand and military strategy is the dominant focus on long-term land operations in Afghanistan and Iraq. The 2010 SDSR was very much constrained in the strategic choices it could make in this respect by the ongoing commitment to Afghanistan. Indeed, the announcement of army-personnel cuts was postponed to a later Army 2020 review, ultimately published in July 2012. Since the 2010 SDSR, a mantra in the MoD has been the 'switch to contingency' from campaigns. There is not a convincing definition of 'contingency' in this context, but the message seems to be very much a return to the 1998 SDR vision of operations that are 'early in, early out'. Prompt participation in operations, particularly alongside the US, is enabled by the UK's constitutional war-powers arrangements, and the proposition is that this will allow for strategic influence if the contribution is sufficiently useful in scale and capability. This needs to be complementary not supplementary, and once initial objectives are achieved, other coalition partners which do not have the same expeditionary agility will take over the caretaking. As such, British forces will need to develop agility, adaptability and interoperability with key partners such as the US, and there are implications for air-sea basing and other capabilities that allow for poise and selective action. Navalists would see this as a return to a more maritime strategic vision, but at a time when maritime capabilities are teetering on the verge of critical mass. The Libya and Mali operations emphasised the use of air power for strategic effect, as well as interdiction and close air support. Moreover, air power would have been the instrument of choice had Western powers decided to intervene militarily in Syria in the summer of 2013. 'Air-maritime' is therefore perhaps a better expression in terms of a strategic choice that offers options for early influence through inducement and that seeks to avoid long-term embroilment on the ground. The implications for the army would be a greater emphasis on elite infantry, lighter in armour and more portable, and greater responsiveness, in terms of domestic arrangements, to expeditionary commitments.[73] This characterisation of the UK's strategic future is contentious. At the end of the day, the country's influence through the use of the military instrument, such as it might be in the future, will be the stronger for commitment, and it is ground forces that demonstrate that in spades.

III. THE STRATEGIC SCORECARD: SIX OUT OF TEN

Malcolm Chalmers

I've been asked ... whether, knowing then what I know now, I would have made the same decision. No, I wouldn't.

(Jack Straw, 2012)[1]

THIS chapter presents a 'strategic scorecard' for the ten most important overseas military operations that the UK has conducted since 1991.[2] It assesses the strategic consequences of each of these actions, and provides a retrospective assessment of whether the interventions were worthwhile or not.

The chapter does not assess whether specific decisions to intervene were right on the basis of information available to leaders at the time. However, it does provide an important reference point for such a judgement. Given the repeated gaps between strategic intent and outcome, moreover, it suggests that leaders were hubristic in their over-ambition and negligent in their failure to take sufficient account of the irreducible uncertainty of major military operations.

Due to this chapter's focus on the strategic level, moreover, it does not seek to assess UK military performance at an operational or tactical level. It does offer some thoughts on whether better performance at the operational level might have made a substantial strategic difference, but expresses some scepticism as to whether this would have been the case.[3] While each had its own distinct characteristics, the ten most important operations can be divided into three broad categories.[4]

Table 1: Scorecard for Intervention.

	Iraq 1991	Iraq 1991–2003	Bosnia 1992–95	Bosnia 1995–2002	Kosovo 1999–2003	Sierra Leone 2000	Afghanistan 2001–05	Iraq 2003–09	Afghanistan 2006–13	Libya 2011
Immediate trigger?	Yes	Yes	Yes	Yes	Yes	Yes	Yes	No	No	Yes
UN approved?	Yes	No	Yes	Yes	No	No	Yes	No	Yes	Yes
NATO involved?	No	No	Yes	Yes	Yes	No	Yes	No	Yes	Yes
Limited objective?	Yes	Yes	Yes	Yes	No	Yes	Yes	No	No	Yes
'Boots on the ground'?	Yes	No	Yes	Yes	Yes	Yes	Yes	Yes	Yes	No
Strong local ally?	Yes	Yes	No	No	Yes	Yes	Yes	No	No	Yes
Real net cost (£ bn)[5]	0.68[6]	0.36	0.28	1.45	1.25	0.08	1.06	9.56	19.59[7]	0.24
Strategic success	Yes	Yes	No	Yes	Yes?	Yes	Yes	No	No	No?

Note: *Iraq 1991–2003 refers to operations related to the no-fly zones over northern and southern Iraq. Bosnia 1992–95 covers the UN Protection Force (UNPROFOR) deployment and related Operations* Deny Flight *and* Sharp Guard. *Subsequent British operations in Bosnia, December 1995–2002, were NATO-led.*

First, there were the **five 'force-for-good' operations** in Bosnia (1992–95 and from 1995), Kosovo (1999–2003), Sierra Leone (2000) and Libya (2011). Each of these operations was launched in direct response to new or imminently anticipated atrocities, and the latter four were successful in achieving this initial objective within a matter of months.

In addition to clear humanitarian gains, the operations in Bosnia in 1995 and Kosovo made an important contribution to stabilisation in the western Balkans, helping to bring an end to the regional conflict that had started in 1991 and putting both territories on the path towards European integration. The UK intervention in Sierra Leone played a key part in re-establishing legitimate government in that country, and contributed to the crucial role that intervention (by the UN, the Economic Community Of West African States and France) played in stabilising the weak states of West Africa after their post-1990 descent into conflict. All three operations, therefore, should be judged as strategic successes.

In contrast, the UN Protection Force (UNPROFOR) mission in Bosnia between 1992 and 1995 must be considered a strategic failure. It is true that UNPROFOR did have some success in containing the conflict to Bosnia. It also delivered significant amounts of humanitarian aid, particularly to the besieged city of Sarajevo where it kept the airport open. As UN troop levels increased, it also had a moderating effect on the conflict and the number of civilian deaths, at least until the large-scale offensives of 1995.[8] However, under-resourced and hampered by a weak mandate, it was unable to prevent the collapse of Bosnia into war in April 1992 and the subsequent overrunning of 70 per cent of the country by the Bosnian Serbs. As British troops began to deploy in Bosnia from October 1992, neither was the mission able to stem the widespread atrocities of the war. The fact that the UNPROFOR mission needed saving, failed to stop Srebrenica and a whole host of other atrocities, and had to be replaced by a NATO-led intervention with a completely different concept of operations, marks it as a strategic failure.

It is too early to judge the strategic impact of the Libyan intervention. It may be hard to believe that leaving Muammar

Qadhafi in power would have contributed to Libyan or regional stability. Since his downfall, however, Libya has failed to establish a workable national government, conflict between rival militias has continued, and large quantities of weapons – previously secured in government arsenals – have potentially become available to illicit international markets.

The second category includes the initial interventions in Iraq (1991) and Afghanistan (2001), which can be seen as **two 'force-for-order' operations**, launched with broad international support in response to new and substantial threats to international order (the invasion of Kuwait and the attacks of 9/11, respectively). Both operations met their main objectives – the expulsion of Iraq from Kuwait and the overthrow of the Taliban regime – within months. Both should also, this chapter argues, be seen as clear strategic successes.

This category could also include the series of Iraq-related operations conducted after the end of the 1991 war, but before the 2003 invasion. Taken together, these achieved important 'force-for-order' objectives – containing Iraq's WMD aspirations – as well as being a 'force for good', in protecting Iraqi Kurdistan. Given their relatively limited cost, they can also be considered to have been a strategic success, especially in their early years.

Third, there were the **two 'force-for-change' operations**, in Iraq (from the invasion of 2003 to the UK's ground-troop exit in 2009) and in Afghanistan (from the UK 'surge' operation that started in 2006 until the UK's military exit in 2014). Rather than being responses to specific triggering events, both were launched as preventive interventions (although, as is subsequently explained, both had other rationales). Functioning modern states were thought to be needed in Iraq and Afghanistan if the international community could be assured that these countries could not in future be used as bases from which new threats (WMD and international terrorism) could emanate. As importantly, both were informed by a belief that outside military forces could play the main role in pushing through such a process of transformation in 'rogue states' (like Iraq) and 'failed states' (like Afghanistan).

Both operations were weakened from the start by a lack of support from the host government (in the case of Afghanistan) or an absence of government (in the case of Iraq). From an early stage, both encountered large-scale insurgencies, generated in part by the interventions themselves and fuelled by logistical and rear-area support from neighbouring countries. This resistance in turn forced the US and its allies (including the UK) into deepening their involvement, at considerable financial and human cost. Yet neither operation achieved the ambitions that had initially been set. This chapter will therefore argue that both operations have proven to be strategic failures. At the time of going to press, whatever happens during the last year of the UK combat presence in Afghanistan seems unlikely to make a material difference to this wider judgement.

Methodology and Assumptions
Even if these latter two interventions did not achieve their ambitious initial aims, some might argue that one or both achieved enough benefits to justify the substantial costs involved. In order to make such a judgement, therefore, it is necessary to conduct a counterfactual analysis, imagining what would have happened in the absence of the interventions. The evidence for this judgement must be fairly assessed in relation to circumstances of great turmoil, where outside intervention is only one of many factors shaping local politics and conflict. The chapter also needs to assess strategic success (or failure) across a variety of dimensions, including the amelioration of direct threats to the UK, the upholding of international order, the protection of affected populations, and the achievement of progressive political change.

This chapter's judgements rely on a further assumption: that it is possible to divide the UK's military involvements in both Iraq and Afghanistan into two phases, the first of which (it argues) yielded significant net gains, but the second of which was a strategic failure. In the case of Iraq, it argues that the operation to expel the country from Kuwait was a success, as were, to a more limited extent, the series of small-scale operations conducted between 1991 and 2003. In contrast, it argues, the invasion of Iraq in 2003 was a failure. For Afghanistan, it argues that the initial expulsion of the Taliban (and associated initial state-building activity) was a strategic gain, but that the surge into the south, starting in 2006, was a failure.

This division corresponds to discrete decisions made by the UK government. Nothing in the nature of either involvement meant that the second strategic decision automatically followed from the first. This chapter argues, moreover, that in each case it is possible to identify a distinct, alternative policy path that would have preserved the gains made from the first operation while avoiding the worst consequences of the second.

Such a judgement depends on being able to construct a plausible counterfactual, in each case, to the second operation. In principle, this could simply involve a slight change to the timing of, or other marginal adjustment to, that operation without much change to its essential elements. The counterfactual to the Iraq invasion of 2003, for example, could have been an invasion in 2004. While such an exercise could expose lessons to be learnt at the operational level, however, it is of little strategic value. The assumption in this chapter, therefore, is that the counterfactual alternatives to the occupation missions would have ruled out any large-scale deployment of ground forces to the south (in the case of Afghanistan) or the threat of regime overthrow and occupation (as in Iraq).

It is assumed, however, that these two alternatives could include a continuation of the military deployments that had been initiated during the first interventions (air patrolling over northern and southern Iraq, and protection of the Kurdish areas in Iraq to 'contain' Saddam Hussein; and more limited, but still significant, Western military support to the Afghan government, as was initiated in 2002).

A further difficulty in assessing the success of UK operations during this period is that nine of the ten most important interventions were undertaken as part of a coalition with the US and other NATO allies. Even the exception to this rule – the UK intervention in Sierra Leone in 2000 – was closely linked to the presence of a much larger, and more expensive, UN intervention force. As a result, any assessment that focuses on the UK effort in isolation would inevitably be restricted to an operational rather than a strategic level. A separate operational scorecard for the UK could examine its performance in Helmand Province and southern Iraq in isolation, with a view to assessing whether the UK armed forces performed well within the overall constraints of the wider coalition mission. This is not the purpose of this chapter.

Such an analysis might be of interest if the main purpose was to ask whether the UK could have reduced the resources expended on these operations by bearing a smaller share of the collective burden. This is further discussed in Chapter IX.

From a British point of view, it could also be argued that the primary UK interest in most of these conflicts was to maintain or deepen its relationship with the US, so as to translate this good will into gains in other areas – as discussed in Chapter VIII. On the basis of this rationale, even if the strategic objectives of an operation are not met, the UK might feel satisfied that it was seen as having been a good and reliable ally.

Yet this argument understates the extent to which, in most if not all of these operations, the UK has played an important and autonomous role of its own, deciding for itself the best course of action, even while aware of the need to work with the US and other allies to achieve its objectives. The UK pushed for further military action while the US was still reluctant in four of the nine cases of coalition operations discussed here: the UNPROFOR mission in Bosnia, in which the US did not take part but France did; the 1999 Kosovo crisis, during which Prime Minister Tony Blair went to the

US to lobby President Clinton to threaten the use of ground forces; the surge of UK forces into southern Afghanistan in 2006, well before the US's own surge in that country in 2009–10; and the UK's support (along with France) for military action against the Libyan regime in 2011. In the case of the first Iraq operation, Prime Minister Margaret Thatcher was as keen for action to be taken as was President George H W Bush, who faced significant domestic opposition. Even in the case of the 2003 Iraq War, it is not convincing to argue that the UK's involvement was driven primarily by a desire to gain credit with the US, although this was a factor. More important was Blair's strong belief in the need for military action in order to overthrow a dangerous dictator. The UK could have gained considerable credit in the US by making a nominal military contribution to the invasion and occupation forces. Yet, despite the serious reservations of senior civilian officials, the prime minister insisted that he wanted the UK to deploy a large military force for the invasion itself, and in the subsequent division of responsibilities for post-war governance.[9] The UK, therefore, is best judged as a full collaborator in this and other operations, and its scorecard for these interventions is best assessed in relation to whether they achieved their strategic objectives.

'Force-for-Good' Operations: Bosnia (1992–95 and 1995–2002), Kosovo (1999–2003), Sierra Leone (2000) and Libya (2011)
All of the UK military interventions during this period were driven by some mixture of interests and values. However, urgent humanitarian concerns over ongoing or feared atrocities were the primary driver for the five operations in Bosnia, Kosovo, Sierra Leone and, most recently, for Libya in 2011. Economic or strategic motives, in contrast, were not important drivers for any of these interventions (even in the case of Libya, where no threat to UK oil interests was posed by the Qadhafi regime).

The first of these interventions – UNPROFOR between 1992 and 1995 – involved substantial numbers of UK troops on the ground, but with a mandate that severely limited their ability to protect the local population. The other four interventions were coercive in nature, and had the effect of reshaping other societies in ways that accorded with UK values. All allowed decisive strategic shifts to take place that otherwise might not have been achieved. The Bosnia (1995–2002) and Kosovo interventions played a key role in creating the conditions for the eventual incorporation of the western Balkans into European political and security structures (the EU and NATO). The intervention in Sierra Leone contributed to the wider process of conflict termination in West Africa, helping to prepare the ground for subsequent economic stabilisation. In Libya, however, it is too early to say what the longer-term results of Qadhafi's overthrow will be. Initial turmoil has shown that the construction of a viable state is far from assured, and a long period of disorder and internal conflict remains likely. Yet compared with the likely alternative – a vengeful Qadhafi family re-establishing its power over the country by force – it is still plausible to argue that Libya is in a better place than it would have been in the absence of NATO intervention.[10]

Air power was the primary means of coercion deployed in Bosnia (in 1995–96), Kosovo and Libya. The coercive role of ground forces in the fourth case, Sierra Leone, was small-scale and short-lived. Yet all three of the earlier, coercive force-for-good operations also involved 'boots on the ground': regular forces deployed in follow-up operations to help provide post-conflict security while local forces were established and developed. What distinguishes these operations from the more problematic later interventions after the turn of the millennium, therefore, is that UK forces in Bosnia, Kosovo and Sierra Leone never had to face a significant armed revolt against their presence.

The UK's commitment to use its military as a force for good (the term used in the 1998 Strategic Defence Review) was vital to the decision to undertake these operations. The government's resolution to support populations in peril from attack was a primary driver for the interventions in Kosovo and Sierra Leone, the two most significant UK operations during Tony Blair's first years as prime minister.

Intervention in Sierra Leone
Even now, Sierra Leone is frequently seen as 'exhibit number one' for the success of humanitarian intervention: a short and decisive coercive effort, followed by a sustained military capacity-building effort, accompanied by a considerable DfID development effort. Yet it has not been used as a model for other interventions, in part because of a lack of interest in sub-Saharan Africa on the part of the UK armed forces, and in part because of the unique character of Sierra Leone as a society. There are few, if any, other African societies where UK forces would have been welcomed so readily, reflecting the country's particular colonial history. It also took place in a small country, and in support of both a UN mission, UNAMSIL, and a democratically elected president, Ahmad Tejan Kabbah.

The strategic success of the UK's operation in Sierra Leone was only made possible, moreover, by the fact that it took place as part of a wider process of regional stabilisation. At first, in the early 1990s, outside powers had stood by as the weakest states of the sub-region were torn apart by civil conflict, driven by corrupt post-colonial rulers, economic decline and porous borders. In retrospect, external intervention should have taken place earlier. When it did begin to occur, moreover, many mistakes were made. However, as increased international military and economic resources began to be devoted to the sub-region, conflicts were resolved and managed. Crucially, for Sierra Leone, international forces in Liberia and Guinea-Bissau helped to stabilise the surrounding neighbourhood. Sierra Leone's stabilisation, for its part, contributed in turn to the security of the wider region. In the absence of the stabilisation that took place in the region during this period, conflicts might well have spread, affecting countries – such as Ghana – whose subsequent economic success has been made possible by the absence of civil war.

Intervention in the Balkans

There is also a strong case that the much larger interventions in Bosnia and Kosovo have delivered real strategic benefits. In Bosnia, the eventual NATO-led military intervention, supported by the UN, helped to bring about an end to the war, forcing the Bosnian Serbs to the negotiating table at Dayton and delivering a lasting (albeit imperfect) political settlement. This followed the ineffective UNPROFOR peacekeeping deployment, which failed to resolve the crisis. Many of the failures associated with UNPROFOR were, at their root, failures of high-level diplomacy and strategic disagreement between the US, the UK and France; the more forceful approach increasingly advocated by Washington sat uneasily with the Europeans, whose troops were on the ground and therefore at risk. Absent US leadership and absent the eventual credible use of force against ground targets by NATO – in other words, no fundamental change in diplomatic and military approach to the Bosnian War – it is difficult to image how the Bosnian Muslims would have achieved Dayton's 51/49 territorial split between Muslims/Croats and Serbs – a substantially better deal for the Muslims than a 70/30 split in favour of Republika Srpska and no alliance with the Croats.

The Bosnian War entered a new phase by mid-1995, as a result of a renewed Croat-Muslim alliance with US support, which resulted in a series of territorial losses for the Bosnian Serbs. In the absence of a more forceful NATO intervention, the violence could have gone on for much longer. Even if an unstable ceasefire had been made possible as a result of the advances by Muslim-Croat Federation and Croatian forces, it would have been vulnerable to breakdown in the absence of a clear political settlement. As it was, the credible threat of NATO military force underpinned a political settlement that ensured the survival of a Bosnian state, albeit with its powers severely limited by its partition into two ethnically defined entities.

The Kosovo intervention in 1999 was more difficult and problematic. It lacked a UN mandate, and probably contributed to the worsening of relations with Russia during this period. Its strategic result – the forced secession of Kosovo from Serbia – sat uneasily with the wider norm of recognising international borders unless there is mutual agreement to change them. Its military and economic costs were also much higher than those in any of the other three force-for-good operations of this period, involving a prolonged air campaign (lasting over eleven weeks), accompanied by a clear threat (backed by the UK) that ground forces could be deployed if Serbia did not withdraw from Kosovo. If such a deployment had been necessary, and had plunged the UK and its allies into a ground war with Serbia, a retrospective scorecard might well have found it to have been a strategic failure.

If NATO had declined to intervene in the Kosovo crisis, however, Serbia would likely have consolidated its hold on the territory through large-scale expulsions of the Kosovar Albanian majority population. This in turn could have contributed to the destabilisation of neighbouring Macedonia (whose own demographic balance would have been altered) and Albania. Success in Kosovo as a result of NATO inaction would have emboldened Slobodan Milosevic, and perhaps encouraged his Serb allies to challenge the terms of the Bosnian peace. The democratisation of Serbia's domestic politics would have been postponed, as would the prospects for reconciliation with the EU and NATO. The costs of inaction, therefore, would have been felt both in Kosovo itself and throughout the region.

As it turned out, moreover, Serbia retreated without the need for a ground campaign. NATO led a stabilisation mission in the country and now, more than a decade later, Kosovo is on the path towards being accepted as a full member of the European community of states. The successful settlement of key outstanding issues between Kosovo and Serbia in April 2013, brokered by the EU's High Representative for Foreign Affairs and Security Policy Catherine Ashton, is further proof that this process continues to enjoy momentum.

An immediate side effect of the Kosovo intervention, moreover, was that it helped to underpin the credibility of NATO and EU preventive diplomacy during the Macedonian crisis of 2001, when that country also seemed set on a course to ethnic conflict. Without a NATO shot being fired, a credible promise of external intervention underpinned the avoidance of Macedonian–Albanian conflict.

There are inherent uncertainties in assessing the strategic value of both the Bosnia and Kosovo interventions. Predictions of how far Serbian ethnic cleansing in Kosovo would have gone, absent intervention threats, are inherently uncertain – and the forced exodus of many Serbs from their Kosovo homes in the months after NATO's victory still casts a cloud over its success. The NATO-led Bosnia operation of 1995 helped make possible a negotiated settlement which benefited the interests of the militarily weakest party (the Bosnian Muslims), strengthening (albeit imperfectly) the forces against partition and population exchanges. The Kosovo operation, in contrast, resulted in the victory of one party to the conflict (the Kosovo Liberation Army) that represented only one of the two main ethnic groups in the territory. Neither in Bosnia nor in Kosovo has military intervention succeeded in creating the conditions for overcoming the legacy of inter-communal divisions. NATO's commitment to maintaining large military forces in both territories for many years after the conflicts ended partially reflects this failure (international forces are still present in both even today).

Neither Bosnia nor Kosovo has been able to create the conditions for sustainable economic development. Despite their low starting points, large volumes of aid and, until recently, favourable international economic conditions, neither has been able to achieve economic take-off. Both remain heavily dependent on state employment and remittances from *émigrés* for their economic survival.

The strategic case for both military interventions, therefore, must rest primarily on the fact that they successfully stopped the wars, and have successfully prevented their recurrence. Given what had been happening in the period immediately before the respective interventions, this alone makes the strategic case that both interventions were probably worthwhile.

Intervention in Libya
The Libyan force-for-good operation took place in a different time period and region, and therefore in a very different political context, from the four other operations in this category. It had a broad base of international legitimacy, with support from the Arab League and from the UN Security Council through Resolution 1970, albeit with some creative interpretation of the latter.[11] No major power supported the Qadhafi regime, in stark contrast to the concurrent war in Syria, in which President Assad could draw on substantial support from Russia and Iran.

The Libya campaign was also informed by the experience of Iraq and Afghanistan, which helped to ensure that putting 'boots on the ground' was never a political possibility. As in Kosovo and the initial operation in Afghanistan, NATO air power acted on behalf of rebel forces seeking to overthrow a regime in place, albeit (in all three cases) with some help from special forces on the ground. As in those operations, NATO was successful in its operational mission.

However, there are still many legitimate questions about whether subsequent security and political developments in Libya constitute a strategic success, and thereby justify the operation. The fall of the regime was followed by large-scale reprisal killings, along with the expulsion of many black migrant workers. Economic and security conditions are better in some parts of the country than in others. But rival groups continue to compete for political power through force of weapons, often holding vital oil resources hostage to their demands. Many large caches of arms, previously secured by the state, are now vulnerable to seizure and dispersal. Questions remain as to whether the political power of radical Islamists could grow further, and Libya is already the source of many of the foreign insurgents operating in Syria. After the 2013 military coup in Egypt, moreover, there are questions as to whether the supposedly positive 'knock-on' effects of the Libyan uprising on the parallel process of political change in Egypt can still be held up as evidence in favour of the 2011 air campaign.[12]

While the direct costs involved in the Libya campaign were relatively modest, moreover, the fall of the regime led to an increased flow of arms over Libya's southern border and on into Mali, probably contributing to subsequent victories (in summer 2012) by secessionist and radical Islamist forces in that country. Given the internal political problems within Mali, it would be unwise to attribute all of the costs of its conflict – including the subsequent Franco-African intervention – to spillover from Libya. Nevertheless, it does increase uncertainty as to whether, on balance, the Libyan intervention has had a positive strategic effect.

'Force-for-Order' Operations: Iraq (1991) and Afghanistan (2001)
Although there was an important humanitarian element in both the operation in Iraq in 1991 and that in Afghanistan a decade later, neither was driven by a commitment to Responsibility to Protect (R2P) objectives. Despite well-known human-rights abuses under the Saddam Hussein and Taliban regimes then in place, neither intervention would have taken place without clear breaches of more universally accepted norms for international behaviour.

In the first case, Iraq had invaded Kuwait in what was one of the most blatant post-1945 examples of the violation of the principle that no country should seek to extinguish another through the use of force. As a result, the operation commanded very wide international support, both globally (at the UN Security Council) and in the region, with major Arab states, including Saudi Arabia, Egypt and Syria, participating in the coalition. The invasion remains the only case since the UN's foundation in which one of its member states has sought to eliminate another.

It is difficult to speculate as to the exact consequences that would have ensued had no international action been taken to reverse Iraq's aggression. The US could still have provided a security guarantee to Saudi Arabia, and thus prevented further Iraqi advances. Yet it is hard to imagine that Saddam would have been prepared to reverse his aggression in response to economic sanctions alone. As a result, other Sunni Arab states might have come to an accommodation with him, if only to ensure a common front with Iran. But it would likely also have led to intensified arms-racing in the region, with small states in particular afraid that other post-colonial borders might be redrawn by stronger neighbours.

With the benefit of hindsight, it is also clear that, by 1990, Iraq's nuclear-weapons programme was well advanced and was on track to produce an elementary capability within a few years. The country already possessed enough weapons-grade uranium for one gun-type or two implosion-type warheads.[13] These capabilities were destroyed either as a result of the US-led bombing in 1991 or the subsequent UN-sanctioned inspection efforts (the latter supported by further military operations in which the UK was involved). Without the 1991 military campaign, in particular, it is reasonable to assume that by 1995 (or 2000 at the latest) Iraq would have possessed a nuclear-weapons arsenal. In these circumstances, it is likely that Iran, in particular, would have accelerated its own efforts to acquire nuclear weapons, and others might have followed suit. Efforts at combating nuclear proliferation, both regionally and globally, would have been dealt a major blow.

The 2001 Afghanistan operation was also in direct response to a clear breach of international law, and was widely supported by states across the world. The US convincingly argued that Afghanistan was guilty of having provided sanctuary (and, indeed, training facilities) to an organisation that had launched attacks on New York and Washington, DC. Working with Saudi diplomats, the US attempted to persuade the Taliban regime to hand over the Al-Qa'ida leadership to face international justice. It refused. As a result, the US had wide international support for its efforts to overthrow the Taliban regime – even from traditional rivals such as Russia and Iran. While the military operation brought about a de facto regime change, it is also significant that the Taliban regime had previously been recognised by only a handful of countries, and was not represented at the UN. By December 2001, the UN had authorised the establishment of an International Security Assistance Force (ISAF) to assist the new political authority that was to be established in the country, and was contributing to the process that led to the creation of that authority.

Both force-for-order operations played to Western military strengths, consisting primarily of efforts to defeat the forces of another state, rather than operations in which technological superiority is less decisive (notably against non-state insurgents). Indeed, the restorative (rather than transformative) objectives of force-for-order operations mean that they can normally be achieved through the use of military force against the armed forces of states. This remains a task which, at least in an era of US military hegemony, is relatively straightforward to achieve.

The judgement of this chapter, therefore, is that both of these operations were well judged and proportionate. Both were wars of choice in the sense that other, non-coercive options were available. More time could have been allowed for diplomacy, economic sanctions and political subversion to work. The chances of success for such alternatives, however, would have been quite limited, especially in a short timeframe. In the meantime, the absence of a forceful response to such clear and massive breaches of international order would have risked doing substantial damage to the fabric of international society, and to the rules of acceptable behaviour on which this fabric depends.

In War, the Result is Never Final
The one reservation to this conclusion, albeit a very significant one, is that it is necessary to reflect on what subsequent events in Iraq

and Afghanistan might say about the wisdom of these two initial interventions. Neither of the operations led to the settlement of underlying political conflicts in either country. The 1991 invasion of Iraq proved to be only the starting point for a prolonged period of confrontation between Iraq and the Western powers, with increasing Iraqi immiseration as a result of economic sanctions punctuated by the effects of limited US military strikes (notably Operation *Desert Fox* in 1998), and culminating in the 2003 invasion. In Afghanistan, the political settlement that followed the first phase of operations failed to find a way of bringing the defeated Taliban movement into the political process, an omission that proved increasingly costly as Taliban strength recovered in the years that followed.

While there is clearly a strong element of continuity between the initial operations and subsequent contested state-building operations, however, they can and should be treated separately. In the case of Iraq, the 2003 invasion was far from being an inevitable consequence of what went before. The survival of Saddam Hussein's regime after his 1991 defeat opened the way for a long period of economic sanctions and confrontation, which in turn undermined the reputation of the major Western powers (including the UK) in the region. The presence of US troops in Saudi Arabia after 1991 (to deter future Iraqi aggression) may have contributed to the radicalisation of some Saudi citizens, including Osama bin Laden. It may be stretching counterfactual analysis too far to argue that a more aggressive 1991 operation ('going to Baghdad') might have prevented the rise of Al-Qa'ida. However, it is certainly plausible to argue that one of the positive results of the 2003 invasion was to allow the US to withdraw its forces from Saudi Arabia, which has always been especially sensitive to the presence of foreign forces on its territory.

It is also possible to draw a clear distinction between the two phases of international military involvement in Afghanistan. Until 2005, and even later for the US, Western powers were committed to a light-footprint military presence in which ISAF only expanded into relatively benign areas of the country (the north and east) and only in order to provide some support for civilian reconstruction efforts. While enough was provided to allow a basic level of security support for Kabul in particular, NATO allies were reluctant to get involved in operations to seize new territory from the control of forces opposed to the central government (whether Taliban-affiliated or linked to regional warlords). This approach may have contributed to the resurgence of the Taliban, which was already occurring by 2005. However, far from halting this resurgence, the UK's decision to lead an effort to extend NATO's military presence into southern Afghanistan had the effect of fuelling the insurgency. The UK intervention in Helmand began with its decision to insist on the dismissal of Governor Sher Mohammad Akhundzada, an ally of Afghan President Hamid Karzai – a step which drove many members of Akhundzada's militia to join the burgeoning insurgency. As the UK became drawn into a growing number of firefights across the province, levels of violence and insecurity grew. Increasing commitments of UK forces, followed by the deployment of a massive force of US Marines to the province from 2009, quelled the conflict that had been started in 2006. It is hard in retrospect to avoid the conclusion, however, that the UK's decision to pick a fight in Helmand was a tactical error.

Humanitarian Outcomes
While both of the force-for-order operations deserve a positive scoring for their contributions to the upholding of international order, their humanitarian consequences, by contrast, have been more mixed. The 1991 liberation of Kuwait was clearly positive for the people of that country. The subsequent, and closely linked, decision to support the establishment of an autonomous Kurdish government in northern Iraq also constituted a significant gain in terms of human security and development. For the rest of the people of Iraq,

however, the 1991 operation was followed by a period of progressive impoverishment and criminalisation for which sanctions must bear much of the responsibility.

There is a case to be made that the US and the UK should have extended their military operations for several days in 1991, providing more cover for the southern rebellion that gathered momentum as Saddam's forces retreated in confusion. A replacement of his regime in 1991, even if his successor had been another Sunni general, might have avoided much of the pain and conflict that followed. On the other hand, such a step could also have triggered a civil war, similar to the process that took place after the 2003 invasion.

Even if the US and its allies had not been prepared to accept such an extension of their objectives, however, there is a compelling case to be made that the sanctions regime that was subsequently adopted was unnecessarily indiscriminate and damaging. The focus on WMD disarmament was understandable in the immediate aftermath of 1991. Yet the insistence on the dismantlement of every last battlefield chemical weapon as the price to be paid for sanctions relaxation was unnecessarily punitive. The excessive focus on strategically inconsequential 'WMD', which was such a central feature of the 2003 debacle, had its roots in the decade after the 1991 war, and in the first UN resolutions that brought that war to an end. Any assessment of the 1991 Iraq operation as a strategic success, therefore, needs to be tempered by an acknowledgement that subsequent Iraq policy (certainly from 1995 onwards, and arguably from 1991) was of diminishing strategic value.

The 2001 Afghanistan operation, in contrast, delivered clear humanitarian benefits from the start. Within a short period after the expulsion of the Taliban, millions of refugees had returned to the country. The economy grew sharply throughout the 2000s, albeit from a low base. And – in stark contrast to Iraq's experience after 1991 – Afghanistan saw significant improvements in the provision of health and education services. Levels of infant and maternal mortality have more than halved,[14] and school enrolment increased from 1 million in 2002 to nearly 7 million in 2010.[15]

While the case for both force-for-order operations remains a strong one, therefore, subsequent events have inevitably cast a particular shadow over the strategic value of post-intervention policies in Iraq in particular. With regard to Afghanistan, by contrast, there is a strong case to be made that the 'economy-of-force' intervention, between 2001 and 2006, achieved significant strategic gains at modest cost.

'Force-for-Change' Operations: Iraq (2003–09) and Afghanistan (2006–13)

As Chapter IX shows, the financial and human costs of these two operations dwarfed those of all of the other operations that the UK conducted during these two decades. Eighty per cent of the total additional financial costs, together with 70 per cent of the total casualties, were incurred during these UK operations. This undoubtedly increases the burden of proof for those who argue that these operations have been strategic successes.

Yet this is not how either operation was seen when it was launched. The decision to launch the military operation to overthrow Saddam Hussein needs to be seen in the context of the US's strong, and understandable, reaction to the attacks on its cities in September 2001. In the months and years that followed, US and UK policy became focused, almost to the exclusion of other threats, on the possibility of further terrorist threats, including the real possibility (as Washington and London perceived it) that future attacks could involve the use of chemical, biological, radiological or even nuclear weapons. In these circumstances, the burden of proof shifted against those who argued that terrorism could be contained through a more cautious approach. Instead, it became conventional wisdom that the only way to win the new global War on Terror was to address the root causes of terrorism, which lay (it was argued) in the existence of the rogue states that were giving (or might, in future, give) terrorists support and sanctuary. The alternative to fighting terrorists in Afghanistan and Iraq, it was argued, was to wait for them to strike again in London and New York.

This new approach – with all its offensive implications – combined with the US's increased confidence in the effectiveness of its armed forces, bolstered by the successes of the previous decade in Iraq and the Balkans. It was also allied with a belief that Western military force could be the midwife of a radical transformation of foreign societies, bringing freedom and democracy to territories suffering under tyrannical rule. From the start, many UK officials – and most of the British public – were instinctively sceptical of such a vision. However, Tony Blair proved to be one of the strongest proponents of this approach, which he saw as completely consistent with the Chicago doctrine that he had espoused in support of the 1999 Kosovo intervention.[16]

The war in Iraq, in particular, continues to cast a deep shadow over UK defence policy, and indeed over political life more generally – as the unprecedented parliamentary vote in the House of Commons against military involvement in Syria in August 2013 demonstrated once again. Some might argue that the UK had no choice but to go along with President George W Bush in 2003. But this underestimates the extent to which the UK can, when it decides to, play an important role in contributing to US internal debates. And, in this case, the US's belief that the British prime minister was a strong supporter of military action from an early stage of the crisis materially strengthened the hawks within the administration.

The UK's direct responsibility for the intensification of NATO operations in Afghanistan in 2006, however, is even clearer. By the end of 2005, the UK was already being given a hard lesson in the difficulties involved in state transformation in southern Iraq. Rather than supporting US efforts for one last push to re-establish control of the situation in the country, however, the British government – mindful of the unpopularity of the Iraq invasion at home – was focused on a 'surge' of its own, agreeing to take responsibility for security in the southern Afghan province of Helmand, and then progressively reinforcing its initial force as it increasingly ran into problems.

The British push into the south was not a unilateral one (Canada and the Netherlands – both close British allies – also took responsibility for the adjacent territories of Kandahar and Uruzgan, respectively). However, the UK was the leading force for NATO's expansion into this region, and was prepared to take the risk of doing so even as the US military continued to treat Afghanistan as an economy-of-force operation until 2008, preoccupied as it was with increasing the tempo of its operation in Iraq.

With the benefit of hindsight, both interventions have been strategic failures.

Flawed Interests: WMD, Terrorism and Narcotics
The initial drivers for both interventions, clearly articulated by the US and supported by the UK, were threats to national security.

Since the end of the Cold War, US and UK security policy had given a high priority to preventing potentially hostile states and non-state groups from obtaining 'weapons of mass destruction'. The period saw some notable failures in this regard, particularly in relation to Pakistan and North Korea. But it also saw some successes. One of the most important of these successes was in Iraq, where the inspection regime established after the 1991 Gulf War, together with the effects of air strikes during that war, had successfully eliminated Saddam's nuclear (and, it turned out, also his chemical and biological) programmes. The misjudgement made in 2003 was based on a desire to push for absolute certainty that no WMD remained in Iraqi hands. This was, in turn, a consequence of the elision of the difference between nuclear and chemical weapons under the catch-all term of 'WMD'. The use of chemical weapons has long been banned under international law. But their effects, especially against well-protected, modern armed forces, are relatively limited compared with nuclear and (some) biological equivalents. If some battlefield chemical weapons had been found after the 2003 invasion, therefore, it would have eased the extreme political embarrassment that American and British leaders subsequently faced at home. It would not, however, have substantially altered the fundamental scorecard as to whether the invasion was strategically justified.

If the coalition had not overthrown Saddam in 2003, he might well have sought an opportunity to rebuild some of his WMD capabilities. Chemical weapons had proven to be an important element in Iraq's efforts to counter superior Iranian forces in the Iran–Iraq War in the 1980s. Saddam must also have been aware that other neighbours – notably Syria – also possessed large chemical-weapons arsenals. Post-war interviews, moreover, strongly suggest that Saddam was concerned that full verification of the dismantlement of his WMD capabilities might have weakened Iraq's ability to deter a future Iranian attack, an all-too-plausible scenario given recent history. While a post-2003 regime under Saddam Hussein might well have rebuilt some chemical-weapons capability, however, it is much less likely that it would have been able to construct a capability that would pose a strategic threat to the US or other more powerful states.

In particular, it would have been much more difficult and expensive for Saddam to build nuclear weapons, as long as international constraints on this programme – via International Atomic Energy Agency (IAEA) monitoring and international nuclear sanctions – remained in place. Some continuing possibility of selective air strikes, for example in response to an expulsion of IAEA inspectors, could have further helped to maintain the containment of Iraqi nuclear ambitions. There would have been risks involved in such a policy, but it could have bought time, and at considerably less cost than the more radical option on which the coalition embarked in 2003.

The decision to invade Iraq in order to destroy its WMD arsenal was watched closely by other potential nuclear proliferators. One immediate, and positive, effect of the invasion of Iraq was that, confronted with evidence gathered by the British and American intelligence services, Libya agreed in December 2003 to dismantle its own WMD programmes under international supervision. Colonel Qadhafi might not have agreed to such a step without the example of Iraq's fate to encourage him.

Yet others may have drawn different lessons from the 2003 invasion, for it had only been possible, paradoxically, because the country was not yet believed to possess a credible nuclear arsenal. The US and UK, as a result, could attack it without fearing any WMD retaliation, except possibly against their troops in the field. The lesson that other internationally isolated states – North Korea and now, possibly, Iran – will have drawn is that, if you can get away with developing them, nuclear weapons are more important than ever as a means of deterring externally imposed regime change.

The invasion of Iraq was justified primarily as a force-for-order operation, designed – like the 1991 liberation of Kuwait – to enforce an international norm that might otherwise have been in danger of falling into abeyance (in this case, against the possession of chemical weapons). There was a case for such action, especially given that the state in question had already used them, both against Iran and against its own people, in the 1980s. This rationale, moreover, provides a credible argument in support of the limited actions – including Operation *Desert Fox* in 1998 – that took place in the decade between the two invasions. The decision to escalate to a full-scale, and inherently risky, regime-change operation, by contrast, crossed the threshold into a force-for-change rationale without the international support that characterised the 1991 war to liberate Kuwait and the 2001 war to expel Al-Qa'ida from Afghanistan, and in the absence of a compelling case for immediate action.

If WMD were the primary driver for the Iraq intervention, the War on Terror was the central narrative underpinning every phase of the UK's involvement in Afghanistan. The initial intervention in that country in 2001 played an important role in this respect, removing a key base for Al-Qa'ida, and forcing its leading cadres and associates across the border into Pakistan.

The UK-led surge into southern Afghanistan after 2006, by contrast, made very little difference to counter-terrorist efforts, for the simple reason that there were very few Al-Qa'ida-associated terrorists in the area in the first place. The use of bases in Afghanistan continued to be important for the US to be able to target terrorist infrastructure and leaders in Pakistan and (to a lesser extent) in eastern Afghanistan. But this mission could have been fulfilled without the UK-led expansion of NATO's mission into the south. The Taliban foot soldiers confronting the British in Helmand were primarily recruited locally, motivated much more by opposition to foreign intervention than by global jihadism.

By the time of the UK's move into Helmand, the Taliban and its associates had begun to recover from their 2001 defeat. Using their sanctuaries in Pakistan, they had started to conduct more military operations within Afghanistan itself, establishing themselves in remote areas and (in some cases) setting up shadow-government structures. By helping to strengthen the presence of the Afghan government in the south, it was argued, NATO was helping to contain further Taliban advances before it developed into a wider strategic threat to the whole country. For, it was argued, the restoration of the Taliban to national power – or even to dominance over the south of the country – could have brought with it a return of international jihadist terrorist groups.

Yet President Karzai was never convinced that such a threat existed, or that the deployment of NATO in the south was the best way to counter it. While he reluctantly acceded to UK pressure to replace his ally Akhundzada as governor of Helmand, he continued to cultivate alternative power networks in the province. As General Karl Eikenberry (combined forces commander Afghanistan from

2005 to 2007, and then US ambassador to Kabul from 2009 to 2011) argues:[17]

> ...while US military commanders argued that a long, costly counterinsurgency campaign in Afghanistan was necessary to decisively defeat al Qaeda in the Central and South Asian region, Karzai consistently held that the so-called insurgency was mostly a 'made-in-Pakistan' product.... He had a point.... The Afghans [then] became angry when the costs of counterinsurgency seemed to far exceed the benefits delivered.... The escalation of the war ... delayed the exercise of real sovereignty, something which all Afghans wanted.

Eikenberry's criticism is directed primarily at the US 'surge', which started in 2009. But it could also have been applied to the UK's own surge, which started in 2006 but reached its peak in 2010, by which time the UK's total military presence reached a total of more than 10,000 personnel.

No one can calculate for certain what would have happened in Afghanistan in the absence of the NATO, and then US, troop surges. But there is a strong case to be made that NATO and the US could have met their counter-terrorist objectives with a much smaller force, focused more strategically on the defence of key Afghan cities while providing a base for counter-terrorist operations in Pakistan and within Afghanistan itself. A less-ambitious effort might have helped to reduce some of the economic and political distortions created by the massive influx of foreign currency into the country to pay for the support of coalition forces, and by the creation of a 'parallel government', working outside the control of Afghan structures. Such an effort, conducted at a much lower economic and human cost, might also have been more sustainable than the 'boom and bust' cycle through which Afghanistan is now going.

Turning to narcotics, the intervention in southern Afghanistan did not succeed in reducing opium production in Helmand – one of the main reasons the UK chose to focus its efforts on what is an otherwise relatively unimportant province in economic or strategic terms. The decision to give the UK the G8 lead for counter-narcotics may also have contributed to the choice of Helmand. Yet Afghanistan remains the world's leading producer and cultivator of opium, producing 74 per cent of global supply in 2012.[18] As Table 2 shows, opium cultivation in Helmand is higher today than it was before the British arrived. Meanwhile, Helmand continues to account for 49 per cent of the total area of land under cultivation in Afghanistan. In counter-narcotics terms at least, therefore, the Afghan War has been a failure.

Table 2: Opium Cultivation in Helmand Province (hectares).

2004	2005	2006	2007	2008
29,393	26,500	69,323	102,770	103,590

2009	2010	2011	2012	2013
69,833	65,045	63,307	75,176	100,693

Source: *UN Office on Drugs and Crime and Islamic Republic of Afghanistan Ministry of Counter Narcotics, 'Afghanistan: Opium Survey 2013', November 2012, p. 16.*

Human Development and Human Security
Nor is the scorecard much better with regard to human security or human development. The populations in both Iraq and southern Afghanistan saw improvements in disposable income and access to social services following the two interventions. However, these have been accompanied by sharply increased levels of violence and outward refugee flows, for which coalition operations must bear some responsibility.

Any measurement of human development related to the Iraq intervention critically depends on whether the counterfactual scenario assumes the continuation of general economic sanctions.

The lifting of sanctions on oil exports, together with increased oil prices, has permitted substantial growth in imports of consumer goods and spending on government employment. On other measures of economic progress, rates of economic development (outside Iraqi Kurdistan) have continued to be disappointing. Investment in infrastructure has remained frustratingly limited. Neither the US nor the UK, in their respective areas of operations, seemed able to keep the lights on (and the millions of new air-conditioners working). While there has been a rapid growth in state oil revenues, Iraq is still some way from its aim of catching up with neighbours (such as Turkey, Iran and Saudi Arabia) with which it had been roughly equivalent in socioeconomic terms in the 1970s. One of the best indicators of social development, the total fertility rate – which measures the number of children that would be born to a woman if she were to live to the end of her childbearing years and bear children in accordance with current age-specific fertility rates – remained at 4.1 per woman in 2011: the highest level in the Middle East (with the exception of Yemen). This compares with rates of 3.3 in Pakistan, 2.8 in Saudi Arabia, 2.1 in Turkey and 1.9 in Iran (with a higher number typically associated with poor social indicators in other areas such as high infant mortality and low education and employment opportunities for women).[19]

US and UK forces proved unable to protect the civilian population from sustained terrorist campaigns, designed primarily as a means of achieving sectarian ends. Estimates vary, but credible ones settle at around 100,000 Iraqis killed, with many more injured and mentally scarred.[20] By 2007, the coalition invasion had been followed by 2 million more refugees fleeing to neighbouring countries, with a similar figure internally displaced.[21]

The US 'surge' in 2007, alongside the parallel Sunni 'awakening', temporarily helped to stem the tide of sectarian violence. But it has now worsened again, this time without the presence of US forces on the ground. Far from reducing international terrorism, moreover, the

2003 invasion had the effect of promoting it. The rise of Al-Qa'ida in the Arabian Peninsula (AQAP) was a reaction to this invasion, and to the consequent marginalisation of Iraq's Sunni population (including de-Ba'athification and army disbandment). Today, AQAP and other radical jihadist groups, stretching across the Iraqi–Syrian border, pose new terrorist threats to the UK and its allies that might not have existed, at least in this form, had Saddam remained in power.

While leaving Saddam in power would have involved other costs in terms of human development and human security, these would probably not have led to casualties on the scale of the civil war that followed the invasion, at least as long as his regime remained secure. Saddam was one of the most brutal dictators of the late twentieth century, responsible for successive atrocities against his own people as well as wars of aggression against two of Iraq's neighbours. By 2003, however, the scale of these misdeeds had been much reduced, not least because of the containment measures put in place after 1991.

Perhaps the greatest uncertainty relates to whether Saddam might have faced a Shia-led rebellion similar to that faced by Assad from Syria's majority Sunni community in 2011. If he had, the resulting conflict might well have proven just as bloody as the civil war taking place in Syria, which has been responsible for around 100,000 deaths in two years, and seems set to lead to many more.[22] Such an outcome would not have been preordained. An uprising may not have taken place at all, given the trauma of past repressions (as has been the case in Algeria). Alternatively, Saddam might have defeated an uprising with less bloodshed than has been witnessed in Syria. It is even possible that, in the absence of the 2003 invasion, Iraq and the West could gradually have moved towards a settlement in which general economic sanctions were eased (allowing living standards to recover), even as nuclear-focused sanctions were retained. None of these less-gloomy alternatives, however, would have been predetermined. The domination of Iraq by a Sunni minority would have continued to make the country vulnerable to fierce internal conflict. Easy access to support from Shia-led Iran would likely have fuelled any rebellion, especially if Saudi Arabia had provided support to Saddam Hussein's regime or its Sunni successor.

The strongest case for the coalition intervention in Iraq in human-security terms is that it helped to create the conditions for a sustainable political settlement, which recognises the rights of all three of the country's main ethno-confessional communities. The consolidation of Kurdish autonomy in the north has brought considerable benefits – in terms of both security and development – to the 6 million residents of Iraqi Kurdistan. Yet the long-term effects on Arab Iraq remain uncertain. Some democratic institutions have been established, resulting in regular elections and public debate. But the country has failed to institutionalise inter-confessional power-sharing based on the Lebanese model, as had been hoped and planned. Indeed, the shift of political power and patronage from Sunni to Shia elites has been accompanied by extraordinarily levels of inter-communal violence, forcible expulsions of populations, and indiscriminate terrorism. This internal conflict has been fuelled by external assistance, from Syria and Saudi Arabia to Sunni militias, and from Iran to their Shia equivalents.

As a result, more than a decade after the 2003 invasion, levels of violence remain high, and are now being exacerbated by increased co-ordination with radical Islamist groups in Syria. The prospect of a full-scale sectarian civil war, leading to attempts to partition Iraq into three states that are even more thoroughly 'cleansed' of ethno-confessional minorities, remains. The 2003 intervention may have helped to provide Iraq with some of the constitutional mechanisms needed to prevent such developments. But it was also the proximate trigger for the Shia–Sunni conflict that began almost as soon as Saddam was toppled and his armed forces were disbanded. It must therefore bear some of the responsibility for the mobilisation of radical Sunni militia that followed, which is now helping to radicalise the opposition to Assad in Syria, leaving Western leaders with some deeply uncomfortable choices.

In terms of human development and security, Afghanistan's post-invasion performance is significantly better than that of Iraq, in part because of its much lower starting point. Since 2001, per capita Afghan GNI (gross national income) has almost doubled; primary-school enrolment has increased from 19 per cent in 2001 to 98 per cent in 2011, with 81 per cent of girls of primary-school age enrolled.[23] Over 5.7 million refugees and internally displaced persons have returned from Pakistan and from elsewhere in Afghanistan,[24] and the population of major Afghan cities, especially Kabul, has swelled sharply, helping millions to escape from crippling rural poverty.

However, given the scale of resources expended on the Western occupation, it is striking how little progress has been made in some areas. The decision to direct so much aid through private contractors, rather than building a more effective Afghan state, owes more to the need for foreign agencies to meet their own performance criteria than to considerations of the long-term interests of Afghanistan. The World Bank estimates that the proportion of aid allocated to Afghanistan that is actually spent *within* Afghanistan amounts to only about 14–25 per cent of the total.[25] Domestic producers of agricultural and manufacturing products have been hit by an overvalued currency, itself a result of increased flows of external aid. Exports as a proportion of national income have, as a consequence, fallen sharply.[26]

Moreover, large parts of the state remain weak and highly corrupt, shaped more by the economic interests of a small elite than by the requirement for broad-based development. This is the context in which the development of Afghanistan's mineral resources, potentially its greatest hope of self-sustained development, lies. It is far from clear that the Afghan state yet has the structures and people in place to manage such resources to the benefit of the economy and society as a whole. But the fact that such a potential is seriously being discussed is a reflection of the considerable development gains that have been made since 2001.

Moreover, in that time, Afghans have never had to face the levels of violence experienced by Iraqis after the 2003 invasion. Taliban-affiliated groups (probably from the Haqqani network) have been responsible for some spectacular attacks in Kabul and other cities. But Afghan cities have not had to face the repeated, high-casualty attacks on mosques and markets that have become such a common feature of urban life in Iraq. Nor has Afghanistan seen a return to the levels of violence it experienced during its post-Soviet civil war, when rival *mujahedeen* groups reduced much of Kabul to rubble.

Afghanistan also has a better record in post-conflict political reconciliation. Its parliament has proved to be an important forum for resolving conflicts between Afghanistan's regions, ethnic groups and ideologies, to an extent never before witnessed in the country's history. The 2014 presidential election will be a critical test, and the political system could yet collapse if this is bungled. Yet there is also a reasonable chance that the trajectory towards elite institutionalisation – turning warlords into businessmen and politicians – has been at least partially successful. Much will depend, in Afghan eyes, on whether Pakistan is prepared to accept an independent Afghanistan and to facilitate reconciliation with the Taliban. There are also substantial risks involved in the withdrawal of foreign funds, especially in relation to the (largely externally financed) Afghan National Army. Overall, however, Afghanistan has made sufficient progress to confirm a positive verdict on the strategic wisdom of the initial 2001 intervention, and the light-footprint international presence that followed.

This comparatively positive record, however, does not prove that the post-2006 surge was worthwhile. Much depends on one's assessment of what would have happened in its absence. This, in turn, must depend on speculation on how the Taliban and Pakistan would have acted in such a scenario, in which there would have been, at most, only a modest growth in NATO's forces in Afghanistan. It could be argued that NATO's southern intervention helped to prevent the development of Pashtun separatism, with all the implications this could have had for stability in the region. Given the continuing strength of wider Afghan nationalism, however, it is not certain that such a development would have occurred without both states concerned co-operating to contain it. Certainly, it is quite a thin basis on which to build a convincing case for the post-2006 British-American surges.

Strategic Success or Failure?
Both Afghanistan and Iraq remain works in progress. Iraq's economic potential should be greater than that of Afghanistan, given its massive, proven oil reserves and its substantial human potential. Afghanistan, for its part, has made considerable advances since 2001, starting the process of economic reconstruction after the depredations of the Taliban, while successfully avoiding a return to sectarian civil war. Nevertheless, it remains to be seen whether either country can achieve a sustainable political settlement or economic development. Even if they do, a question will remain as to whether they could have achieved such success more rapidly, or with less pain, without the military-led state-building interventions spearheaded by the US and the UK during the last decade.

Yet analysts need to be careful not to overstate either the positive or the negative impacts of these interventions. Despite their considerable expense, each of these interventions may, in time, be seen as only one more point along long, national histories, rather than as radical ruptures. Longer-term societal trends can often be more important in national development than outside powers – focused on assessing their own activities – like to believe. At a social level, both countries continue to be subject to all the disruptive processes that accompany economic and social modernisation around the world in differing ways, and would have been subject to these broader trends even in the absence of intervention. Both continue to be profoundly shaped by the ideological and inter-confessional conflicts that are affecting the wider Muslim and Arab worlds. As relatively small and weak states, both are also victims of enduring rivalries between stronger neighbours, all of which will retain an interest, and a material stake, in their fates long after US and UK interest has receded.

Perhaps the underlying flaw in both of these operations, therefore, was that US and UK leaders thought that their superior military power, along with large amounts of money, could shift foreign societies onto quite different paths of political development. As these interventions come to an end, debate will continue as to whether or not they made a difference for the better. The most important conclusion, however, may be that in the end their contribution to change was much lower than that resulting from other factors, most of which have proven remarkably resistant to shaping by outside powers.

The Limits of Power and the Failure of COIN
The limits of Western strategic influence in both Iraq and Afghanistan were mirrored, and indeed perhaps amplified, at an operational level. Despite the resources expended, both interventions showed that there are severe limits to what military power can achieve in a counter-insurgency operation in support of a weak or dysfunctional foreign government, even when deployed by the most powerful military machine the world has ever known (the US armed forces) against rather poorly armed, albeit well-motivated, insurgent militias.

This renewed awareness of the limits of military power has been particularly evident in the UK. All British politicians are obliged to say that the UK has the 'best armed forces in the world'; and this extravagant claim gained validation from successive operations in Northern Ireland, Bosnia, Kosovo and Sierra Leone. Confidence in the effectiveness of the UK military was, however, badly shaken by its experience in southern Iraq during 2004–07. Poor preparation, inadequate resources and the failure to develop an adequate understanding of local political dynamics all helped to create a situation in which Shia militias were able to conduct a campaign of ruthless ethnic cleansing without any serious UK opposition. Police reform further empowered the same militias, armed and supported by supplies coming across the porous border with Iran. By early 2007, following the underwhelming Operation *Sinbad* (see Chapter II), the British force had withdrawn to wait out the war from the relative safety of Basra Air Base, courtesy of a safe-passage escort provided by the Jaish Al-Mahdi (JAM) militia. The Iraqi army did eventually re-establish control of Basra in 2008, through the US-supported Operation *Charge of the Knights*. By this stage, however, the UK had become a relatively marginal player in a region for which, after the invasion, it had taken lead responsibility. Both at the time and subsequently, fingers have been pointed at the lack of resources available for the operation, driven by London's desire (given the unpopularity of the initial intervention) to get out of Iraq as quickly as possible. But, as a number of analyses have shown, this was far from the whole story.[27]

The experience in Afghanistan was better, but not that much better. It is now commonly argued that 'far from helping to secure Helmand, the arrival of the British triggered a violent intensification of the insurgency.... [they] sent a force too small to stop the Taliban advance, but just large enough to antagonize the local population and drive them further into the arms of the insurgency'.[28] The UK increased its presence in response to the worsening security situation, from 3,300 in 2006 to 5,800 in 2007, to a peak of more than 10,000 military personnel in 2010. This latter level was by far the largest European contingent deployed in Afghanistan, and was near the limits of what the UK was able to deploy on a sustainable basis. More and better equipment was also introduced, and a series of offensive operations were launched to push back the Taliban from major centres of population. Even so, it was only after the arrival of 11,000 US Marines after the spring of 2009 (as part of President Barack Obama's surge) that the UK and NATO were able to achieve a significant reduction in levels of insurgency-generated violence in the province. The UK had learnt the hard lesson that it simply did not have the resources to conduct a large and sustained counter-insurgency operation on its own: a conclusion that would be reinforced by the cuts announced in the 2010 Strategic Defence and Security Review. In future, if it wanted to take part in such operations, it would have to plan to do so in close coalition with others from the beginning.

Aversion to service casualties also played a key role in domestic British politics concerning both Iraq and Afghanistan, limiting military options and greatly increasing financial costs. While military commanders have typically been robust in their acceptance that casualties are an inevitable by-product of having 'boots on the ground', the British public proved to be less tolerant. Fear of the political consequences of casualties played an important role in the Labour government's determination to draw down rapidly from Iraq after 2006. Prime Minister David Cameron's unconditional commitment to withdraw all UK combat forces from Afghanistan by 2014, made soon after he entered office in 2010, appears to have been driven most of all by domestic political imperatives.

A June 2013 Supreme Court judgement, which held the Ministry of Defence (MoD) and military commanders subject to prosecution for deploying soldiers without adequate equipment, has further increased the sense that the domestic conditions for sustained discretionary operations on the ground no longer exist.[29] Such conditions would no doubt be set aside if the military were to be engaged in a desperate battle for national survival. However, it does reflect widespread public understanding of governmental responsibilities to servicemen and women sent to fight in discretionary operations.

Yet the difficulties that the UK has experienced in Iraq and Afghanistan do not result only from inadequate resources or the lack of domestic public support. Even more importantly, they reflect the difficulties involved – given the constraints of domestic public tolerance, limited political and military capabilities, and the intrinsic complexity of the task – in seeking to transform other societies while combating a strong local insurgency. The US and the UK went further towards creating occupation regimes in Iraq and Afghanistan than they had since the occupations of West Germany and Japan after the Second World War. But the limits of Western power in such operations have been clearly demonstrated.

If Only: The Roads Not Taken
Many argue, in retrospect, that one or both of these operations could have worked better 'if only' a different approach to achieving their strategic aims had been adopted. Perhaps the Iraq intervention would have gone better had it more closely resembled the light-footprint operation in Afghanistan, been more respectful of existing power structures and less determined to rebuild the whole society from scratch. In Afghanistan, by contrast, it is often argued that a more 'full-on', Iraq-type approach, confronting local power-broker elites at an early stage after the overthrow of the Taliban, would have stood a better chance of success. Neither argument is convincing.

In the case of Iraq, particularly strong criticism is often made of the decision, finalised in May 2003, to disband the Iraqi army and remove Ba'ath party members from official positions, instead governing the country directly through the Coalition Provisional Authority. This decision was made with remarkably little prior discussion or planning by the US. By contrast, a reconstitution of the old army and a decision to maintain Ba'athists in most of their government roles, under new leadership, could have been quite effective in restoring law and order in Iraq's cities, halting the widespread looting and reprisal killings that took place in the post-invasion security vacuum. It might also have prevented, or at least subdued, the armed Sunni uprising that quickly developed, most of whose participants were drawn from the ranks of those suddenly deprived of a livelihood by the coalition. Yet such a decision would have created other problems. It would have allowed Sunni and Ba'athist elites to reconsolidate their grip on the levers of state power, and would have been bitterly opposed by the majority Shia population and by the Kurds. Uprisings by these groups (for example, in Shia-dominated southern Iraq) would have been almost certain to follow, and the occupying authorities would have been faced with some unenviable choices. It is possible to imagine, in such a scenario, that the coalition might have used its military presence to underpin a negotiated power-sharing settlement between the country's leaders, with a gradual shift of power in favour of hitherto-oppressed Shia and Kurdish communities, backed up by a phased process of military demobilisation (paying soldiers to remain in camps) and reform. However, there would have been no guarantee that such a path would have been effective in preventing conflict from spreading. On the other hand, coalition forces would have been under strong pressure to stay in place long enough to deter a Sunni coup, given the risks of sectarian conflict this would have involved. Given the deep fracturing of Iraqi society and the Iraqi state, there was probably no easy 'exit strategy' available, unless the coalition had been prepared to accept Iraq's rapid descent into widespread civil conflict. In the case of Afghanistan, by contrast, critics often argue that the main problem with the 2009 surge by US forces is that it did not take place earlier. As a consequence, they argue, the first five to seven years after 2002 were 'wasted years', allowing the Taliban to regroup and expand into the vacuum created by the US decision to adopt a light-footprint approach in the country.

On this argument, the intervening powers should have acted more forcefully, in the months after the expulsion of the Taliban, to disband the militia structures of Northern Alliance power-brokers, thereby giving President Karzai the political space within which a new, more liberal and democratic state could be built. Rather than wait until 2009 to deploy a NATO force of 100,000, by which time the Taliban was on the ascendancy, the US and its allies should have deployed a surge-like force across the country in 2002 or 2003, before the Taliban had time to recover. Such a force, backed up by a massive economic aid effort, would have allowed (it is argued) Karzai to impose the writ of the central government nationwide, replacing local warlords with competent Westernised bureaucrats, and laying the ground for a new Afghanistan.

It will never be known whether such an option might have worked. Much would have depended on how those excluded from such a settlement (the 'warlords') would have reacted. One scenario would have been that NATO's occupation forces – now spread across the country in support of the drive to establish a modern Afghan state – would have been successful in rallying support for the government in Kabul, either co-opting or marginalising former *mujahedeen* leaders. Yet it is also possible, and probably likely, that an early surge of this sort could have added to the ranks of the resistance to foreign occupation, much as the later UK and US surges did when they reached the Pashtun south after 2006. Far from preventing conflict, such an approach could have widened it to encompass the whole country, provoking displaced elites to unite against the outsiders. Success, in such a scenario, would have depended on the ability rapidly to build an effective Afghan state from a very low baseline, and without support from many of the country's key power-brokers.

One's judgement on which scenario is more probable may depend on how far one thinks that foreign forces have themselves been a driver for Taliban recruitment since 2006. To the extent that this is true, one can reasonably argue that an earlier surge would have had the same effect, but this time with the ranks of the resistance broadened to include many of the non-Pashtun groups.

It can be argued, more plausibly, that the 'original sin' of the Afghan campaign was the failure to make serious efforts to achieve an inclusive political settlement – including the Taliban – from the beginning. Given the availability of a safe haven across the border, it would never have been possible to defeat the Taliban militarily. But it is possible, in the immediate aftermath of their 2001 defeat, that many elements of their leadership (and indeed their membership) would have been prepared to accept secondary roles in the new political and economic dispensation. Such a proposal would have required other Afghan leaders – including Pashtun notables – to accept greater power-sharing. It would also have been difficult for the US to accept, so soon after 9/11. Yet there is some chance that it might have avoided the subsequent decade of conflict, as a result of which both the Afghan government and the main Western powers accepted the need for a negotiated settlement.

There are many other 'if only' variations that could be envisaged. If only modern counter-insurgency practices had been followed from the beginning, then the US and the UK could have avoided the mistakes that were made. More could have been done to understand, through more extensive language training and anthropological study, the complexities of the societies that outside powers sought to shape. Tour lengths could have been increased, and incentives for task-group commanders to reinvent the wheel every six months reduced. A more 'comprehensive' approach could have been adopted. And so on. So many things went wrong during these large and complex operations that it will always be tempting to imagine that, if only things had been done differently, the strategic outcome would have been transformed.

Operational practice can be improved, and much can and must be learnt from the UK's experiences in Iraq and Afghanistan. As in the US after Vietnam, there will be a strong temptation to say 'never again', and to relegate discussion of counter-insurgency to a footnote in training curricula. Yet 'never' is a long time, and the UK could still find itself – for reasons that cannot now be foreseen – involved in a similar operation in future. Remembering the operational lessons from these two interventions, therefore, should continue to be a vital part of what the armed forces are asked to do.

Wars Not Fought
The focus of this chapter has been on whether the wars that were fought were successful in achieving their strategic objectives. All of these wars were, to some extent, controversial. Some, the chapter has argued, were strategic failures.

Yet it does not necessarily follow that the UK should have done less during this period. These two decades have seen a number of cases in which military action was debated and seriously considered, but in which, in the end, a decision not to intervene was made. It is possible to argue both that some of the operations that did take place were unwise and ill-judged; but it is also possible to assert that there are cases in which the UK and its allies should have done more.

The earliest and clearest example of an intervention that should have taken place, but did not, was in Yugoslavia at the start of the 1990s. The UK armed forces were absent from this developing crisis (from summer 1990 until September 1992), but made an important contribution to the UN peacekeeping forces that were deployed to Croatia and Bosnia in 1992. However, this response proved entirely inadequate for the storm of conflict that engulfed the region. In Bosnia, over four years, nearly 100,000 are estimated to have died as a direct result of the war, at least half of whom were civilians – 82 per cent of Bosnian Muslim dead, 28 per cent of Bosnian Croat dead and 16 per cent of Bosnian Serb dead.[30] By the end of 1993 – when the conflict had become a three-way fight between Muslims, Serbs and Croats – the UNHCR, the UN's Refugee Agency, had registered over 600,000 refugees and 1.2 million internally displaced persons, out of a pre-war population of only 4.3 million.[31]

Despite a storm of public protest (not least in the UK, as shown in Chapter V), Western governments resisted a sustained, robust military response until August 1995. The second bombing of the

Markale marketplace in Sarajevo precipitated NATO air strikes on Serb positions – via Operation *Deliberate Force* – which were shortly followed by the US-brokered peace talks at Dayton, Ohio. This experience played a decisive role in convincing much of the UK political elite of the need for a more muscular approach to the use of military force for humanitarian purposes, and helped to explain the commitment of the Blair government, elected in 1997, to make the UK military a force for good.

An earlier intervention could have had, as its central objective, the provision of credible security guarantees for any new states which the EU and US agreed should be recognised as independent. As a condition of such guarantees, however, Western powers could have insisted that all new states should negotiate the terms of any separation between themselves and, in particular, could have insisted on European standards of respect for human and minority rights.

Fragmentation would still have been inevitable. But the concurrent examples of Czechoslovakia and the Soviet Union (excepting the Caucasus) showed that this could take place without large-scale warfare. By providing a credible guarantor for any political agreement that was reached, outside powers could have alleviated the security dilemma faced by ethnic groups and parties, each of which felt their survival depended on rearmament and territorial expansion. A NATO intervention in former Yugoslavia could have been costly and difficult, and would have raised difficult issues regarding when to intervene in order to police internal conflicts. In order to demonstrate its commitment to protecting state sovereignty, NATO would have had to attack the Yugoslav tank columns when they crossed the border into Croatia. But it is less clear, even in retrospect, whether and how it should have intervened in response to escalating tensions between the potentially separatist Serb minority in Croatian Krajina and Slavonia and the special police units that President Franjo Tudjman mobilised to suppress them. Even allowing for such uncertainties, it is now clear that a robust NATO intervention at this early stage could have prevented (or greatly limited) one of the most damaging conflicts of the post-Cold War period. States such as Serbia and Bosnia could, if such an operation had been successful, now be on an economic and political par with Poland and Slovakia, rather than decades behind.

The Sierra Leone operation in 2000 is widely acknowledged to have been a successful force-for-good intervention. But it proved to be the only case of significant UK intervention in sub-Saharan Africa during this period. Rwanda and the Democratic Republic of the Congo (DRC) in the 1990s are the most well-known examples of cases in which, in retrospect, more might have been done to respond to ongoing, or imminent, humanitarian catastrophes. It has also been suggested, more recently, that the UK and other European powers could have done more to provide military support to Ugandan forces in their operations against the Lord's Resistance Army, and to UN forces deployed in eastern DRC.

Resource constraints may help to explain why so little was done in these cases. But the more substantive explanation lies in the fact that, with some exceptions, the UK security-policy elite does not believe that the sub-continent's strategic importance justifies it being given a priority comparable to that of the Middle East. Even if this is accepted, however, a case can perhaps be made that there were (and continue to be) some conflicts in sub-Saharan Africa where the possibility of some form of light-footprint intervention – working to strengthen local and African Union (AU) forces, for example, through the provision of logistical support and special-force capability – can be of significant value.

This is not to argue that the UK and the US should have committed themselves to major combat operations on the African continent, as proposals during 2007 for the establishment of a no-fly zone over Darfur would have required. Such an intervention could have developed into a large and highly expensive operation that might ultimately have spread beyond Darfur into other parts of

Sudan. In this case, the UK approach was broadly correct, devoting considerable resources to conflict resolution and development aid, as well as to the AU and UN forces that were subsequently established. The UK has also played a major role in helping to support the security forces of the new government of South Sudan in the run-up to, and beyond, its formal independence in 2011.

More generally, there is a credible case to be made that the considerable external involvement in sub-Saharan Africa during the last two decades – comprising UN peacekeeping and diplomacy, economic assistance, and operations to build African institutions – has played an important role in gradually reducing the number of conflicts on the sub-continent and limiting the damage in those that do occur. Given the economic and political fragility of most of the region's states, new conflicts will continue to erupt. Nevertheless, international action can be effective in curbing and containing new problems, as seen most recently in the French-led intervention (alongside regional forces) in Mali. There will remain a strong case for the UK, as one of Europe's strongest military powers, to continue to be ready to play a part in African conflict management.

Finally, and again in retrospect, it can be argued that international diplomatic intervention in Afghanistan in 1990–91, backed up if necessary by UN-led military forces, could have helped to broker a government of national unity for Afghanistan in the difficult period after the abrupt withdrawal of Soviet aid after 1991, thereby forestalling the post-Najibullah descent into a civil war so destructive that the Taliban was eventually to emerge as a force for stability and peace.

Conclusion
This chapter's review of the UK's most important military operations of the last two decades suggests that the most successful interventions were those with clear but limited strategic objectives. Two cases in particular – the expulsion of Iraq from Kuwait in 1991 and the

overthrow of the Taliban in 2001 – made vital contributions to the maintenance of international order, and they did so at reasonable cost and with widespread international backing. Without these two force-for-order operations, the UK's overarching commitment to the maintenance of a rules-based international system could have been severely compromised.

The interventions which most clearly deserve to be called strategic failures, by contrast, were characterised by implied strategic objectives that were both radical and, as it turned out, unachievable. Both the invasion of Iraq in 2003 and the post-2006 surge in Afghanistan were justified in terms of more limited normative or national interests – the threats posed by WMD, international terrorism and opium production. Yet these never quite provided a full and convincing explanation for why the interventions were necessary. In any case, both campaigns soon became open-ended programmes for societal transformation – force-for-change operations – designed to support the US and the UK in their roles as occupying powers. The ambition that this entailed was the primary reason that the cost of these two operations far exceeded those of all other military operations during this period put together.

Nor can either of these operations be dismissed as simply 'the wars of 9/11', in which the UK was obliged to participate in order to preserve good relations with the US. The UK was an active participant in all of the strategic decisions leading up to both operations, and must accordingly share responsibility for the strategic failures that resulted.

In contrast to the two force-for-change failures, four of the five force-for-good operations in which the UK participated during this period – Bosnia (1992–95 and 1995–2002), Kosovo, Sierra Leone and Libya – achieved positive strategic outcomes at a reasonable cost. The greatest uncertainty in this regard is in relation to Libya, where it is still too early to say whether current difficulties are temporary or the harbinger of further conflict.

As the last section of this chapter indicates, a comprehensive scorecard should also take account of wars not fought. The decision not to intervene earlier or more strongly as Yugoslavia disintegrated proved a major strategic failure. Non-interventions in Afghanistan (1991) and Rwanda (1994) probably also fall into the same category. Yet political reality means that no intervention ever takes place in isolation from those that preceded it, irrespective of differences in context or feasibility. There is a limit to how many operations the UK can take part in at once, imposed as much by considerations of political as of military capability. Thus, one of the reasons nothing was done as the Balkans and Afghanistan fell apart in the early 1990s was that so much attention was instead focused on the collapsing Soviet Union and on the confrontation with Iraq.

At every stage of the evolution of intervention during these two decades, moreover, leaders have tended to 'overlearn' from recent experience. One of the costs of the successful operations in the Balkans in the late 1990s is that it persuaded politicians that military force could deliver societal transformation, a hubris that helped to create the conditions for the failed interventions in Iraq and Afghanistan.

Yet it is also true that one of the costs of failure is that it may blind leaders to the possibility of strategic success. The costs of US failure in Somalia in 1993 were paid by the people of Rwanda in 1994. In 2013, discussions on possible UK intervention in Syria took place in the shadow of Iraq. Now, as ever, a decision not to intervene can have as much strategic consequence as one to intervene. Neither course of action can relieve major powers, including the UK, of responsibility for what then takes place.

IV. THE DOMESTIC BALANCE

David Omand

THE period 1991–2013 opened as British forces deployed and fought in the First Gulf War to expel Saddam Hussein from Kuwait whilst continuing to implement the restructuring of the 1990 post-Cold War 'Options for Change' defence review.[1] Over the twenty years that followed, the British armed forces were active in significant operations in Bosnia and Kosovo in the Balkans, Sierra Leone, East Timor, Iraq, Afghanistan (twice) and Libya, as well as engaging in counter-piracy and counter-narcotics operations and training missions overseas. As other chapters observe, these were mostly operations of choice in pursuit of the ends of foreign policy, including exercising the responsibilities of the UK as a permanent member of the UN Security Council and a leading member of NATO.

Some operations, however, were felt to be necessary to protect the British public from a range of threats, including countering terrorism – notably in Northern Ireland, but also, more controversially, in Afghanistan – and countering narcotics trafficking in Afghanistan (heroin) and in Central America and the Caribbean (cocaine). At many points over this twenty-year period, British forces were also engaged in supporting the civil authorities in operations within the UK, to protect the public from terrorism (an example of military aid to the civil power – MACP);[2] to keep essential supplies flowing during periods of disruption (military aid to other government departments/civil ministries – MAGD); and to help with recovery from the effects of natural calamities and hazards (military aid to the civil community – MACC).

This chapter attempts a strategic audit of the British military contribution to the protection of the modern equivalent of the home front – what could thus be described as operations of modern national security – and examines the extent to which such missions achieved their goals. In each case, the question goes beyond simply whether, with hindsight, the gains appear to have justified the costs. Indeed, it must always be considered what might have happened, given the uncertain pressure of events, had such action not been taken and whether, given these counterfactual considerations, the gains could have been achieved at a lesser cost had different policies been followed.

It is during this period that intelligence and law enforcement came to span the traditional divide between domestic and overseas theatres of operations, as events overseas increasingly came to affect security at home, and vice versa. Old certainties about what would justify armed response to 'clear and present dangers' also became less convincing in the world that followed the attacks of 9/11. Future risks – for example of the acquisition of weapons of mass destruction by terrorists – became the justification for acting 'upstream', on the grounds that, although the threat was not yet present, the danger seemed clear enough to warrant this. The return in strength to Afghanistan in 2006 was thus justified as necessary 'to keep the streets of Britain safe',[3] and to prevent the country from serving as a safe haven for Al-Qa'ida, from which it might plan attacks on the UK or its allies.[4]

The forces deployed were those maintained for the UK contribution to NATO's defence. As the 1967 *Statement on the Defence Estimates* concluded,[5] 'it is not perhaps inconceivable that, because of some fundamental change in the world situation, the threat to Western Europe might revive. But such a change is most unlikely to develop overnight'. Over forty years later, the 2010 National Security Strategy similarly concluded that 'we do not currently face, as we have so often in our past, a conventional threat of attack on our territory by a hostile power', but warned that 'Today, Britain faces a different and more complex range of threats from a myriad of sources. Terrorism, cyber attack, unconventional attacks using chemical, nuclear or biological weapons, as well as large scale accidents or natural hazards – any one could do grave damage to our country' and, by implication, require the services of the armed forces.[6]

Nevertheless, even today the military forces dedicated to direct home defence remain largely limited to special forces and an air-interception capability, together with reservists. There has therefore been little in the way of a direct relationship between, on the one hand, the stationing, posture and equipping of the armed forces in the UK – the base for the country's contribution to UN, NATO and other intervention operations – and, on the other, the types and level of direct threat faced by the public on these islands – the home front. Over the last twenty years, it has taken all the skills of Ministry of Defence (MoD) planners to ensure that the former can continue to serve the pressing needs of the latter.

Military Aid to the Civil Power

Northern Ireland
In 1992, the dominant theatre of operations was still Northern Ireland, with 17,750 members of the armed forces engaged in the counter-terrorist campaign Operation *Banner*.[7] The numbers deployed fell thereafter with the campaign's entry into its final phase of operations, as the army's posture was rebalanced in response to – and in some ways anticipating – improvements in the security situation that would pave the way eventually to the Good Friday Agreement of 1998. When, in July 2007, the close of Operation *Banner* was declared, it ended the direct involvement of the British

Army on the streets in what is still the longest continuous operation in its history. It had taken twenty years of painful struggle with the Provisional IRA and Loyalist paramilitaries – as well as twenty years of sometimes bitter arguments within the British security establishment – to create the conditions for a strategic resolution of the conflict. Although in 1969 the army had been welcomed across all communities as an impartial upholder of civil order, London had been unable to develop a political strategy to address the causes of the disturbances. What then occurred was a mutation of the threat under the pressure applied by security forces, altering the mission from one of protecting the community to one focused on fighting a counter-insurgency campaign against the Provisional IRA, which had emerged as the self-styled defender of the Catholic enclaves. The army had some significant initial tactical success against a Provisional IRA organised into brigades and battalions, but failed to achieve operational and strategic dominance. This allowed the Provisional IRA to reorganise itself into 'active service units', making it difficult to frustrate attacks which extended into Great Britain and to British diplomatic and military targets across Europe.

Crucially, there was no link between the tempo and type of security operations and a political strategy. Increasing violence led to the internment of 342 suspected Republican terrorists (against the advice of local army commanders),[8] coupled with the enhanced, or 'deep', interrogation of a small number of suspects.[9] The result was a strategic propaganda disaster, leading to condemnation of the British Army's methods by the European Court of Human Rights as amounting to inhumane and degrading treatment,[10] the suspension of the Northern Ireland government at Stormont and the imposition of direct rule from London. Finally, in 1975, under the subtle manoeuvring of Frank Cooper, the permanent under-secretary of the Northern Ireland Office,[11] a new strategy of 'police primacy' was adopted, in which the army would return to a classic posture of MACP, supporting and building up the capability of the police. The Templer solution of a 'supremo' was strongly advocated by many army commanders, but ran contrary to the theme of restoring normality, with strategic direction coming instead from a hierarchy of joint Northern Ireland Office, army and Royal Ulster Constabulary security committees – a slower mechanism, but one more in tune with British constitutional principles.

Gradually, entering into the period under consideration here, army operations became increasingly intelligence-led,[12] as the intelligence that had been so absent during the counter-insurgency phase of the campaign began to flow, with growing coverage of the Provisional IRA and Loyalist terror gangs using specialist military and civilian capabilities. A joint intelligence-assessment organisation had been set up at Stormont to support the political strategy and link it to security developments on the ground. The security forces began to take the initiative and the army at last assumed the correct relationship with the civil power (although tensions continued to the end), producing the confidence to pursue a political strategy using the leverage that security and intelligence operations provided.

The Provisional IRA leadership became aware that the organisation had been penetrated by British intelligence, leading to considerable disruption of its activity – including the ambush by special forces of a number of Provisional IRA units attempting to carry out attacks.

By the early 1990s, leading figures in the Provisional IRA and its political wing, Sinn Féin, had doubts about whether their political goals could be achieved through terrorism. Secret discussions began with the British and Irish governments, using covert intelligence channels. This contact was kept a close secret; that Prime Minister Margaret Thatcher and her successor John Major were prepared to sanction the discussions probably speaks to the quality of the intelligence that convinced them that important figures within the Republican movement genuinely wanted to bring the campaign to an end.

A unilateral Provisional IRA ceasefire was called in 1994, but was broken in 1996 when the group attempted to exert pressure on negotiations through a bombing campaign in the UK. The British political strategy paid off when the Clinton administration excluded Sinn Féin leaders from the White House, making US disapproval of terrorism clear. Another Provisional IRA ceasefire in July 1997 led to the Good Friday Agreement in 1998 that brought the Provisional IRA campaign to an end. The army history commissioned by the Chief of the General Staff, published internally in 2006, rightly concluded that whilst the army had failed to defeat the Provisional IRA, it had made it impossible for the organisation to win through violence and had also substantially reduced the death toll in the last years of the conflict.[13]

The final years of Operation *Banner* thus illustrate MACP in its most effective form, having witnessed well-motivated, trained and equipped armed forces supporting a credible civil administration, following a defined political strategy, working in conjunction with an effective and impartial police service and judicial system, and, above all, with the intelligence to enable operations to be conducted sensitively to lower the level of terrorist violence, whilst minimising civil disorder and hostile propaganda opportunities.

The overall 'audit' of the Northern Ireland campaign must therefore be positive; although, as the army itself concluded, earlier strategic misappreciation by politicians and soldiers alike meant that the price paid by the population and security forces throughout the campaign was higher than it need have been. As noted in 'Operation Banner: An Analysis of Military Operations in Northern Ireland', 'Looking at the events of the Troubles in retrospect, it is apparent that many of them could have been avoided or reduced in impact if effective measures had been taken early on'. It also observes that 'similar patterns can be seen in many situations elsewhere', and, specifically, that 'circumstances will often suggest that … senior commanders deployed on the ground have the duty and the obligation to attract, at the earliest opportunity, the attention of government ministers (or political administrators) to the range of problems, and to recommend and enable non-military as well as military action in order to address the underlying causes of the unrest'.[14]

Countering Terrorism in the UK
Spurred by Provisional IRA and international terrorist incidents, the 1990s saw the evolution of doctrine governing the use of military personnel for MACP duties in the UK involving senior ministers meeting in the Cabinet Office Briefing Room (COBR) and a defence minister authorising deployment following a request by the Gold Commander – the senior police officer in charge of managing an incident. The Gold Commander, as the representative of the civil power, is then able to request intervention from the assigned military commander, should circumstances appear to demand it.[15] This pragmatic blending of efficient military command with the independent operational responsibility of the senior police officer, under the law (and the democratically elected government's right to provide strategic direction) has been much studied – and envied – by security authorities overseas. Throughout the period, the relevant senior ministers became familiar with the doctrine through regular COBR exercises – including live special-forces play – experiencing the type of decision-making that falls to ministers in dealing with terrorist incidents.

The main terrorist threat in the UK as the period under consideration opened came from the Provisional IRA, whose active service units conducted attacks on the mainland, causing a total of 125 fatalities (including fifty members of the security forces), through almost 500 attacks or attempted attacks, including two attempts to kill the prime minister. The economic cost of the urban bombings of the period (including that of the Baltic Exchange in 1992, Bishopsgate in 1993, and Canary Wharf and Manchester Arndale Centre in 1996) ran into the billions of pounds.

The main weight of the day-to-day work of countering this threat fell not on MACP forces but on the Metropolitan Police and local Special Branches, supported by the Security Service; with the role of the armed forces largely confined to the protection and guarding of military bases, the contribution of defence research and development (R&D), the development of non-lethal technologies such as baton rounds, improvised explosive device (IED) inhibition and explosive-ordnance disposal methods. The Metropolitan Police developed its own capability to use such technologies, but for most mainland police forces the first recourse for specialist IED support was to the army.

MoD R&D resources were also used to develop capabilities to deal with any incident involving chemical, biological, radioactive or nuclear agents (assistance was provided to help with the anthrax scares of October and November 2001, for example) and to collocate civilian chemical, biological, radiological and nuclear (CBRN) training at the Defence Chemical, Biological, Radiological and Nuclear Centre at Winterbourne Gunner. Industry was used to dealing with well-established MoD processes, but found civilian security requirements fragmented between departments, agencies and fifty-four separate police services. Only in the aftermath of 9/11 did the Home Office and MoD really bring together scientific and technical expertise from the military, civilian and industrial domains,[16] having previously been hindered by the competing needs of defence for scarce technical resources, and perhaps by a fear, on the civil side, of domination by the much greater resources of the MoD.

Of importance, in terms of the development of peacetime MACP arrangements, was the continuous availability of special forces – the Special Air Service (SAS) and Special Boat Service (SBS) – supported by dedicated air transport and with covert surveillance capabilities on call, to help resolve hostage and hijacking situations, including those taking place at sea. Although not often called upon, the capability provided by SAS and SBS units remains highly valued by chief constables, both offering reassurance that extreme terrorist situations can be resolved and acting as a deterrent to prospective hijackers.

In 2003, the UK government-wide counter-terrorism strategy CONTEST was adopted with the strategic aim of 'reducing the threat from terrorism so that people can go about their normal business, freely and with confidence'.[17] The part played by the armed forces in support of CONTEST since 2003 represents a specialised but essential military task for the twenty-first century. It involves the military playing key roles in CONTEST's four strategic campaigns: in Pursue and Prevent, to reduce the likelihood of terrorist attack, including through the provision of intelligence capabilities and training missions overseas;[18] in Protect, to reduce vulnerability to attack through the protection of defence infrastructure and facilities, and defence R&D; and in Prepare, to provide specialist capabilities to improve the ability of the emergency services to respond, especially in the event of a CBRN incident or where extensive consequence management is needed. The CONTEST campaign of Prevent (to counter jihadist radicalisation) has remained the least-developed and most-controversial to date. An unintended and unwelcome consequence of the campaigns in Iraq and Afghanistan after 2003 has been the radicalising impact of images on jihadist websites – especially of civilian casualties and allegations of ill-treatment – an example of the blurring of the distinction between overseas and domestic theatres.

Armed MACP support in the UK as part of CONTEST was only infrequently required during the decade after 2003, but notably included the February 2003 deployment to Heathrow of a Blues and Royals cavalry squadron based at Windsor following what turned out to be unfounded intelligence on the possession of surface-to-air missiles by jihadist terrorists (this contingency plan had last been activated at Heathrow in 1994 after the Provisional IRA mortared the airport). Much of the contemporary 'tanks at Heathrow' coverage in the media reflected cynicism over what was seen as the government exaggerating the threat to justify its policies, and recalled the British tradition of suspicion over a greater role for the armed forces in domestic security.[19] In July 2005, however, after the 7/7 London bombings, specialist intelligence support and MoD Police were deployed to assist with the provision of security in the capital, without controversy.

RAF Quick Reaction Alert (QRA) fast-jet interceptors continue to provide MACP support over the UK as part of an effort to maintain the integrity of UK airspace and counter the threat of a 'rogue' airliner entering UK airspace by intercepting, identifying and attempting to communicate with pilots, and in certain circumstances – if ministers so authorise – shooting down the aircraft to avoid greater casualties were it to appear to be heading for a crowded target. QRA Typhoon fighters were on standby at Northolt airfield during the London 2012 Olympic Games. Also available were surface-to-air missile batteries around the Olympic Park, service marksmen in helicopters based on HMS *Ocean* moored on the Thames, and special forces and pre-positioned armed-response units in readiness. There were, in the event, no security incidents during the 2012 Olympics that required an armed response; the visible armed-forces deployment, in addition to widespread speculation about enhanced intelligence coverage, may have helped to persuade jihadists to lie low.

Large numbers of unarmed but uniformed service personnel were also needed at short notice for the Olympics following the failure of the civilian contractor G4S to provide sufficient personnel. The episode illustrated a common theme of MACP deployments over the period, whereby the armed forces were used as a last resort, placing considerable strain on the individuals concerned and their families. It is inevitable, when all else fails, that ministers will turn to the armed forces, with their 'can-do' attitude in the face of the unexpected but, at the same time, senior MoD staff do not want to make this too easy for the civil ministries, lest it creates a dependence on the military for functions that fall under the business of civil government.

The complex command, control, communications and intelligence (C3I) arrangements for the 2012 Olympics showed the overall robustness of the MACP model, even for what was the largest UK security operation since the Second World War, as well as the value of being able to tap into existing defence experience. The security exercise programme for the Olympics was managed by Air Vice Marshal Clive Bairsto and an MoD team used to evaluating tactical performance. In the Home Office, the responsible Under Secretary Robert Raine was seconded from the MoD, and he was advised by a group of 'critical friends', chaired by the author, which included a retired commander in chief, a retired deputy assistant commissioner of the Metropolitan Police and a retired deputy director of the Security Service.

Overall, the CONTEST counter-terrorist strategy sets normality as the goal.[20] According to its own terms, it has been a success since, despite the continued jihadist threat and occasional attacks (both successful and attempted), the public and visitors to the UK remain confident that the risk is being managed by the civil security authorities in ways that allow normal life to continue, with armed-forces support essential but largely in the background.

Another example of MACP during the period was the use of the armed forces in counter-narcotics operations, including efforts to stem the heroin supply in Afghanistan and the naval interdiction of cocaine shipments in the Caribbean. The ultimate purpose of these operations – to help protect the British population from the evils of narcotics abuse – is clear. Well-publicised successes in the seizure of drugs and the destruction of both poppy crop and heroin base have been commendably frequent, with the street value of seizures many times greater than the cost of interdiction. However, the street price of the drugs remains stubbornly resistant to such measures and it is likely that traffickers take such losses into account in their business models. It is therefore doubtful that these supply-side operations would pass a strict cost-benefit test in relation to expenditure on demand-side measures. Engagement in most of these operations would be worthwhile only if the units and personnel were in any case required for other essential defence tasks in these areas.

Over the whole period from 1991 to 2012, however, MACP peacetime deployments for the armed forces – with associated C3I, training and exercising – represent a good national return on the relatively modest investment made principally by the MoD, Cabinet Office and Home Office, and have done much to enhance the reputation of the armed forces as an essential backstop.[21]

Military Aid to other Government Departments/Civil Ministries
In contrast to the doctrine for MACP, the evolution of mechanisms for the management of civil emergencies in the early part of the period was slow, always seeming to be behind the demands of the situation. This caused considerable ministerial concern over the maintenance of supplies and services essential to the life, health and safety of the British people. The Cold War structure of civil defence to help protect the general public was a civil responsibility under the Home Office, but by 1992 it had been run down to a small central grant that funded a number of emergency planners in local authorities.[22] At the start of the 1990s, the government thus had little civil capability to anticipate, plan for or manage emergencies, inevitably meaning that it would have to look to the armed forces when problems arose – a consequence not fully recognised at the time within the MoD.

It must be assumed that there will be similar calls by government departments for assistance in the future, for instance when industrial disputes threaten the life of the nation. Defence planners would be prudent to bear this in mind. Saying 'no' is not a realistic option for the MoD, as shown by the 2003 firefighter strike, which required the deployment, under Operation *Fresco*, of large numbers of troops to provide emergency fire cover for the population, coinciding with the final preparations for the Iraq operation and depriving some service personnel of the chance to spend time with their families prior to deployment overseas. On the other hand, the success of the armed forces over the period in responding to requests from government departments for support at times of crisis has undoubtedly earned them the gratitude of successive governments.

Around the turn of the century, the lessons learned from a succession of problems associated with the national disruption of fuel supplies, industrial action by firefighters, foot-and-mouth disease, and the rescue-and-recovery effort necessitated by extensive flooding led to the creation of a Civil Contingencies Secretariat in the Cabinet Office in July 2001.[23] New legislation – the Civil Contingencies Act 2004 – placed duties on new local and regional resilience bodies, with the participation of dedicated army planning cells, formed in each region of the UK. These changes became an essential part of the process of preparing to deal with the consequences for the life of the community of catastrophic events, from terrorism – as part of the Prepare strand of CONTEST[24] – to natural disasters on a national scale.

The MoD has maintained that it should charge the relevant civil department for the use of the armed forces in MAGD to maintain essential supplies and services when these are disrupted by industrial action. Examples over the years have included using service personnel to clear rubbish, unload supplies at docks, run power stations, man fire engines and drive oil tankers. Such activity has traditionally not been seen as a proper military task for which forces should be maintained and funded from the defence budget. The MoD has also been nervous about drawing the armed forces into political controversy were they to come to be seen as 'strike breaking', rather than a last resort to protect the 'life' of the population. The devolved governments in Scotland and Northern Ireland were not, during this period, given authority for MAGD, which was reserved by the Westminster government.

The MAGD operations conducted during the period were, however, mostly in response to natural emergencies, and were conducted in ways that retained widespread public support and enhanced the reputation of the services. Thus, for example, the military was asked for help by the Ministry of Agriculture, Fisheries and Food in early 2001 as foot-and-mouth disease spread out of control and the mass culling of animals was required. The situation was rescued by the injection of military staff planners and logistics units. The number of service personnel involved – including reservists – reached a peak of 2,000. Another notable example was the response to severe flooding in the West Country in July 2007 when a month's rain fell in sixteen hours, and only the work of the armed services prevented Bristol from being deprived of electricity for weeks when a substation was at risk of being flooded. A typical task was organising the distribution of bottled water to some 35,000 people after a major water-filtration plant became contaminated.

Civil Defence and Military Aid to the Civil Community

A traditional 'home-front' peacetime activity conducted by the armed services has been the provision of (unarmed) assistance at the request of local communities, to prevent or deal with the aftermath of a natural disaster or a major incident, or to assist civil sponsors, either by carrying out special projects of significant social value to the community or by attaching individual volunteers to specific projects,[25] such as to local charitable organisations. The 1966 defence review announced that, with a higher proportion of British forces stationed in the UK, there would be 'scope for developing further the peaceful use of military forces in this country',[26] with examples since then including road repair in remote areas, bridge building and demolition – all of which have training value for the units concerned as well as direct value for the local community. Such activity continued throughout the period – the MoD sensibly allowing charging for the use of some of its equipment and facilities at marginal cost – to encourage local participation and provide a valued means of connecting the armed services to their wider recruiting base.

In the case of emergencies, local military commanders have discretion under MACC arrangements should they consider their contribution to be urgently required in order to alleviate distress and to preserve and safeguard lives and property in times of disaster. There were many such minor deployments over the period in question, although the principal use of the armed forces in disaster relief took place under centrally mandated MAGD arrangements.

Over this period, the armed forces also maintained, as funded military tasks, a year-round, twenty-four-hour search-and-rescue service at locations around the British Isles to answer calls of distress around the coast, as well as an RAF mountain rescue service. The pressure for cost savings through contracting out services will inevitably mean that less of this activity is conducted by the armed forces in future.

Military Assistance: Lessons Learned
Central to resilience thinking in government after 9/11 is the role that the armed forces would play in the event of any form of major disruption through their ability to plan, deploy and command complex operations. An 'all-risks' approach is adopted,[27] since very much the same arrangements for military assistance would be needed to maintain the life of the population, whether the disruption were caused by malign threats such as terrorism, major accidents or forces of nature. New legislation – the Civil Contingencies Act 2004 – wrote the armed forces into the script for national resilience through their role in regional and local resilience fora. The 2002 Strategic Defence Review 'New Chapter'[28] introduced several domestic defence and security measures aimed at developing the machinery whereby the civil authorities could request appropriate support from the armed forces, with emphasis on improving command and control (C2), liaison, communications and the role of the reserves. Fourteen Civil Contingency Reaction Forces (CCRF) were created from the reserve forces to provide

assistance at short notice and boost military planning capacity at regional level. These changes have introduced a sound framework for C3I, with the capacity to escalate if the situation worsens, but has blurred the doctrinal distinctions between MAGD and MACC, with the real distinction for ministers being within the MAGD category, between the sensitive cases of support for the public during industrial action on the one hand, and support in response to terrorist action, accidents or natural disasters on the other.

Examples of major civil disruptions over the last decade have been triggered by threatened disruption of fuel supplies (in 2000, 2002, 2005, 2008 and 2012), animal disease and pandemics (in 2001, 2003, twice in 2007 and in 2009), and weather and natural hazards (twice in 2004, twice in 2005, in 2007, twice in 2009, twice in 2010 and in 2012). To take another example, large-scale maritime pollution from accidents at sea around the UK remains an unpredictable risk (with examples in 1996, 2007, 2009 and 2012), with a spill of 1 million tonnes or more in UK waters probable once every seventeen years and a spill of at least 4,000 tonnes likely to occur every other year, the risk increasing as the oil and gas fields to the west of the Shetlands are exploited and increasing numbers of large tankers and cruise ships pass through UK waters.

When – as is almost certain – there is a major disruptive challenge to normal life in the UK, the armed forces will be expected to be available to support the civil power to provide command, control and communications and disciplined personnel within a reliable chain of command in order to help rescue the situation. Such a call for support is even more likely than in the past, since one beneficial effect of the 2012 Olympics has been a significant reconnection of the armed forces to the people and a recognition that in times of national need the armed forces provide the backstop of public safety and security. Lack of funding has slowed the adaptation by the MoD to this reality, in terms of strengthening joint planning and command-and-control infrastructure for UK operations, and maintaining recognised maritime and air pictures from UK headquarters co-located with the relevant civil institutions. The direction of travel is, however, clear and recognised in the National Security Strategy.

Protecting the Public at Home through Operations Abroad

Afghanistan
George Orwell's remark that 'We sleep safely in our beds because rough men stand ready in the night to visit violence on those who would harm us' could have been written about the dramatic 2001 coalition intervention in Afghanistan to destroy the terrorist infrastructure built up by Al-Qa'ida and sheltered by the Taliban. 9/11 was the 'sudden-impact' emergency writ large as the politics of terrorism changed overnight with the sudden public realisation of danger – what Fawaz Gerges later called the Al-Qa'ida strategy to attack the 'far enemy' in its own homeland.[29] In response to the 9/11 attacks, the UK MoD identified four main goals in its campaign – Operation *Veritas* – against international terrorism: to deny Al-Qa'ida its Afghan base; to deny it an alternative base outside of Afghanistan; to attack the organisation internationally; and to support other states in their efforts against Al-Qa'ida.

The UK contributed forces to the first coalition intervention in Afghanistan (the US's Operation *Enduring Freedom*) which succeeded, with the help of the Northern Alliance, in dislodging the Taliban swiftly and without major allied casualties. The Al-Qa'ida terrorist infrastructure had represented a real menace to the UK, as well as to other European nations and the US, specifically due to the existence of a cadre of dedicated, trained and equipped jihadist terrorists, including potential suicide bombers, some with UK passports or right of entry to the UK. The training manuals and notebooks seized in Afghanistan during Operation *Enduring Freedom* included instruction in the use of primitive (but in some circumstances potentially deadly) means of chemical and biological terrorism.

On the other side of the ledger, Osama bin Laden and his deputy (and eventual successor) Ayman Al-Zawahiri escaped after failures in the planning and resourcing of the US-led operation intended to net them (the Battle of Tora Bora). The battle itself saw some 250 Al-Qa'ida and Taliban fighters killed. The key terrorist planners, however, dispersed to distribute the seed of their ideology and know-how more widely. The flight of Al-Qa'ida leaders to the Federally Administered Tribal Areas (FATA) in Pakistan made contact between UK-based extremists of Pakistani descent – who could easily travel legitimately to Pakistan – and terrorist facilitators and trainers in Pakistan, such as Rashid Rauf, easier. The UK security authorities began to see more and more domestic networks of jihadist activists, with increasing talk of action against the UK itself.

We can only speculate as to how much of the global spread of the jihadist ideology and how much of the suffering of the decade that followed might have been avoided had Bin Laden and Al-Zawahiri been captured or killed in mid-December 2001, thus bringing at least partial closure to the US need for justice to be meted out to those principally responsible for conceiving the attacks on the US on 9/11. For future historians, this will be one of the great 'what ifs'. The Al-Qa'ida terrorist infrastructure uncovered in Afghanistan nevertheless fully justifies the British decision, in light of knowledge at the time, to launch the coalition operation aimed at averting threats to the UK and its interests around the world.

Iraq
In the aftermath of 9/11, Prime Minister Tony Blair (reasonably) concluded that the suicidal jihadists who carried out the attacks would not have hesitated to use a dirty bomb or bio-terror weapon if they had had access to them, or even a nuclear weapon if this had been passed on by a rogue state. Advanced Western societies

appeared fragile and vulnerable. For the prime minister, it was no longer prudent to wait for the proliferator to develop his weapons and for the enemy to strike the first blow.[30] That became his – and to some extent, at least, the US's – strategic rationale for the highly controversial 2003 invasion of Iraq, as justified by what was later found to be flawed intelligence on Saddam Hussein's failure to comply with UN Security Council Resolutions on weapons of mass destruction.

The Iraq campaign coincided, however, with a rise in jihadist activism in the UK, accelerating radicalisation – as the Joint Intelligence Committee (JIC) had warned that the UK's participation in the invasion would. The subsequent four-and-a-half-year occupation of the Basra region by British forces, although a consequence of the decision to join the US in the invasion, had only an indirect link to British security interests. As the then-director general of the Security Service stated to the Iraq Inquiry chaired by Sir John Chilcot:[31]

> ... our involvement in Iraq radicalised, for want of a better word, a whole generation of young people, some British citizens – not a whole generation, a few among a generation – who ... saw our involvement in Iraq, on top of our involvement in Afghanistan, as being an attack on Islam ... So it undoubtedly increased the threat and by 2004 we were pretty well swamped – that's possibly an exaggeration – but we were very overburdened by intelligence on a broad scale that was pretty well more than we could cope with in terms of leads to threat plots and things that we needed to pursue. Of course, also we were dealing at that time with a number of young British citizens who went to Iraq to fight not with Her Majesty's forces but against them ... if you take the video wills that were retrieved on various occasions after various plots, where terrorists who had expected to be dead explained why they had done what they did, it [Iraq] features. It is part of what we call the single narrative, which is the view of some that everything the west was doing was part of a fundamental hostility to the Muslim world and to Islam.

That assessment, in itself, would not necessarily have been a reason for declining to participate in the invasion, if the wider strategic arguments in favour had been strong enough. A final judgement must await the publication of the inquiry's report, but there seems little doubt that the campaign, as it turned out, substantially exacerbated the domestic threat, an effect intensified by the imagery of the bloody aftermath of occupation which the rapidly expanding Internet carried globally.

Renewal of Effort in Afghanistan
Another, predictable consequence of the Iraq War was the significant distraction of US and UK effort – framework security, military training and aid – from the unstable situation in Afghanistan, which rapidly deteriorated as the Taliban began their insurgency against the newly installed Afghan government. In 2003, NATO had assumed control of the International Security Assistance Force in Afghanistan under a UN mandate but, in 2006, as the Iraq campaign wound down, the UK volunteered the UK-led NATO ACE (Allied Command Europe) Rapid Reaction Force (ARRC) to allow NATO's mission to be extended and strengthened, with overall troop levels rising from 9,000 to 36,000. The mission contained inherent contradictions, however, between the counter-insurgency task, in support of the Afghan government, and the counter-narcotics mission that had, for the UK, been an important part of the mission's original justification. The very significant UK contribution, and the casualties suffered, were nevertheless justified by Prime Minister Gordon Brown as part of a 'clear strategy' and a 'patriotic duty' to clear terrorist networks from Afghanistan and Pakistan: 'It comes back to terrorism on the streets of Britain. If we were to allow the Taliban to be back in power in Afghanistan – and al-Qaeda then to have the freedom of manoeuvre it had before 2001 – then we would be less safe as a country.'[32] This line of justification, that the campaign has been pursued to protect the UK's own national security by preventing the

return of international terrorist groups, has been maintained by the current coalition government.³³ The overall effect of the war in Iraq and the second intervention in Afghanistan, taken with the excesses of the original US War on Terror, has, however, been to make it much harder, over the period, to counter the jihadist message and thus to protect the British public at home and abroad.

One other consequence of the Iraq and Afghan experiences has been a recognition that it would now be difficult for a government to engage in armed conflict without parliamentary support; indeed, in then-Prime Minister Blair's own words: 'I cannot think of a set of circumstances in which a Government can go to war without the support of Parliament'.³⁴

Conclusion

Over the last twenty years, the dominant threat to the life of the nation has been terrorism, both Irish and international. A series of plots in the UK have been uncovered and pre-empted, or were launched but failed in their intent – perhaps as many as a dozen after the 7/7 attacks in London – and notable arrests and convictions have followed. That pace of work by the security authorities has not faltered, and significant arrests continue to be made and suspects charged with terrorist offences. The statistics on global terrorist incidents over the period, produced by the US National Counterterrorism Center, paint a broadly encouraging picture. In 2011, the number of terrorist attacks across the globe fell to a five-year low despite the activities of so-called affiliated groups.³⁵ Osama bin Laden's vision of global jihad has been rejected by mainstream Islamic opinion and the central structure of Al-Qa'ida, which he led until his death in 2011, is in disarray.

The aim of the counter-terrorism strategy CONTEST, followed by the last three British governments, has been to reduce the risk to the UK and its overseas interests from terrorism, so that the British people can go about their lives freely and with confidence. That aim has clearly been secured, not least through the demonstration of a safe, secure and highly successful Olympics in 2012.

It would be reasonable, therefore, to look back over the last decade and conclude that, overall, the UK is safer today than on the eve of 9/11, when Al-Qa'ida had bases and training camps in Afghanistan, and a cadre of dedicated and experienced terrorist operational planners to call on. The terrorist threat level in the UK is nevertheless still (at the time of writing) substantial, and in Northern Ireland specifically, severe: the UK cannot reasonably be accused of over-reacting over the course of the last decade due to exaggerated perceptions of the Al-Qa'ida threat. If anything, the authorities might be criticised for not pressing for a major increase in the domestic security and resilience effort a little earlier.

The hard, counterfactual question is, of course, whether the UK could have been even safer had different counter-terrorism and overseas policies been adopted. There can be more than one point of view on the matter. Iraq did bolster the radicalisation process, even though it did not create it. Bush-era rendition and interrogation policies helped to create a sense of double standards over key Western values of freedom, democracy and human rights. The very term 'War on Terror' may have helped to create the sense of an inevitable conflict between the West and the world of Islam. Some measures in UK counter-terrorism legislation may have been counterproductive in discouraging active intelligence co-operation with Muslim communities. There may therefore have been a higher price paid than need have been, but this is with the benefit of hindsight. Events never appear so clear at the time they are played out; had the US not acted against the Al-Qa'ida leadership, for example, and had it not been prepared to share its intelligence with the British authorities, and vice versa, the current domestic security situation might be very different.

Today, national security itself can usefully be defined as a state of confidence on the part of the public that major risks, be they malign threats or natural hazards, are being satisfactorily managed so that people can get on with making the most of their lives.[36] Public protection thus requires that there are effective emergency responses available against the widest range of major threats and hazards. Those responses in turn depend upon prior investment in the resilience of society and its critical infrastructure and networks – human as well as electronic – in the knowledge that the armed forces will continue to devote the resources necessary to play their part and will continue to innovate in developing their roles in domestic security. It is very much in their interests that they do. The armed forces represent a unique national asset that the public expects to be there when all else falters.

V. OF TAILS AND DOGS: PUBLIC SUPPORT AND ELITE OPINION

Joel Faulkner Rogers and Jonathan Eyal

OPINION polls are often used to reinforce the familiar maxim that 'all politics is local' – or national at best – and that come the next election, domestic issues will predominate while foreign affairs can be largely ignored. The question of when public opinion matters to foreign policy, and vice versa, is hardly new. Political scientists Gabriel Almond and Walter Lippmann coined the so-called 'Almond-Lippmann consensus' in the 1950s, suggesting that popular views were erratic, ill-informed and unlikely to have much impact on foreign policy. The Vietnam War challenged this consensus, highlighting a more complex relationship between the two and helping to expand the social sciences into the study of public opinion on foreign affairs and military intervention.

This chapter documents the public-opinion drivers for a number of crises in which British military forces were engaged in the two decades following the Soviet Union's collapse. At various times during this period, policy aligned naturally with a majority of public opinion over questions of military intervention. However, the two also diverged in several cases, from the Balkans to Afghanistan to Iraq, although with arguably limited impact on the direction of policy. In the process, wider British attitudes to military action saw a fundamental change of mood, though not, perhaps, the kind of shift to isolationism that many proclaimed after the dramatic House of Commons vote against Syrian intervention in August 2013.

The polling evidence presented in this chapter is not always comparable: almost by definition, the methodologies used and questions asked varied in different periods. Nor is it comprehensive: in some cases, it is possible to know in some detail about what the British public thought at the start of a particular crisis but not how opinions evolved as the crisis dragged on or reached a particular conclusion.

Still, the picture that emerges is a continuing canvas of broad trends. It starts with robust public willingness to support the use of force, and particularly air power, during the first decade after the collapse of the Soviet Union. Crucially, this support extended to the insertion of 'boots on the ground', even in conflicts that appeared potentially intractable from the start. By contrast, it ends with a deeply weary public attitude to the danger of 'mission creep', greater yearning for strong international endorsement of any operation in which British troops are involved, a deeper reverence for the legalities of intervention, and diminished willingness to trust British leaders, either with framing the aims of military action or pursuing them to successful conclusion.

'The Glorious Interventionist Decade': From 1990 to 2001
The post-Cold War era began with an 'easy' war for the relationship between public opinion and foreign policy: namely Saddam Hussein's invasion of Kuwait, a conflict that pitted a brutal dictator in charge of a large country against a small, oil-rich, vulnerable state. It was an easy conflict to understand and a clear violation of international law. Unsurprisingly, therefore, British support for action was high from the outset and was duly bolstered by the five months of diplomatic negotiations that preceded the start of operations to liberate Kuwait on 17 January 1991.

As Gallup polling showed soon after Iraqi forces invaded Kuwait on 2 August 1990, 85 per cent of the Britons surveyed approved of US forces being sent to the region to prevent an Iraqi invasion of

Saudi Arabia. A further 88 per cent supported the British government sending units of the Royal Navy and Royal Air Force to do the same. Between August 1990 and the first weeks of 1991, strong majorities consistently supported intervention with ground troops to invade Iraq 'if Britain and America did decide to use force against Iraq'. This ranged from 74 per cent in favour of such an operation in early September 1990 to 65 per cent in late October, and back to 74 per cent in early January 1991. As Figure 1 shows, stable majorities also continued to support the potential use of British forces for a range of purposes, including the defence of Gulf States, restoring independence to Kuwait, toppling Saddam Hussein and protecting Western oil supplies.[1]

Figure 1: 'Could you tell me for each of the following whether you support the use of British forces or not?' (%)

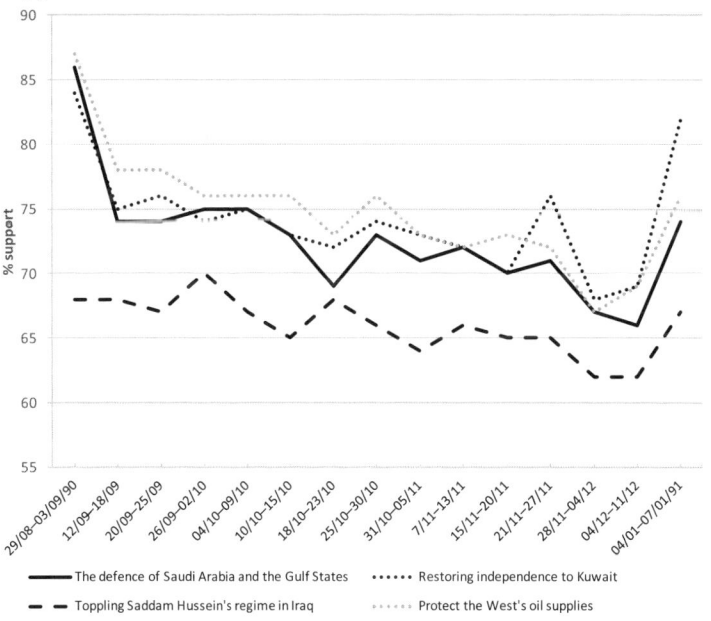

Source: Anthony King (ed.), British Political Opinion 1937–2000: The Gallup Polls, compiled by Robert J Wybrow (London: Politico's Publishing, 2001), p. 347.

Similarly, the percentage of Britons saying it was right to launch an assault on Iraq once the UN ultimatum for Iraqi withdrawal from Kuwait had passed remained consistently high from the beginning of January 1991 to the end of operations six weeks later, ranging from 79 per cent in January to 82 per cent at the beginning of March that year.[2]

Interestingly, then, it seems the British public imposed few limits on the options of decision-makers in this period, including that of escalating the mission and overthrowing Saddam Hussein. The decision not to do so was, therefore, dominated by political and strategic considerations in the capitals of those countries contributing to the military operation, rather than by the constraints of public opinion.

Either way, these were confident times for British attitudes to military intervention, both among policy-makers and the general population. This kind of public–political alignment was short-lived, however, as the simplicity of repelling a cross-border invasion was soon replaced with the complexity of a civil war.

In the first wave of substantial British polling on the subject of Bosnia in August 1992 (with the war having begun in April), a National Opinion Polls (NOP) survey showed that a 53 per cent majority was already dissatisfied with how the British government was handling the crisis, while 86 per cent supported sending British troops under UN authorisation to protect humanitarian supplies. The latter figure dropped when respondents were confronted with the scenario of an intervention force but still remained high at 61 per cent.[3]

By the time that MORI (before its merger with Ipsos UK in 2005), Gallup and other research agencies were surveying British attitudes to the Yugoslav crisis in 1993, the focus of attention had moved from initial clashes in Slovenia to the war in Croatia and then to tragic, bloody attrition in the Bosnian War. While much of the British public struggled to understand the conflict, it also supported the deployment of troops – at least to the vague end of doing 'something useful'.[4] As Tables 1 and 2 suggest, this included strong and sustained support for putting boots on the ground to protect convoys and enforce peace settlements.

Table 1: 'Do you approve or disapprove of the use of British troops in Bosnia to protect humanitarian convoys?' (%)

	April 1993	June 1993	August 1993	January 1994	June 1995	October 1995
Approve	72	67	73	74	62	72
Disapprove	20	25	21	21	27	20
Don't know	8	7	7	6	11	9

Source: King (ed.), British Political Opinion 1937–2000, *pp. 356–57.*

Table 2: 'If an international force were trying to enforce a peace settlement in Bosnia, would you personally like to see British troops forming part of that force or not?' (%)

	April 1993	June 1993	August 1993	1–6 June 1995	8–13 June 1995
Yes	67	64	69	75	62
No	22	25	21	17	24
Don't know	11	11	10	8	14

Source: King (ed.), British Political Opinion 1937–2000, *pp. 356–57.*

This is not to imply the absence of public concern regarding the risks of military involvement. Between spring 1993 and autumn 1995, Gallup conducted repeat polling on the question of what should happen if British troops were to suffer serious casualties while protecting aid supplies, with the options in response being to pull out the troops, to limit their remit to fighting back only when attacked, or to take steps to reinforce them.

As results from sequential waves of polling indicate, the preference to 'reinforce' competed constantly with the option of pulling out, while support for the middle option of fighting back only when attacked remained low, in a range of 14–17 per cent. In April 1993, for instance, 43 per cent of those polled claimed they would rather 'reinforce' the troops versus 32 per cent preferring to 'pull out'. Two months later, these numbers had converged somewhat to 34 per cent preferring to 'reinforce' versus 39 per cent to 'pull out'. Responses to subsequent waves of polling continued to fluctuate, with the preference for reinforcement just about keeping ahead: 41 per cent 'reinforce' versus 36 per cent 'pull out' in August 1993; then, 43 per cent 'reinforce' versus 32 per cent 'pull out' in January 1994; 35 per cent 'reinforce' versus 38 per cent 'pull out' in June 1995; and 43 per cent 'reinforce' versus 30 per cent 'pull out' in October 1995.[5]

Nonetheless, as then-Defence Secretary Malcolm Rifkind noted early in the conflict, the fears held by ministers about a slippery slope towards costly engagement by British forces in Bosnia were clearly challenged by a less risk-averse British public.[6]

Other repeat surveys between April 1993 and July 1995 show general stability in this regard. In April 1993, 60 per cent of respondents told MORI they were dissatisfied with the way the government was handling the situation in Bosnia, while only 20 per cent said they were satisfied. Fifty-two per cent also said that Britain 'isn't doing enough' to deal with the Bosnian War versus 35 per cent saying it was 'doing all it can' and only 9 per cent saying it was 'too involved'.[7] Two years later, these figures were broadly similar, with a small increase in both dissatisfaction and opposition to involvement: 65 per cent said they were dissatisfied versus 14 per cent satisfied; 47 per cent thought Britain 'isn't doing enough' versus 35 per cent saying it was 'doing all it can' and 14 per cent saying it was 'too involved' already.[8]

A public sense of the responsibility to protect seemed stronger still when the long-simmering Kosovo crisis erupted into full warfare in late 1998. The polling record only sparsely documents public opinion in the build-up to that war but various agencies conducted repeat polling from around the time that NATO began its air campaign on 24 March 1999.

Levels of British support for air strikes were high from the outset. They also reflected a commonplace phenomenon among democracies going to war, namely a 'rally round the flag' effect, where support is initially and substantially boosted by the action itself.

A MORI survey conducted shortly after the beginning of Operation *Allied Force* showed 55 per cent of those Britons polled saying the country was right to join the NATO operation versus 27 per cent saying it was wrong, and 18 per cent giving the response 'don't know' (see Table 3).[9] When MORI fielded a similar survey at the start of April, the figure for those saying it was 'right' jumped to 76 per cent (versus 16 per cent 'wrong' and 8 per cent 'don't know').[10] Answers to a third run of the survey in early May showed sustained, albeit slightly lower, levels of support (with 70 per cent saying it was 'right', 21 per cent 'wrong' and 8 per cent 'don't know').[11]

Repeat polling by Gallup reveals a similar pattern. Initial results from late March 1999 show 58 per cent saying they approved of the action versus 33 per cent saying they disapproved and 9 per cent choosing 'neither/don't know'. When the survey was repeated in April, answers jumped to 72 per cent 'approve' versus 23 per cent 'disapprove', with 4 per cent opting for 'neither/don't know'. By May, the percentage approving had dipped again but still remained high (67 per cent 'approve', while 28 per cent 'disapprove' and 5 per cent 'neither/don't know').[12] It is also worth mentioning in this context that the Yugoslav army and Serb paramilitaries were reported to have stepped up the pace of 'ethnic cleansing' against Kosovo Albanians after the bombing began, which may have affected the figures.

Table 3: 'On balance, do you believe that Britain is right or wrong to have joined in the NATO bombing of Yugoslavia?' (%)

	28 March 1999	2 April 1999	2 May 1999
Right	55	76	70
Wrong	27	16	21
Don't know	18	8	8

Source: Ipsos MORI, 'Mail on Sunday – Kosovo Poll', 28 March 1999, <http://bit.ly/LCns3k>, accessed 7 February 2014; Ipsos MORI, 'Mail on Sunday – Kosovo Poll', 2 April 1999, <http://bit.ly/1dN0LW9>, accessed 7 February 2014; Ipsos MORI, 'Local Elections, Kosovo and the Tory Leadership', 2 May 1999, <http://bit.ly/LCoz2N>, accessed 7 February 2014.

Attitudes to sending ground troops were both less certain or stable than for air strikes over this period but appeared to settle on support from roughly half of the population by early May 1999. In the initial March survey by MORI, only 26 per cent agreed that the UK should send ground troops into the conflict (versus 62 per cent who disagreed and 11 per cent responding 'don't know').[13] MORI results from a survey a month later suggested that 47 per cent now agreed with sending ground troops (versus 43 per cent who disagreed and 10 per cent responding 'don't know').[14] Finally, in May, repeat polling showed a majority of 51 per cent agreed with sending troops (versus 40 per cent who disagreed and 9 per cent responding 'don't know').[15]

Notwithstanding fluctuations in support, therefore, public opinion towards the Kosovo crisis suggested a generally receptive environment for the language of liberal interventionism emanating from Downing Street at the time. As MORI's first survey relating to the crisis duly showed in late March, a striking 87 per cent thought Britain had a 'moral duty' to help prevent further killings and human-rights abuses in the country.[16] This attitude was also likely helped by the nature of the Kosovo operation, which involved a Serb-dominated Yugoslav army already identified as a serial aggressor during recent Balkan conflicts; a local Albanian population that was allegedly defenceless; a precise objective to prevent massacres and put a stop to ethnic cleansing; and a high degree of international support.

Thus, when Prime Minister Tony Blair made his now famous 'Chicago speech' in April 1999, he clearly had his country behind him. The Kosovo War would also mark a high point for the humanitarian zeal of British attitudes to military intervention in the years since the Cold War. The Afghan intervention that began two years later came to challenge most of these attitudes, although, as explained below, the initial phase of the Afghan operation enjoyed strident public support.

Afghanistan: Elite Unity versus Public Consensus
An ICM poll conducted just after the beginning of Operation *Enduring Freedom* did well to capture the atmosphere of British public opinion between the September 2001 attacks on the United States and the end of initial operations to eliminate the Taliban leadership in Afghanistan. A full 74 per cent of respondents said they approved of military action by the US and the UK in Afghanistan, with high approval ratings among supporters of all of the major parties. This included 83 per cent of Conservatives, 76 per cent of Labour voters and 69 per cent of Liberal Democrats (Lib Dems). A still higher 85 per cent overall said British operations should continue even if there were retaliation against the UK for helping its ally, including 90 per cent support from Conservatives, 86 per cent from Labour and 82 per cent from Lib Dems.[17] Accordingly, those who have subsequently criticised British involvement in the Afghan War for allegedly encouraging domestic terrorism in the UK would do well to remember that this danger was discussed right at the beginning of the war in 2001, and seemingly had little impact on public attitudes at the time.

A subsequent history of the conflict needs no retelling here but, suffice it to say, public opinion soon followed a typical pattern for long counter-insurgency operations: initial enthusiasm wanes as costs and casualties mount; the 'rally around the flag' effect dissipates and underlying rationales for the operation are increasingly questioned, often in the context of concerns about growing expenditure.[18] In the process, however, the Afghan War also became notable for another phenomenon: the divergence between elite and public consensus.[19]

As public-opinion theorists suggest, popular support for ground deployments or tolerance for casualties are commonly based upon a weighing of benefits and costs, which in turn can be heavily influenced by the presence or absence of consensus among political leaders. Elite unity can mediate the impact of problematic deployments on wider political and electoral dynamics, while even low costs can erode public support for missions and their leaders when this consensus is absent.[20]

Accordingly, several analysts have described the importance of British elite agreement over Afghanistan, as political leaders quickly united behind the war, forming a cross-party consensus that remained broadly intact over the subsequent decade. Politicians naturally argued over military means; however, they circled wagons around the fundamental ends of the campaign, remaining loyal to the basic idea that Afghan operations were vital to the broader fight against terrorism.

In reality, public support for continued involvement decreased substantially over the duration of several parliamentary periods. There is, unfortunately, a dearth of opinion data on British attitudes to the Afghan War between initial operations to remove the Taliban in 2001 and the more forceful expansion of British troops into southern Afghanistan during 2005–06. Notwithstanding this omission, as Douglas Kriner and Graham Wilson note in their 2010 paper on elite support for the war in Afghanistan, high levels of public support soon diminished after the initial operation in 2001, falling to levels nearer to 40 per cent in several polls by 2006.[21]

By the time YouGov began tracking attitudes to the subject in October 2006, 64 per cent of the public believed that there was no clear strategy guiding the use of British troops in Afghanistan. Moreover, 53 per cent said the government should withdraw troops – including 22 per cent who wanted this to happen 'immediately' and 31 per cent who preferred 'within the next 12 months' – compared with 35 per cent saying they should remain in-theatre until Afghanistan's own security forces were able to take over, and the remaining 12 per cent saying 'don't know'.[22]

Over the next couple of years, the balance between those who thought that the UK would eventually win the war and those predicting it would be lost changed dramatically: in 2007, a roughly even 39 per cent forecasted an eventual 'win' versus 36 per cent predicting the UK would 'lose'; by 2009, this had shifted to 28 per cent saying 'win' versus 57 per cent saying 'lose'. YouGov trackers have also shown a large increase in the percentage wanting troops to come home either immediately or soon (see Figure 2) – rising to 65 per cent overall in August 2007 and levelling out in the 70 per cent range thereafter: 73 per cent in November 2009; 71 per cent in November 2010; 76 per cent in November 2011; and 78 per cent in July 2012.[23]

Interestingly, however, Afghanistan did not become the war that destroyed political careers, as Vietnam had for a previous generation of US politicians. According to a set of leading survey researchers, including Thomas J Scotto, Jason Reifler, Harold D Clarke, Julio Amador Diaz Lopez, David Sanders, Marianne C Stewart and Paul Whiteley, the absence of elite opposition in the case of Afghanistan – and the fact that political elites were largely united and supportive of the operation – limited the ability of the war to weigh on the fortunes of British leaders.[24] Political parties have to take opposing positions, theorists argue, for this kind of issue to become particularly relevant in electoral politics. However, since the Conservatives – then in opposition – broadly supported the government's objectives in relation to the conflict, this meant that the Labour administration did not suffer unduly, even if it was increasingly attacked for allegedly failing to fund and equip the Afghanistan operation adequately.

Figure 2: 'Should British troops be brought back home from Afghanistan?' (%)

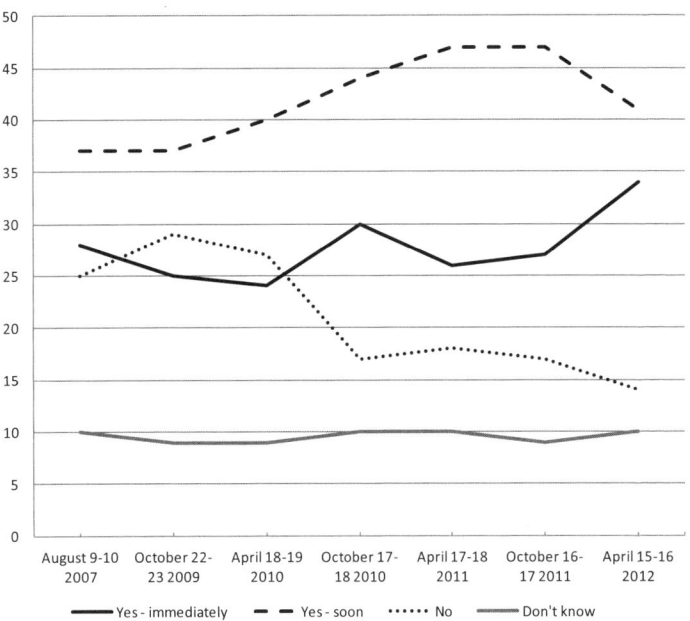

Source: *YouGov Archive, 'Afghanistan Tracker', <http://bit.ly/1jycDLq>, accessed 14 February 2014. Fieldwork was conducted online and sample sizes vary above n=1,000 in each case. The data have been weighted and the results are representative of all British adults aged 18+.*

Iraq and the 'Rally around the Flag' Effect

If elite unity over Afghanistan helped to contain the political fallout from growing public opposition, then elite dissension over the UK's involvement in Iraq had the opposite effect. As noted by Clarke, Sanders, Stewart and Whiteley in their 2009 publication *Performance Politics and the British Voter*, the public was exposed from the earliest stages of debate to 'sharply contrasting arguments' about the morality, benefits and costs of intervention, and about the likelihood of its success.[25]

Perhaps all the more striking, then, that the Iraq debate saw an arguably greater suppression of the democratic pulse via different means. This time, in the face of backbench revolts and mass street protests, then-Prime Minister Tony Blair took the unprecedented step of giving Parliament an explicit vote on the use of force. The gamble worked (by some measures), delivering a questionable form of democratic blessing from a relatively pliant House of Commons in the face of overwhelming public opposition.[26]

Even so, the initial phase of operations saw a bold demonstration of the 'rally around the flag' effect, as contemporary YouGov polling shows.

Two months before the war began, only 13 per cent said they supported sending British troops into action against Iraq 'no matter what', while 32 per cent opposed intervention entirely. Just over half (53 per cent) said they would support military action but only with UN approval.[27]

Another poll conducted two weeks later, in mid-January 2003, similarly shows only 23 per cent agreeing that the UK should contribute troops to a US-led force 'if the UN does not take action', versus 67 per cent saying it 'should not' and 10 per cent responding 'don't know'.[28] By the end of January, the percentage of those opposing action entirely had fallen slightly – but not by much – from 32 to 25 per cent, while the figures for those supporting 'no matter what' or only with UN approval remained about the same (at 17 and

55 per cent respectively).[29] Repeat polling over the following six weeks in the build-up to war show these numbers essentially unchanged, with YouGov's final pre-war poll of 14–16 March indicating 32 per cent in favour of joining the US-led action without a second UN Security Council resolution compared with 60 per cent against.[30]

Figure 3: 'Do you think the US/Britain are/were right or wrong to take military action against Iraq?' (%)

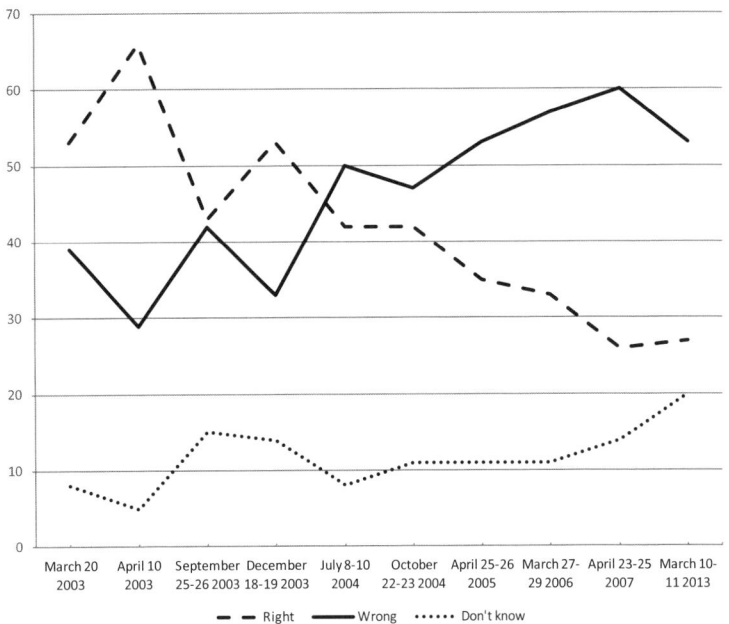

Source: *YouGov Archive, 'Iraq Tracker', <http://bit.ly/1bhAPMz>, accessed 14 February 2014. Fieldwork was conducted online and sample sizes vary above n=1,000 in each case. The data have been weighted and the results are representative of all British adults aged 18+.*

Polling results suggest that the weight of public opinion then shifted dramatically and suddenly in favour of intervention a week later, just after the war began, with 56 per cent now saying that the US and the UK were right to take military action against Iraq, compared with 36 per cent calling it wrong and 9 per cent responding 'don't know'.[31]

Levels of support remained strong – and stable – over the following two months, peaking around 10 April as US troops entered central Baghdad, with 66 per cent saying intervention was 'right' versus 29 per cent deeming it 'wrong' and 5 per cent responding 'don't know'.[32]

Approval then zig-zagged gradually towards opposition over the following year. By the middle of 2003, results suggest that the 'Bliar' story had begun to take hold, with the public roughly split between 43 per cent saying that the prime minister had told the truth over Iraq's supposed weapons of mass destruction versus 46 per cent saying he had distorted the evidence.[33]

By the end of 2003, the percentage of those saying the intervention was 'right' and those believing that it was 'wrong' fell roughly even, before the capture of Saddam Hussein prompted a brief spike in public support around the middle of December. As Figure 3 shows, the proportion of those saying intervention was 'wrong' then permanently overtook the number giving other responses around the time that the Butler Report was published in the summer of 2004, reaching the mid-50 per cent range by early 2005, where it largely remained thereafter.[34]

Libya, Mali and Whither the Spirit of Kosovo?
If the post-9/11 period took its toll on public attitudes to military intervention, then events in Libya, Mali and Syria brought the realities of this legacy into view. When the British people were asked to support action in Libya in 2011, it carried UN authorisation, involved no ground troops and was aimed at preventing widespread bloodletting by the Libyan leader Muammar Qadhafi, whose intentions were barely in doubt.[35] All the same, those surveyed were divided on military action while opposition to the potential use of

ground troops was vehement, with 21 per cent agreeing that the UK should send ground troops if necessary, versus 69 per cent who disagreed.[36]

There were noticeable contrasts, moreover, with YouGov polling from the eve of intervention in Iraq nearly a decade earlier (as seen in Table 4): 53 per cent supported military action in Iraq on 20 March 2003; 45 per cent supported it in Libya on 20 March 2011, showing only a nine-point lead over those who opposed. The proportion giving the response 'don't know' was 19 per cent in 2011, more than double that in 2003, at 8 per cent.[37]

Levels of trust had also changed: in March 2003, 62 per cent said they trusted Tony Blair to tell the truth about what was happening in Iraq; in March 2011, only 43 per cent said the same about Prime Minister David Cameron regarding Libya. Trust in the armed forces had similarly dropped substantially, with 83 per cent saying they trusted the British armed forces to tell the truth about events in March 2003, compared with 64 per cent saying the same in March 2011.[38]

A comparable mood emerged among the British public towards the Mali crisis in January 2013: 49 per cent said they supported sending transport planes to help the French intervene versus 31 per cent who opposed and 21 per cent who gave the response 'don't know'. However, only 15 per cent supported deploying British troops to help the French army fight the rebels versus 63 per cent who were opposed and 21 per cent responding 'don't know'.[39]

While Mali remained largely the subject of policy wonks, the question of Syria, only months later, quickly grew into a national debate on the UK's place in the world. It was clear from the very earliest stages of this debate, however, that Cameron was out of step with his public.

Table 4: Attitudes to intervention in Iraq (2003) and Libya (2011) compared (%).

Do you think [Britain/coalition forces] are right or wrong to take military action in [Iraq/Libya]?	20 March 2003 (Iraq)	20–21 March 2011 (Libya)
Right	53	45
Wrong	39	36
Don't know	8	19

How big an effort do you believe [Britain/coalition forces] are making to avoid casualties among [Iraqi/Libyan civilians]?	27 March 2003 (Iraq)	20–21 March 2011 (Libya)
A very great effort	62	30
Some effort	30	37
Not much effort	6	13
No effort	1	3
Don't know	1	17

How much do you trust the following to tell the truth about what is happening in the military action against [Iraq/Libya]?	25–26 March 2003 (Iraq)	20–21 March 2011 (Libya)
The British Military		
Trust a great deal/trust a fair amount	83	64
Do not trust much/do not trust at all	16	26
Don't know	1	10
Blair vs Cameron	*Blair*	*Cameron*
Trust a great deal/trust a fair amount	62	43
Do not trust much/do not trust at all	37	47
Don't know	1	10
Bush vs Obama	*Bush*	*Obama*
Trust a great deal/trust a fair amount	40	38
Do not trust much/do not trust at all	60	51
Don't know	1	11

Source: YouGov Archive, 'Comparative Survey Results on Iraq and Libya', <http://bit.ly/1ey0jJr>, accessed 17 February 2014. Fieldwork was conducted online and sample sizes vary above n=1,000 in each case. The data have been weighted and the results are representative of all British adults aged 18+.

Syria and the 'Red Lines' of Public Opinion

Around the time that Cameron and French President François Hollande began asking foreign ministers to lift the EU arms embargo on Syria in March 2013, YouGov polling showed strong British support for sending food, medicine and humanitarian supplies to civilians in Syria (75 per cent), plus still notable, though lower, support for sending protective clothing such as flak jackets and helmets to rebel forces fighting to overthrow the Assad regime (48 per cent). However, there was scant support for any kind of harder commitment, such as sending defensive military supplies like anti-aircraft guns (23 per cent), small arms such as handguns (18 per cent), full-scale military supplies including tanks and heavy artillery (12 per cent), and – least of all – troops to fight alongside anti-Assad rebels (8 per cent).[40]

Repeat polling a month later suggested the scenario of Syrian government forces crossing the political 'red line' by using chemical weapons made little difference. YouGov asked the following, amended version of the question [emphasis added]:[41]

> In recent weeks some Western countries have expressed concerns that the Syrian regime is using chemical weapons against rebels. The Syrian government has said it will never use chemical weapons against its own people and has said such allegations are lies. *If Syria were to use chemical weapons against rebel fighters or civilians, would you support or oppose the following actions?*

As Figure 4 shows, there were small increases in support for sending protective clothing, defensive military supplies, small arms, full-scale military supplies and even British troops, but not in ways that alter the balance of opinion.[42]

When serious reports of a chemical attack did emerge in late August 2013, YouGov polling showed that the public was opposed to a missile attack by two-to-one (with 50 per cent opposed versus 25 per cent supportive). Crucially, both Prime Minister David Cameron and Deputy Prime Minister Nick Clegg also lacked the support of their own parties, with Conservatives divided 45 per cent against and 33 per cent for, and Lib Dems 42 per cent against and 27 per cent for.[43]

Figure 4: 'Thinking about the conflict in Syria, here are some things Britain could do. Would you support sending...' (%)

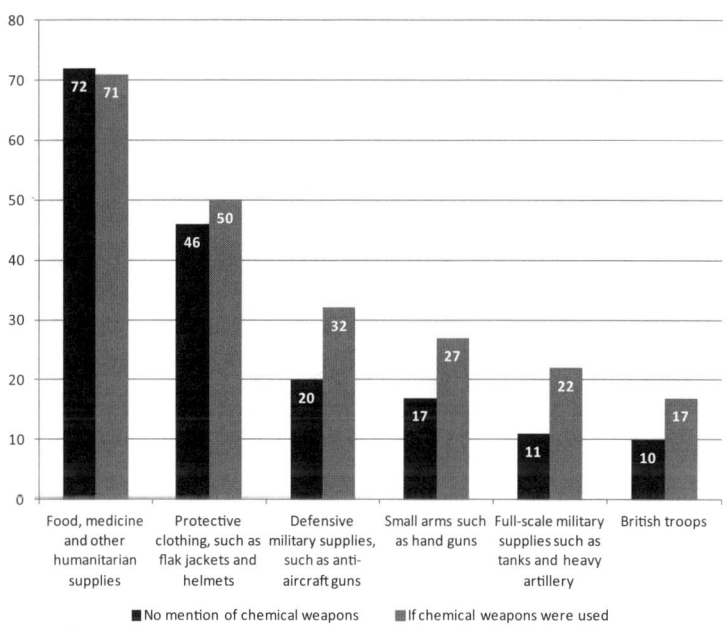

Source: *YouGov.com, 'YouGov Survey Results', <http://bit.ly/1dOIacq>, accessed 17 February 2014. Fieldwork was conducted online between 28–29 April 2013, with a total sample of 1,632 British adults. The data have been weighted and the results are representative of all British adults aged 18+.*

Only days before the House of Commons voted against military action in Syria on 29 August, YouGov conducted a further survey experiment for the annual YouGov-Cambridge Forum (in which

RUSI was a partner), testing the potential impact of UN authorisation on levels of support for intervention.

Respondents were first asked if they supported or opposed several forms of intervention in Syria, including air strikes and sending arms, non-lethal support or troops. The overall sample was then split into two: subsample 1 was asked if it would support or oppose the same measures as part of a UN operation; subsample 2 was asked whether it would support or oppose these measures if they were not part of a UN operation.[44]

As Table 5 shows, the presence or absence of UN support makes a perceptible difference but only a small one. For instance, support for sending troops to protect civilians climbed from 18 per cent to 33 per cent if they were to be part of a UN operation, and fell to 12 per cent if they were not.

In other words, even the variable of UN support does little to change the overall balance of opinion in each case.

A New Role for Parliament and the Public?
YouGov polling shortly after the House of Commons vote against intervention in Syria showed that Britons believed Parliament to have made the right decision by a ratio of four to one (68:16 per cent). Further results suggest that this outcome rested on two factors: first, the public had limited faith in the government's word, with 43 per cent believing that the Syrian government had used chemical weapons, versus a striking 43 per cent giving the response 'don't know'; second, a majority also believed limited missile strikes would likely end up pulling the UK into deeper involvement, with troops getting stuck in fighting on the ground.[45]

Consequently, the Syrian vote *does* mark a democratic turning point of sorts, helping to highlight several reasons why domestic public opinion is likely to have greater influence in future debates on British military intervention.

Table 5: YouGov/RUSI study on support for action [in Syria] with/without the UN. (%)

	Non-Specified	With UN (subsample 1)	Without UN (subsample 1)
	(n=1,954)	(n=1,004)	(n=950)
Providing arms to the Syrian rebels			
Support	11	18	11
Oppose	66	60	72
Don't know	23	22	17
Providing 'non-lethal' support to the Syrian rebels			
Support	52	59	39
Oppose	29	26	43
Don't know	19	15	18
Sending British/allied troops into Syria to protect civilians			
Support	18	33	12
Oppose	63	49	71
Don't know	18	18	17
Sending British/allied troops to overthrow President Assad			
Support	9	17	6
Oppose	72	63	78
Don't know	19	21	17
Launching air strikes on Syrian government targets			
Support	18	29	12
Oppose	59	49	72
Don't know	23	23	16

Source: *YouGov.com, 'YouGov-Cambridge Survey Results', <http://bit.ly/1dONAnB>, accessed 17 February 2014. Fieldwork was conducted online between 28–29 August 2013, with a total sample of 1,954 British adults. Data from the whole sample have been weighted and these results are representative of all British adults aged 18+. Subsample 1 (with UN support) included 1,004 respondents. Subsample 2 (without UN support) included 950 respondents.*

First, people are simply less trusting than they have been previously in the need for intervention, while those making the case for such action will need to meet a higher threshold of evidence for doing so.

Britons also now exhibit a firm reluctance to act without strong, international or multilateral endorsement, and they need some persuading that British troops will avoid the quagmire of long and costly deployments.

Finally, politicians are generally less able to ignore the contemporary force of public opinion, and are also less inclined to do so after the Iraq experience weighed so heavily on the legacy of Tony Blair and New Labour.

Looking at Parliament's role, meanwhile, it remains to be seen, at the time of writing, whether a line has been permanently redrawn on military action between those decisions that are properly left to ministers and those that should be made by Parliament.

Nevertheless, it is possible to explore the extent to which the Syrian debate represented a fundamental change of public mood on constitutional convention. In a further study to support the YouGov-Cambridge Forum 2013, YouGov asked two samples of British respondents how the nation should decide on a range of foreign-policy actions, including declaring war on another country.

In the first survey, people were shown the following introductory text:

> At the moment, Britain's armed forces operate in the name of the Queen. In practice, all major decisions are taken by government ministers acting in the Queen's name. Sometimes, but not always, MPs debate the issues in Parliament before British troops are sent into action. But Parliament has no formal powers to approve or veto military action.

Respondents were then asked how the decision to declare war should be taken. The answer options offered (see Table 6) spanned a democratic scale from ministers acting entirely alone to following the current convention, to Parliament having *ex post facto* or full war powers, and finally to the 'democracy max' option: a public referendum.

Table 6: Answer Options for Survey 1 on Parliamentary Oversight.

Answer Options	Democratic Scale
Decision should be taken by ministers alone, without involving Parliament	Zero involvement for Parliament
Ministers should have the right to take the decision and choose when it is appropriate to consult Parliament	Current convention
Ministers should have the right to authorise urgent action, but Parliament should have the power subsequently to instruct ministers when to stop	*Ex post facto* powers for Parliament
Decision should be taken by Parliament before the action is taken	Full powers for Parliament
Decision should be taken by a referendum of voters and no action taken for the two to three months it would take to set up and hold the referendum	Democracy max

In the second survey, respondents were given a slightly altered form of introductory text, this time emphasising that the prime minister and full Cabinet take the decision together, having received wider legal and military advice [emphasis added]:[46]

> At the moment, Britain's armed forces operate in the name of the Queen. In practice, all major decisions of this kind are taken by *the Prime Minister and full cabinet who act in the Queen's name after taking legal and military advice*. Sometimes, but not always, MPs debate the issues in Parliament before British troops are sent into action. But Parliament has no formal powers to approve or veto military action.

This change was also included in the answer options offered, as shown in Table 7 (on the following page), with the changes italicised.

As Figure 5 shows, spelling out the nature of wider involvement by ministers and advisers at the top of government has a noticeable impact on the willingness of respondents to allow the government to act without prior parliamentary approval or a direct referendum, increasing from 28 per cent to 49 per cent overall, while the proportion wanting to give full war powers to Parliament falls from 46 per cent to 27 per cent.[47]

Table 7: Answer Options for Survey 2 on Parliamentary Oversight.

Answer Options	Democratic Scale
Decision should be taken by the prime minister and full Cabinet after taking legal and military advice, but without involving Parliament	Zero involvement for Parliament
Decision should be taken by the prime minister and full Cabinet after taking legal and military advice, and then choosing when it is appropriate to consult Parliament	Current convention
The prime minister and full Cabinet should have the right to authorise urgent action, but Parliament should have the power subsequently to instruct ministers when to stop	*Ex post facto* powers for Parliament
Decision should be taken by Parliament before the action is taken	Full powers for Parliament
Decision should be taken by a referendum of voters and no action taken for the two to three months it would take to set up and hold the referendum	Democracy max

With such a short passage of time having passed since the Syrian vote in the House of Commons, it is – at the time of writing – impossible to predict how Parliament or the public might behave in the face of the next debate on military action. Yet it is notable, in theory at least, that nearly half of those polled say ministers should have the right to authorise initial military action, while only 27 per cent say the decision should be taken by Parliament and 12 per cent by a referendum.[48] These results, gathered only days after the Commons debate in August 2013, suggest that the prime minister lost public support for military intervention in Syria more because of how he handled that particular crisis, and less because voters rejected the principle of the government acting on their behalf in such matters.

Figure 5: 'How do you think the following type of action should be decided?' (%)

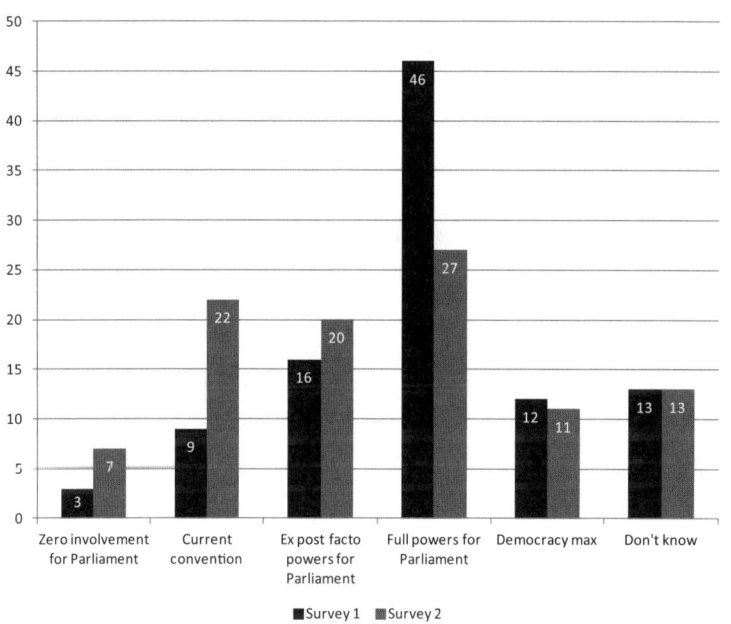

Source: For Survey 1, see YouGov.com, 'YouGov-Cambridge Survey Results', <http://bit.ly/KFFx0f>, accessed 17 February 2014. Fieldwork for Survey 1 was conducted online between 21–23 August 2013 with a total sample of 1,948 British adults. For Survey 2, see YouGov.com, 'YouGov-Cambridge Survey Results', <http://bit.ly/1jzpTiW>, accessed 17 February 2014. Fieldwork for Survey 2 was conducted online between 9–10 September 2013 with a total sample of 1,579 British adults. n each case, the data have been weighted and the results are representative of all British adults aged 18+.

Great-Power Expectations and Domestic Retrenchment

Caution is in order, therefore, in interpreting the public's verdict on Syria and what it says more broadly about attitudes to the UK's role in the world. While YouGov polling showed strong opposition to direct action, it also showed high levels of support for helping the US to conduct its own strikes: 70 per cent said this should include sharing intelligence about Syria (versus 15 per cent who said it should not and 15 per cent responding 'don't know'); 64 per cent said this should include providing diplomatic support for US military action at the UN (versus 16 per cent who said it should not and 20 per cent responding 'don't know'); and 48 per cent said this should include providing access to British military facilities in Cyprus (versus 31 per cent who said it should not and 21 per cent responding 'don't know').[49]

In the same survey, YouGov also tested voters' attitudes – *in principle* – to British involvement in a range of possible scenarios for military action in the future. Opinion data from this kind of survey should be treated with caution, because it faces at least two challenges: the first is the reliance on hypothetical questions that provide little guarantee of how respondents might feel in reality; the second is the problem of surveying 'non-attitudes', with respondents providing answers on subjects about which they hold no living, breathing opinion at the time.

Nevertheless, the survey still illustrates a general direction of opinion. Respondents were shown several different circumstances in which the UK might send its forces into action in countries beyond Europe. The results show that most people believe the government should definitely or seriously consider taking part in each of the seven cases: in particular, 72 per cent said the UK should definitely or seriously consider taking action to help a friendly country that had been invaded; 67 per cent said the same for attacking bases used by terrorist groups such as Al-Qa'ida; 53 per cent supported the use of force for stopping an unfriendly country from acquiring nuclear weapons; and 75 per cent supported taking part in an operation authorised by the UN Security Council.[50]

As YouGov President Peter Kellner argues, these figures suggest important nuances in the British mindset: opposition to British military action in 2013 did not indicate – as some feared and others hoped – a shift in public opinion towards a new doctrine of disengagement from the world's problems; rather, it was participation in military action in those particular circumstances that people rejected.[51]

By a similar token, YouGov polling suggests that the UK still clearly regards itself as a great power, whose prosperity and security both depend on keeping its historic place at the high table of leading nations. According to research produced for the YouGov-Cambridge Programme in early 2013, 65 per cent of those polled thought that the UK still needs a major role in the world to protect its own national security while 75 per cent said the same was necessary to protect its economic interests. Meanwhile, 73 per cent said the UK needs to keep a leading voice in NATO while 78 per cent said the same was true in relation to the UN Security Council (see Table 8 on the following page).[52]

Perhaps notably, the same survey further showed high levels of overall support for being a leading voice in the EU (at 70 per cent), including strong endorsement from supporters of the three largest political parties (68 per cent of Conservative, 75 per cent of Labour and 87 per cent of Lib Dem supporters). These figures are not to be confused with attitudes to EU membership itself, but still emphasise an underlying resistance to the notion of strategic shrinkage, even within Europe.[53]

This is not to deny that the British public was experiencing a period of domestic retrenchment by the end of 2013, following five years of economic slump and twelve years of war: immigration vied with the economy as a top concern for voters; the public seemed divided on the wisdom of defence cuts; Euroscepticism had gone

Table 8: 'In your view, how important or unimportant are the following activities in serving the United Kingdom's national interests?' (%)

	Important	Unimportant	Don't Know
Being a leading voice in NATO (the North Atlantic Treaty Organization)	73	16	11
Being a leading voice in the European Union (EU)	70	23	8
Being a leading voice on the United Nations Security Council, as one of the Big Five Permanent Members (the others are the United States, Russia, China and France)	78	13	8
Having aircraft carriers to send our armed forces anywhere in the world	69	23	8
Acting as a bridge between the United States and Europe	60	30	9
Helping to finance international efforts to tackle global warming	51	41	8
Having our own nuclear weapons	54	34	12
Using military force to protect human rights in other countries	45	43	11
Sending financial aid to the developing world	36	57	7

Source: YouGov.com, 'YouGov Survey Results', <http://bit.ly/KFXbRt>, accessed 17 February 2014. Fieldwork was conducted online between 23–24 April 2013, with a total sample of 1,976 British adults. The data have been weighted and the results are representative of all British adults aged 18+.

mainstream; while the Syria debate underscored a new reluctance to act together with the country's longstanding superpower ally.

However, it would be premature to declare a new age of isolationism. A raft of British politicians and the public might see merits in reducing the size of the UK's armed forces or the scope of its international commitments; but as polling suggests, the appetite for exercising influence on the world stage seemed as strong as ever in 2013.

Conclusion
Several trends stand out from this survey of what is essentially a quarter of a century of UK military interventions. The first is that the British public remains instinctively and determinedly internationalist – if not interventionist – in outlook. Instead of retreating into a shell of peaceful existence at the end of the Cold War, the overwhelming majority of the UK's voters supported international intervention, and the level of that support continued throughout the 1990s. Furthermore, even in those conflicts in which the public did not wish to see British troops involved, such as in Syria in 2013, the UK's voters were not against the use of force per se: they understood that this could serve a useful purpose. So, almost twenty-five years since the end of the Cold War, the UK is not gripped by a bout of pacifism, even if the public is now jaded about military operations.

Second, the public-opinion obstacles that politicians claim to have encountered over this period in conducting military operations were, on several occasions, more imaginary than real – bar the obvious exception of the invasion of Iraq in 2003. There was little opposition, at least initially, to widening the war for the liberation of Kuwait in 1991 into one for the liberation of Iraq itself from Saddam Hussein; that was a self-denying ordinance that Western leaders then sought to justify by invoking supposed public opinion. There was little opposition to playing a bigger military role in the Balkans during the 1990s; again, the main opposition came from within government itself. Likewise, there was little reluctance for an all-out effort to reshape Afghanistan in the immediate aftermath of the Taliban's removal in 2001; that opposition only came later, with politicians having wasted years doing little in this regard before suddenly deciding to pick up the job of recreating Afghanistan after the Taliban and other insurgents had regrouped.

Third, despite the fact that politicians were perceived to have failed at various times in their handling of the conflicts analysed in this chapter, none of these played a critical role in domestic British politics, save for the 2003 Iraq intervention and the much-debated 'Iraq effect' on support for the Labour Party. The Conservatives were driven out of office in May 1997 not because they were perceived to have made errors in the Balkans, but because of other, largely domestic issues. Labour lost power in 2010 not because it 'messed up' in Afghanistan and Iraq. Cruel as it may seem, the number of European migrants arriving and settling in the UK likely cost the incumbent government more votes in the 2010 general election than the number of body bags making the sad journey home from Helmand Province. Nor did the public image of Britain's armed forces suffer unduly as a result of these conflicts: support and even admiration for the men and women in uniform remains high, even though confidence in the ability of politicians to use these armed forces in an efficient manner is now low.

Ultimately, however, it is a fact that the UK's interventionist phase in the two decades following the collapse of the Soviet Union was not an invention of the country's politicians alone. Whether by accident or design, it was a trend largely supported by the public. Whether Tony Blair, the man who led the UK during much of this period, did more to shape those times or was more their subject is a question for future historians. However, as this chapter has sought to argue through a variety of polling evidence, both positions are partially correct, with an internationalist elite supported, for much of the time at least, by an instinctively internationalist public.

VI. ON THE OFFENSIVE

Malcolm Chalmers

UK involvement in overseas military conflicts grew sharply in the period after 1990, in terms of both the number and size of operations, to levels not seen since the immediate post-1945 period. The contrast with the last two decades of the Cold War was especially striking. During the period from 1971 to 1989, the UK was involved in only two significant military campaigns – in Northern Ireland and the Falklands – both of which were fought to preserve control of sovereign British territory.[1] The US was similarly reluctant to become embroiled in costly overseas military operations. Between its final withdrawal from Vietnam in 1975 and the start of Operation *Desert Storm* in 1991, the largest operational deployments of US forces were to Lebanon in 1982–83, Grenada in 1983 and Panama in 1989. For both countries, the primary purpose of their armed forces was strategically defensive: to deter the Soviet Union from underestimating Western resolve to defend the territorial status quo in Europe and, in the case of the US, in East Asia.

The UK had never entirely withdrawn from 'east of Suez' after 1971, with small detachments of forces remaining in Brunei, Hong Kong, the Falklands and, until 1975, Oman. However, these 'out-of-area' commitments were viewed, during the Cold War, predominantly as residual colonial responsibilities, largely unconnected to broader foreign-policy ambitions and taking second place to the armed forces' primary NATO mission.

It did not take long for this Europe-centric approach to be dropped once the Cold War ended. At the time of writing, the prospect that the UK's military presence in the smaller Gulf kingdoms may soon be reinforced has elicited much comment, to the effect that there may now be a UK military return 'east of Suez'.[2] However, the true return to Asia took place in the summer of 1990, when, barely nine months after the fall of the Berlin Wall, Prime Minister Margaret Thatcher promised that the UK would stand 'shoulder-to-shoulder' with US President George H W Bush in seeking to reverse Saddam Hussein's invasion of Kuwait.

The conduct of the 1991 Gulf War, which sought only to restore the *status quo ante* in Kuwait, remained broadly consistent with the defensive strategic objectives that had generally informed UK policy during the Cold War. Thereafter, however – and in part because of the ease with which Saddam Hussein was defeated – the UK and the US became increasingly comfortable with a more expansive concept for the use of their military power. The first instance of this shift, led from London, came with Prime Minister John Major's decision in April 1991 to support the establishment of a 'safe haven' in Iraqi Kurdistan, thereby intervening in a sovereign state in order to prevent further atrocities.

The Tide of History
The narrative of justification for each post-1991 campaign has been constructed around specific threats: migration for the Balkan wars; the threat from international terrorism for the invasion and occupation of Afghanistan; and the threats posed by WMD and terrorism in the case of Iraq. Yet none of these problems were unique to this period. As such, in order to explain why two decades of intervention followed two decades of little or no intervention, it is also necessary to look at how the end of the Cold War affected the tolerance for what had, before 1990, been significant but still secondary concerns compared to the primary objective of preventing a major war with the Soviet Union.

First and most important, the end of the Soviet Union's role as a world power meant that the risk of escalation to major-power conflict ceased to be an important restraining factor when considering military deployments outside the NATO area. If NATO or the US had threatened a large-scale military intervention in Yugoslavia, Iraq or Iran during the 1980s, it would have been seen by the Soviet Union as an attempt to shift the strategic balance of power in the West's favour, and could well have led to dangerous escalatory responses. Since 1991, however – with the exception of a short, albeit dangerous, moment at the end of the Kosovo conflict – the Russian military response to Western interventions has been very limited. Similarly, in the one case in which Russian forces were used beyond their own national territory during this period, namely in the 2008 invasion of Georgia, there was no significant military response from the West.

Second, because after 1990 the Soviet Union had neither the capability nor the intent seriously to threaten Western Europe with invasion, UK (and US) forces were able to redeploy safely from their German bases without leaving the European front undefended. This proved vital during mobilisation for the 1991 liberation of Kuwait, and in subsequent operations in the Balkans, Iraq and Afghanistan. The 1994 Provisional IRA ceasefire in Northern Ireland, followed by the Good Friday Agreement in April 1998, also helped to release UK military resources for potential use elsewhere.

Third, humanitarian motivations were a clear element in all of the UK military campaigns of this period. All combatants, stretching back to ancient times, seek to demonise their foes and idealise their own motives. But ethical factors have played a more profound, and genuine, role in shaping the UK's approach to intervention during the last two decades. The strength of this commitment has been based on a continuing sense of obligation, especially amongst political elites, to the UK's role as a power that takes its international security responsibilities seriously. This was not simply a reflection of the UK's place as one of only five permanent members of the UN Security Council, or of its relationship with the US. It was also rooted in its historical experience as a major world power, as one of the key shapers of the post-1945 liberal world order and, not least, as a country for which ethical considerations have long played a role in foreign policy. As former Secretary of State for Defence George Robertson argued in the 1998 Strategic Defence Review, 'The British are, by instinct, an internationalist people.... We do not want to stand idly by and watch humanitarian disasters or the aggression of dictators go unchecked. We want to give a lead, we want to be a force for good.'[3]

The UK has, as a result, 'punched above its weight' in most of the key interventions of this period, from the Balkans to Iraq to Afghanistan. However, instincts are not enough to explain the extent to which the UK has done more than other European states. The UK's ability to punch more strongly than other states was only made possible by previous years of investment in the capabilities that were necessary to turn these inclinations into reality.

Fourth, the new era of intervention also had the fortuitous effect of granting the armed forces a new and challenging role at a time when they might otherwise have been vulnerable to calls for a larger 'peace dividend'. Throughout the 1970s and 1980s, the UK's military had been overstretched and under-equipped, facing the dual challenges of conventional deterrence in Central Europe and continuing operations in Northern Ireland. By the time the Soviet Union collapsed in December 1991, however, the first task had become virtually irrelevant. Successful negotiations with Sinn Féin, capped by the Belfast agreement of 1998, led to further pressure on army-personnel numbers as a result of the sharp reduction in the forces needed for deployment in the province. There is little doubt that, if the post-1990 armed forces had been confined to their previous roles of national and alliance defence, the cuts in their budgets would have been much deeper than they turned out to be.

The end of the Cold War not only created the permissive conditions in which the UK's 'offensive turn' was possible. It was also central to the belief, on the part of both the UK and the US, that increased intervention was now desirable. The Cold War had been, at its heart, an ideological competition pitting two incompatible models for how society should be organised against each other. The collapse of the Warsaw Pact, and subsequently of the Soviet Union, was not primarily a military defeat (the two parties to the Cold War had, after all, never come to blows). Rather, it was the end of an ideology, and the beginning of a process through which the former European members of the 'socialist bloc' would transform themselves into capitalist, liberal democracies.

The triumph of democratic capitalism in Europe produced a historic opportunity to expand the community of democratic allies and friends. During the Cold War, both the US and the UK had often felt compelled to make deals with repressive regimes in order to further their common interests in containing the Soviet Union and its developing-world allies. Yet now, with the radical reduction in Russia's international role, Western interests and values were in happy coincidence. The UK and its allies could support the cause of democratisation both because it was in their interests (both economic and strategic) to do so, and because it accorded with their longstanding (if often unrealised) commitment to the promotion of human rights and democracy.

There were good reasons to think that the tide of history was on the side of democratic capitalism. As late as the 1970s, dictatorships dominated much of the developing world. By the 1990s, however, democracy was being successfully consolidated as the predominant form of government in Latin America, in East Asia and, albeit more unevenly, in sub-Saharan Africa. The emergence of democracies in Central and Eastern Europe (most successfully in Poland, the former Czechoslovakia and the Baltic republics) was thus seen as part of a wider historical trend. Any remaining dictators were anachronistic hold-outs, likely to be swept aside sooner or later.

The result of this mentality was that, at senior levels in both the UK and US governments, a pronounced hubris began to develop as to the feasibility of accelerating democratisation through external intervention. If the 'natural state' of human societies is a democratic one, it was argued, history could be given a nudge in order to accelerate the process. This shift towards a more transformative agenda was greatly accelerated in the aftermath of the 9/11 attacks, as a result of which the risks of inaction (rather than the costs of action) came to dominate the thinking of US and UK leaders.

The assumption that democratisation could be quickly delivered, however, was to prove gravely mistaken in both Afghanistan and Iraq, not least because it was much more difficult to achieve these gains than was predicted when these interventions were conceived. The government's 'force-for-good' narrative turned into something much less palatable on the ground, where UK forces struggled to provide the human security to local populations which their leaders at home had promised. Even as ambitions became much more limited, moreover, the human and financial costs of the UK's interventions soared beyond anything that had previously been predicted.

Discretion and Values

The discretionary nature of military operations during this period also distinguished the campaigns of the last two decades from either the Second World War or the Cold War. The UK had to make hard choices in both of those conflicts. It could have chosen not to declare war in September 1939, and it could (as many urged) have sued for peace during the Phoney War that ran between the occupation of Poland and the invasion of France. It could, during the Cold War, have chosen to adopt a more maritime approach, specialising in those conventional capabilities most necessary for national defence and global operations, rather than investing such a high proportion of its limited resources in the direct defence of West Germany. Indeed, both of these decisions provoked serious disagreements, some of which were along lines – the merits and risks of overseas intervention for an island power – that continue to reverberate today.[4]

Where these choices differed from those made in recent years, however, was in the fact that the decisions made would have had a direct impact on vital UK national interests, and could well have determined whether or not the UK survived as an independent state. No comparably important national interest was at stake in the decisions taken after 1991.

There is a closer parallel between recent interventions and the string of extra-European operations that the armed forces fought during the withdrawal from empire. As in the last decade, the growing cost of these operations was to prove one of the main reasons many of them were wound up, often with suboptimal political outcomes. Yet, compared with these earlier campaigns, post-Cold War interventions have been significantly more discretionary in nature. Colonial operations resulted from events in territories over which the UK had sole and clear responsibility. In 1982, the same was also true for the Falklands, where the war was a discretionary one only in the sense that the UK government could have decided to accept the *fait accompli* created by the Argentinean invasion (and, under a different prime minister, it might well have done so).

After 1991, by contrast, the main operations in which the UK took part were more obviously wars of choice. None of the operations conducted in this period was in a territory for which the UK was solely responsible, and all were launched as part or in support of a wider coalition. All the post-1991 operations involved taking the war to the enemy – a decision that tends, by its very nature, to be more a matter of choice than the decision to resist an attack.

No cost-benefit calculus is appropriate for wars of necessity, except insofar as a state always has a choice (before, and indeed after, the start of a war) as to whether to accept defeat and invasion. However, a calculation is appropriate, and indeed inevitable, when the use of military force is a matter of choice at every stage. It is this discretionary character of recent interventions that came to form a key element in wider public unease over the 'New Age of Intervention'. This unease was reinforced by the duration of operations in Afghanistan and Iraq, associated as this was with a growing lack of clarity as to mission objectives. It cannot be healthy that while the armed forces have never been held in higher esteem by the British public, the two main, extended operations in which they have been deployed have come to be viewed with considerable scepticism by a majority of those same citizens.[5]

This domestic 'legitimacy gap' has been one of the main reasons why Prime Minister David Cameron decided to set a firm deadline for the withdrawal of all British combat forces from Afghanistan, and stuck to this timetable despite some gentle pushback from the armed forces (though not from the White House, which has moved in a similar direction). It was perhaps the most important sign that the peak of interventionism had passed for the UK, at least in the form in which this had been expressed since 2003.

On the Offensive

The removal of the Soviet threat after 1990 gave the US and the UK an opportunity to adopt a more strategically offensive military policy, fighting away from home in order to alter the course of events in other societies, and seeking to transform the structures of those societies in line with Western interests and values.

The Western powers did not begin with such ambitious objectives. The twenty-year conflict with and in Iraq (from 1990 to 2010) began with the self-limiting purpose of reversing the invasion of Kuwait, and was halted once this had been achieved. Coalition forces then stood by as Saddam Hussein crushed Shia rebels who had been encouraged by the disarray in which the Iraqi army found itself.

In one of the first precursors of the more assertive Responsibility to Protect (R2P) missions that followed, however, the UK and the US also used the threat of force to help to establish the safe haven in Iraqi Kurdistan. Thereafter, policy became incrementally more interventionist. Concern over Iraq's continuing WMD programmes led to an intensifying programme of economic sanctions, no-fly zones that limited Iraqi military aircraft to barely half of the national territory, and a major bombing campaign (targeted at WMD-relevant sites) in 1998. By 1999, long before President George W Bush entered office, 'regime change' was the declared objective of the US government. Then, in 2003, the US and the UK led a full-scale invasion of Iraq, followed by the most ambitious programme for transformation through occupation that has been seen since the aftermath of the Second World War, although without the resources – the large armies and detailed reconstruction plans – that had accompanied those post-war efforts.

In the case of the West's twelve-year military engagement in Afghanistan, a similar pattern – a short, sharp initial campaign, followed by progressive entanglement – was evident. The US responded to the September 2001 attacks on New York and Washington, DC by launching a military campaign to overthrow the Taliban regime in Kabul. With UN support, it then convened a conference in Germany, led by Hamid Karzai, to agree Afghanistan's new constitution and government. A comparatively light-footprint approach was subsequently adopted, with a relatively small in-country UN presence, and with forces from NATO member states totalling only around 10,000 in late 2005 (before the expansion to the south), and only 35,000 as late as early 2007.[6] In part as a result of UK urging, however, force levels then progressively increased, reaching a peak of more than 130,000 military personnel by late 2010.[7]

In Bosnia, after the humiliating failure of a traditional UN peacekeeping operation, NATO led a 'peace-enforcement' operation designed to compel the Bosnian Serbs to the negotiating table and then, in the form of the Dayton Accords, to accept an imposed peace. Four years later, NATO launched an attack on Serbia to force it to withdraw from part of its own territory, Kosovo, before (as in Bosnia) deploying a large, permanent, international presence, both military and civilian, to support subsequent state-building.

Viewed strategically, UK military campaigns in all three of these major theatres of operations were thus about coercion, not direct self-defence. By 2013, the UK had been involved in military operations that forcibly changed the government of three UN member states (Afghanistan, Iraq and Libya), installed a new regime in a breakaway province (Kosovo) of a fourth (Serbia), and used lethal force to oblige warring parties within a fifth UN member state (Bosnia) to sign up to an internationally brokered settlement.

Challenging the Non-Intervention Norm
The more transformatory nature of the UK's strategic objectives since the end of the Cold War was made possible by the wider transition from a world in which NATO was obliged to focus its resources on the containment of the Soviet Union to one in which great-power military rivalry was no longer a serious concern, at least in the short term. This shift towards a more ambitious military posture was paralleled, and indeed made possible, by increased questioning of the non-interference principles established in the 1945 UN Charter. *Inter alia*, the charter had set out that:

> The Organization is based on the principle of the sovereign equality of all its Members. (Article 2.1)

> All Members shall refrain in their international relations from the threat or use of force against the territorial integrity or political independence of any state. (Article 2.4)

> Nothing contained in the present Charter shall authorize the United Nations to intervene in matters which are essentially within the domestic jurisdiction of any state or shall require the Members to submit such matters to settlement under the present Charter... (Article 2.7)

None of these principles were observed in their entirety during the Cold War that followed the founding of the UN. Both as a result of the charter and of wider considerations of mutual interest, however, the Cold War period was marked by a far-reaching shift in state behaviour. The norm against direct military intervention by one state in the territory of another state became widely accepted. Even the smallest and weakest state gained a remarkable degree of protection from invasion and elimination. No member of the UN has ever been wiped off the map by force, and no independent state, once recognised as such, has been successfully occupied for long.[8] Iraq's attempt to annex Kuwait proves the point, given the unprecedented international coalition that was then formed to reverse it.

This was a remarkable achievement, in stark contrast to previous centuries in which – often successful – attempts to change international borders by force were a primary driver of international conflict. Together with regional agreements to accept colonial borders as the basis for newly independent states in Africa and the Middle East, these norms helped to ensure that a world containing many more states was also a world characterised by much less armed conflict. Given the intensity of the Cold War stand-off between the US and the Soviet Union, this achievement was even more remarkable.

Yet the results of the non-intervention norm were hard to accept when faced with the human suffering that authoritarian regimes often imposed on their own peoples. India's 1971 invasion of East Pakistan in support of the secession of Bangladesh, Vietnam's invasion and overthrow of the Khmer Rouge in Cambodia in 1978–79, and Tanzania's 1978–79 intervention against Idi Amin's Uganda, all took place without support from the UN or any other international organisation. In each case, however, these invasions occurred only after sustained and widespread atrocities had been perpetuated by governments against their own citizens.[9]

International, or at least Western, attitudes towards 'humanitarian intervention' began to change soon after 1990. In April 1991, the

UN established a safe haven for Iraqi Kurds in order to prevent a repetition of the brutal treatment previously meted out to them by Saddam Hussein, and the UK, France and the US used this as justification for establishing a no-fly zone over parts of northern Iraq. In 1992, the US joined a UN force deployed to protect humanitarian supplies, and restore stability, in Somalia. Both interventions were driven, in large part, by humanitarian motives.

Soon after Bill Clinton came to power in the US in January 1993, however, he ordered the withdrawal of US forces from Somalia in response to the loss of eighteen soldiers at the hands of a Somali warlord; a humiliation that was shortly to be followed by renewed conflict and humanitarian suffering. This failure was soon followed by the Western powers' failure to respond meaningfully to the 1994 genocide in Rwanda, in which it is estimated that more than 500,000 were killed.[10] Meanwhile, war erupted on the territory of Europe for the first time since the end of the Cold War, and continued despite the presence of 'blue helmet' UN missions in Croatia and Bosnia. In Bosnia alone, an estimated 96,000 lives were lost as a result of the war, and around half of the population was displaced from their homes.[11]

The combined experiences of Rwanda and the Balkans, however, had a profound impact on British thinking on the role of military intervention. Across the political spectrum, a new climate developed in support of a more interventionist approach to the use of military force. This was evident first in practice, with the commitment of NATO (including UK) military power to coerce Bosnian Serbs, and Serbia itself, to support the Dayton Accords. It was then translated into UK politico-military doctrine, first in the 'force-for-good' concept that underpinned the expeditionary focus of the 1998 Strategic Defence Review, and then by Prime Minister Tony Blair's 1999 speech in Chicago, during the Kosovo War, in which he argued for a new 'doctrine of the international community':[12]

... the principle of non-interference must be qualified in important respects. Acts of genocide can never be a purely internal matter. When oppression produces massive flows of refugees which unsettle neighbouring countries then they can properly be described as 'threats to international peace and security'.

Yet the dividing line between large-scale atrocities and 'ordinary' repression can be a thin one, with authoritarian regimes often fluctuating between the two as circumstances dictate. Non-Western governments (including democracies such as Brazil, India and South Africa) also feared that it would be the most powerful states that would decide when, and whether, repression was sufficiently serious as to warrant invasion and regime change. Both for its supporters and detractors, 'humanitarian intervention' was often seen as part of a wider 'democracy crusade', in which Western powers took it upon themselves to spread democracy worldwide.

Even without military intervention, the end of the Cold War had seen dramatic advances in terms of democratisation. The threat of international communism having receded, the US withdrew support from military-dominated regimes in Latin America and East Asia, helping to pave the way for the 'democracy waves' of the 1980s and 1990s in those regions. On the other side of Europe's Iron Curtain, the transition to democracy was achieved with relatively little upheaval. Even within the former Soviet Union, despite conflict in Georgia and Nagorno-Karabakh, democratic norms and practices appeared to be starting to take root.

Given these wider trends, the world's remaining non-democratic regimes came increasingly to be seen, by influential Western intellectuals and policy-makers, as anomalies that would be unable to withstand the onward march of history. The apparently strong association between democracy and peace (the so-called democratic-peace theory) added academic credibility to the belief that democracies were more peaceful, stable and friendly to Western interests.[13]

Until the Arab uprisings began in the spring of 2011, most Middle Eastern regimes seemed impervious to democratisation pressures. It was precisely for this reason, advocates of democratisation argued, that the region was the locus of so much instability and risk. Dictators who had shown their willingness to use violence against their own peoples, it was argued, were more likely to use it irresponsibly against others. One of the objectives of US and UK policy in the Middle East over the two decades before 2011, therefore, was to promote democracy, especially in those states – such as Iraq and Iran – that were seen as most antagonistic to Western interests. As the experience of the last decade has shown, however, military force is an expensive, blunt and unpredictable means for achieving this objective. The chaotic aftermath of the Arab uprisings, moreover, showed once more (as had the Balkans) that the process of democratisation often leads at first to *more* conflict rather than less.[14]

Of Coalitions and the International Community
Most of the international military interventions carried out since the end of the Cold War were not led by the US and the UK, but by the United Nations. Between 1989 and 2013, the UN authorised fifty-three new peacekeeping missions, supported (and in part funded) by all five permanent members of the Security Council. As of April 2013, 92,000 uniformed personnel from 116 countries were serving with fifteen UN missions, along with 17,000 civilian personnel.[15] Regional organisations, notably the African Union, also established large peacekeeping missions of their own. These operations had their own difficulties and failures. However, the overall picture has been one of considerable success, achieved with an annual global budget that peaked at less than $8 billion. None of these operations involved large-scale war-fighting campaigns comparable to those that helped to drive the costs of Afghanistan and Iraq to such high levels for the US and the UK. Even so, the United Nations' member states have been increasingly willing to give its commanders more robust mandates.[16]

Peacekeeping missions would not be effective, and have not been attempted, in situations where large and effective armies are already present, such as in Iraq in 2003. Yet they have made a strong contribution to the stabilisation of post-conflict countries that required international assistance to fill the security vacuum left by the absence of strong, and unified, indigenous security forces. The available academic literature suggests that UN peacekeeping forces, supported by international diplomatic engagement and development aid, has substantially reduced the rate at which states return to civil war. This increased international engagement in conflict zones was, in turn, one of the most important explanations for the overall decline in the incidence and severity of civil war since 1990.[17]

Yet UK armed forces were, at best, only peripherally involved in the UN's peacekeeping surge. While sub-Saharan Africa has been one of the main foci of the increase in the UK's aid effort over the last decade, the UK armed forces, in contrast to those of France and the US, have continued to see the region (where most UN peacekeeping operations take place) as a relatively low priority for the use of their limited resources. The exception of the UK's short campaign in Sierra Leone in May 2000 proved this rule: the intervention, which proved to be a turning point in the defeat of the Revolutionary United Front (RUF), began as a limited evacuation operation for foreign citizens, with the initiative of the local military commander, then-Brigadier David Richards, playing a decisive role in expanding its mandate into support for the local government's effort to defeat the RUF. The UK then followed up its initial success with a sustained programme of security and development assistance, working alongside a large UN peacekeeping force.

Despite its success in Sierra Leone, however, there has been no subsequent British operation in Africa on anything approaching the scale seen in 2000. This has not been because of a lack of demand for external military assistance on the continent, as multiple UN peacekeeping operations can testify. The UK armed forces have also been reluctant, in subsequent years, to provide even relatively small numbers of personnel for advisory and capacity-building roles – for example, in support of UN peacekeeping efforts in Sudan and in support of the Ugandan government's campaign against Lord's Resistance Army (LRA) rebels.

Since 2010 (perhaps coincidentally the period during which Sir David Richards was Chief of the Defence Staff – a post he held between 2009 and 2013), there are some signs that this may have been beginning to change. Over the period under study in this chapter, however, the US and the UK were focused on a relatively small number of high-intensity, regime-change operations in Europe and the Middle East, organised outside of the UN framework and, in the case of both Kosovo and Iraq in 2003, without a UN mandate. The nature of the post-9/11 campaigns – large-scale invasions followed by counter-insurgency – was very different from those conducted under UN auspices, being more difficult, much more costly and inherently more controversial.

As a consequence of these factors, the US and the UK were unable, in these campaigns, to build an operative coalition that encompassed more than a narrow group of close allies. This was especially true of the 2003 invasion, and subsequent occupation, of Iraq, in which many of the UK's NATO allies refused take part. As a result, of the 173,000 foreign forces deployed in Iraq at the end of 2005, 166,000 were from the US and the UK.[18] The coalition of nations represented in Afghanistan was bigger, and expanded further once NATO was given the lead responsibility for organising nationwide military support for the government. As a result, by December 2010, NATO's International Security Assistance Force (ISAF) included force contributions from forty-eight countries. Yet most of these contributions were very small (thirty-seven states provided fewer than 1,000 troops). The main commitments to the area experiencing the greatest level of conflict (the southern provinces around Kandahar) were made by the US, the UK and their closest NATO allies (Canada, the Netherlands and Denmark).

The lack of a more serious commitment by the US's other allies reflected two wider features of the post-Cold War international community. First, some of these other allies, most notably Germany and Japan – the two most economically powerful – have been deeply reluctant to use their armed forces for purposes beyond national self-defence. They had, moreover, deliberately refrained from investment in military capabilities for expeditionary warfare in order to avoid such a temptation. Second, some NATO member states (most notably in Central and Eastern Europe) were concerned that the Alliance's involvement in Afghanistan was at the expense of its core business back in Europe. For all the publicity given to the proposition, common in Washington policy circles, that NATO should go 'out of area or out of business', some of the US's key European allies (most notably France) were not convinced.[19]

British and American attempts to build a broader international community in support of robust intervention were also less than successful outside their circle of formal allies, all of which have a strong interest in cementing their defence relationships with the US. The leading democracies of the developing world, such as India, Brazil and South Africa, might have been expected to welcome campaigns designed to combat atrocities and promote democracy. Yet all of these states proved to be less than enthusiastic about what became codified as the universal concept of the Responsibility to Protect. Together with many other developing-country democracies, they were concerned that the new interventionism was eroding the UN Charter's protection of national sovereignty, which they saw as a key principle of the post-1945 international order. UK policy, they suspected, continued to be shaped by an imperial past in which European powers, rather than local actors, played the decisive role in shaping the future of occupied peoples. There was also a widespread belief that, as in the colonial era, the UK was motivated largely by its own selfish economic and strategic interests.

The Great Game

The British-American approach to military intervention during this period may also have overstated the extent to which the two countries could ignore Russian concerns without incurring any serious costs to their shared interests. Russia no longer had the military power or political influence credibly to deter Western military campaigns, as the Soviet Union could have done during the Cold War (for example, by pinning down NATO forces in Europe in order to prevent their redeployment to the Middle East). Precisely because of its relative weakness, however, the new Russia was concerned that the US was seeking to use the opportunity presented by the end of the Cold War to pursue an offensive strategy that would further undermine its interests. It feared that the US was seeking to expand its sphere of influence at the expense of that of Russia, even when – as in the case of NATO enlargement – this was justified through a narrative of universal values. Russian concern was deepened by the enthusiasm for membership amongst its former allies, which were keen to emphasise NATO's continuing role in collective defence.

The military campaigns in Kosovo and Iraq, in particular, may have had a role in contributing to the worsening of Russia's relations with the West after the late 1990s. As late as 1998, these relations were relatively co-operative in nature. Russia supported the UN's authorisation for the deployment of a NATO-led military mission to Bosnia after the 1995 Dayton Accords, contributing its own forces to the mission. In May 1997, NATO and Russia signed the Founding Act on Mutual Relations, Cooperation and Security, which signalled a desire for a new institutionalisation of their post-Cold War relationship.

NATO's air campaign against Serbia in the spring of 1999, however, dealt a serious blow to the West's relations with Russia. President Boris Yeltsin refused to provide UN Security Council authorisation for an attack on one of Russia's few remaining friends in the region. Along with China (itself furious at the bombing of its embassy in Belgrade), Russia was alive to the precedent that the Kosovo campaign would set for separatists elsewhere in the world.

This was the international context within which Yeltsin appointed Vladimir Putin as his prime minister in August 1999, only two months after Serbia admitted defeat in the Kosovo campaign. Putin quickly moved to strengthen his position by launching the Second Chechen War, determined to combat a separatist threat that, for Russians, seemed alarmingly similar to that faced by Serbia in relation to Kosovo.[20] By December of that year, Putin was president of Russia.

For a short period in the immediate aftermath of the Al-Qa'ida attacks on the US in 2001, it appeared that a new Russo–American *détente* had emerged. Putin gave his support to the US-led campaign to oust the Taliban from Afghanistan, not least because of a belief that the US now understood better the problems that Russia faced in the northern Caucasus. Yet the period of rapprochement did not last long. As preparations for the invasion of Iraq proceeded during the following year, Putin increasingly expressed his concern that the US was determined to impose its will on Iraq, irrespective of international law. His determination to oppose the Iraq invasion at the UN Security Council was further strengthened by meetings with French President Jacques Chirac in February 2003, who urged him to oppose US hegemonic ambitions. As Fyodor Lukyanov argues:[21]

> The conclusions drawn by Putin from the situation surrounding Iraq were concerned less with Russia-American relations, and more with the general idea of how the world works in the twenty-first century. The strong do what they want: they don't contemplate international law, global reality or the costs incurred by themselves and others. The only rational way of behaving in such a world is to increase one's own power and capabilities...

These years proved to be a 'perfect storm' for Russia, and may have played a decisive role in reshaping its perceptions of the US's intentions, and thus the prospects for a co-operative relationship between the two countries. Even as the US and the UK were fighting in Iraq, they were also supporting the 'colour revolution' street protests in Ukraine, which resulted in Viktor Yushchenko defeating Viktor Yanukovych (whom Russia had supported) to become president. American and British support for political change in, and NATO membership for, Ukraine and Georgia was not only seen as a geostrategic threat to Russia, potentially bringing NATO's infrastructure into the heart of the former Soviet Union; it was also seen as constituting a potential threat of political change within Russia itself.

This was the wider context within which Russia launched its invasion of Georgia in August 2008, sparking fears across NATO that this might augur a more aggressive policy throughout the region. The shift towards a more assertive Russian posture towards NATO may have been inevitable even in the absence of the Kosovo and Iraq interventions in 1999 and 2003, respectively. Moreover, the extent of the deterioration in relations should not be overstated. Today, even as Russia and the US support competing parties in the Syrian civil war, Russia continues to provide vital support for NATO's operations in Afghanistan. While their positions are not identical, the US, the UK and Russia are also still able to co-operate on UN Security Council efforts to tackle the North Korean and Iranian nuclear files.

Some have argued that tension and conflict with the US is inevitable as long as Russia (and China) remain fundamentally undemocratic. If one accepts this premise, it is then argued, the post-Cold War period has provided a time-limited opportunity for the US and its allies to improve their own positions, which they were right to take while they could, before the revival of Russia's military power and China's remarkable economic growth made such adventures progressively more difficult.[22]

Such an argument may have had some merit when it delivered results, as it did in large measure in the decisions to press ahead with NATO enlargement and Balkan stabilisation. However, the hubris that has underlain this argument must bear much of the responsibility both for the decision to invade Iraq in 2003, and for the appallingly poor execution of the occupation that followed. It will never be possible to know whether relations with Russia might have improved had the US and the UK taken a more cautious path during the aftermath of the 9/11 attacks (as a President Al Gore might have done). Yet it is certainly plausible that, without the Iraq invasion, US relations with Russia in the decade that followed might have been rather less fraught than they proved to be. Insofar as this may be the case, it is one additional possible cost of those campaigns that should be weighed in the overall audit of the wars of this period.

On the other hand, it is also plausible to argue that intervention has strengthened the credibility of US military deterrence against a range of potential foes. The US made clear, in a series of conflicts and against a wide range of opponents, that it was willing to take risks, and incur significant human and financial costs, when deploying its armed forces in operations. It demonstrated on the battlefield that the massive resources that it has spent on defence since the end of the Cold War have resulted in a range of deployed military technologies which no other state can match. It has provided its armed forces with an unparalleled depth and width of combat experience, allowing them to improve their techniques and training further. The last decade therefore helped to demonstrate to potential adversaries that they will have to live under the shadow of US military superiority for some time to come.

Conclusion
The UK's armed forces have been continuously involved in large-scale overseas operations – with thousands of troops on the ground – since 1992. After the gap between July 1991 (the end of UK assistance to Operation *Safe Haven* in northern Iraq) and September 1992 (the reinforcement of UK forces assigned to UNPROFOR in

Bosnia), successive state-building missions in Bosnia, Kosovo, Iraq and Afghanistan provided the main focus for UK operational activity for more than two decades.

The high point of this 'boots on the ground' intervention has probably now passed. Yet the wider strategic context for UK defence policy remains relatively unchanged in three key respects. First, the forces driving further democratisation (and associated political turmoil) in the wider world remain unabated; and, as the UK reaction to the Arab uprisings demonstrates, there remains a strong political desire to support this trend. Second, it will still be more than a decade – probably longer – before China is able to emerge as a military 'peer competitor' to the US, comparable to the Soviet Union during the Cold War. Third, despite the retrenchment in its defence budget as a result of fiscal austerity, the US's military continues to maintain unmatched capabilities for power projection, its operational edge further enhanced through a decade of conflict. While the UK is clearly in a different league from its principal ally, it retains some of Europe's most powerful forces for long-range intervention and continues to prioritise investments in capabilities for such operations.

Given these enduring realities, it seems unlikely that the era of the strategic offensive – for either the US or the UK – is now over. There are strong pressures to correct some of the excesses of the last decade, evident in particular in the operations in Iraq and Afghanistan. Such operations have proven highly costly, played into the hands of the West's opponents, and largely failed to achieve their strategic objectives. Rather than signalling total disengagement, though, the end of such operations is more likely to be replaced by a range of more limited 'economy-of-force' interventions, emphasising financial and training support for local partners, together with a continuing role for air power and other stand-off capabilities. There is also likely to be greater focus on the creation of coalitions that stretch beyond traditional partnerships. If the UK were to become more engaged in conflict prevention in Africa, for example, this is likely to involve increased support for UN peacekeeping missions, especially in the provision of enabling capabilities and training. If there is to be increased operational involvement in the Middle East, this is likely to draw more heavily on the capabilities of regional states than in the past (as indeed was the case in Libya in 2011).

There will also continue to be strong support for UK military forces to remain available for what might be called, in this context, 'strategic defence'. Protection of the post-1945, rule-based international order – in which states cannot be extinguished by force, and in which freedom of movement over the high seas is guaranteed – remains central to UK national interests. Even as the offensive overstretch of the last decade is reined back, this fundamental commitment is likely to remain a cornerstone of UK defence policy.

VII. STRATEGY AND OPERATIONS
Robert Fry

IN many ways, the period 1991–2012 has the look of an historical aberration. It was preceded by the 'short twentieth century',[1] a period of demonstrable historical continuity centred on Europe, involving the machinations of great powers, and classical in the grand-strategic sense that it was defined by the aggregate of all instruments of power of states, or alliances of states, in a series of adversarial relationships. That the period 1914–89 witnessed the collapse of successive empires, a second Thirty Years War, the twin abominations of communism and fascism, the Holocaust and nuclear use concentrates attention on individual events, such is their scale and hideous novelty. Yet there is an unbroken narrative that links German aggression in 1914 to Soviet exhaustion in 1989, marking the start and finish of a recognisable and unified passage of history. A history, moreover, that in 1989 would have been recognised by the participants of the Congress of Vienna in 1814–15, defined as it was by the application of state power in pursuit of competing grand-strategic visions. Both Castlereagh and Kissinger would recognise themselves as players in a grand-strategic contest whose rules had changed little between centuries and where power was both a means and an end in a competitive international system.

It may also be that a return to classical strategic mores in the future can be anticipated. Transnational terrorism will not go away, but it might look like a minor chord in international affairs in comparison to, say, a Sino–Japanese conflict in the South China Sea or an Israeli attack on Iran; the very existence of the BRIC acronym speaks to the rising power of the nation-state. And while the centennial echoes of 1914 may have invited over-literal comparisons between the UK at the beginning of the First World War and the US today as a 'weary titan, staggering under the too vast orb of its fate'[2] which is bound to share imperial decline, great-power relationships look set to return as the currency of strategic exchange. The instruments of engagement will fit the twenty-first century and might include the use of cyber or currency weapons, but the strategy that combines those instruments in pursuit of a defined outcome is likely again to have a classical form.

So what changed between 1991 and 2012 to mark it as an aberration, historically and strategically? At first, very little; the UN was at the heart of a unified international response to Iraqi aggression that President George H W Bush eulogised as indicative of a 'new world order'. The Iraqi army that invaded Kuwait had the misfortune of finding the US forces that formed the core of the coalition at the height of their post-Cold War powers, with a capacity for military violence shaped by the assumptions of classical grand strategy to fight the Warsaw Pact in northern Europe. The subsequent mismatch was brief, decisive and entirely contained within the boundaries set by the UN Security Council. So far, so classical. Yet in the subsequent chaos within Iraq, both Kurdish and Shia minorities seized what they saw as an historic opportunity to rise against the regime of Saddam Hussein. The response was sufficiently brutal to provoke a reaction beyond the Westphalian boundaries of grand strategy and into the affairs of a state that, however reprehensible its actions, remained sovereign. UN Security Council Resolution 688 of April 1991 did not authorise any specific action but it created an atmosphere sufficiently permissive to allow a ground intervention in Iraqi Kurdistan and the imposition of two no-fly zones,[3] to wide international applause.

This represents the first aberrant step away from a classical tradition of war as the means through which to resolve the balance of power *between* states and towards war as an instrument used to address the balance of power *within* states. In 1991 this still had a one-off look, justified by localised and exceptional conditions. However, as the decade proceeded, those conditions looked increasingly ubiquitous and habitual, as the Balkan conflict, East Timor and Sierra Leone saw successive interventions of increasing diplomatic and military fluency. This process culminated in Tony Blair's speech in Chicago in April 1999, laying out a formalised manifesto for liberal intervention, which itself followed a British Strategic Defence Review (SDR) in 1998 that had identified the military as a 'force for good' rather than an instrument of national power to be rationally applied in the classical, realist tradition. At that point, and following a seductive run of military and political successes, the Chicago doctrine was a powerful contribution to the debate about the nature of power in the post-Cold War world, but it did not yet provide the intellectual underpinning for British grand strategy; after 9/11, it would.

The 9/11 attacks created a unifying theme for Western grand strategy that would have as its centrepiece the global War on Terror.[4] Despite the near-universal support for the US in the aftermath of 9/11, such a war was always problematic in strategic terms. To be effective, military strategy needs clear objectives, a definable enemy and a recognisable theatre of operations. In particular, fighting a condition – at best a tactic – is hardly consistent with the clarity that is the first prerequisite for success. Also, while recourse to war was always understandable at a visceral level, it had the further disadvantage of making the terrorist groups it targeted cohere in a manner that would have been unlikely had the attacks been regarded as criminal and subject to a civil response. Finally, a global condition that demanded to be addressed wherever it became manifest created an automatic asymmetry between ends and means that would eventually exhaust the strategic inventory of even the US. Therefore the grand strategy declared in 2001, after a decade in gestation, contained a series of tensions that would test its military dimension repeatedly in the wars that followed.

The Chicago doctrine was not an immaculate intellectual conception and drew on a long tradition, represented not least by Michael Howard.[5] Liberal wars present a philosophical challenge in that, being nasty, brutish and not necessarily short, they have an inherently illiberal quality. But leaving semantics aside, they also bring practical problems. Wars in defence of liberal values are what the British people fought throughout the twentieth century, and these were wars of unnegotiable necessity. Wars in promotion of liberal values are what the British armed forces have fought since 1991 and, by their very nature, they have been discretionary. Because issues of national survival are not involved, the means available are also discretionary and often less than the vaulting ambition of nation-building demands. There is also the logical conundrum that the UK seeks to promote liberal values in the least liberal of places. Indeed, there is in the very idea of promoting liberal values a central conceit that assumes that the Western idea of what a state should be – an entity that dispenses goods and services based on formal procedures such as the rule of law and democratic process – is a universal model. To impose this in places where the state is a mechanism for pursuing patronage on the basis of class, tribe or ethnicity is to invite a further tension, of which Afghanistan provides vivid testimony.

The period under study therefore has a certain self-contained quality. That its start point marked the end of a distinctive historical continuum associated with the actions of great powers pursuing classical grand strategies seems to be supported by the available scholarship. That it might be followed by another period of great-power hegemony supported by similar strategies looks like a reasonable assumption. Within the period, American exceptionalism, unconfined by the dialectic of classical strategy, moved towards liberal intervention; a doctrine with immediate British intellectual provenance but with costs which would be borne mainly by the US. Within the doctrine, there were a series of tensions that distanced grand-strategic ambition from military strategic execution and this is the issue to which this chapter now turns.

'To focus on strategy is to emphasise the importance of choice'.[6] At one level, this is a self-evident statement; at another, it defines the key decision that shaped the British experience during the period: the choice to engage simultaneously in operations in Afghanistan and Iraq. The historical chapters of this book have provided an operational narrative of the entire period 1991–2012 and this chapter will make no attempt to repeat that, or to examine the strategic issues involved; rather it will focus on strategic choice and strategic consequence in the defining period of 2001–09.

Having to service two theatres simultaneously is hardly a novelty within the British experience. The Easterner-Westerner debate in the early years of the First World War is probably the best example of the recurring dilemma that had appeared previously in 1812 and would emerge again after 1942. It is when claims on strategic means are made by the competing demands of strategic ends that the process of military strategy justifies its title. To service a single theatre can be operationally exhausting but it remains a strategically linear process, however complicated. If choice is the defining characteristic of strategy, then decisions between, rather than within, theatres represent its acid test.

The US Military Experience after 9/11

There are a number of ways to try to put a shape on events from the joint invasion of Afghanistan in 2001 to the US reinforcement of Helmand Province in 2009, but the vehicle this chapter will use is the four armies the US employed during that time.[7] The first never took the field in the wars of 9/11,[8] but dominated the intellectual assumptions around the application of American force in the lead-up to 2001. The Powell doctrine[9] made clear that US forces would only be deployed in overwhelming strength, in pursuit of clear objectives and with a clear route to exit. In this, it showed the legacy of messy engagements in Lebanon and Somalia but also its firm roots in the classical strategic tradition. In the aftermath of 9/11, US Secretary of Defense Donald Rumsfeld almost immediately sought to revise this approach in favour of a force with the speed and agility to match the operational conditions. The solution comprised huge volumes of indirect fire from invulnerable platforms in the air and at sea, CIA agents playing a twenty-first-century version of the Great Game and dispensing comparable volumes of cash to anyone claiming an ability to fight the Taliban; a ready-made infantry in the shape of the Northern Alliance; and an urbane and, at least then, compliant political-leader-in-waiting in Hamid Karzai. In a seminal example of asymmetric engagement, the second US army within the period shattered the Taliban and drove its remnants into Pakistan or back to their villages.

The outcome was an apparent vindication of the Rumsfeld economy-of-force strategy, and, though victory was more complete within the Washington Beltway than in the field, a new orthodoxy shaped the plans for the invasion of Iraq. As a result, General Tommy Franks commanded a manoeuvre force sufficient only for the conventional phase of the war; the Kurds and Shia were assigned the role of auxiliaries and Ahmed Chalabi provided the requisite political urbanity and compliance. That Afghanistan, with its strong society and weak state, was never going to be a model for Iraq, with its highly centralised tradition of governance, would only become apparent later. Iraq's descent into chaos is well documented and led to the crisis of the campaign in the summer of 2006. By this stage it was clear that three things had to happen if the Western intervention was to have any historic claim to success: Al-Qa'ida in Iraq had to be destroyed, the Sunni had to be reconciled and the Shia had to be contained; each outcome set the preconditions for the next and the whole was dependent on the sequenced effect of its parts. By 2007, sufficient progress had been made to allow President George W Bush his Lincoln moment in ordering the 'surge' of American forces, now re-trained and equipped for the counter-insurgency campaign they never originally intended to fight. The arrival of this, the third US army since 2001, marked the mastery of the counter-insurgency military discipline they had always abhorred, and defined the techniques that they would then take to Afghanistan. Yet already, by 2009, there were moves in the Obama White House to end the uncongenial burden of residential soldiering in other people's countries, and a shift was already apparent to the fourth, counter-terrorist army of drones and Special Forces raids that would find full expression in the operation to kill Osama bin Laden.

Each of the four armies was the material form of the military strategies from which they were derived. The classical provenance of the Powell doctrine has already been noted and need not be discussed further. The Rumsfeld economy-of-force strategy was, arguably, right as the immediate and essentially punitive response to 9/11, but it was wholly inadequate for the subsequent operation in Iraq or the mature Afghan campaign. By 2003, the promotion of liberal values was represented by the slogan 'regime change' and implied a level of grand-strategic ambition incomparably greater than the scattering of the Afghan Taliban. Yet essentially the same military instrument that had prevailed in Afghanistan in 2002 entered the field in Iraq in 2003 in what amounts to a fundamental failure of strategic imagination and, more practically, a failure to match military strategic means to grand-strategic ends. The price was paid in the following years as the coalition forces struggled first to comprehend and then to address the energies they had released in Iraq. By the time the military strategic means and ways were more closely reconciled with grand-strategic ends, the high-point of liberal intervention had passed and the US had begun to seek a more limited liability, expressed through indigenous capacity-building and the ability to strike remotely in a selective and punitive way.

It therefore becomes apparent that the grand and military strategies of the major player in the wars of 9/11 bore little relation to each other and passed as ships in the night between 2006–09, travelling in opposite directions. This owes something to the surprise of the 9/11 attacks, the speed with which operations subsequently developed and a great deal to the hubris of soldiers and statesmen. But, above all, it illustrates the disjunction between the elements of strategy during a period when US grand strategy was briefly emancipated from the balance-of-power considerations of the classical tradition and could write its own script.

The UK Military Experience after 9/11

While the American experience sets an essential context, it is British strategy and operations with which this chapter is concerned and to which it returns, in late 2001. But before doing so, one might compare how the British Army evolved in parallel to the clearly separate armies that the US deployed into the field between 2001 and 2009. The American experience draws on a long tradition of renewal in public life; indeed, a capacity for re-invention is probably the defining national characteristic. In military terms, the armies that took the field in 1862 (on the Union side), 1917 and 1942 bore little resemblance to those that completed successive conflicts. In Britain too, the *ingénue* army that entered the war in 1914 did not look like the corps of hardened professionals that defeated the German field army at the top of its game in 1918. However, in examining the British Army in the wars of 9/11 it is difficult to see any adaptation that shadows the American experience. Quantity does, of course, bring its own quality and the scale of US forces allowed greater scope for re-organisation, but this is a plea in mitigation rather than an adequate explanation. The UK entered the era confident in its vocation for small wars and lost no opportunity to proselytise;[10] a message the Americans were grateful to hear initially but quickly tired of, especially when their transformation from a conventional to a counter-insurgency army between 2003 and 2006 created an instrument more capable than anything that the UK had deployed throughout the wars of colonial disengagement or in

Northern Ireland. The UK started ahead for the particular demands of the 9/11 wars, but the British equivalent to four American armies is at most two; a point those responsible for British training and doctrine might choose to ponder.

Grand Strategy

Returning to 2001, the UK policy response to 9/11 was immediate and categorical: the ungoverned space of Afghanistan must be denied to Al-Qa'ida as a haven and prospective mounting base for future operations – a position that gained formal and general expression with the publication of the 2002 'New Chapter' addendum to the 1998 SDR.[11] The New Chapter made clear that, in the British view, terrorism at home had to be addressed by forward defence in Central Asia or wherever the contingent threat emanated from. This view can be, and was latterly, criticised as supine conformity to US policy, but whatever else it was, it was certainly a tract for liberal-interventionist times.

The UK's coincidence of strategic purpose with the US stemmed from a deep-rooted sense of security being indivisible in the face of a potent transnational threat. There was also a recognition that Afghanistan had been abandoned after the Soviet withdrawal and the result had been civil war, Taliban government and a secure base for Al-Qa'ida. NATO's invocation of Article V of the founding treaty provided a broader context for the sense of collective threat and an inalienable responsibility to respond. This combination of factors led, initially, to the deployment of forces under national command, which were subsequently brought under NATO auspices in 2003. It is arguable that the rapid defeat of the Taliban regime deprived Al-Qa'ida of its client sponsor and so achieved the strategic end. That was not the view taken at the time, either nationally or within the UN Security Council; on the contrary, it was judged that any enduring solution had to be underwritten by effective governance of a unitary Afghan state from Kabul.

This view was given clear expression at the Bonn Conference of 2001, which ushered in a wider political process involving an interim Afghan government and the negotiation of a new constitution, followed by phased elections; all underwritten by the UN. In parallel, Provincial Reconstruction Teams (PRTs) were conceived and their deployment initiated on an exploratory basis in the north of Afghanistan, first under national command and later under NATO. The NATO plan included a British PRT in Mazar-e-Sharif which provided a broadly successful model for development elsewhere, though there was no single, universal template.

As the plan rolled out, the northern half of Afghanistan entered into a broadly compliant relationship with NATO forces and the Karzai government. The operation was not without its flaws, amongst which the role of atavistic warlordism and the associated limitations of central governance were prominent. At the level of theatre command, the bifurcation of NATO-led framework operations and US-led counter-terrorist operations was a mortal doctrinal sin to those seeking unified campaign effect. However, seen in its early stages, British involvement in Afghanistan was regarded as essential and proportional and it enjoyed broad-based political and popular support. The invasion of Iraq would change that.

The indivisible nature of the British–American response to 9/11 has already been noted and the possibility clearly exists that, while apparently pursuing the objective of neutralising Iraqi WMD and links to Al-Qa'ida, the maintenance of the transatlantic relationship was also an unstated grand-strategic end in its own right. It may be necessary to await the findings of the Chilcot Inquiry – launched in July 2009 – for a more definitive view on this, but to regard the US relationship as simultaneously an end, a means and a way within the British strategic calculus was, at the very least, to risk confusion. In addition, London suffered from the same distance between ends and means that characterised the planning process in Washington, and with the same consequences. It has already been observed that liberal wars are, by their very nature, discretionary. The initial response to 9/11 in Afghanistan was almost reflexive, was certainly punitive and had little to do with the promotion of liberal values; that would come later with the consolidation of the operation under NATO. There is no such mitigation for the invasion of Iraq, which, even if WMD had been found, would still have been a discretionary operation; if regime change was planned to proceed regardless, it moves beyond the discretionary and towards the wilful. Either way, it is now possible to identify three grand-strategic consequences arising from the invasion.

The Impact of Iraq 2003

The first is the attenuation, confusion and perhaps long-term compromise of the campaign in Afghanistan. In 2002, the Taliban did not exist as a coherent entity and Pakistan, having been bluntly asked if it was 'with or against America',[12] was proving an amenable partner, as the capture of Khalid Sheikh Mohammed and the purging of its Inter-Services Intelligence (ISI) showed.[13] Within Afghanistan, the sense of a better future was palpable: 'everywhere one travelled … one found the expectation of a new era of security, stability and prosperity was dawning'.[14] The use of the word 'victory' is perhaps oxymoronic in Afghanistan, but had the West been able to maintain enough momentum to sustain that expectation, this book might now contain a quite different historical review. That it did not is the result of two factors: strategic confusion and the distraction of Iraq. In 2001–02, the US saw Afghanistan as a place to kill 'bad guys' that in no way resembled a prospective site for liberal intervention. And, indeed, the West could have completed that business and walked away, leaving Afghanistan to revert to medievalism. Instead it managed the worst of all possible worlds, which was to stay but without the appetite or resources to make a real difference, and the moment passed and eventually soured. To be fair to US military strategy at this stage, it did not claim to be anything other than punitive and could easily have taken the title of Pollock's 'Army of Retribution',[15] deployed by the British in 1842. But at the same time, US grand strategy was moving in the direction, perhaps unconsciously, of liberal intervention in Iraq and so, again, grand and military strategy were going in different directions. By the time the West returned with serious intent to Afghanistan in 2006, it would face a different situation. The material result of this distraction was a complete lack of interest in Washington regarding Afghanistan, beyond the narrow confines of counter-terrorism. When Sandy Gall observes, 'Why did it all go wrong in Afghanistan? It can be summed up in one word: Iraq',[16] he may be over-simplifying, but not by much.

The second consequence is a re-definition of the strategic terms of engagement in the Middle East. Before 9/11, Shia Iran had faced a Sunni encirclement, with Iraq and Saudi Arabia to the west and Pakistan and Taliban-controlled Afghanistan to the east. At a stroke, the invasion of Iraq in 2003 broke down the western part of the Sunni wall and replaced it with a Shia-led client state and the luxury of strategic depth between the Iranian homeland and its main prospective enemies. At the same time, traditional Iranian influence was re-established in the west of Afghanistan and a contiguous area formed which bears a passing resemblance to the seventeenth-century Iranian Safavid Empire and within which Tehran pulls the strings. No matter how fortuitous the cause, the Iranians were not slow to consolidate their power amongst the 140 million Shia living between Lebanon and Pakistan in what King Abdullah of Jordan has demonised as the 'Shia Crescent'. Through a range of proxies, Iran has indulged in adventurism in Shia-dominated Bahrain, the eastern Saudi provinces and, above all, Syria – at the same time engaging Israel through the surrogate of Hizbullah. Without Iranian support, the Assad regime may already have fallen from power. Whatever the motives, the existential legacy of Western intervention has been to transform the geostrategic position of Iran by neutralising its immediate enemies, extending its influence in the near-abroad and encouraging unrequited national ambitions. In doing so, it has exacerbated sectarian tensions throughout the region and added confessional conflict as another dimension within the mutating Arab uprisings. Within this crucible, the next generation of jihadists is learning its trade, with untold consequences for the region and the West.[17]

The third consequence is the forfeit by British political and military elites of the confidence of the British people. The utility of force has been a core assumption of British public life for at least a century and is the legacy of wars fought in defence of liberal values. The unwritten compact assumed that British military force would be used in rules-governed situations, that it would prevail, and that the results would be defensible and beneficial. At the outset, Afghanistan met these criteria but Iraq did not, of which the presence of hundreds of thousands of protesting British citizens on the streets of London in March 2003 gave warning. Many of the subsequent rituals of British life, from the phenomenon of Royal Wootton Bassett to the prodigious achievements of the Help for Heroes charity, speak to the desire of the British people to conduct a dialogue with the British armed forces over the heads of the intervening elites. For the moment, the compact is broken and may or may not be reformed; in the spirit of Clausewitz's trinity,[18] this is a matter of fundamental strategic importance.

These consequences emerge with greater clarity now than they did in 2006, the year when the intensity of the wars of 9/11 was at its height and crucial British military strategic decisions were executed. This chapter has given broad equivalence to the campaigns in Iraq and Afghanistan and so, probably, does folk memory, but that was not the way it seemed then. The campaign in Iraq was reaching its denouement, and incipient confessional civil war and a broad-based jihadist insurgency dominated the public debate. Taken against this backdrop, the British deployment to Helmand Province looked like a subordinate clause within the wider picture of Western engagement. It has since attracted considerable comment from official,[19] informed,[20] and popular[21] sources, little of it generous. In terms of the often-cited lack of strategic coherence, this is entirely fair. For the nation that won two wars of national survival in the twentieth century on the basis of its strategic rather than its operational competence,[22] this loss of national vocation is salutary. The very fact that the British had to invent the title the 'comprehensive approach' to describe a process their forebears would have understood instinctively as strategy illustrates the poverty of the approach. It is a truism that the UK failed to pull together the military, economic, political and developmental strands of its engagement in any mutually supporting form; indeed, one commentator, though hardly disinterested, judges that the UK's failure to engage at an appropriate diplomatic level was total.[23] Some structural failures have been addressed, and the creation of the National Security Council in 2010 was a significant reform, formally placing, as it does, the head of the executive function of government with the whip hand over the often-fissiparous departments of state charged with strategic execution. That grand and military strategy were out of step, and that grand strategy failed to observe the most basic tenet of producing compound effect, is also clear. What then can be claimed in mitigation of such a comprehensive indictment?

The first thing is to observe that this was not an easy business. The statement that Britain 'punches above its weight' has entered the language, but the vacuity at its heart was only revealed when, to pursue the analogy, it entered into a strategic catch-weight contest in two theatres with the resources to service only one. In a war of national survival it would have been self-evidently necessary, and entirely possible, to increase the means to match the ends, but, in a series of discretionary engagements which, after it became clear that neither WMD nor links to Al-Qa'ida existed in Iraq, were only tenuously connected to vital national interests, this proved impossible. As a result, once the decision to become involved in Iraq was taken, a systemic asymmetry within strategy arose that would never permit a reconciliation of means and ends while the UK pursued two, simultaneous campaigns.

A second is that military strategy has throughout been faithful to the core policy that informed grand strategy. From Tony Blair's definitive speech in support of enlightened intervention at the post-9/11 Labour Party Conference in 2001 to David Cameron's warnings of a 'generational struggle',[24] the stated political intent has always been to seek the forward defence of the UK in the places from which operational threats arise, rather than to meet those same threats in the metropolitan homeland. Indeed, this has been one of the very few elements of the British strategic debate that has remained consistent since 9/11, and it shaped major decisions that found material form in 2006.

The UK's Strategic Focus on Afghanistan, 2006

By 2006, while the violence on the ground reached a climax, the only strategic objective that remained in Iraq was to honourably discharge the residual responsibilities of an occupying power under international law and return a functioning polity to the international community.[25] Liberal intervention as a mechanism of forward defence had proved chimerical; indeed, such was the response within Iraq and internationally that a continued Western presence seemed more likely to generate terrorist attacks than to neutralise them. Meanwhile, in Afghanistan the major part of the country lay beyond the writ of Kabul and was policed with the very lightest of touches by NATO and Afghan security forces. At the same time, the US was pursuing its singular counter-terrorist objectives in a campaign both unconnected and inimical to the wider NATO campaign in the country. It was therefore entirely clear that only by combining the separate counter-terrorist and nation-building strands into a single campaign under unified command would the NATO operation have any chance of success. Equally clear was the fact that only the commitment of large-scale US resources could sustain the NATO plan through to its completion, and that, until that happened, the southern provinces that had harboured Al-Qa'ida and so led directly to the doctrine of forward defence would remain ungoverned.

In addition, the stalled NATO plan had effectively partitioned Afghanistan between north and south, so feeding both Pakistan's fears and ambitions. The former were based on the possibility of Afghanistan, under the rule of its non-Pashtun nationalities, becoming a client state of India and completing the strategic encirclement of Pakistan. These fears were further fed by Indian sponsorship of Baloch separatists and the increasing cosiness of the Indo–American relationship. Pakistan's ambitions derived from a judgement that the West would follow the Soviet Union to failure in Afghanistan, and in the ensuing chaos Pakistan would need its Pashtun allies to prevent encirclement and to provide the strategic depth its obsession with India demands. These concerns count because, as Anatol Lieven points out, Pakistan's size (six times the population of Afghanistan or Iraq; two-thirds the size of the entire Arab world), the role of its at least semi-compliant intelligence services in fighting terrorism, the quality of its armed forces, its possession of nuclear weapons, and, in Britain's case, its diaspora, make it 'quite simply far more important to the region, the West and the world than is Afghanistan'.[26] In so doing, Lieven again makes the cherished Foreign Office case for regional engagement and shows why seeing Afghanistan through to a conclusion was, and is, strategically imperative.

Given an inability to service both theatres adequately, the choice was between an Iraq campaign whose strategic objectives were best served by its conclusion and an Afghan campaign where the credibility of NATO, the international position of the US, a fundamental tenet of UK political policy and the stability of a nuclear-armed state were all at stake. Some commentators observe that other, institutional motives were also at play, such as the British Army's search for a redemptive mission after the relative failure of Iraq, and there is some truth in that.²⁷ However, the strategic calculus makes its own case, and diverting subplots were neither necessary nor decisive. The choice of where the UK should place its strategic main effort was therefore clear; the reasons why it also felt it had to lead the process of re-engagement in Afghanistan may, however, not be.

The UK led the NATO plan into the south of Afghanistan in mid-2006 because of the aggregate power of the strategic case, the increasing autonomy of a de facto Pashtunistan under Pakistani tutelage, and because nobody else would. At the post-Samarra height of the campaign, American eyes were firmly fixed on Iraq as the global War on Terror became concentrated on the geographic confines of Baghdad and Anbar Province. Afghanistan was seen as a minor theatre in comparison, and it was only after the Iraq surge of 2007 showed the virtues of comprehensive counter-insurgency techniques, well applied, that the US preoccupation with counter-terrorism in theatre would change. Meanwhile, and in sharp contrast to 2001 when then-Pakistani President Pervez Musharraf saw advantage in supporting the West (not least as a potential lever in Kashmir),²⁸ Pakistan saw NATO's lack of resolution in prosecuting its Afghan plan as implying failure, and was hedging towards its reserve position of supporting the Taliban as its only ally in a rough neighbourhood. Breathing life into the moribund NATO plan therefore seemed timely and necessary. That British execution of the move was poor has become conventional wisdom, but that should not obscure the strategic clarity that informed it. To have undertaken an unfinished intervention in Afghanistan, the main legacy of which might have been to define the start line of the next round of regional conflict, could seem historically irresponsible and must form part of the eventual judgement on this passage of events.

The British Approach to Operations
Finally, this section moves from strategic generalities to operational specifics. In doing this, no attempt will be made to focus on

established *bêtes noires* like the withdrawal from Basra or the entry into Helmand; neither will equipment or the conduct of the tactical fight be examined. Rather, it will concentrate on the institutional framework within which operations were conducted and the consequential results.

In 'A Good War Gone Wrong?', Theo Farrell reviews the emerging literature on Afghanistan and draws conclusions that broadly echo his title.[29] One of his observations concerns the constantly changing tactical designs at brigade level, caricatured by one of the authors he quotes as providing 'work experience for generals'.[30] It may be that, but it most certainly is not the systematic execution of military strategy which should be its only purpose. Operations at formation level must have some quality of unified design and consistency if they are to make any claim to be faithful to the military strategy they serve; to be fair, this seems to have become more the case latterly. The question is, though, why early operations in both Iraq and Afghanistan amounted to a series of cameo performances rather than the delivery of a single script.

The first reason is the exaggerated deference to the commander on the ground that has characterised the British approach. This is not entirely without virtue and may derive from empire or be a legacy of Northern Ireland, where the battalion was probably the largest coherent unit of manoeuvre. Either way, the tendency has been to concentrate command at relatively junior levels and trust that professional training and native wit will suffice. Except for brief periods in the wars of 9/11, British generals have not commanded in the field; they have provided a long line of deputies to US commanders at various levels and led the staffs in the Ministry of Defence (MoD) and Permanent Joint Headquarters (PJHQ), but they have not performed their titular function. In turn, this derives from the fact that the UK has not itself conducted any *campaigns*, no matter how hard we try to dress up the tactical engagements in southern Iraq and Helmand Province in campaign clothing. It is

American commanders like Casey, McChrystal and Petraeus who have orchestrated campaigns, and with a clarity, rigour and access to military and other resources that Britain has rarely matched. The UK's response has been to create small but rather imperfectly formed localised operations which have often been sufficiently different in character to the overall campaign to both reassure the country of its sovereign independence and intensely irritate the theatre commander and his staff. This author exaggerates for effect, but at their most egregious, British structures have been designed on a principle of inverse deference, where successive layers of command, with no autonomous function in directing operations in the major theatres, act as facilitators to, typically, a one-star commander on the ground that does. Under these circumstances it is hardly surprising that individuals feel they have the mandate to extemporise.

The dilemma is probably most perfectly captured in the role of the Chief of Joint Operations (CJO). The institutional reforms that created the post were informed by the requirement, clearly illustrated in the First Gulf War and subsequent engagements, to concentrate the joint instruments of military power in a single individual who would become habituated to command. But command – in the sense of designing and executing campaigns at theatre level, rather than command as the formal condition regulating successive layers of military hierarchy – is something the incumbents have rarely exercised since the inception of the post. Successive CJOs have provided a briefing function to the chiefs of staff and ministers and a sounding board to deployed commanders; ensured the sustainment of deployed forces; and, exceptionally, played a national 'red card' on those occasions that the UK fell out with the US. These are important functions, but they should not be confused with the design and conduct of campaigns in pursuit of military strategic ends for which the post was conceived and around which national command doctrine has been based.

Current British military institutional assumptions might be recognised by Montgomery in North Africa or Slim in Burma, and they may serve the UK again in a future era not dominated by counter-insurgency operations in a coalition framework. In the wars of 9/11, however, they have created an illusion of independence and a tendency to assume that parochial outcomes in limited geographies have significance at the campaign level; yet, on the few occasions that this has been true, such as in Operation *Charge of the Knights*, the British have not necessarily emerged with credit. This 'Helmandshire' mentality is not only a military phenomenon. The UK's more authoritative newspapers have rarely offered any sense of, say, Canadian casualties or operations in Ghazni Province, and this is as much a reflection of the introspection borne of the disillusionment identified earlier as of any institutional predilection. Moreover, while the effects the UK has created are localised, that has not discouraged its more outspoken deputy commanders or in-theatre diplomats demanding a voice in, or offering a running commentary on, events to which the British are essentially observers. The Americans have indulged the British in public, recognising that coalition cohesion is a prerequisite of international legitimacy; their private reflections might not be so accommodating.

Much of this improved after 2009, when the greater weight of US military power, which had always been the precondition to campaign success, began to be felt. At a military technical level, NATO Communication and Information Systems (CIS) became the only means of battle management and served a newly created International Security Assistance Force (ISAF) Joint Command that concentrated on operational-level management; focus and interoperability improved significantly as a result. General Stanley McChrystal built on the population focus of his predecessor, General David McKiernan, in a way that gave a greater unity of purpose to operations and provided a sharp contrast to the previous binary and divisive sub-campaigns. In the UK, the need to properly resource an enduring campaign was recognised and began to be addressed, but, above all, the application of American military resources created a contiguous battlespace that resembled a properly constituted campaign, rather than a series of isolated national enclaves conducting separate tactical engagements. In doing so, more recent operations in Afghanistan give an insight into what is possible when strategic ends are both limited and more closely matched by the means available to discharge them.

Conclusion

No historical period is entirely insulated from what went before and what comes after, but the process of liberal intervention that started in 1991 took the post-1945 US policy of international deep engagement to a new level. The country will not want to repeat the experience any time soon and a counter-terrorist military strategy will seek to ensure that it does not have to. But neither can it abandon its responsibilities or interests, as public statements of policy make clear,[31] and an animated national debate between those who wish to 'lean forward'[32] and those who take greater comfort in strategic reticence[33] continues. We may therefore not have seen the end of US-led, Western liberal intervention, but we might have seen its most vigorous expression. The same is true for Britain. However chastened the UK may feel at the end of the wars of 9/11, a nation that makes its living from international trade and is defined by its international roles cannot simply revert to autarky, and its stake in continued access to the 'global commons' will remain.[34]

Neither is the historical record since 1991 a bad one. Political stability and sound institutions in the Balkans and a functioning state in Sierra Leone are adornments to the international system and the jury on Afghanistan will remain out for some time yet; even Somalia gives cause for hope. Yet the experience of Iraq continues to shape the period and taint the doctrine that defined it. Liberal intervention will always play to mixed reviews in open societies that flourish on debate; it also runs the global risk of looking like neo-colonialism dressed in Jeffersonian clothing. That there might be a sound case at its core has been obscured by the loss of the moral and material argument in Iraq that has subsequently dominated the wider debate and acts as a disincentive to current and future interventions that might serve national and wider purposes. The full audit of the wars of 9/11 will only be possible when we can see both the good and the bad that has resulted from them, a process that is not yet complete.

VIII. BROTHERS IN ARMS: THE BRITISH-AMERICAN ALIGNMENT

Michael Clarke

THERE is nothing inevitable about the unique closeness of the policy establishments of the United States and the United Kingdom, despite the cultural and historical affinity between American and British society.[1] The two states were still potential adversaries during the first half of the nineteenth century, and US isolationism in the first half of the twentieth forced the British to attempt to maintain European stability through a partnership with only the enfeebled French Third Republic. A strong identity of international interests, in Europe and beyond, did not emerge between Washington and London until mid-1940 and was not cemented until 1942 following the US entry into the Second World War.

Certainly, it was an act of astonishing strategic vision for President Franklin D Roosevelt, having witnessed an attack on America's Pacific front at Pearl Harbor in December 1941, to respond by sending most of his forces to the Atlantic front from 1942. Yet it was nevertheless the unique circumstances of the war that created the relationship that British politicians and the public have often taken for granted, as if it were somehow natural and historically determined. In fact, it was the intensity and scale of that conflict which created the depth of a relationship that has since come to seem inevitable.[2] The war created high-level connections between the two countries as well as strong and immediate relationships between the two defence establishments.

The Cold War had the effect of institutionalising these links, and giving them an enduring quality. They have generally withstood some significant policy disagreements, such as those over the Suez Crisis in 1956 or the Vietnam War in the 1960s, and created a relationship that cast the UK in a leading role on European security, with the UK acting as a 'transatlantic bridge' in security matters, despite its more peripheral role in European economic and social integration.

In reality, the relationship between the US and the UK has been a mixture of the very general at the political level and the very specific at the level of defence and security policy. For senior political leaders, atmosphere and symbolism count for a great deal and there have been genuine personal friendships between leaders which have smoothed the way through all but the most severe policy disagreements. Key relationships have included that between Roosevelt and Winston Churchill; John F Kennedy and Harold Macmillan; Jimmy Carter and James Callaghan; Ronald Reagan and Margaret Thatcher; and George W Bush and Tony Blair. Certainly, the British feel the chill when the atmospherics have not been good, as between Dwight D Eisenhower and Anthony Eden; Lyndon B Johnson and Harold Wilson; or Richard Nixon and Edward Heath. Outside the security and defence sphere, however, it is difficult to translate these atmospherics into specific, day-to-day policy outputs (either good or bad), although officials and observers on both sides of the Atlantic have generally maintained they make a significant difference.

The other pole of the relationship, however, is different and rests on very specific legacies of the Second World War that were carried into the Cold War; namely, doctrinal and operational co-operation between the individual armed services of both countries; a good deal of training and exercise co-operation at all levels; nuclear co-operation that has been fundamental to the UK's independent deterrent; and a uniquely close intelligence arrangement whereby the two countries share information and jointly monitor global media and communications on a daily basis. The Cold War was good for the

British end of the transatlantic relationship since it emphasised the UK's strengths in the defence and security field and minimised its weaknesses, flowing from its declining relative economic power and progressive post-imperial overstretch. The Cold War, and the UK's enduring commitment to NATO missions in all major aspects of the Alliance's military posture, had the effect of maintaining the UK's armed forces at higher levels than might otherwise have been the case. The commitment to keep 60,000 British troops in the British Army of the Rhine; to be the backbone of NATO's Second Allied Tactical Air Force; and to police the Greenland-Iceland-UK gap, the Western Approaches, and parts of the Mediterranean; and to maintain an independent nuclear deterrent as part of the US Single Integrated Operational Plan from 1961 and 2003, in preparation for general nuclear war, all provided force drivers that ensured the UK maintained military capacities at a level and of a type that the US was bound to take seriously.

These were the overt policy elements of the US–UK relationship. Less obvious, but arguably more important than any of them, was the intelligence relationship, forged during the Second World War and refined throughout the Cold War in crisis after crisis. For the UK's three main intelligence agencies – and particularly for the GCHQ signals-intelligence monitoring organisation and the Secret Intelligence Service (MI6), both of which deal essentially with foreign intelligence – the relationship with the CIA and the FBI was critical. Indeed, the CIA had worried in the late 1940s that it might not escape from the shadow of British intelligence after the Second World War and that the service must be prepared to 'stand on its own two feet', so much had it relied on its UK partners.[3] There were, of course, many tensions in the relationship over specific issues, not least leaks and defections in both the US and the UK as well as some bad faith between the two. Yet none of this ever overwhelmed the essential trust between them as intelligence partners, which, in fact, has expanded in the modern era. The role of GCHQ, working intimately with the

US National Security Agency (NSA), naturally grew in importance as the communications revolution set ever-tougher technical challenges for global monitoring. As the official history of MI6 puts it, 'the "special intelligence relationship" remained a central feature of the foreign policy of successive British governments, lasting, indeed, for a long time after the end of the Cold War during which it was forged.'[4]

It was this military and intelligence legacy that defined US–UK relations when the Cold War ended in 1989 and it has evolved and been redefined in light of military and intelligence relationships in the wars and operations the US and the UK have conducted since. The story of the defence and security relationship between Washington and London during almost twenty-five years of continuous military operations since the Cold War is not just important in its own right. Like the Second World War itself, the experience of operations has become the most tangible yardstick for politicians and the public to assess the state of US–UK relations at any given moment.

Military Co-operation since the End of the Cold War
At least at the level of military and security matters there is general agreement about the main features of the Washington–London axis. In Hew Strachan's words, 'Britain's defence relationship with the US in the 1990s had been a mixture of operational awe and strategic uncertainty'; a judgement that also applies to the decade thereafter.[5] The two countries' strategic cultures are not identical but, with relatively minor variations and some time lags, the British military has tried to mirror US thinking and practice in all of the operations they have shared, as well as in those they have not.

The UK's military establishment was keen to adjust to US thinking in the 1990s about the arrival of a 'revolution in military affairs' (RMA) and all that implied. In truth, the RMA was more evolutionary than revolutionary, but the process had nevertheless reached some tipping points by the late 1990s in the ability of US forces to integrate information and action across many spheres of activity. As the quarter of a century since the end of the Cold War has progressed, the US has made significant breakthroughs in genuinely integrated systems and action across all six domains of warfare – on land, at sea, sub-surface, in the air, in space and in the cybersphere. The UK has worked hard to keep up with such progress, choosing carefully those systems in which to invest. Examples included Sentinel surveillance aircraft – an airborne, stand-off radar system (ASTOR) – to provide better integrated targeting; considerable improvements in electronic monitoring and intelligence assets, such as those that are present at GCHQ; and upgraded battlefield communications such as Skynet 5 (a system of military communications satellites) and the Bowman system.[6]

As the US sought to exploit this growing technical maturity, the logical extension was to articulate a concept of 'network-centric warfare' (NCW) as a way of achieving dominance over any currently conceivable adversary. Although NCW was out of the UK's price range in its initial conception, the UK eventually developed a concept of 'network-enabled operations', which at once seemed more affordable and a subtle enhancement of the more human scale on which British forces went to war. Network-centric operations, whatever they were called, suggested a reversion to greater emphasis on the political purposes of military operations, in recognition of the fact that mere destruction and dominance is meaningless unless it also ultimately has the desired political effect on an adversary. 'Effects-based operations' (EBO) became fashionable, translated in the UK, and eventually also in the US, as an 'effects-based approach to operations' (EBAO). Ultimately, however, this fell out of fashion in the US and was also quietly dropped by the UK.

This technical evolution and the strategic uncertainties over how it would be exploited set a context in which US and UK forces found themselves revising their counter-insurgency doctrines in Iraq and then in Afghanistan after 2004. No matter that, as Emile Simpson points out, operations in Afghanistan and Iraq seemed increasingly to confuse the use of armed force to establish the *military conditions* for a political outcome with that seeking a *direct political outcome*, regardless of the actual military result.⁷ Both powers tried to apply their technical superiority to the asymmetry of the insurgency landscape in two large countries of over 30 million people each and found that their approaches to counter-insurgency needed constant adjustment and adaptation. While the US had largely eschewed counter-insurgency as a key military skill during the Cold War, the British reckoned they were naturally good at it after dealing with so many post-colonial insurgencies and the experience of operating in Northern Ireland.⁸ However, the US drastically revised its view of counter-insurgency, learned fast, and adopted its own approach to this re-emergent style of warfare, using the full panoply of its new technical capabilities. The UK was slow to follow suit and was forced to recognise that its previous conceptions of counter-insurgency were not sufficiently relevant, nor sufficiently well equipped, to deal with major conflicts in Iraq and Afghanistan – campaigns which did not sit well with some of the existing structures and practices of the British Army. In truth, the most enduring lesson of all of the UK's post-colonial wars was that the lessons of counter-insurgency had to be re-learned on each occasion.⁹ The reality of this in Iraq and Afghanistan came as an unpleasant surprise to a generation of officers taught in a military system that had prepared them primarily for a defensive, high-tempo war in Europe – notwithstanding the operational experience gained by most of them in Northern Ireland – who were then sent east of Suez for prolonged and difficult operations that have defined their military careers since.

In fact, US and UK operations after the Cold War generally seem to have been marked by a confusion of the tactical and the strategic. Both countries had impressive technical advantages available to their militaries, which, in this period, mostly faced weak or insignificant opposition from traditional military forces: trivial opposition in Somalia, Haiti, Sierra Leone and Libya; and weak traditional military opposition in Bosnia, Iraq, Kosovo and Afghanistan. However, asymmetric military opposition – from political cunning to criminal and guerrilla tactics, to outright insurgency – became prevalent throughout, particularly in Somalia, Bosnia, Kosovo, Iraq post-2003 and Afghanistan. As both countries struggled first to make the most of their technical military potential and then to bring their counter-insurgency methods up-to-date to deal with modern insurgent behaviour, so 'strategy' increasingly seemed to be defined on the battlefield itself.[10] Indeed, there seemed to be a binary relationship between strategy as pursued in national capitals and strategy as pursued in the theatre of operations, and the gap between the two was increasing, with greater significance laid on the latter.[11] It was as if the political decision to engage in intervention in the first instance was the only meaningful strategic decision taken by the governments and that thereafter the responsibility for real strategy lay with the military, dealing day-to-day with criminals, warlords and insurgents in the battlespace.[12] There are exceptions, such as the decisions taken by Washington to launch the military 'surges' in Iraq and then Afghanistan, where a rethink at the strategic level translated into a new tactical reality, but it is difficult to find examples of this happening in London since the end of the Cold War.

This may be regarded as an inevitable feature of contemporary conflict. Having already grappled with it for some time now, US and UK military establishments could be seen as being ahead of other Western militaries in their consideration of the problem. A serious debate has taken place about strategic compression and whether the 'operational' level – situated between the political direction provided by the national capital and the tactics of the battlespace – is meaningful anymore. Perhaps all strategy, it is argued, has to be seen as a straight dumbbell between politicians and the battlespace commanders.[13] Whether or not this approach is inevitable or even sustainable, it epitomises the strategic uncertainty in the military establishments of the US and the UK over the last quarter of a century and perhaps the failure of military leaders to understand, or interpret, the strategic intent of their political masters – ambiguously though that political intent is frequently expressed.

It was an uncertainty that had growing political implications throughout the period. There were twelve significant military operations in which the US and UK were involved, separately or together, from 1991 (see Table 1).[14] Over this period, the US engaged in ten significant military operations; the UK also in ten. The two allies were involved together in eight of the twelve operations and significantly, in three of the biggest and most expensive – in Afghanistan between 2001 and 2005, and then between 2006 and 2014, and in Iraq from 2003 to 2009. (The list does not include other operations in which US or UK allies were separately involved, such as the Italian-led operation in Albania in 1997 or French operations in Côte d'Ivoire during the 2000s or Mali in 2013.)

Certainly, *military* success can be said to have been achieved unambiguously in eight of the twelve cases, with either failure or highly contested success in only four of them (though these include the two largest campaigns, in Afghanistan between 2006 and 2014 and Iraq after 2003). More significantly, however, the operations have generally been regarded as having had disproportionate political cost or negative political impacts (failing to achieve their political objectives) in six of the twelve cases. Two involved Iraq; in the 1991-2003 campaign where the no fly zones were successful in restricting Saddam Hussein's air operations but did not prevent his persecution of the Kurds in the north or the marsh Arabs in the south, which was the original object; and then again in 2003 where order could not be secured in Iraq after the toppling of Saddam. Other politically costly or failed objectives were evident in Somalia, Bosnia in the early phase and in Afghanistan and Libya. Clearly the military instruments deployed by the US and the UK have worked in their own terms most of the time. The only unambiguous military failures since 1991 were for the US in Somalia and for the UK in Bosnia during the UN

Protection Force (UNPROFOR) period, and even this was rectified during 1995–96, when the UK and then NATO – led by the US – went into high-gear, first to drive back Bosnian Serb forces within Bosnia and then to enforce a tough peace deal via NATO following the 1995 Dayton Accords.

Table 1: Significant Military Interventions by the US and UK, 1989–2013.

Operation	US involved	UK involved	Military Success
Iraq, 1991	Y	Y	Y
Iraq, 1991–2003	Y	Y	Y
Somalia, 1991–94	Y	N	N
Bosnia, 1992–95	N	Y	N
Haiti, 1994	Y	N	Y
Bosnia, 1995–2002	Y	Y	Y
Kosovo, 1999–2003	Y	Y	Y
Sierra Leone, 2000	N	Y	Y
Afghanistan, 2001–05	Y	Y	Y
Iraq, 2003–09	Y	Y	?
Afghanistan, 2006–13	Y	Y	?
Libya, 2011	Y	Y	Y

Note: Iraq 1991–2003 refers to operations related to the no-fly zones over northern and southern Iraq. Bosnia 1992–95 covers the UN Protection Force (UNPROFOR) deployment and related Operations Deny Flight *and* Sharp Guard. *Subsequent British operations in Bosnia, December 1995–2002, were NATO-led.*

For both countries it is not a bad record overall, but it also indicates something that was changing in terms of the way, and the purposes for which, military force has been used by the allies. It also indicates that after a good record of military and political success during the early years of relatively small operations (and eventual success in the case of Bosnia and Croatia), there is a dearth of such clear-cut success, either militarily or politically, in the generally bigger operations after 2001.

Table 1 elucidates quite a trend line. Indeed, the record of operations indicates that 2001 marked the beginning of an important turning point in both political and military terms. Such a turning point may have been partly disguised by the close working relationships between military and security officials on both sides of the Atlantic, but it cannot be ignored in the US–UK story of this period.

Pre-2001 Operations
Conservative leaders in the early 1990s may have seen UK military operations in Kuwait, Iraq, and Bosnia and Croatia as essentially individual responses as needs arose, albeit there were many such cases. However, Labour leaders after 1997 fashioned the trend into a doctrine of 'liberal interventionism' that assumed a natural coincidence of interests with the US. Blair's Chicago speech in April 1999 certainly assumed that the 'doctrine of the international community' was based on shared ideas, and a shared commitment to act, between Washington and London. In the view of the Blair government, there was a continuum in the operations carried out by the UK and the US, both separately and together. There were important points to make to the world. Bosnia in 1995 had shown that 'muscular peacekeeping' could be effective. The gainsayers who had argued fearfully against any slippage from strict UN-based neutrality were proved wrong. Leadership and political courage could achieve satisfactory outcomes for the liberal democracies that would have been impossible in the Cold War – and the global environment was not so benign after the Cold War that the liberal democracies could afford to relax. As Blair himself put it, there were 'many dark forces' that threatened freedom in the world. From a political point of view, the friendships between John Major and George H W Bush and between Tony Blair and Bill Clinton, and then George W Bush, all had echoes of the Thatcher–

Reagan relationship during the Cold War. The UK was a junior partner of some military and political significance to the US. In times of military adversity, British prime ministers appeared to have more clout in Washington, and both John Major and Tony Blair, and their staffs, certainly benefited from the sense of 'business-as-usual' continuity in the military and security spheres. It is evident that UK political leaders had no serious qualms during these years about using British military force. It reinforced the relationship with the US and helped to maintain the military commitment of the US to the defence and security of the European continent.

From the armed forces' point of view the problem was less simple. While UK military planners were struggling to keep up with the emerging revolution in US military power and did not look with great confidence to a future in which the UK would occupy ever-smaller niches in the US military spectrum, the effect of actual operations prior to 2001 also served to reassure them. Operations require the technologies that are immediately available and allies cannot move too far ahead of each other, so the pressure of fighting tends to take over from the worries of long-term planning. As such, both politicians and military chiefs in the UK saw the immediate advantages of operating closely with the US wherever possible.

In the five significant operations prior to 2001 in which US and UK forces fought together, there were certainly technical strains and political disagreements over objectives, but not at a level that seriously questioned the value of the defence and security partnership itself. In the 1991 First Gulf War to liberate Kuwait, the UK fielded an armoured division and commensurate air and naval assets. As the UK commander, General Sir Peter de la Billière, noted:[15]

> If we went to war in the desert with one armoured brigade, it would have to be attached to an American division ... which would severely limit its freedom of action. If, on the other hand, we had a British division, it would have far more scope to do itself justice.

As such, the UK controlled a corresponding sector of the battlespace within the international coalition and ran its own war on the ground within that space. It also operated smoothly with the US Air Force (USAF) and US Navy elsewhere. Logistics aside (where UK forces did struggle), there was no relevant technological gap to be addressed.[16] The international coalition against Saddam Hussein operated formally under Saudi direction, but there was no doubt that the UK was the principal military partner to the US military leadership in the whole endeavour. There were no significant differences other than in the sheer numbers – the military capacity – that each country brought to bear,[17] and the multinational command-and-control process was handled well by the US to create an effective combined headquarters. The establishment and operation of two no-fly zones over Iraq in 1991 and 1992 was even more technically integrative for the British. The air-enforcement operation (originally also conducted with France, which withdrew from it in 1998) ran until the Second Gulf War in 2003. It involved joint surveillance, counter-air operations, and bombing against Iraqi air-defence systems in the north and south of the country. It had the effect of reinforcing the ability of the USAF and the Royal Air Force (RAF), and of their intelligence support services, to work together in a limited but highly sensitive, long-term campaign.

Strains over military tactics and political objectives were more evident in Bosnia and Croatia both before and after the key turning point of 1995, when the commitment changed from UN peacekeeping to a NATO-led peace-enforcement operation. Disagreements between Washington and London were more about strategy than technology, with the US wanting to 'lift and strike' – that is, to lift the arms embargo in order to supply Bosnian Muslim and then Bosnian Muslim/Croat Federation forces, and to strike Serb forces through NATO air power. For UK forces operating as peacekeepers on the ground, this was a dangerous prospect. In response to repeated Serb provocations, however, British, French and Dutch forces formed a rapid-reaction force in June

1995 to take, reluctantly, a more muscular approach to peacekeeping and peace-support activities. This was partly also to forestall the US going ahead unilaterally with a 'lift and strike' policy. In the event, the US entered the arena decisively in 1995 to impose the Dayton peace process on all parties without much reference to its European allies and their gradual creation of more effective civil–military partnerships in such delicate operations. The result, as Strachan puts it, was that 'the 1995 Dayton Peace Accords left the two allies dissatisfied with each other and with themselves'.[18]

The 1990s witnessed a slow and painful learning process among European forces, particularly in how to conduct themselves within what became known as 'operations other than war' – a condition which was assumed to be prevalent and was expected to be enduring in the post-Cold War world of the 1990s. A good example was the effective prevention of war in Macedonia in 2001. The presence of a small US military contingent in Macedonia acted to deter warlord destabilisation and some fast political and military footwork on the part of NATO Secretary General George Robertson, and of UK and other NATO forces, effectively prevented another Balkan war from breaking out when ethnic tensions appeared likely to boil over.[19] It was a neat and largely unsung US, NATO and UK success in keeping the Balkan conflict contained, ultimately stopping the war and saving an unspecified number of lives.

By this time, however, the Kosovo operation of 1999 had already begun to expose more serious differences between the two allies, even though it did not feature public disagreements between Washington and London. The US was determined to pursue a coercive strategy against the Serb leadership in Belgrade and Serb forces on the ground in Kosovo. This would be delivered through air power. Ground troops were ruled out by Washington, as were any significant risks in mounting air attacks, which relied on stand-off missiles and bombers operating – less effectively – well above the range of Serbian air defences.[20] However, British leaders and military commanders feared that this effort was failing and that European troops would be left poised in Albania and Macedonia over the winter of 1999, dealing with increasing flows of refugees from Kosovo. Consequently, they prepared to spearhead a ground-invasion plan, independent of the US if necessary, at least to seize a large portion of southern Kosovo before the winter, thereby putting President Milosevic of Serbia under more pressure than the air campaign seemed to be achieving.[21] It was a desperate plan, born out of a sense of impending, US-led strategic failure. In the event, Milosevic capitulated, declared victory and withdrew his forces from Kosovo – for motives that are still a matter of debate. Nevertheless, the uncomfortable truth of the Kosovo campaign, successful as it was, is that it revealed key differences in the political stakes that the US and the UK had in Balkan crises, a difference in thinking about the way military force should best be used – a 'casualty aversion' in the US which the British felt was debilitating – and a different approach to all the grey areas of civil–military and humanitarian co-ordination which the British felt they had finally mastered but which US forces regarded as marginal to their combat tasks.[22] And beneath these differences, UK forces were, for the first time, struggling like other European NATO forces to keep up with the advanced technologies deployed in the campaign by the USAF.[23] Just as significantly, Kosovo reignited the burden-sharing debate between the US and its allies. The US was making a disproportionate contribution to European security while the Europeans struggled to mobilise even comparable forces in an operation that was much more in their interests than it was in those of the US. The fact that the UK and France were at the forefront of every effort ameliorated this for London, but could not disguise it.

At least some of the writing was on the wall in the Kosovo crisis but it ended luckily and prematurely, and the UK's very successful independent operation in Sierra Leone in 2000 – quickly in, quickly out, using all arms of the three services in a largely national rather than multinational campaign – disguised some of the problems to come. The UK helped to rescue the failing UN operation in Sierra Leone (UNAMSIL) as the local situation deteriorated in May 2000.[24] In fact, the strategy of the Sierra Leone operation was determined more by the commander, then-Brigadier David Richards, than by politicians in London, on the basis of opportunities that presented themselves in the theatre of operations, and the aftermath was prolonged for both UK and UN forces. However, the public image of the Sierra Leone operation was that it was a model of the efficient use of military force that built on all of the lessons learned in Bosnia and Croatia.[25] By 2001, it appeared that the Balkans had set the parameters of the most likely future operations. At the same time, it seemed that US–UK military relations could be managed and enhanced, were uniquely productive for both parties, and provided an enduring means for the UK to enhance its role and prestige in the world.

Overall, the first decade after the Cold War had bolstered London's longstanding view of the US–UK relationship. Military operations played to the strong and specific elements in the relationship and although the partnership would always be unequal, the UK could remain strategically significant to the US in both military and political terms. Neither Conservative nor Labour leaders had any doubts that it was an international role that the UK should play. While political leaders would never admit to writing the US blank cheques for joint military action, there were no serious political reservations about any of these operations. As long as the military continued to deliver success at surprisingly low cost, there was growing confidence in the strategic consistency behind it all. Economic growth, liberal interventionism and a renewed global purpose to the US–UK relationship all sat well with the UK's self-perception as a post-modern, globalised, warrior nation.

Post-2001 Operations

The wars in Iraq and Afghanistan following the turn of the millennium represented a step change in the size of military operations as well as a distinctly new political purpose. The hard-won lessons of previous operations since the end of the Cold War were now to be tested on new political and social canvases in the Middle East, South Asia and North Africa. The growing confidence that politicians and military leaders in both Washington and London had developed in the 1990s, and their belief in the efficacy of assertive and precise military action, diminished more mundane doubts about getting into quagmires. For the British, the 'jolt' back to reality was a prolonged process of painful realisation that became more evident as the decade went on.

The reactions of the US to the September 2001 attacks on New York and Washington created a sequence of events that progressively strained British–American relations – and not necessarily in the most obvious ways. In some respects, the immediate political response seemed to bolster the relationship in this unique adversity. Prime Minister Tony Blair and his staff were in no doubt on the evening of the attacks that this marked the beginning of a long struggle – Blair decided even then that 'it was war' – in which some of those 'dark forces' the prime minister had previously cited were set to attack Western society.[26] His reassertion of the closeness of the relationship between Washington and London, and his sense that this was a moment in history when allies really mattered – whatever policy choices the US made in response to the attack – harked back to the very roots of the kith-and-kin relationship. As it happened, the UK also had 23,000 troops in Oman, taking part in the *Saif Sareea* military exercise, at that moment and expected that they might be redeployed quickly into operations should the US request it.[27] Meanwhile, George Robertson, then NATO secretary general, engineered a rapid invocation of Article V of the Washington Treaty, for the first time ever, to place NATO at the forefront of the defence of North America. It was a curious reversal of the longstanding supposition that Article V was designed to bring the US and Canada to the defence of Europe, not the other way around. However, British policy-makers, in Downing Street and Brussels, were reacting instinctively on the assumption that the UK was the natural transatlantic bridge between North America and Europe and that in this moment of crisis the importance of such a bridge was necessarily increased. Indeed, Tony Blair's aspirations during 2002 to act as a proactive – rather than passive – diplomatic fulcrum between President Bush, the UN, the other European allies and a revived Middle East peace process was the most ambitious formulation of the 'transatlantic bridge' role since the days of Harold Macmillan and John F Kennedy.

This sense of a renewed transatlantic mission was also reinforced by the enhanced relevance of the intelligence relationship between the US and the UK in the new circumstances that the 9/11 attacks had created. Now, the UK's knowledge of and links with Pakistan; its joint monitoring of the Al-Qa'ida organisation and its growing offshoots; and the UK intelligence services' human-intelligence links (particularly with the Tajiks and Hazaras in northern and central Afghanistan) all came to the fore.[28] In a manner that harked back to the height of the Cold War, it was in the intelligence relationship that the UK could most credibly claim to be the most important partner of the US – not in terms of the resources or facilities that could be deployed, but certainly in the value and relevance of the intelligence output.[29] The years since 9/11 have not diminished this perspective. Indeed, the intelligence relationship has been strengthened and extended by the struggle against violent Islamic extremism. It is a less apparent form of cement that helps to keep the US–UK relationship together when other aspects are diverging.

The unambiguous strengthening of the intelligence relationship, however, has not been reflected in other areas of the partnership, with the wars in Iraq and Afghanistan leaving an uncertain legacy between Washington and London. Of course, the UK joined the US in invading two countries that mattered more to the Americans than to the British. Indeed, the UK went to war in Iraq in a highly unpopular coalition of just three states, including Australia,[30] and it was also one of the few countries involved in Afghanistan from the very beginning in late 2001, contributing intelligence assets, special forces and some elite units. All this may be counted as an example of the deep sense of strategic community between the two partners.

And yet the policy reality began to diverge from this grand perspective, first in Iraq in 2004 and then in Afghanistan from 2006. This divergence took several forms. For the first time since the Cold War, the two allies seemed to be fighting in the same wars for different strategic purposes. Policy-makers in the UK never signed up to the George W Bush administration's rhetoric of a War on Terror – notwithstanding Tony Blair's personal commitment to it – and still less to the Bush notion that Iraq, Iran and North Korea formed a meaningful 'axis of evil'. The invasion of Iraq was far more controversial in the UK than in the US and even a total and rapid victory on the battlefield did not assuage a sense that the UK had participated in an unnecessary war and a strategic blunder. After the invasion, having taken on the policing of Basra and the surrounding southern provinces, UK forces wanted to conduct a rapid stabilisation operation – and, incidentally, to use this to open up a quiet diplomatic channel to Iran for wider strategic purposes. However, stabilisation was quickly overtaken during 2004 by a growing insurgency that drew UK forces into an operation that became ever-more taxing and difficult to explain to the UK public. Meanwhile, the attempt by Foreign Secretary Jack Straw to open up a diplomatic channel to Iran was not much supported by US policy-makers and, anyway, failed to make headway.[31]

If the US intended to remake Iraq as an effective democracy – and to do whatever it took to achieve that – the UK just wanted to work with the grain in southern Iraq and to leave a territory functioning in its own way, even if that meant accepting a disproportionate role for the criminal groups operating across the border with Iran and a predominant role for the Shia militias, which British commanders insisted were only local warlords rather than part of a national sectarian force inspired through Iran. In any case, the British presence in southern Iraq was not sufficient to do more than influence stabilisation trends. It was never great enough to impose stabilisation *against* the trend, still less to have a transformative effect on the south of the country. In Basra city, the UK's three battalions constituted, at most, a quarter of the force that would be required to assure basic security for the more than a million people who lived there.[32]

While both Washington and London had failed to plan adequately for 'Phase IV' post-conflict operations,[33] the US had some margin of error and could re-orientate its strategy. The UK could not without a significant increase in military deployments at a time when the government was under domestic pressure to withdraw. Indeed, it became an acute bind for the Gordon Brown government from 2007. Whereas his predecessor Tony Blair had toyed with the idea that UK forces should be sent to operate even in Baghdad, and was dissuaded from pressing the idea, Gordon Brown was anxious to speed up the withdrawal from Basra and was continually frustrated by military advice that it was too dangerous to do so. The US operated in the most populous area of the country; it dominated what happened in Baghdad and beyond from the huge Green Zone. For the British, this created all the responsibility of coping with national political trends – in particular, the growing insurgency and failure of governance – as they affected the south, without the political power, and certainly without the military power, to take control of the situation. One view has it that from the outset there was 'a desire in Whitehall to turn southern Iraq into a model of stability, brought about solely through British influence'.[34] Whether or not this is true, political pressures were pulling in different directions for the two allies. For the British, the conditions were unlike any previous counter-insurgency operation they had known. Furthermore, though UK officials played a role in Baghdad and had helped the US to form the interim government in Iraq, Washington's influence over the Iraqi government steadily diminished and UK forces found themselves operating as a spoke in someone else's political wheel.[35]

The simple fact was that the UK had assumed a common strategic purpose with the US in invading Iraq in 2003 but found it increasingly difficult to maintain this commonality as the commitment extended to countering a long, full-scale insurgency. Standing staunchly by the US in 2001 and thereby following in the wake of the reckless US War on Terror may have appealed to a higher strategic logic which had the effect of taking the UK to war in 2003, but that was never spelt out explicitly by the government even to itself, let alone to the British public. The strategic purposes of trying to stabilise southern Iraq when instability in the area was driven by its own political dynamics were difficult to sustain. UK policy, instead of remaining in close harmony with a grander US strategy, effectively settled on mere tactical competence in its theatre of operations. 'Politically and strategically,' says Richard Iron, then-chief UK military adviser to Iraqi forces in Basra, 'we had become de-linked from our ally the USA'.[36]

With strategy awry between Washington and London, the operational level also suffered. While US forces were moving proactively in central Iraq to create and support a 'Sunni awakening' accompanied by a surge of reinforcing troops, the British, now also under pressure to increase forces in Afghanistan, were trying to run down their operations and were preparing to leave. UK commanders judged that the situation in the south could be progressively handed over to newly trained local forces; British units could remain within the Basra Palace complex and the airport, and then consolidate just at the airport, prior to withdrawal. This was logical as long as the strategic aim was not to create a different society in southern Iraq. However, neither the US nor, more importantly, the interim Iraqi government saw it in the same way. In March 2008, Prime Minister Nouri Al-Maliki personally led a major operation to take Basra city back from the Jaysh Al-Mahdi militias – in the very heart of the UK's area of responsibility. UK forces looked on during Maliki's Operation *Charge of the Knights* and provided some back-up support, and then some direct engagement, in the later stages. Commanders argued that this was precisely the hands-off situation they had been working towards, but few others in Iraq, the US or even the UK saw it as anything other than an expression of inadequacy.[37] When it came, the final drawdown of UK ground troops from their airport base the following year was as an act of orderly tactical withdrawal rather than an act of evident strategic success.

By that time, UK forces were already deeply involved in operations throughout Helmand Province in Afghanistan. Here, the logic of British–American relations had worked differently. Critical commentary that the UK was simply driven by the US into this new phase of an Afghan war is a caricature of more complex circumstances.[38] US attention had been diverted away from Afghanistan by Iraq early in 2002 and the two separate military operations that continued in Afghanistan, a nation-building operation and a counter-terrorist sweep, were both faltering badly by 2004. Along with Canadian and Dutch military planners, British officials and military officers devised a plan to reinvigorate the Afghan operation to prevent its outright failure. This would ultimately depend on US military forces coming into a reorganised Afghan operation in some numbers. But given that the US was still heavily involved in Iraq, that would only happen if European NATO nations took the lead. Turning the Afghan operation around, in other words, depended on the ability of the Europeans to trigger a renewed US commitment to it. This, and a need to mend transatlantic fences after the Iraq controversies of 2003, led the UK, with Canada and the Netherlands, to press NATO to take responsibility for stabilisation across the whole of Afghanistan.[39] NATO was at once the trigger and the vehicle for US troops to move into the Afghan theatre in some force and then, eventually, to surge in numbers to deal with the fractured but persistent insurgency in the south and east of the country, and especially in the Pashtun areas.

If the origins of the 2006 campaign were different, however, the outcome was in some respects similar to that of Iraq. UK forces were numerically small and therefore dispersed across a wide area where they received little real help from locals, just as in southern Iraq.[40] The International Security and Assistance Force (ISAF), which had come under NATO leadership in 2003, was a large and unwieldy coalition. UK forces and their allies were stretched too thinly across a large swath of territory – which was also the province most affected by insurgency. Indeed, Helmand was considered the major 'narco-province' when the UK had taken on a counter-narcotics role in 2002 with no internationally agreed strategy on how to address it. This military overstretch in Helmand Province was only exacerbated by the fact that the UK did not have meaningful political influence in Kabul or even in Kandahar and, again, was doing the best it could at the tactical level while coalition strategy in the country was in a state of flux. The same strategic disconnect between several of the ISAF nations was apparent, not because of disagreements over what the strategy should be, but more because stated ISAF strategies were unrealistic in the circumstances of Afghanistan; they were simply beyond implementation given the meagre resources that had been committed to them. It was hardly surprising that ISAF partners were pursuing different objectives in their own areas of responsibility. The result was that, in effect, there was no meaningful ISAF strategy for the first eight years of the campaign. The arrival of General Stanley McChrystal as commander of ISAF forces in 2009 and his replacement by General David Petraeus in 2010 certainly gave some clarity to a nation-wide strategy but by then so much time, and ground, had already been lost – not really to the insurgents as such; more to the destructive vacuum of political drift, corruption and ineffective action programmes. By the time US counter-insurgency policy was well underway in Afghanistan and the British Army had geared itself up properly to take on modern counter-insurgency, the expanding strategic purposes of intervening in Afghanistan after

2001 – to deny it to Al-Qa'ida as a base, to squeeze the Taliban out of the political equation, to put Afghanistan on a new development path and to defuse growing Afghan–Pakistani (and Indian) tensions – had almost all been scaled back to not much more than the original objectives of 2001 in chasing Al-Qa'ida out of the country. Indeed, with the exception of denying Al-Qa'ida a base in Afghanistan and the considerable achievement of dismantling its core organisation in the Pakistani border territories, Afghanistan must still be judged as a long war waged for confused and shifting objectives.

The operational relationship between the US and the UK was a mirror image of that in Iraq and no happier. It was the US that was reluctant to engage fully and anxious to exit quickly. UK forces had been operating fairly aggressively in Helmand from 2006 while the incoming US president in 2009, Barack Obama, took some time to decide on another surge of US troops into theatre. Indeed, he announced the decision almost a year after taking office, in December 2009. The UK had got its wish of triggering a greater US commitment to the Afghan strategy, though a good deal later than it had hoped. And in the time that had elapsed, British political fatigue for the operation was also evident. Prime Minister Gordon Brown was struggling to hold the line within his own government against a unilateral announcement of withdrawal, and UK commanders were keen to transfer responsibility for Sangin and Musa Qala to incoming US forces.[41] At the same time that President Obama announced the troop surge, he also committed to begin the withdrawal of troops by 2011 and confirmed that the whole operation would be wound up by the end of 2014 if conditions were right. The president was not to be saddled with 'Obama's war' and was determined to disengage from it after a brief period of more intense operations. Meanwhile, as incoming prime minister following a general election in May 2010, David Cameron repeatedly signalled a reduction in UK force strengths and then announced in July 2011 that there had to be an 'endpoint', making clear that full withdrawal of UK troops would take place 'by 2015' regardless of the conditions.⁴²

The surge of US troops added greatly to the tactical effectiveness of ISAF operations in Helmand. As a result, British forces can claim that, at least in relative terms, they will be leaving Helmand in a more improved social and economic state than they had left the more prosperous Basra. With the help of US Marine Corps units which operated in Helmand during the surge, they can claim to have achieved tactical success. Yet this has made little difference to the essential strategic equation. Helmand was not unimportant, given that the Afghan campaign could certainly have been lost there; however, the war could never have been won in Helmand. It was clear that the UK made a big commitment to rescue the ISAF mission by engaging with its European allies across the south of the country. That commitment was not echoed by a commensurate US effort at the political level, and despite the temporary US surge, the UK's military found itself under pressure in a part of Afghanistan that has little bearing on the future political direction of the country as a whole.

In 2011, the Libya operation restored some confidence in the allies' ability to apply military force precisely and for a clear strategic purpose. The unintended consequences of the fall of the Qadhafi regime are still being felt across the Sahel region, no less than in Libya itself; but US and allied forces achieved their primary purpose of unseating the Qadhafi regime and preventing a series of massacres by government forces, albeit by intervening in a civil war.⁴³ The military success of the operation, however, did not disguise growing divergence between British and American approaches to such events. After the opening salvos of the campaign, the US withdrew from front-line operations to play a critically important role in 'enabling' the forces of its allies through NATO, but thrust the leadership of the military campaign firmly onto the UK and France. It was evident that the US stake in the conflict was less than that of the Europeans. It was also obvious that the European allies found it technically and operationally difficult to work under such taxing rules of engagement – no innocent casualties, no mistakes, no regular NATO troops on the ground, not much time to achieve a result – and were visibly stretched in a relatively minor campaign.[44] Indeed, NATO was far from united in its response, with only some European allies participating in the action, alongside some new, non-NATO partners. Ironically, NATO's success in Libya exposed more of its military and political weaknesses than strengths, and increased the determination of the US not to keep on propping up inadequate military capabilities in Europe.[45]

As Washington's strategic vision shifts to a new conception of its interests in the Middle East and a sense of historical destiny in its 'pivot' to Asia, the military success of the Libya campaign seems less relevant than the asymmetry of interests, commitments and resources that it highlighted between the US and its European allies, including the UK. In the decade since 2001, the traditional currency of British–American relations seemed to have been devalued by the curious circumstances of the Libya operation. Conditional military success in UK operations in the wars of Iraq and Afghanistan and the strategically marginal success of the military operation in Libya left an impression on both sides of the Atlantic that strategic interests and military compatibility between the US and the UK were diverging, perhaps irreversibly.[46]

Conclusion

The armed forces of the US and UK have marched down a long, hard road since the end of the Cold War and have journeyed together for much of the time. Their travails when working together have been both symptom and driver of the broader political relationship between them.

At the senior political level there were inevitable variations in approach. Five prime ministers spanned the period, from the last months of the Thatcher premiership through to John Major, Tony

Blair, Gordon Brown and then David Cameron. They coincided with four presidents in George H W Bush, Bill Clinton, George W Bush and then Barack Obama. Margaret Thatcher and Tony Blair gave strong and instinctive support for US actions in the Middle East and then over the Balkans and in Afghanistan. The administration of John Major was consistently exasperated that Bill Clinton was not more decisive, at an earlier stage, in the Balkans. Gordon Brown and David Cameron were primarily concerned with the extraction of UK forces from operations in Iraq and Afghanistan as soon as politically possible and both found it difficult to synchronise their timing more closely with shifting US approaches to success and withdrawal in these two operations. Not surprisingly, their political instincts were all different when considering the relationship with the US, ranging from the Churchillian reactions of Thatcher and Blair that a higher strategic purpose was served by supporting the US regardless, to the more conditional support offered by Gordon Brown and even David Cameron in light of operations that had become highly controversial.

During these twenty-five years, however, the UK's military and security establishments have clung to their close relationship with the US with some tenacity. They have tried to maintain the high-quality relationship they have traditionally had with their American counterparts and to provide some ballast against the rough waters that political change and electoral cycles always bring.

In these respects, balancing the political and the military aspects of the relationship, current uncertainties between the US and the UK could be compared with the much more difficult moments created by events such as the Suez Crisis in 1956 or the festering sore of Vietnam in 1968. The relationship is cyclical and the record of eight joint operations undertaken by the two allies since 1991 is still impressive. To be sure, there were some real disagreements over the Bosnia and Kosovo campaigns in the 1990s, but they did not prevent a close identification of national interests subsequently in Iraq and Afghanistan, and now in counter-terrorism in the Horn of

Africa or across the Levant. On this reasoning, the difficulties of the Iraq, Afghanistan and Libya campaigns should be kept in perspective and not allowed to unbalance an overall judgement on the US–UK military relationship since the end of the Cold War.

Nevertheless, it is difficult to escape the conclusion that the last three operations in particular have pointed to trends that are not cyclical and which, if anything, will have a cumulative effect on the relationship for both military and political reasons. The Iraq and Afghanistan operations have been considerably larger than any of the others and have lasted for much longer. Their effect has been to magnify tensions between the allies more than to stimulate coping mechanisms. Most significantly, both the military and the political contexts in which the relationship was set have been shifting in cumulative ways.

One problem is the scale of UK capabilities deployable without some significant national mobilisation. The declining size of UK forces has become a serious handicap to their ability to take a piece of the battlespace, as they did in 1991, and run it successfully with largely their own resources. The UK's 'manoeuvrist approach' to operations has sustained an expectation that small forces can perform large tasks as long as they are very capable, agile and well commanded. This had its limitations in both Iraq and Afghanistan, especially in the years when UK forces were in both theatres simultaneously. Expectations of what they could achieve simply exceeded the abilities of the small forces that could be deployed and sustained in each case. Operations in Libya, fought primarily in the air domain, showed something similar. UK (and other) air forces were ultimately successful but they struggled to deploy the numbers – particularly of aircraft capable of using the precision-guided munitions that were politically required – to make the rapid impact that was anticipated. Whereas US forces can always be deployed at levels that have real punch, UK forces of similar quality lack comparable combat power without US help.

Nor is it a matter only of numbers. The UK tries hard to define the key areas where it can keep up militarily with US technology, and while the intelligence relationship remains strong, these defence and security attributes appear to be of diminishing value to US policymakers. If the US is able to integrate the six domains of warfare – from sub-surface to space and cyber domains – in the way it presently intends, under the Air-Sea Battle concept,[47] then it will be increasingly difficult for UK forces to take a strategically significant part of the battlespace, as they tried to do in southern Iraq and Afghanistan, and run it autonomously as a UK theatre of operations. In reality, the last three operations have highlighted the UK's struggle to counter a growing perception in Washington that its loyalty as a political ally is no longer matched by its capabilities; that it can be a valued and useful partner, 'plugging into' a US deployment, but not an autonomous, strategically significant partner in the battlespace itself.

At the political level, the US reorientation towards Asia is a symbol of other deeper changes which indicate a widening gap in the respective perceptions of national security between London and Washington. The US 'rebalancing' may be regarded as historically inevitable in the unfolding 'Asian Century'. But it implies that the natural military overlap between the two allies in defending Europe during the Cold War, and in trying to maintain European order in the decade afterwards, will not exist to the same extent. US security interests now lie further afield and even a bigger UK military might struggle to make a strategically important contribution to common interests. Fighting a NATO-style war in Iraq in 1991 was seen by both allies at the time as an investment in a 'new global order' that would have an important effect on post-Cold War Europe as well as the Middle East. Fighting a COIN-style war in Iraq after 2003 was not based on a similar strategic consensus and, as with the campaign in Afghanistan, became notable for the differences in global perspective between Washington and London.

The UK's political support for US security strategy, willingly given and gratefully received for the most part, does not flow so easily to a superpower whose direct security interests in Europe and the Mediterranean are visibly diminished; whose energy relationship with the Middle East is rapidly changing; and whose future seems more bound up with Asia and the Pacific. The defence and security relationship is unlikely to provide so much ballast against the political vagaries created by two leaderships with different national priorities on their minds. The military experience of the last two decades may come to seem like the busy conclusion of a close security relationship more than a continuation; one that has not created new habits of working and thinking as previous operations had done; and one that has latterly been marked more by strategic differences than by growing consensus. This was evident in the Clinton years in dealing with Bosnia, throughout the George W Bush administration and now again, deep into the second term of the Obama presidency. In over four presidential terms – almost twenty years – this strategic uncertainty has left the UK without the strong strategic lead from the US that in the past has played to its military and security strengths. This seems unlikely to be a blip and more the beginning of a new trend that should make UK policy-makers think carefully about their priorities, particularly in light of the limited military capacity the UK plans to deploy after 2020.

The author would like to thank Laura Dawson of RUSI for her research assistance in the preparation of this chapter.

IX. THE SINEWS OF WAR

Malcolm Chalmers

BECAUSE of the manner in which the British government finances military operations, it should be relatively straightforward to calculate how much has been spent on defence as a result of such operations over this period. The 'core' budget of the Ministry of Defence (MoD), agreed in regular spending reviews led by the Treasury, does not include a contingency for use in new military operations. When the government authorises the use of UK forces in such operations, therefore, it is now long-established practice (at least since Operation *Granby* in 1990–91) for the MoD to receive a supplementary allocation to cover any additional costs, officially labelled Net Additional Costs of Military Operations (NACMO).[1]

Over the period from April 1990 to March 2013, as Table 1 shows, spending on NACMO totalled £34.77 billion (at 2012/13 prices). This accounted for 4.26 per cent of the total of £816 billion spent on defence during this period. The proportion was higher during the peak years – 2009/10 and 2010/11 – of operations in Afghanistan, when it accounted for around 10 per cent of total defence spending.[2]

The NACMO arrangement was not used for the extended operations in Northern Ireland that began in 1969 and continued through to the present day. Nor has the MoD been able to provide the author with a record of any additional allocation being made for the cost of the UK's substantial contribution to the UN's forces in Bosnia in the early 1990s, so alternative sources have been used.

Because the NACMO system does not provide extra funding for tasks that do not constitute 'military operations', moreover, it is often seen as having created a disincentive for taking on new non-operational commitments, for example in relation to defence-engagement tasks.

Table 1: Summary of Net Additional Costs of Military Operations (2012/13 prices).

Theatre	Cost (bn)
Afghanistan, 2006–13	£19.59
Iraq, 2003–09	£9.56
Afghanistan, 2001–06	£1.06
Iraq, 1990–91	£0.68
Iraq, 1991–2003	£0.36
Wider Gulf[3]	£0.23
Bosnia, 1992–95[4]	£0.28
Bosnia,1995–2002	£1.45
Kosovo, 1999–2003	£1.25
Libya, 2011	£0.24
Sierra Leone, 2000	£0.08
Total	**£34.77**

As Table 1 shows, the wars fought in Afghanistan (after 2006) and Iraq (from 2003) were the most expensive military operations of the period, accounting for 84 per cent of total operational spending: £19.59 billion on Afghanistan from April 2006 to March 2013; and £9.56 billion on Iraq between 2003 and 2009. Around a further £3 billion of spending may be incurred before the bulk of UK troops leave Afghanistan by the end of 2014. Total additional MoD spending incurred as a result of post-2006 Afghanistan operations, therefore, is likely to total around £23 billion in real terms. The two campaigns were the UK's most expensive military operations since the late 1940s. Both exceeded the extra direct costs incurred by either the UK's limited involvement in the Korean War, or by its counter-insurgency operations in colonial Malaya and Kenya.

A further £2.1 billion, as Table 1 shows, was spent on the preceding 'force-for-order' operations in Iraq (1991–2003) and Afghanistan (2001–06). Together, these accounted for 6 per cent of total operational costs for the period. Most of the costs of the initial operation to expel Iraq from Kuwait in 1991 were reimbursed through burden-sharing contributions from Saudi Arabia, Kuwait, Germany and Japan, which totalled £3.2 billion (at 2012/13 prices).[5] The net cost to the UK of this operation, therefore, amounted to only £0.68 billion. A further £0.36 billion was spent on Iraq-related operations during the period from 1991 to 2003, primarily on the UK contribution to no-fly zones over northern and southern Iraq.

The UK also spent around £1.06 billion on Afghanistan-related operations in the first five years (to March 2006). This corresponds to the first-phase Afghan operation, as identified in the scorecard in Chapter III. Most of this spending was incurred during the two years after 9/11, after which UK investment in Afghan security declined to a low of £57 million in 2003/04, reflecting the economy-of-force approach adopted as attention shifted towards Iraq.

In Bosnia, to December 1995, a net figure of £0.28 billion was paid by the UK for operations. This included British troops deployed to UN Protection Force (UNPROFOR), for which the Foreign Office reimbursed the cost of £387 million to the MoD (and the UN in turn reimbursed £255 million to the Foreign Office), and the related Operations *Deny Flight* and *Sharp Guard*, which cost the MoD about £144 million. Thereafter, a further £2.7 billion was spent on military operations in Bosnia and Kosovo, accounting for 8 per cent of total operations spending over these two decades. Finally, at the lowest end of the scale, only 1 per cent of total spending was devoted to the two operations in Sierra Leone and Libya, as a result of their limited scope and duration.

Broader Costs

Even at its peak, additional spending on Afghanistan by the UK amounted to only 10 per cent of annual defence spending, equivalent to 0.6 per cent of total government spending. Yet this understates the impact that these operations have had, for two reasons.

First, it fails to account for the use of resources for which additional NACMO funding was not provided, but which nevertheless had to be made available for the operations to take place. Had these operations not taken place, the government might have decided to use these resources – whether people, equipment or infrastructure – for other purposes. Alternatively, in the absence of some or all of the operations of this period, the government might have decided to cease funding some elements of the 'core' budget completely. Examining such counterfactuals can help to provide insights into the costs of the UK's wider defence posture during this period, of which individual operations were the most important expression.

Second, the NACMO methodology does not account for the human costs of war for those involved, including the fatalities and serious injuries suffered by service personnel. The additional costs of aftercare for those injured are largely hidden as a result of the public nature of healthcare provision in the UK. Projections for US veteran care needs, however, suggest that comparable UK costs could be considerable, and could last decades into the future.

Estimating Total Costs through Counterfactual Analysis

The provision made for NACMO, used in the figures above, is well documented. Yet this forms only one element of the total costs of military operations. A large proportion – perhaps almost half – of the UK's ground forces were involved in supporting the peak level of operations in Afghanistan: training for active service, preparing to deploy, supporting deployments from UK bases, deploying and resting after deployment. A large proportion of the UK's equipment inventory was also being used, or being prepared for use, in theatre. Even when items of equipment did not have to be replaced, they often suffered a reduction in service life as a result of operational deployment. Not least, as already noted, any individual deployment has an opportunity cost: military capabilities used in one operation are not available for use elsewhere. Thus, for example, one of the costs of the UK's Afghan 'surge' in 2006 was that the forces available for continued deployment in Iraq were reduced. Most of the capabilities used in UK military operations (but funded from the core budget) during these two decades could have been redeployed had appropriate alternative operations – or deterrent roles – been pursued.

Cost estimates relating to each of these elements could reasonably be included in an estimate of the total costs of the operations of the last two decades. One could, for example, seek to apportion a share of the cost of all those defence assets used in an operation to its total cost. On such a basis, the total cost of military operations over the last two decades might be several times as large as the £34.77 billion figure for net additional costs that is used above.

By contrast, where the alternative to a particular deployment was non-deployment, an estimate of total cost based simply on apportionment of the costs of those capabilities used – taking the share of front-line units, maintenance crews, training facilities and headquarters used for an operation, and adding an appropriate share of the total cost of these elements to the marginal cost – has more limited policy utility. For, as long as the capabilities in question would have been maintained in service even in the absence of the operation, such an estimate would significantly overstate how much would have been saved had the operation not taken place.

Yet this does not mean that the financial costs of the UK's post-Cold War military operations have been limited to the net marginal cost of £34.77 billion identified above. Rather, in order to get a sense of the full costs of operations, it is necessary to use counterfactual analysis. Specifically, what financial savings could have been made had the UK not reoriented its defence posture towards long-range operations outside the NATO area? And, even if such a reorientation had taken place, what savings would there have been had the UK not taken a major part in the large, opposed state-building operations of the last decade in Iraq (post-2003) and Afghanistan (post-2005)? This chapter considers these two illustrative scenarios in turn.

The Eurocentric Option
Only months after the Berlin Wall fell, the invasion of Kuwait confronted the UK with a new challenge for which its previously Eurocentric defence posture had left it unprepared. Its military response was clear and strong. It deployed a division-strength force, accompanied by aircraft and a naval task force: by far the largest European contribution to the US-led (and UN-authorised) force charged with liberating Kuwait. A new pattern of alliance burden-sharing, fundamentally different from that established in the Cold War, was being established.

During the latter part of the Cold War, the UK's strategic posture had been largely subsumed in its commitment to NATO. During this period, the UK was one of the three-largest European contributors to the Alliance, alongside France and Germany. Its contribution was smaller, in relative terms, in some areas (notably ground forces) and relatively stronger in others (notably naval and nuclear forces).

When the importance of Central Europe as a potential theatre for conflict diminished after the fall of the Berlin Wall, however, the UK again – along, to a lesser extent, with France – became an exception to the European rule. While other European states maintained conventional forces that were still primarily oriented to territorial defence, the UK took the lead in embracing a more offensive 'out-of-area' strategic orientation. In both public statements and capability planning, operations outside the NATO area came to the forefront of its defence posture. Following the precedent established in the 1991 Gulf War, the UK emerged as by far the largest European contributor to operations beyond the continent. British exceptionalism was reborn.

This new British exceptionalism was given momentum by political personality, and in particular by the robust stances taken by Prime Ministers Margaret Thatcher (in the immediate aftermath of the invasion of Kuwait) and Tony Blair (successively over Kosovo, Afghanistan and Iraq). Alternative prime ministers might have taken a more cautious approach to foreign intervention, as indeed would John Major over Rwanda, Croatia and Bosnia in the early 1990s. Yet both Thatcher and Blair drew on a deep well of internationalism within the nation's political elite. In contrast to Germany or Italy, for which the idea of returning to former imperial territories would be viewed with trepidation and concern, the UK's collective memory of empire is generally more positive and sympathetic. Indeed, the return of UK forces to Afghanistan or Iraq, sites of many previous campaigns, was widely seen as an opportunity to demonstrate the country's traditional military strengths.

British exceptionalism during this period was reinforced by widespread (albeit far from universal) public support for the use of military force in the pursuit of ethical objectives, as a 'force for good'. It is not a coincidence that the UK is the only one of NATO's major European members to have consistently met its target of spending at least 2 per cent of national income on defence, while at the same time being the only such state within reach of meeting the UN's 0.7 per cent target for overseas aid.[6] Far from competing against each other, UK adherence to both targets stems from a common cause: its determination to remain one of the most important powers on the international stage. As a result, the UK is now Europe's biggest military spender by some margin (only France comes close), and is also its largest aid donor (albeit by a smaller margin). This dual commitment reflects the strength of the UK's political commitment to internationalist policies, across parties, even in the austere economic circumstances in which it currently finds itself.

Yet, increasingly, both of these commitments are under pressure from the wider push for austerity in government spending. Unless government ministers are prepared to give higher priority to defence than they did in the 2010 spending review, UK defence spending could fall below the 2 per cent target soon after 2015. Across all three main parties, moreover, the 0.7 per cent aid commitment is also under increasing pressure. It may be only a matter of time before both manifestations of the UK's commitment to an outsized international role fall victim to competing claims at home.

In the absence of any of the operations of the post-1990 period, a reduction in the MoD's budget to below 2 per cent of national income would probably have taken place earlier, and more steeply. With the end of the Cold War, the UK became more secure from the threat of invasion than at any time in its history. It soon became clear that Russia would be a shadow of its former Soviet self in terms of military capabilities, and the possibility of China becoming a peer military competitor to the US was still far into the future. Moreover, the UK no longer had a substantial global empire, with its non-NATO obligations limited to a few legacy commitments (such as the Falklands). In these newly benign strategic circumstances, a much more dramatic decline in UK defence spending might have been expected, comparable to those that occurred after both the Napoleonic Wars and the First World War.

The end of the Cold War still saw the realisation of a significant 'peace dividend'. Between 1990/91 and 1997/98, defence spending fell by 16 per cent in real terms.[7] As a proportion of GDP, it dropped even more sharply: from 4.1 to 2.7 per cent.[8] In the aftermath of the 1998 Strategic Defence Review, however, the defence budget started to increase again in real terms. As late as 2010, the proportion of GDP spent on defence remained steady at 2.7 per cent: significantly higher than the average defence burden (around 1.6 per cent) carried by the UK's European allies. Once the full effect of the Afghan withdrawal and 2010 Strategic Defence and Security Review (SDSR) force reductions is felt, real defence spending is due to fall by around 21 per cent from 2010/11 levels, and by proportion of GDP to around 1.9 per cent by 2015/16.[9] Yet the UK will still be NATO's second-largest military spender, and Europe's most-capable military power.

Contractual and moral commitments to personnel and defence contractors, together with the political support these constituencies enjoyed, limited the pace at which defence spending could realistically have been reduced after 1990. Yet these conservative factors are not enough, on their own, to explain the about-turn in spending trends after 1998. The main explanation for this, instead, is to be found in the shift towards a more interventionist defence posture, starting with the 1991 Gulf War, and gathering pace over the next two decades.

Such a turn was not inevitable at the time, not least because it marked a significant shift in what had, until 1990, been the predominant post-1945 trend. In the quarter of a century since the end of the Second World War, the UK went through a process of radical retrenchment in its global security commitments, culminating in the decisions to withdraw finally from east of Suez (Southeast Asia and the Gulf) by 1971. Thereafter, during the 1970s and 1980s, the UK adopted a NATO-centric defence posture, with out-of-area military commitments largely confined to defence of dependent territories (such as the Falklands and Gibraltar).

With the end of the Cold War, the government might well have decided to continue such an approach, hedging against the possible future re-emergence of an existential threat and maintaining uniquely national commitments (such as to Northern Ireland and the Falklands), but declining to rebuild the expeditionary commitments and capabilities that had been wound down as part of its withdrawal from east of Suez in the early 1970s.

Such a posture would not have required the UK to refrain entirely from taking part in collective operations outside NATO territory, for example in the Balkans. But, in such a scenario, the UK would have declined to make extra-European expeditionary operations a primary force driver. Its contributions to such operations would have been proportionally comparable to, but not much greater than, those of European states such as Germany, Italy or the Netherlands (France's defence posture was more closely comparable to that of the UK in its emphasis on extra-European commitments).

The continuation of a Eurocentric defence posture after 1990 could have allowed the UK to make larger savings in its defence budget. Rather than shifting defence resources from the demands of Cold War deterrence towards enhanced capabilities for projecting power at distance, savings from the former could have been shifted out of defence altogether. Those commitments necessary to hedge against long-term threats – such as renewal of the strategic nuclear force, and suitably reduced conventional capabilities for air defence and anti-submarine warfare in the Atlantic – would have been maintained, alongside those needed for continuing national commitments, notably in Northern Ireland and the Falklands. But, in such a scenario, the government would probably have invested much less in the new capabilities required primarily for long-range power projection. The programme for two new aircraft carriers for the Royal Navy (along with associated aircraft) would probably have fallen foul of this more Eurocentric (and parsimonious) approach, as would the programmes – which are now well advanced – to buy greatly enhanced capabilities for long-range air transport and refuelling.

Sharper reductions could also have been expected in the army, which had been receiving more than its historic budgetary share as a result of the commitment to maintain a large contingent in Germany as part of NATO's forward defences against the Warsaw Pact countries. Such reductions did indeed take place in the immediate post-Cold War period, with the size of the regular army falling from 153,000 in 1990 to 109,000 in 1997 as a result of the programme of cuts initiated in the government's 'Options for Change' defence review, the results of which were announced in July 1990.[10]

Despite the peace settlement in Northern Ireland, however, successive operations during the second post-Cold War decade (especially in Iraq and Afghanistan) made it more difficult to further reduce army personnel numbers. Only in 2011, after a date had been set for full Afghan withdrawal, was it possible to order significant reductions in the size of the regular army. Even then, the pill was sweetened by a programme for significantly enhancing reservist numbers, the main value of which was to support future expeditionary operations.

The continuation of a Eurocentric strategic posture after 1990 would, in contrast, have allowed the UK to reduce army numbers more rapidly. Current post-Afghanistan targets – for a regular British Army of 82,000 by around 2016 – could have been achieved a decade earlier, soon after Northern Ireland reductions had been completed. This could, in turn, have allowed for an earlier relocation of remaining UK troops from Germany, with subsequent recurrent cost savings.

A Eurocentric defence posture along these lines might have allowed the UK to make significant savings in defence spending, over and above direct savings in the net costs of operations. Such a posture would have left the UK as one of two European nuclear powers in NATO, with conventional capabilities roughly on a par with those of France and Germany, but with significantly less capacity for power projection than is currently planned. Such a posture might plausibly have been financed by a 2010/11 defence budget of around £25 billion, equivalent to 1.7 per cent of GDP: £14 billion (or 1.0 per cent of GDP) less than the £39 billion that was actually spent that year.[11] Because of subsequent savings in both core and operational spending under current plans, this gap would have been halved by 2015/16. Even so, a Eurocentric posture might still have cost around £7 billion less than currently planned spending (£32 billion) for 2015/16, equivalent to around

0.6 per cent of GDP. This figure is a plausible, if very approximate, representation of the net financial costs of the UK's new strategic orientation after the Cold War, over and above the additional costs of specific military operations. If such a reorientation had taken full effect by the late 1990s, it could have delivered cumulative savings of more than £100 billion by today, over and above NACMO savings of more than £30 billion.

While a Eurocentric posture could have delivered considerable potential financial savings, however, it would also have involved significant strategic risk, both to the UK itself and to NATO cohesion. If the UK had limited the extent of its involvement in post-1990 interventions to a level comparable to that of other European powers, and had cut its defence budget to the NATO European average, this would have represented a major and deliberate shift towards a more modest strategic posture. It is unlikely that further UK cuts would have persuaded the country's European allies to do more. Europe's options for responding militarily to the new instabilities being generated in its neighbourhood and near abroad – for example, in Libya, Syria, Mali and Sudan – would therefore have been even more limited than they are today. The UK's ability to hedge against the re-emergence of major state threats would have been further reduced. A more modest posture might have risked an erosion in the UK's relations with the US, for example in relation to the uniquely close arrangements for nuclear and intelligence co-operation that exist between the two. The quid pro quo for becoming a more 'normal' European state in military terms would have been that the UK could no longer have retained the 'special' strategic role which, for all its vulnerabilities, still constitutes an important element in how others see the UK's place in the international system, and in how the UK sees itself. Despite the financial savings that could have been generated, therefore, a radical Eurocentric option was never a serious or plausible option for the UK during this period.

The Option of Selective Interventionism

There is a second, more plausible, counterfactual. Rather than abstaining altogether from turning towards a more interventionist posture, the UK could have done so selectively. In particular, it could have remained ready for a wide range of extra-European interventions, but declined to take the leading European role in either of the two operations (post-2003 Iraq and post-2006 Afghanistan) which, with the benefit of hindsight, are widely believed to have been strategic failures. In such a scenario, the UK would still have played a major role in the liberation of Kuwait and the overthrow of the Taliban, as well as taking part in the humanitarian interventions in Bosnia, Kosovo, Sierra Leone and Libya. But it would have refused to take part in the two operations that accounted for 84 per cent of total post-Cold War NACMO.

An evaluation of the likely path of UK defence spending in this scenario can help to provide an indication of the total cost of the opposed state-building operations in Iraq and Afghanistan. The savings that would have resulted from this counterfactual would not have been as large as those from a more radical rejection of interventionism. Many of the investments in expeditionary capabilities that have been made, or started, since 1990 would still have been necessary. However, less emphasis would have been placed on developing capabilities for sustained ground operations at a distance, and relatively higher priority given to other capabilities now planned for introduction by 2020 or shortly thereafter.

Perhaps the greatest potential budgeting benefit from such a scenario is that the absence of intense ongoing operations could have allowed the MoD to conduct a proper defence review after the 2005 general election, balancing forward defence plans against the likely availability of resources. In particular, a 2005 budget-balancing review could have helped the MoD to avoid the inefficiencies and capability gaps that were to result from the attempt to manage a substantially overcommitted budget during the five years from 2005 to 2010.

Such a review might, for example, have involved taking decisions – such as the move to an 82,000-strong regular army – that had been mooted as options ever since the completion of the withdrawal from Northern Ireland, but which operations in Iraq and Afghanistan had made much more difficult to carry through. In this scenario, a book-balancing 2005 review would only have allowed major programmes to proceed provided that the resources were available to fund them.

It is unlikely that the total post-Afghanistan core defence budget (for 2015/16) would have been much less than is now planned. The path through which the core budget reached this level – slow growth of 1 per cent per annum up to 2010, followed by a real cut of around 10 per cent in the subsequent five years – would probably have remained the same. Without the constraints imposed by the Iraq and Afghanistan commitments, however, this scenario could have allowed a smoother path of capability adjustments and reforms between 2005 and 2015, rather than having to concentrate all of the economies needed to get to the same end point during the short period following the 2010 SDSR.

The Costs of Care

Some of the most serious costs of operations during this period have been felt by UK military personnel, thousands of whom have suffered life-changing injuries as a result of operational service.

Frank Ledwidge estimates that casualties sustained in Afghanistan will lead to a further £1 billion of spending on the Armed Forces Compensation Scheme, together with around £1 billion spent, over time, by the National Health Service (NHS) or charities on the ongoing costs of treating injured veterans.[12] In calculating the total costs of the Afghan War, Ledwidge also assigns a statistical value to the loss of lives (£1 billion) and loss of quality of life (£0.8 billion). When combined, he estimates, these four factors add a further £3.8 billion to the cost of the Afghan War to the UK.[13]

In addition to the 448 UK military personnel killed in Afghanistan (at the time of going to press), 178 UK military personnel lost their lives in Iraq in the 2003–09 conflict, forty-five in Operation *Granby*, seventy-one in the Balkans, and one each in Sierra Leone and Libya.[14] If Ledwidge's methodology were to be applied to all of these operations, therefore, the total cost of military casualties, not included in NACMO, could be around £6–7 billion: adding around a further 20 per cent to total operational costs. All of these figures are indications of orders of magnitude, rather than precise estimates.

The American Perspective

The gap between UK military activism and that of its main European allies widened significantly since the end of the Cold War, with the UK shifting more rapidly towards a more expeditionary posture. Yet this differentiation between European states took place within the context of a wider shift in the relative balance of total military effort within NATO from Europe towards the US. This reflected the global nature of US security concerns, compared to the regional focus of the foreign and security policy of most European states.

While NATO military efforts were focused primarily in Europe – in Bosnia and Kosovo – European states contributed a large share of personnel and other resources, even as they remained uncomfortably dependent on the US for key assets and capabilities. Yet once the focus of collective military operations shifted to the wider Middle East – to Iraq and Afghanistan – the disparity of effort became much more marked. For the US, these two campaigns were the largest and most expensive in which it had been involved since the 1960s. Operations in Iraq cost the US a total of $784 billion (in 2011 prices) between 2003 and 2010, and Afghanistan has so far cost it around $600 billion. In real dollars, both Iraq and Afghanistan will each have cost the US budget about the same amount as the Vietnam War.[15] Together, they will in real terms have cost more than three times as much as America's short, but intensive, involvement in the First

World War, and more than a quarter of the costs incurred in fighting the Second.

The casualties incurred by the US in the last decade's wars have been much lower than in Vietnam or Korea, both because of technological advances in the US's own forces and because of the relatively low level of technology deployed by its main insurgent opponents. Moreover, the Vietnam War was more expensive as a proportion of US national income (2.3 per cent of GDP at its 1968 peak) than Iraq (1.0 per cent in 2008) or Afghanistan (0.7 per cent in 2010). Yet, unlike the 1960s, the last decade saw the US fighting these two major campaigns in overlapping sequence.[16]

The UK made the largest European contribution to coalition operations in both Iraq and Afghanistan, exceeding the next-largest European state (at peak levels) by margins of 5:1 and 3:1 in Iraq and Afghanistan respectively. But even the UK's contribution was dwarfed by the massive American commitments of human resources, as Tables 2 and 3 show. The US commitment of personnel to these two operations typically exceeded that of the UK by a margin of around 10:1. The US also bore the brunt of military casualties in these two campaigns, with around ten times as many American as British fatalities incurred.

The disparity between US and UK contributions is even more marked in financial terms, as a result of the much-higher levels of per capita funding for US armed forces. Between September 2001 and March 2013, the US Congress appropriated about $1.3 trillion to the Department of Defense for operations in Afghanistan and Iraq, and related activities.[17] This was equivalent to £800 billion at current exchange rates. The comparable figure for the UK for the same period was £27.8 billion: approximately 3.5 per cent of the US level.[18] In contrast, the UK had regular armed forces that were 13.5 per cent as large as those of the US (in 2011), and a total population equivalent to 20.1 per cent of that of the US (in 2012) (as shown in Table 4).[19]

Table 2: Alliance Contributions Compared, Iraq and Afghanistan (Peak Levels of Military Personnel).

	Iraq	Afghanistan
US	157,000–162,000	101,000
UK	45,000	9,500
Next-largest European	2,000 (Poland)	5,000 (Germany)

Source: *On US data, See Amy Belasco, 'Troop Levels in the Afghan and Iraq Wars, FY2001–FY2012: Cost and Other Potential Issues', Congressional Research Service, 2 July 2009;* CBS News, *'U.S. to Cut Afghanistan Force 1/3 in a Year', 29 November 2011;* BBC News, *'US Forces in Iraq Reach New Peak', 8 August 2007. On UK data for Iraq, see Geoffrey Hoon,* Hansard, *HC Debates, 20 March 2003, Col. 1087; on Afghanistan, see House of Commons Defence Committee, 'Operations in Afghanistan: Memorandum from the Ministry of Defence', Session 2010–11, 2 November 2010, <http://www.publications.parliament.uk/pa/cm201011/cmselect/cmdfence/writev/afghanistan/opa7.htm>, accessed 21 February 2014.*

Table 3: Alliance Contributions Compared, Iraq and Afghanistan (Total Fatalities).

	Iraq	Afghanistan (by 6 December 2012)
US	4,486	2,156
UK	178	438
Next-largest European	33 (Italy)	88 (France)

Note: *In terms of next-largest NATO member fatalities, the losses suffered by Canada in Afghanistan total 158.*

Source: *For Afghanistan, see Susan G Chesser, 'Afghanistan Casualties: Military Forces and Civilians', Congressional Research Service, 6 December 2012; for Iraq, see Iraq Coalition Casualty Count, 'Operation Iraqi Freedom', <http://icasualties.org/Iraq/index.aspx>, accessed 21 February 2014.*

Table 4: Comparing the Financial Costs of Military Operations, UK and US.

	US	UK	UK as a proportion of US
Population (2012)	313.9m	63.2m	20.1%
GDP (2012)	$15.7tn	$2.4tn	15.3%
Regular military forces (2011)	1,427,000	192,000	13.5%
Spending on military operations in Iraq and Afghanistan (Pentagon/ MoD only, cash)	£800bn	£28bn	3.5%

Moreover, in addition to costs incurred by the Pentagon, the Department of Veterans Affairs (VA) is estimated to have spent $134 billion on Iraq- and Afghanistan-related medical and disability costs. Linda J Bilmes, a senior lecturer in public policy at Harvard, also estimates that 'the present value of accrued costs – that is, future medical and disability benefits already committed but not yet disbursed for OEC/OIF/OND [Operation *Enduring Freedom*, Operation *Iraqi Freedom* and Operation *New Dawn*] veterans – is … a further $836.1 billion.'[20] Furthermore, spending related to past wars has often not reached peak levels until decades after the conflicts themselves (four decades later in the case of the Second World War). As Bilmes notes, 'Higher survival rates, more generous benefits and new, expensive medical treatments' are likely to lead to higher levels of expenditure in future.[21]

Few efforts have been made to estimate the additional costs to the UK government of caring for those injured as a result of the Iraq and Afghanistan conflicts. As noted above, Ledwidge estimates that UK casualties sustained in Afghanistan could lead to a further £1 billion of spending on the Armed Forces Compensation Scheme, together with around £1 billion on ongoing costs for treating injured veterans.[22] Using relative casualty levels to generate an initial estimate, this might suggest that the government might incur a further £0.8 billion in veterans' costs related to the 2003–09 Iraq War. On Ledwidge's methodology, therefore, UK veterans' costs from these two conflicts could amount to around £3 billion.

Table 5: Estimating the Financial Costs of Caring for Veterans of Iraq and Afghanistan, UK and US.

	US	UK	UK as a proportion of US
Total fatalities (Iraq and Afghanistan after 2001)	6,642	626	9.4%
Spending as a result of Iraq and Afghanistan (veteran care, cash and [for future liabilities] present value)	£600bn	£3bn	0.5%

Source: US spending from Linda J Bilmes, 'The Financial Legacy of Iraq and Afghanistan: How Wartime Spending Decisions Will Constrain Future National Security Budgets', Kennedy School Faculty Research Working Paper RWP13-006, March 2013, p. 9. UK spending extrapolated from Frank Ledwidge, Investment in Blood: The True Cost of Britain's Afghan War *(New Haven, CT: Yale University Press, 2013),* chapter 5, to include Iraq (see the text for further explanation).

Yet when viewed in the context of projected US spending on veterans, this figure looks too low (see Table 5). Taking these two operations together, and in light of the information available, it is reasonable to estimate that the UK armed forces have probably incurred a total number of serious life-changing injuries that is around 9 per cent of the level of those suffered by their US comrades. There is also strong, and continuing, public support for measures to ensure that those injured in these conflicts are given a high level of medical treatment and other benefits. Even allowing for the greater cost-effectiveness of the UK's NHS and relevant charitable organisations, as well as making some allowance for the relatively less-generous treatment of veterans in the UK, it is hard to imagine that the government will not find itself spending at least half as much per capita as does the US. On this (admittedly, very rough) basis, total UK spending on veterans related to these two conflicts could reach around £25–30 billion at today's prices over the next few decades.[23] As in the US, therefore, the aftercare costs of the wars in Iraq and Afghanistan for the UK could prove to be almost as great as the direct operational costs of the wars themselves.

Even at these increased levels, however, total US spending related to military operations in Iraq and Afghanistan will still have been some twenty-five times higher than that of the UK. This comparison should encourage a degree of caution in relation to claims that the UK's armed forces, in either of these two conflicts, have been of sufficient weight to have made a significant difference at a strategic level. Indeed, given this disparity in resources expended, it is remarkable that the UK has managed to exercise the degree of influence it has on the course of events.

The relative level of the UK's contribution (and, not unrelated, influence) was greater in some other post-1990 coalition interventions, for example in Kosovo and Libya. And, as President Barack Obama's reaction to the vote in the House of Commons on Syria in August 2013 demonstrated, UK views on war and peace still have powerful resonance in US politics. Even in operations in which European states have taken the political lead, however, the relatively small size of UK forces, together with the lack of comparably effective European allies, has made it hard for the UK to punch as much above its weight as its declaratory policy sometimes suggests that it would like to.

Conclusion

The additional costs of the UK's military operations since 1990 have amounted to £34.77 billion (see Table 6), equivalent to an extra 5 per cent on the average annual defence budget. Depending on the assumptions made, long-term costs associated with veteran care over the next few decades could come to perhaps a further

£25–30 billion (or £1 billion a year) at today's prices.[24] The large discretionary operations in Iraq (from 2003) and Afghanistan (after 2005) were particularly costly, accounting for some 84 per cent of total operational costs.

These two operations must also share some of the responsibility for the budgetary over-commitment which developed in the years leading up to the 2010 SDSR, and which ensured that this review had to make much sharper capability cuts than the headline budget cut of 8 per cent would, in itself, have necessitated. In the absence of these two operations, it is possible that the MoD would have grappled with its over-commitment at an earlier stage, perhaps through a defence review after the 2005 election. Such a review would probably not have resulted in a 2020 force structure and budget very different from the one towards which the MoD is now heading. But the process for moving towards this objective would have been smoother and more deliberate, and could perhaps have avoided some of the capability gaps which the current, more sudden, rush to make savings has required.

Yet the costs of the UK's shift to a more ambitious strategic posture after 1990 have gone beyond those that can be attributed to individual operations. This shift was widely supported by all of the major political parties, and accorded with the UK's long tradition as a global power. However, it did require significant investment in new and revived capabilities, many of which had been allowed to atrophy after the 1968 decision to withdraw the military from east of Suez.

Deeper savings in defence spending could have been made had the UK been prepared to retain the Eurocentric defence posture to which it had retreated in the last decades of the Cold War. In such a scenario, based around territorial defence and hedging (with both conventional and nuclear forces) against the re-emergence of a major power threat, the UK might have been able to reduce defence spending to perhaps 1.4 per cent of GDP by 2015, saving as much as £7 billion annually compared to current plans, and more than

£130 billion over the period since the mid-1990s. In return for these savings, the UK would have had to give up most of its capability for power projection outside northwest Europe (including aircraft carriers), abandon its position as Europe's most capable military power, greatly reduce its ability to use its military as a 'force for good', and permit much deeper cuts in numbers of active personnel. Yet the governments of the last two decades have been consistent in their belief that such a policy would not be acceptable, and that these extra costs have been a price worth paying for the security and foreign-policy benefits they bring.

Table 6: Net Additional Costs of Military Operations in Cash and Real Terms, 1990/91–2012/13.

Theatre	Operation	Duration	Cash Cost (£m)	Real Cost (£m)
Gulf	Granby[25]	1990/91–98/99	441.8	675.5
Gulf	Warden[26]	1991/92–98/99	40.5	58.3
Gulf	Jural[27]	1992/93–98/99	33.6	47.9
Gulf	Driver[28]	1993/94–94/95	-2.2	-3.3
Gulf	Bolton[29]	1997/98–98/99	32.5	34.6
Gulf	Desert Fox[30]	1998/99	3.0	4.1
Gulf	[Various][31]	1999/00–2002/03	159.0	206.8
Iraq	Telic[32]	2002/03–09/10	8,164.2	9,559.1
Afghanistan	Herrick[33]	2001/02–12/13	19,438.8	20,646.4
Kosovo		1998/99–2002/03	806.0	1,064.3
Bosnia		1993/94–95/96	191.0	276.0
Bosnia		1997/98–2002/03	935.0	1,265.9
Balkans	Oculus[34]	2003/04–06/07	309.6	373.2
Sierra Leone		2000/01–03/04	57.9	75.6
EU – FYRoM		2003/04	1.0	1.2
DRC		2003/04	1.0	1.2
Libya	Ellamy[35]	2010/11–11/12	234.0	238.0
Wider Gulf	[Various][36]	2010/11–12/13	221.3	226.8
Mali	Newcombe[37]	2012/13	17.4	17.4
Grand Total (£ millions)				**34,769.0**

Notes: The real cost is adjusted to 2012/13 prices, using a GDP deflator. The 'cash cost' figures between 1990/91 and 2000/01 have been calculated on a cash basis; the figures from 2001/02 onwards have been calculated on a full cost basis following introduction of the Resource Accounting and Budgeting regime in that year across government.

Source: Response to a Freedom of Information request to the Defence Resources Secretariat, MoD, accurate as of 24 September 2013. Data for Bosnia 1993/94–95/96 was not included in this response, and is derived from National Audit Office, 'Ministry of Defence: The Financial Management of the Military Operation in the Former Yugoslavia'.

X. INDUSTRY AND THE MILITARY INSTRUMENT

Trevor Taylor, John Louth and Henrik Heidenkamp

> *The United States must have an industrial and technological base capable of meeting national defense requirements and capable of contributing to the technological superiority of its national defense equipment in peacetime and in times of national emergency. The domestic industrial and technological base is the foundation for national defense preparedness.*
>
> (President Barack Obama, 2012)[1]

> *Grand Strategy is the application of national resources to achieve national policy objectives. Military strategy is the application of military resources to help achieve grand strategic objectives. Operations are concerned with the direction of military resources to achieve military strategic objectives.*
>
> (British Defence Doctrine, 1999)[2]

THE Cold War period represented a remarkable break in modern history in that the central military task – that of deterrence – no longer required access during armed conflict to a capable, agile and, most of all, reliable source of supply of the many goods and services that are needed to sustain fighting over a prolonged period. Immediately prior to this era, the Second World had been, to a significant degree, a competition between the industrialised economies of the Allies on the one hand and the Axis powers on the other, as to which could produce the most and best equipment and materials for use primarily by conventional forces. The Cold War, in contrast, involved no scenarios in which industry was to be mobilised for a protracted conflict: the ability to deter was seen to rely on weapons that had been deployed and the fuel and ammunition that was in stock. In order to underline the credibility of Western readiness to use nuclear weapons, NATO forces never sought the capability to undertake a protracted conventional war.

In these circumstances, having a significant national defence industry could, in part, be a means of mitigating the costs of deterrence through the generation of employment and, perhaps, the benefits of advances in technology. There was also a sense of the advantage available to countries in exporting the equipment they had developed and manufactured, thus gaining a further instrument in their foreign-policy toolboxes. Only the rare surprise – and in the UK the Falklands War was the prime example – provided a reminder that, for unforeseen campaigns of uncertain duration, assured access to defence industry was an important element of military capability. Happily for the UK, in 1982 the US opted, after some hesitation, to support it in its dispute with Argentina, providing access to US supplies, including the advanced short-range, air-to-air missiles of the day. Yet US support notwithstanding, industry in the UK was called on to make a range of contributions to the campaign, the likes of which had simply not been conceptualised as part of the conventional deterrence playbook.

Since the end of the Cold War, the UK has become engaged in a range of campaigns of varied size, mission and duration. With the possible exceptions of the 1999 Kosovo and 2003 Iraq campaigns, each would have been difficult to predict even a year before. Almost all of them required the private sector to perform a large number of short-notice tasks to enhance the chances of success and lower the risk to British forces. The term Urgent Operational Requirement

(UOR) has become a regular element in the day-to-day vocabulary of those dealing with defence.

The central lesson of what is now more than twenty years of operational experience is that assured access to an agile, capable and reliable source of supply for products and services is a key element of national military capability.

The structure of the basic equation is relatively simple: if a country wishes to play an active military role on the international stage, where the unexpected is not unusual, the defence industry under its direction is likely to be an important element of its agility and capability. In contrast, if a state opts to concern itself only with territorial self-defence, and is confident about the duration, form and intensity of any campaign, then stockpiles from external suppliers may be a militarily acceptable option, although the financial and foreign-exchange costs may be significant. Had the UK adopted a much more modest defence policy after 1990 and not sought external intervention capabilities, the shape of the British defence industry today would therefore likely be rather different.

The implication of this argument is apparent. If, in the twenty-first century, the industrial dimension is a significant element of military capability, then the Labour government's 2002 Defence Industrial Policy and 2005 Defence Industrial Strategy were at least pointing in an appropriate direction, while the current government's 2012 *National Security Through Technology* White Paper, which indicated a predisposition to buy from the global market, looks more problematic. Moreover, defence co-operation projects with friendly states should be assessed not just in terms of what equipment they place in the UK inventory, but also in terms of the UK's capacity to use that equipment in accordance with perceived national needs.

The other chapters in this book deal with the front-line and strategic aspects of the various operations that UK forces have been called upon to conduct since the end of the Cold War. The concern here is with the industrial activities that supported these operations

– activities that were frequently less visible or newsworthy than the actions of uniformed personnel.

Methodological Issues and Data
A study concerned with the importance of industrial support for military operations has obvious methodological problems. First, either for national-security or commercial reasons, information is seldom readily available within the public domain. Information about contracts placed with industry, demands made beyond the contractual, industrial performance and so on, may be hidden from view. In times of conflict, secret arrangements with industry may be made that are not revealed afterwards. In some cases, the National Audit Office (NAO) and parliamentary committees in the UK have investigated such matters explicitly – including, for example, the placing of UORs – and anecdotal and statistical information has been forthcoming as a result. This chapter relies significantly on this information, as well as on press reports from reliable sources, while bearing in mind the real possibility that the involvement of industry in UK military campaigns has been understated as a result of information shortages.

Second, even if the relationship between military results and political outcomes is ignored, there are clearly many interdependencies and causal relationships between an industrial input into military capability and the success, or otherwise, of a military operation. In this area, experiments are impossible and the counterfactual is unavailable: it is not possible to re-run a campaign to see how it would have turned out without the efforts of industry associated with it. In 2011, for the Libyan campaign, for instance, MBDA and its partners significantly increased production of the dual-mode Brimstone missile, although delivery did not reach the levels the Royal Air Force (RAF) would have liked. The enhanced production still had a notable impact on the shape of the operation, enabling precise and agile strikes with a small warhead that minimised collateral damage. However, it is impossible to know how the Libyan campaign would have turned out had the dual-mode Brimstone not been available.

This chapter therefore reflects a supposition that the Ministry of Defence (MoD) would not have asked industry to respond had it not judged that the extra industrial contribution would provide a valuable input into a campaign. Yet there is no assumption here that British forces would inevitably have failed without the industrial backing that was put in place. It can, however, be asserted that on-shore industrial effort is a key component of the military instrument, as seen in the above example, and one heavily implicated in the success, or otherwise, of British contributions to post-war campaigns.

The UK Defence Management System
Industrial involvement in military operations has to take account of a government's national defence management system. In the UK, the system has evolved significantly since the beginning of the period covered in this book, but the key elements that have been in place since 1998, and in some ways before, are as follows.

The regular defence budget is for the preparation of defence capability. If a government opts to use that capability in an operation, additional resources to cover the extra costs of using that capability are provided by the government, and then Parliament – with the Treasury playing a key role, in conjunction with the MoD, in deciding what those extra costs comprise. This is the same system, in conceptual terms, as that in operation in the US.

In return for the use of the regular defence budget, the MoD is expected to build specific, and maintain specified, capabilities. While the specification of capabilities, missions, tasks and force structures has evolved through a number of defence White Papers, the core and enduring idea is that the MoD should use its money to generate force structures available at varying degrees of readiness to undertake a number of identified missions and roles.[3]

For the armed forces, the specified outputs imply force elements at varying levels of readiness and sustainability (FEAR and FEAS) as they proceed through training cycles, with personnel available for deployment only within the 'Harmony Guidelines' (which specify that people should have a twenty-four-month interval between six-month deployed operational tours).

Within this guiding defence managerial taxonomy, industry is noteworthy in its absence. In principle, therefore, the UK defence management system would appear not to require any mobilisation of industry in the event of an operation, since the highest-readiness units are supposed to be 'ready' in relation to all requirements, including equipment and weapons.

In practice, however, it is neither desirable nor feasible for UK forces to be ready for any operation anywhere within the parameters set out in the 1998 Strategic Defence Review and its successor documents. The 'undesirable' derives from the costs of holding large stocks of equipment and consumables that might not be needed if no operation is called for and which have a finite shelf-life. This applies to many ammunition types and to products that could be supplied in bulk from the civil economy, such as small batteries. The 'unfeasible' relates to the government's inability to forecast with any accuracy every campaign that it might wish to conduct. This also refletcs an increasing recognition of the costs of ownership, tying down large sums of public money to stock rooms and storage facilities. When feasible, purchasing items 'just-in-time' – through UORs – is seen as a much smarter commercial model. As the National Audit Office (NAO) explained in its 2004 report:[4]

> Urgent Operational Requirements are a major and increasingly important feature of today's operations and other countries procure capabilities urgently similarly to the United Kingdom. The varied nature of operations and operational environments that may be encountered and the different strategies that may be employed mean that existing capabilities

often need to be enhanced to adapt to circumstances or new capabilities need to be procured rapidly to fill previously unidentified gaps. Given that the Department does not have the money to buy all the equipment it may need for all types of operations, it must therefore prioritise and have to work on the basis that it will have to fill some capability gaps by Urgent Operational Requirements.

The MoD identified four principles for UORs. First, it must be impossible to meet the requirement through the redeployment of existing in-service assets; second, the requirement must be theatre-specific; third, it must be possible for the requested capability to be deployed in time to make a contribution to an operation; and fourth, the quantity procured should only be that required to support the operation, unless the value-for-money case for procuring additional capability is compelling.[5]

Inventory management also became a more prominent and challenging topic, primarily involving the MoD's struggles to keep track of stores held, as well as efforts to balance the stocks it could afford, industrial responsiveness and reliability, the potential impacts of stock-outs and risk management.

By the time Labour left office in 2010, the model the MoD was using identified eight elements associated with Force Element at Readiness and Sustainability metrics – training, equipment, people, infrastructure, doctrine, organisation, information and logistics (TEPIDOIL) – while also acknowledging that whether a unit was actually capable of executing a specific mission would depend on the threat (including the capabilities of any opposition), the environment (for example, the presence of deserts, mountains or heat) and the contribution of allies. Essentially, extra spending (and securing additional, targeted effort from industry) could be justified by any gaps between FEAR and FEAS and the specific needs of an operation, as well as by obviously justifiable elements such as increased fuel consumption. The need to go to industry for further supplies of goods and services was not, in itself, a failure properly to prepare force elements at high readiness, but rather reflected the recognition of an interdependence with industry, usually on-shore.

In 2004, in addition to TEPIDOIL, defence-acquisition professionals made much of the need to integrate purchases, so that the ninth metric, for a while, became that of integration.[6] This, however, was quietly wished away as it became increasingly clear that integration was not necessarily a natural consequence of just-in-time purchasing from industry.

The Campaign Record

This chapter will not discuss each of the campaigns covered in this book, but examines illustrative examples, primarily drawn from the 1991 Iraq War, to highlight the different ways in which industry can be called on to support a campaign – in this case one that took the armed forces themselves over six months to prepare for. In order to do so, the equipment-related activity of industry is analysed according to five categories.

Preparation, Maintenance and Support of (Deployed) Equipment

Because military operations usually involve enhanced rates of usage of equipment – often in novel and demanding locations – and because, in the current era, contracting occurs for equipment rather than just the supply of spare parts, special demands are often made on industry in the support domain. During past operations, industry could be called upon to demonstrate flexibility by enhancing its support efforts and by deploying employees into theatres of operations to provide advice to uniformed personnel looking after equipment.

In 1990, personnel from GKN and Perkins (the manufacturers of the Warrior infantry fighting vehicle and its engine) visited units in theatre to help with defect reporting and the fitting of modification kits. They also supplied equipment and worked with the Royal

Electrical and Mechanical Engineers to set up a deep, second-line repair and rebuild facility for diesel engines in Saudi Arabia in just three weeks.[7]

Vickers Defence Systems had just over a dozen people in theatre during the campaign providing technical help on the Challenger tank in order to maximise its performance and availability.[8] These personnel were linked to the Vickers Granby Operations Room in Leeds (which was open twenty-four hours a day), which, in turn, was connected to all component and materials suppliers. This generated a timely problem-solving capability and a capacity rapidly to realise material requests.[9]

BAE Systems already had large numbers of contractors (about 3,500) in theatre, involved in supporting the Royal Saudi Air Force, with their expertise also available to deployed RAF units.[10]

Overall, in the UK experience, although some individuals have proven reluctant to accept the risks of deployment in or near to an operational theatre, industry has generally been able to provide personnel for this purpose. Often, this has been on an ad hoc rather than a planned, pre-contracted basis, reflecting individual and corporate commercial interests as well as a sense of emotional commitment to British forces and the national interest of the UK within the companies concerned. However, in a few cases, including the Tornado aircraft, the UK has planned and contracted for 'mission availability', rather than simply for platform or spares availability. Such arrangements entail the deployment of contractors with uniformed personnel on operation and require a close and trusted relationship with the firms concerned. It should be noted that such arrangements are most feasible for combat aircraft – and most difficult for land equipment – given that the bases to which planes are deployed are normally secure, safe places for contractors to work.

To some extent, the possibilities for more intense equipment usage are a function of the support arrangements put in place in times of peace: the MoD has recognised that the contracting-for-availability arrangements and close Rolls-Royce–RAF relations were an element in enabling the Tornados and Typhoons used in the Libya campaign to double their regular flight hours. Meanwhile, the Defence Equipment and Support (DE&S) house magazine *Desider* observed that 'a flexible and open partnering arrangement can bring significant benefits to both manufacturer and customer'.[11]

Operation *Ellamy* (the campaign against the Qadhafi regime) also benefited from the close working relations between the RAF and BAE Systems in terms of support for the aircraft, as described by Stan Ralph, director of UK Force Readiness at BAE Systems:[12]

> Basically both at Marham and Coningsby we had teams in, working 24 hours a day helping the RAF to prepare the aircraft to go. They worked solidly round the clock. Forget what they're normally asked to work, or contracted to work, people just accepted what was happening and knuckled down to get the job done.... It was all hands to the pump.... During that period quite a few people were working almost 24 hours, a lot of others were putting in very long days and 'enjoying' very short nights. That was the level of commitment from our people. We're talking about a couple of hundred people on each base who were involved.

Accelerated Development of Systems

Military operations can mean that equipment still technically in the development and testing phases is rushed into service, which requires help from the firms concerned. In 1991, the most prominent example was the deployment of the GEC Thermal Imaging Airborne Laser Designator (TIALD) pod on to the Tornado to enable precision strikes. Some twelve years later, as the coalition moved against Iraq, Storm Shadow missiles were brought into service on a truncated timetable, performing reliably and accurately. Both of these systems were part of British defence plans and had been funded for some years; the operations essentially increased the urgency involved in their production. In the case of operations lasting only a few days or weeks, there is obviously little time for accelerated progress into service to be organised, and thus such cases are relatively rare. However, even in the case of Libya, BAE Systems expedited and completed various software advances and incorporated the changes on simulators to support mission training.[13]

In operations lasting a number of years, such as those in Iraq and Afghanistan, there is more scope for such activity, as well as for the speedy development and production of new systems that have not previously been part of defence plans (see below). Yet protracted conflicts involve de facto arms races, in which one side brings in changes that the other then seeks to offset or override.

Accelerated and Surged Production

The accelerated procurement of planned programmes or contracts and the corresponding high responsiveness of industry in this regard also played a decisive role in preparing for military operations in the past.

During the First Gulf War, Vickers Defence Systems hurried the production of Challenger armoured repair and recovery vehicles, producing twelve systems some seven months ahead of the planned delivery date and shipping them direct from the production line to the Gulf.[14] GKN, Pilkington, Dowty and GEC were also involved in supporting accelerated training to operators and maintenance personnel to allow the Warrior artillery observation vehicle to be brought more quickly into service.[15] Furthermore, the RAF brought into service and used the TIALD, which was officially in the project-definition stage, giving it the capability to hit targets such as command posts and bridges by day or night.[16]

As a further illustration, consider Royal Ordnance, which adapted an armour-piercing tank round developed in the Challenger 2 development programme so that it could be fired from a Challenger 1 gun. Production was sped up and the round used in the 1991 Gulf War.[17] BAE, together with GKN, was also among those companies involved in expanding the production of spare parts for armoured vehicles, especially of the air filters and rubber seals which were a requirement in the desert. There were also short-notice orders for larger items such as power packs and cranes.[18] Yet, while production was increased in the UK, London had to use continental sources of supply for extra tanks and artillery ammunition.

The British Flight Refuelling Group, a specialist government service, provided a range of goods, including ammunition containers, satellite communication antennas, and search-and-rescue avionics equipment. It also provided and installed additional fuel tanks on Chinook helicopters, activities which required the company to engage in seven-day working and to station company personnel in the Gulf for a period of weeks.

Arguably, an increase in the rate of production of modern defence platforms containing many sub-systems and tens of thousands of components at short notice is often not possible. In some cases, however, the MoD, acknowledging past experience, has contracted companies to maintain a surge capability even during peacetime, as is the case with UK small-arms ammunition made at Radway Green by BAE Systems under the 2008 Munitions Acquisition Supply Solution arrangement. Enhanced production of missiles is also facilitated to a limited extent by the MoD's Portfolio Management Agreement with MBDA and its suppliers under the Team Complex Weapons construct.

As noted, the 2011 air campaign in Libya saw MBDA significantly step up its dual-mode Brimstone production, as well as the refurbishment of missiles that were out of 'carriage life'[19] (after a number of take-offs, flights and landings, given the sensitivity of the electronics and other elements in the weapons, missiles are deemed to have diminished reliability and to need disassembling, re-building and re-testing). The number of missiles that MBDA could make available was a significant determinant of the pattern of RAF activity. There was no comfortable alternative to Brimstone, with its unique capacity for minimal collateral damage, given its limited size of warhead and extreme precision.

The MoD has portrayed the process as planned and orderly, with the government recognising that its contracts and relationships with industry enabled it to pre-arrange enhanced production of weapons and to better manage the maintenance of expensive war stocks.[20] Indeed, one of the functions of the MoD's Team Complex Weapons approach is to develop these possibilities and close relationships with industry. However, enhanced production still required MBDA and its key suppliers to make particular efforts in this case. MBDA, for instance, switched to a twenty-four-hour-per-day, seven-day-per-week production arrangement and used innovative labour mechanisms to deliver as many missiles as possible. It conducted at least some work off-contract.[21] Moreover, the special procurement of Brimstone for Libya could reasonably be seen as a UOR arising from another UOR, rather than from a regular procurement: dual-mode Brimstone was not part of the core weapons programme of the time but had been funded as a UOR for Afghanistan.[22]

Raytheon UK played a similar role in stepping up its production of Paveway IV precision bombs. In both cases, Raytheon and MBDA were able to demonstrate this flexibility only because particular circumstances meant that they had available a stockpile of key elements of the systems concerned.

The principle that the MoD's 'current stockpiles are based on an assessment of likely contingent scenarios in accordance with Defence Planning Assumptions' has suffered from the reality that UK defence operations almost throughout the period after 1998 exceeded the levels envisaged in the assumptions.[23] As a result, stockpiles were sometimes insufficient.[24] This leads directly to the wider debate about whether defence policy is resource-led, with governments since 1990 having been reluctant to admit that they decide first how much they are willing to make available for defence, and then assess defence needs and priorities. Certainly, Defence Planning Assumptions must be seen within government to be leading to affordable demands. Then, of course, the world outside government has an influence on whether the assumptions bear a decent relationship to reality. In this sense, assured access to a capable and agile supply base provides flexibility to governments whose planning assumptions do not quite come to pass.

Modification of Extant Equipment
While every campaign is different, deployed military operations frequently require the modification of equipment in response to a particular adversary or physical environment. Even when items are bought from a foreign supplier, they often require important modifications by British firms to make them usable by the UK's armed forces (see Table 1 for a range of illustrations). Even for the campaign against Libya in 2011, British Typhoon and Tornado aircraft had to be fine-tuned in response to the characteristics of Libyan air defences, work in which BAE Systems and other companies' staff were extensively engaged at short notice. Because of the industrial capabilities in the UK and technology transfer that had taken place from the US, the UK was also able to modify some of its Apaches so that they could be deployed on HMS *Ocean* and make a contribution to the campaign.

The 1991 campaign in Iraq required a large number of upgrades and modifications to equipment to take account of the climate and terrain, and of the expected disorderly nature of the battlefield where attack from the side was perceived to be a much greater possibility than was the case in scenarios for the inner German frontier during the Cold War. Vickers Defence Systems, for example, supplied passive armour for the hull side of the Challenger and an armour package for the Warrior. The up-armouring packages were ordered in October and December 1990 and delivered to the Gulf in January 1991. All work was then carried out in theatre. Vickers further accelerated the design and installation of Challenger modifications for air filtration and power-pack cooling.[25]

GKN also received a contract for appliqué armour kits on 19 November 1990. All of these kits were produced and delivered to the Gulf and fitted before the ground offensive on 24 February 1991.[26] Moreover, GKN delivered kit to enable the MILAN anti-tank missile to be fired from the Warrior for the first time. After receiving the order on 22 October 1990, the first kits were designed, developed and produced in a week, allowing the conversion of the Warriors of three armoured infantry battalions to the anti-tank, guided-missile role.[27]

Another modification to the UK's ground-combat equipment was the rebuilding of all of the British Army's Mk 2 all-terrain vehicles in Saudi Arabia during Operation *Granby* by Supacat Ltd. The extensive modifications included the installation of a special heat-resistant canopy that also formed a storm cover and shelter, and stowage for equipment, fuel, water and weapons.[28]

With regard to aircraft, there were numerous modifications involving the installation of (better) radar warning receivers and other defensive aids. In all there were about sixty modifications to BAE Systems combat aircraft, including the design and installation of extra missile pylons and increases in engine thrust.[29]

Even operations in relatively non-hostile environments can result in the more intensive use of equipment and thus require an increased supply of spares, perhaps over a sustained period. Moreover, the UN Protection Force (UNPROFOR) deployment in Bosnia exposed the need for a greater range and number of campaign stores, not least for the support of deployed people, than had previously been put in place.[30]

Further, the armed forces' operational capacity has often been dependent on the modification of UORs. In 2000, during the British peace-support operations in the Balkans, the MoD contracted BAE Systems to provide a highly automated communications network to replace the manpower-intensive mobile system, which had been designed

Table 1: Examples of Modifications to UOR Equipment.

Vehicle	No.	Manufacturer	Role	Country	Known Modifications in UK
Mastiff (6x6) (Cougar in US)	299	Force Protection Inc	Patrol (people carrier)	US	NP Aerospace in the UK integrating electronics and the British armour package.
Cougar (4x4)	30	Force Protection Inc	Patrol (people carrier)	US	A British version of the Cougar 4x4 from FPII base vehicles with a British armour package and electronics, including installation of Enforcer remote weapon stations on some vehicles.
Ridgebacks	177	Force Protection Inc	Protected patrol	US	A British version of the Cougar 4x4 with a British armour package and electronics, including installation of Enforcer remote weapon stations on some vehicles.
Wolfhound (6x6)	101	Force Protection Inc	Heavy tactical support (goods)	US	NP Aerospace in the UK integrating electronics and the British armour package.
Jackals	455	Supacat Ltd with Babcock	Reconnaissance, rapid assault and fire support; used for convoy protection	UK	The Jackal or Mobility Weapon-Mounted Installation Kit (MWMIK) is a family of vehicles designed and developed by Supacat Ltd at its factory in Devon for use by the British Army. It involved the modification of existing commercially available platforms.
Coyote (6x6)	76	Supacat Ltd with Babcock	Artillery tractor and goods transport	UK	A large version of the Jackal.
Husky (4x4)	333	Navistar	Light utility	US	The Husky is a variant of the US-built MXT-MVA modified to satisfy the UK MoD's Tactical Support Vehicle (TSV) requirements for the British Army.

Name	Number	Manufacturer	Role	Country	Description
Snatch Vixen (4x4)	132	Land Rover	Light protected patrol	UK	Between 2008 and 2010, Land Rover upgraded the standard Snatch used in Afghanistan to the 'Vixen' type, which possesses more power and provides better protection.
Vector (6x6)	198	Pinzgauer/ BAE Systems	Light cross-country patrol	UK	BAE Systems opted to develop and modify this vehicle in its plants in South Africa.
Warthog (tracked)	115	Singapore Technologies Kinetics with DSTA	Light tracked ambulance, command, troop transport, vehicle recovery	Singapore	The Warthog is a modified and better-protected version of the Singapore Army's Bronco. It is equipped with an upgraded cooling and filtration system, Bowman BCIP 5 communications, mine-blast protection and electronic counter-measures by the Thales facility in Wales.
Foxhound (4x4)	376	Force Protection Inc/Ricardo	(small) patrol	UK	The Foxhound has been specifically designed and built in the UK to protect against the threats faced by troops in Afghanistan.

Sources: Defence Industry Daily, 'Blast Hounds: Britain's Army is Keeping Their Mine-Resistant Vehicles', 12 January 2014; Defence Industry Daily, 'Days of the Jackal: Supacat's HMT Vehicles', 9 January 2014; armytechnology.com, 'Husky Tactical Support Vehicle (TSV), United Kingdom', <http://www.army-technology.com/projects/ousky-tsv/>; Thomas Harding, 'MoD spends £700m Protecting Troops in Afghanistan against Roadside Bombs', Daily Telegraph, 29 October 2008; Army Guide, 'Pinzgauer', <http://www.army-guide.com/eng/product4397.html>; British Army, 'Warthog', <http://www.army.mod.uk/equipment/23251.aspx#>, all accessed 17 July 2013.

for fluid battlefield manoeuvring and found to be unsuitable for the more static character of British operations in stabilised security environments.

In a daunting twenty-eight-week programme, from start to finish, and with the harsh Balkan winter setting a clear deadline for the system's operability, BAE Systems developed the technology from commercially available materials, tested and then deployed it. This involved organising the production of sixty system containers, sourcing all of the products to go inside them, providing interfaces to UK cryptographic devices where necessary, establishing a microwave backbone in Kosovo, interfacing into a satellite communications network and building up a UK capability hub in Whitehall.

The automated system allowed the reassignment of 260 Royal Signals Corps personnel and provided modern voice, data and facsimile links to the UK-led multinational division in Bosnia and Herzegovina composed of British, Canadian, Dutch and Czech units and British forces in Kosovo, thereby significantly increasing the commanders' operational capability on the ground.[31]

The operations in Afghanistan from 2006 also required many modifications to, and even the delivery of new, equipment as the initial optimism about the task proved misplaced. For instance, several helicopter types needed improvements to enable them to operate in hot climates at high altitudes. In both Afghanistan and Iraq, as adversaries grew more capable, vehicles needed to be up-armoured and generally given better active and passive defences.

The Development of New Equipment
Short-notice and short-duration operations do not provide time for the development of new equipment, but in Iraq and Afghanistan British forces found themselves involved in hazardous operations against dynamic and innovative adversaries that went on for much longer than had been envisaged. The result was that many UORs were approved and delivered for equipment that needed rapid development work and provided novel capabilities.

The UK sourced such development and production work from the global defence market, including better-protected vehicles such as the Mastiff and Jackal, and the Predator unmanned aerial vehicle from the US, although it did use British firms for some of the work. In some cases, the reliance on other countries' industries did cause problems, as in the case of the Mastiff. The UK had originally bought this vehicle from the US for use in Iraq, where tarmac roads were the norm. When it subsequently took the vehicle to Afghanistan because of the high level of protection it offered, the frequency of breakdown – due to the absence of tarmac roads – increased significantly, not least as far as axles were concerned. However, under US law, the priority customer for Mastiff spare parts was the US armed forces and the UK found itself having to establish separate production arrangements beyond the US for the manufacture of Mastiff spares. Indeed, generally, from 2006 until 2009, parts shortages related to UOR vehicles were associated particularly with systems procured from overseas.

A 2009 NAO report on Iraq and Afghanistan observed that the MoD had used industry on a large scale to good effect to meet a range of short-notice demands in the equipment area for the modification of in-service kit and the procurement of new capabilities.[37]

> The Department has approved £4.2 billion on Urgent Operational Requirements as at March 2009, including modifications to helicopters and aircraft, better protection for existing vehicles, early attack warning systems for bases and electronic counter-measures. While additional armour and electronic counter-measures have improved protection, together with communications equipment they increase vehicle weights and power requirements. The availability of vehicles procured or upgraded as Urgent Operational Requirements has generally met or exceeded the Department's targets, except for the Vector vehicle, whose suspension and wheel hub reliability has been poor. There have also been shortages of spares for some fleets, particularly when the vehicle has been used in a role different to

that intended, such as the Mastiff vehicle in Afghanistan. Armed Forces personnel throughout the chain of command in both theatres told us that Urgent Operational Requirement equipments had performed well overall, including those procured to enhance protected mobility.

It is important to realise the scale of the UORs that could be generated by operations in environmentally and politically difficult environments: while UOR expenditure was falling by 2008/09, it was running, even then, at around £800 million a year, while a UOR budget of £635 million was agreed with the Treasury for 2009/10. The operations in Afghanistan and Iraq generated hundreds of UORs, and at times required the commitment of more than 1,000 staff in DE&S. That the great majority of the UORs could be successfully delivered – and within months rather than years – was a function of the level of access to a capable and responsive set of businesses. As expressed in an NAO report: 'The Department has approved £4.2 billion on Urgent Operational requirements as at March 2009, including modifications to helicopters and aircraft, better protection for existing vehicles, early attack warning systems for bases and electronic counter-measures'.[33]

Variations

Not all military operations over the period under study involved a significant need to turn to industry. The British intervention in Sierra Leone in 2000 was an operation in which this was not required to a large extent. Meanwhile, the Kosovo campaign of 1999 was a much smaller and more focused operation than the 1991 campaign in the Gulf, requiring little mobilisation of defence industry as such: many of the UORs involved (almost half by value) were concerned with the provision of camp infrastructure for UK troops. Munitions, aircraft and vehicle enhancements accounted for only £34 million of the total cost of the Kosovo operation in 1999/2000.[34] Nevertheless, data provided by the MoD was a reminder of the extent to which the delivery of even a limited campaign in Kosovo relied on mobilisation of the private sector in general, as the NAO report *Kosovo: The Financial Management of Military Operations* demonstrates in Figure 1.[35]

Figure 1: Estimates of the Additional Costs of the Kosovo Operation 1998/99–2002/03.

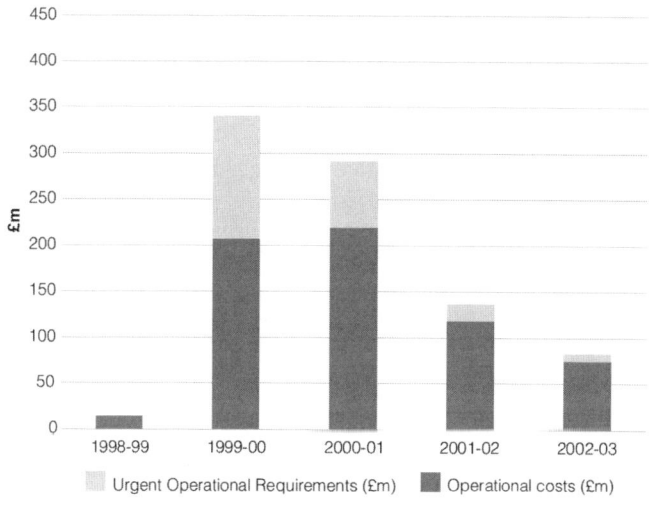

Source: NAO, *'Kosovo: The Financial Management of Military Operations, Report by the Comptroller and Auditor General'*, HC 530 (London: The Stationery Office, June 2000), p. 23.

Consequently, even operations that are modest in nature would seem to require industrial and commercial engagement and support if they are to be conducted effectively. This is not surprising as defence doctrine in the UK is, after all, built around the mobilisation of national resources to meet national objectives.

Contractor Support to Operations
In addition to the role played by industry outside or close to the actual theatre of operations, contractor support to operations (CSO) has become an essential component of the UK's ability to sustain its military operations on the ground.[36] As outlined above, contractors deployed in theatre played an important role during Operation *Desert Storm* in 1991 in the support, maintenance and modification of British military equipment, including the Warrior and the Challenger 1, while BAE Systems produced military aircraft for the Royal Saudi Air Force. Since the First Gulf War, the role of contractors deployed in theatre has evolved substantially. The final MoD report on operations in Iraq (2003) states, with regard to the task of force generation, that: 'The very considerable success in delivering equipment against very demanding time and performance criteria owed much to the excellent contribution of contractors in the face of relatively late changes to the force composition and constraints on early consultation with industry'.[37]

The involvement of contractors in the sustainment of defence efforts has grown in recent years and is now significant. Andrew Higginson estimates that British expenditure on CSO in 2010 was around £2.6 billion.[38] The net additional cost of UK operations in Afghanistan (£3.8 billion) and Iraq (£95 million) totalled to around £3.9 billion in the fiscal year 2010/11,[39] suggesting by best estimate that CSO expenditure accounted for at least 60 per cent of the UK's overseas operational defence sustainment effort in 2010. By way of comparison, British CSO expenditure in 1982 for the Falklands War is statistically insignificant.

Further, on Operation *Herrick*, the number of companies supporting the UK in theatre rose from twenty-two (with 2,030 employees) in July 2008, to sixty-seven (with 4,867 employees) in July 2010.[40] In Afghanistan, UK contractors comprise around 40 per cent of the MoD's total workforce, according to figures released by the Office of the US Deputy Assistant Secretary of Defense (Program Support).[41]

At present, contractors provide essentially two key functions to the British armed forces on operations: equipment support and people support. With regard to the former, contractors provide for the servicing, maintenance and repair of items required for operational capability in theatre. People support, meanwhile, includes the provision of shelter, food and water, personal-hygiene facilities, laundry services, mail and other communication services, as well as medical support, recreation and entertainment facilities for troops within their bases. So far, the UK has been very reluctant to contract companies to provide services directly related to operational effect, including interrogation, intelligence analysis, the operation of military equipment and offensive military operations. Of course, this policy stance, being dependent upon political preferences, attitudes and decision-making, may change in the future, leading to a further expanded use of armed contractors.[42]

As an illustration of equipment support to operations, consider General Dynamics and the Defence Support Group (DSG). In March 2011, General Dynamics was awarded a £2 million contract by the MoD to support the newly elaborated Equipment Sustainability System (ESS), run by the DSG at Camp Bastion in Afghanistan.[43] The ESS delivers an in-theatre equipment regeneration capability that would otherwise only be achievable by sending the equipment back to the UK, thus reducing the costs and turnaround time required to regenerate vital front-line equipment. The DSG, whose team grew incrementally from an initial twenty-nine staff members in October 2009 to over 100 in May 2011, was awarded main-contractor status to operate the ESS until 2013.[44]

In the field of people support, the British arm of the US-based global engineering, construction and service company KBR is one of the largest single providers of support services to British forces. From 2004 to 2012, it ran the Contractor Logistics contract – a non-exclusive enabling contract to secure a wide range of logistical-support services for operations and exercises when the military requires them. It then won its successor – the Operational Support Capability Contract – in early 2012.[45]

Through the MoD's Afghanistan Soft Multi Activity Contract,[46] KBR also provides life-support and healthcare services, as well as facilities management, infrastructure support and hardened accommodation in Afghanistan. The company delivers a comprehensive suite of services such as medical support (including nursing and medical supplies), sustenance, laundry and environmental services, and it also provides British troops with essential services including running water, bottling plants and catering. As the holder of the Temporary Deployable Accommodation contract,[47] and as the Prime Contract Infrastructure Support Provider (ISP) in Afghanistan since November 2006,[48] KBR was also responsible for the construction of shelters and other buildings. At the end of 2011, KBR successfully bid again for the ISP contract.[49]

Another example of people support to operations provided by industry is Purple Foodservice Solutions, a company composed of Vestey Foods UK and Supreme Foodservice Solutions. Since October 2006, the company has been the prime contractor for the MoD's Worldwide Food Supply and Operational Rations Contract, and also operates the overseas depot locations in Afghanistan. The contract initially ran until September 2013 with a value for the company of £150 million in the first year,[50] and has since been extended by two years to September 2015.[51]

The MoD has developed a range of measures to manage contractors, both before they deploy into theatre and during operations. Key elements include the generation of a CSO policy and legal framework, including Joint Service Publication 567, and incorporating sponsored reserve, contractors on deployed operations (CONDO) and private military and security companies' policies, MoD Defence Standard 05-129 outlining CONDO processes and requirements, and MoD Defence Condition 697.[52]

Furthermore, in 2012–13 the MoD adopted the US Synchronized Predeployment and Operational Tracker system[53] to improve tracking of UK contractors both before deployment and when deployed, linking contractor personnel to the contracts they support, thus allowing ready-use data on the contractor landscape in terms of locations, numbers, and the tasks or contracts they support.[54]

Despite these improvements, however, the UK's CSO experience in Iraq and Afghanistan, although positive overall, suggests that the British government and armed forces must continue to improve their CSO contracting, management and oversight capabilities. In particular, there still appear to be too few experienced acquisition personnel with in-depth knowledge of the CSO commercial base to manage the funds and workload entailed by such significant CSO demands.

More fundamentally, the UK may well require a defence industrial policy that acknowledges the service sector as a core component of the defence industrial base, and is capable of addressing the sector's specific challenges, not only on overseas operations but also domestically.

Conclusion

This chapter has analysed the different ways in which the private sector can support military operations, and illustrated how such mechanisms were put into practice by the UK following the end of the Cold War. While the cases cited are not comprehensive and their specific impact cannot be easily assessed, an audit of the conflicts in which UK forces have been involved since 1990 suggests that the UK derived significant benefit from access to the defence industrial capabilities available in the country. The placing of significant numbers of UORs has become the norm in the preparation for and conduct of major operations – even when of short-duration. Indeed, the capacity to place such contracts has become a formal part of defence planning, not least in the area of ammunition and missiles, where the Portfolio Management Agreement in the Team Complex Weapons domain, for example, has a central place in the way capability is delivered.

Yet industry has not shown indefinite capability and flexibility. For instance, it is understood that, during Operation *Ellamy*, the MoD would have had uses for even more than the additional Brimstone missiles that MBDA and its partners were able to generate. It is also obviously not being claimed that British operations would have been unsuccessful or have ended in disaster without access to the industrial sector in the UK: as was noted earlier, there is no access to the counterfactual, and UK forces are prepared specifically to be able to generate workarounds in the face of unexpected problems. Yet there is no escape from the fundamental point that countries with assured access to a capable and flexible supply chain are better placed to conduct military operations than states without such access.

In general, support in the equipment domain for defence operations has been a success story for British defence firms: most UORs (based on both volume and contract value) were probably placed with British companies (although this information is not known to have been collected or published by government), and across the board deliveries were on time and to the specified performance. Almost inevitably, when decisions are taken quickly, there are errors, but overall the MoD and industry worked well together. As outlined above, a similar assessment can be made with regard to the CSO domain. An excerpt from the November 2007 NAO report 'Performance of the Ministry of Defence 2006–07' reflected an assumption that the MoD would have access to an agile and responsive industry: 'The Department is funded to prepare forces for operations, receiving additional resources for actual operations. Similarly, the Urgent Operational Requirements process can deliver additional equipment and specific training can be provided through pre-deployment packages.'[55]

Given that an important lesson of the past twenty-three years has been to highlight the 'catch-22' dimension of future military operations – namely that the only thing about which there can be confidence going forward is that the next operation will include a significant element of surprise, involving unexpected adversaries with unique attributes, a novel geographic environment or an unforeseen mission – the practice of turning to industry to contribute to the success of a mission is unlikely to disappear. This assessment also holds true for the in-theatre support of contractors to British operations, given the apparent political and societal demand for a light military footprint on operations and the need for specialist technological capabilities and niche skills which the armed forces struggle to generate in the time and with the resources available.

Moreover, the cost of holding 'just-in-case' stocks and capability elements at a time when defence budgets are under increasing pressure means that the MoD is likely to accept more risks as far as relying on last-minute help from industry is concerned. Finally, the practice of contracting for availability as far as major platforms – rather than the supply of spare parts – is concerned, implies that more contractors will become involved in the support of equipment on deployed operations than has been the case in the past. Indeed, in many ways, this method of contracting is a dominant thread across the government–defence industrial relationship since the late 1990s.

The experiences of the past two decades have clearly been reflected in the development of British policy. The 2002 Defence Industrial Policy document sent a signal of recognition of the importance of the industrial element in terms of defence capability and not just in terms of employment and the economy. Its chief innovation could be seen as an acceptance of the inevitable, given the investment in British defence facilities by foreign-owned firms that successive governments had allowed: the policy stated that firms which added significant value in the UK would be treated as British.

The Defence Industrial Strategy of 2005 took things much further, spelling out the sectors in which the UK needed to maintain industrial development, production and support capability if it were to achieve its ambition of remaining (or rather becoming) a major military player with sovereign control over the use of its armed forces.

Yet the coalition government that came to power in 2010 arrived with a reluctance to grant special protected-and-supported status to any part of the economy, and also concluded that it could not afford the continued implementation of the 2005 Defence Industrial Strategy.

However, it was also unwilling to acknowledge that British military freedom would have to be constrained by a reliance on externally supplying companies and governments. The result was the *Security Through Technology* White Paper, which included a number of messages which were difficult to reconcile[56] – including a default position of buying off-the-shelf from world markets, a desire to promote UK defence exports, and a recognition of the importance of freedom of action in the defence domain:[57]

> 53. Freedom of action is the ability to determine our internal and external affairs and act in the country's interests free from intervention by other states or entities, in accordance with our legal obligations. This freedom is the essence of national sovereignty. It is also essential to be able to use a capability effectively …
>
> 54. For national security capabilities in general, freedom of action rests on the assurance that we will be able to use them – or continue to use them – whenever we need to; and that when we do so, they will perform as we require. In the field of defence, freedom of action includes being able to conduct combat operations at a time and place of our choosing.

With regard to the importance of contractors on deployed operations, the White Paper states:[58]

> 45. In recent years, industry has increased its role in providing logistics and service support to our Armed Forces on operations. This is known as Contractor Support to Operations (CSO) and has been important in Afghanistan and Libya. We expect to see an active and relatively

increasing role for industry in supporting our Armed Forces in the future.

To its credit, the government was ready to acknowledge the multidimensional contribution made by twenty companies, plus their sub-contractors, to the success of the campaign against the Qadhafi regime. The minister for defence equipment, support and technology wrote to the chief executives concerned thanking them 'for the additional efforts they had made to meet the MoD's requirements during the operation'. To give just a number of examples, it was recognised that 'Ultra Electronics provided additional training and resources at very short notice to keep Litening III pods fully supported in theatre', while 'EADS won praise for providing vital secure communications facilities for RAF Typhoons'.[59]

This chapter cannot point to an inexpensive set of techniques through which the government can maintain a wide range of defence industrial capabilities in the UK at low risk. However, it has presented evidence underlying the view that a state cannot claim, in the modern age, to be a major military power without having assured access to a flexible and capable source of industrial supply. It is clear that the major campaigns of the era since the end of the Cold War have not been 'come as you are' wars conducted with troops, equipment and support that was already in place. The US, whose government pays constant attention to its defence industrial base, is well aware of these considerations, having mobilised its private sector to support operations on a larger scale than even the UK, as emphasised in the quotation from President Obama at the start of the chapter.

This is not a message that the current UK government is keen to promote, preferring to stress the relative size of the UK defence budget, the quality of its uniformed personnel and the inventory of major items as a sign of the UK's military significance.[60] It appears not to wish to draw attention to either the number of these systems that are on a virtual leash that could be tugged at any time by political authorities elsewhere, or to the areas of capability – including satellite surveillance – in which the UK has to rely on the US. Yet foreign governments contemplating the significance of the UK in world affairs will surely be conscious of the limits on UK freedom of action and capabilities.

Looking ahead, the British approach to the provision of industrial support in the area of equipment for military operations will be based on a blend of emotional, financial and risk drivers. A key aspect of this approach concerns the level of psychological comfort of individuals and groups with reliance and dependence on the US, as opposed to the apparent alternative of interdependence with other European countries. As noted at the beginning of the chapter, any consideration of British equipment co-operation and collaborative activities should take account of how such arrangements would work in the event of deployed military operations. In addition, the issue of the extent to which the UK should have nationally controlled defence industrial resources will not go away, and it is also within the bounds of possibility that the British ambition to play a significant military role on the international stage may diminish significantly. None of this lies within any technical management domain but is the very lifeblood of defence policy and doctrine.

CONCLUSION

Michael Clarke

THROUGHOUT the Cold War, the UK maintained a determinedly defensive posture to meet the threat it perceived from the Soviet bloc. Europe was the most militarised region on the planet and the UK prepared a defensive strategy to withstand, collectively, a major onslaught from the Warsaw Pact towards the British homeland. Everything else UK forces did during the Cold War – in Malaya, Kenya, Cyprus, Borneo, Oman and even the Falklands – was essentially peripheral to the central task of using military means to defend liberal democracy, whilst relying on the passage of time and the global marketplace to promote these values. It was a practical and successful implementation of real 'containment' as its architects had intended in the late 1940s. The UK withdrawal from east of Suez, in the 1970s, increased this solid defensive commitment to the Atlantic and European theatres.

Once the Cold War was over, however, UK policy swung effortlessly and only half-consciously into a different posture. Though policy-makers were responding to the pressures of immediate crises, the practical effect was that the UK entered into campaigns where it used the military increasingly to facilitate and promote democracy, sometimes precisely because it was not prepared to let time and the market do their work messily and over too long a period. Free from the prospects of having to plan for a major war to protect the British homeland and its near neighbours, UK policy moved from an essentially defensive posture to an essentially offensive one. The period since 1990 has seen 'expeditionary operations', 'strategic raiding', and 'operations other than war' from the Gulf to the Balkans, from West Africa to Central Asia and back again to North Africa. These operations have been undertaken on the basis of a range of world-order and humanitarian motives that have all been regarded as in the UK's own national interests as a significant power that stands to do well in a globalised, free-trade world still dominated by the United States. This seemed to be in tune with the onward march of liberal market forces and a widespread desire around the world in the 1990s to embrace something like Western democracy. Though the switch from military defence to military offence was highly significant, it seemed natural enough at the time to want to protect innocent people, confront petty tyrants and prevent disorder and chaos on emerging states' roads to democracy and economic development.

It was also completely in tune with US thinking; a factor which, in itself, gave this new orientation a strong flavour of national interest in the UK. To stay close to the US in global security affairs as it contemplated the twenty-first century was axiomatic to the British policy establishment and supported, too, by the major trends of British public opinion. President George H W Bush spoke of a 'new world order' emerging from the Gulf War in 1991 and though that aspiration was quickly dropped, President George W Bush, staunch Republican though he was, was positively Wilsonian in his 2001 view that the active promotion of liberal democracy across the world constituted the best and most practical investment in peace and prosperity.

The chapters by Michael Codner, Malcolm Chalmers, Joel Faulkner Rogers and Jonathan Eyal trace this evolution that was at once dramatic yet also seemed to policy-makers like a form of continuity. It certainly represented continuity of ends in ideological terms, but it was a new expression of means in terms of the way the military was used to achieve this ideological purpose. Tony Blair's famous

Chicago speech of 1999, in which he defined a concept of liberal interventionism, was an eloquent expression of these converging strands of thought. The speech was given in the US and paralleled thinking on that side of the Atlantic; it expressed confidence in the use of the military instrument for just and honourable purposes; it was consistent with emerging doctrine within the United Nations that powerful states had a 'responsibility to protect' those in danger, even from their own governments; and it was consistent with a bullish mood in British public opinion that had seen military forces act with professionalism and success both in war in the Gulf and in promoting peace in the Balkans.

In the event, the speech was also the high watermark of this approach. All of this book's contributors share the view that 2001 marked a turning point in the story. Before the 9/11 attacks, the international environment was favourable to the sort of collective expeditionary operations the US was keen to lead, or at least participate in, to uphold or promote Western values. After 9/11, and particularly after 2002, US leadership in Afghanistan and Iraq became increasingly inconsistent and at times reckless, and has partly created an international environment where the two largest and longest military commitments have changed the conditions and expectations for success in such assertive, confident operations.

As the UK approaches the end of its Afghanistan combat commitment, and the US president asserts that 'a decade of war is ending', both the policy establishment and public opinion in the UK are in a subdued mood as the country contemplates future security and its next defence review. Policy choices should not be based on the last five years of an electoral cycle, whether good or bad, any more than they should hark back to previous generations. But a clear view of the experience of the last twenty-five years to establish mid- to long-term trends should be the bedrock of the important policy decisions that must now be made.

As such, it might be asked how the balance sheet looks across the military history that Michael Codner outlines in Chapters I and II.

The Balance of Consequences and the Costs

On the positive side of the equation, this analysis judges that the military achieved successful strategic outcomes in six of the ten cases assessed, though the less than successful cases include the two biggest operations in the latter stages of the Iraq and Afghanistan campaigns. Overall, this is regarded as a 'six-out-of-ten' scorecard, with the smaller successes weighed against the fewer, but larger, relative failures.

Over this time, UK forces certainly adapted to new conditions. It would be very odd if they had not over two decades of constant operations. But as Robert Fry's chapter makes clear, that adaptation was neither agile nor particularly smooth, and though the UK's military instrument was serving a relatively consistent political grand strategy – the continuity of ideological objectives – it underestimated the political and operational stresses of adopting more offensive military means. Campaign planning, particularly in the early phases of the 2006 Afghanistan operation, was inadequate and took some time to improve. This was exacerbated, Fry stresses, by the fact that in both Afghanistan and the second phase of the Iraq operation, the UK's military was not actually conducting campaigns so much as a series of extensive tactical engagements. By contrast, in the no-fly zones over Iraq and in operations in Bosnia, Sierra Leone and Libya, the UK conducted – or contributed to – the planning and execution of major military campaigns.

In the later stages of Iraq and Afghanistan, however, it did not. In these larger operations, US commanders orchestrated vigorous military campaigns with access to considerable resources, while UK commanders strove to maintain a distinctive British identity in their essentially tactical operations, albeit with a 'whole-of-government' approach. In a sense, the UK tried to take the hard-won lessons of operations in the Balkans and Sierra Leone, particularly the value of integrating all of the instruments of government – military, intelligence, foreign aid and civilian co-ordination – and apply them as a UK campaign plan in southern Iraq and Helmand when, in reality, the UK was not in a position to direct a genuine campaign in either of those theatres. Nor did the UK prove able to maintain clarity of essential objectives in the later stages of Iraq or Afghanistan, when a 'whole-of-government' approach eventually came to hinder the unity of purpose. For all the tactical success the military achieved, it was difficult to translate its efforts into the intended strategic outcomes without influence at the political centre in the capital, and without genuine strategic coherence in the theatre of operations itself.

Nevertheless, UK military forces have derived the benefits of operational expertise and the rapid technological evolution that goes with continuous engagements. A generation of senior officers and chiefs with both combat and combat-command experience have moved up through the system and are now moving into senior posts. Some of the best military technologies have been rushed into battle theatres and integrated into operations. The military must now rebalance itself after a decade of ground-centric counter-insurgency operations, but has a valuable legacy upon which to draw, for instance, in state-of-the-art command-and-control systems and the C4ISTAR technologies and experience to use them effectively in a range of circumstances.

Over this period, the armed forces and defence establishment also enjoyed a good and evolving relationship with the defence industry, which proved able to deliver military equipment very efficiently to operations. As the chapter by Trevor Taylor, John Louth and Henrik Heidenkamp demonstrates, accelerated and surged production occurred in some cases to meet military needs; deployed equipment was frequently modified while in-theatre; new equipment was developed and produced; and contractor support to operations grew exponentially throughout the two decades – to the point where it would now be difficult for UK forces to fight effectively without a high degree of contractor support. The system of urgent operational requirements – whereby systems or components could rapidly be brought straight into the combat area – generally worked well in all operations and benefited UK defence firms more than others. The evolution of the relationship between the defence industry and the military leaves many difficult questions to be addressed, concerning how defence-equipment procurement will be organised for the future; how the government should react to the intrinsically high levels of contractor support now evident in operations; and, not least, the government's attitude in defining strategic defence-industry elements that should be maintained as national assets as opposed, simply, to accepting greater reliance on the international market. These are difficult issues that have now become critical with the squeeze on defence budgets. But one of the reasons they are now critical is that two decades of continuous operations have taken the UK further than any of its partner countries down the road of military and industrial co-operation and integration. The general success of these relationships, forged in the heat and urgency of operations, has now to be normalised in the different circumstances of planning for longer-term contingencies, more than short-term operations. Importantly, this must take place amidst a looming reorientation in defence thinking about how much sophisticated high-tech equipment the armed forces can now afford to maintain effectively.

On the domestic security scene, the experiences of Bosnia served to radicalise a small number of British nationals who later turned to terrorism, though mainstream violent jihadism in the UK has deeper roots. There is no longer any serious disagreement over the fact that the UK's active involvement in the Iraq War, in particular, served to channel and increase those domestic sources of radicalisation. The government's close association with the policies of the Bush administration and its conception of a War on Terror may have helped, creating, as Sir David Omand observes, among some of the UK's Muslims 'a sense of an inevitable conflict between the West and the world of Islam'. Nevertheless, during the years in which the UK was fighting to defend a Muslim community in Bosnia and Kosovo, and then becoming engaged in counter-insurgency in two large Muslim countries in Iraq and Afghanistan, the terror threat in the UK was largely contained. If the UK's foreign and security policies created some deep disquiet among its Muslim citizens which translated into a higher incidence of jihadist terrorism, the security services proved up to the challenge. Indeed, despite the channelling of radicalisation motives, there is no evidence that the domestic security scene was decisively affected by the UK's participation in these conflicts, though, of course, the fact that UK troops were operating in Muslim countries was always cited by terrorist and support organisations in the UK as justification for their actions.

During these years, the armed forces took on a better defined role in the increasingly integrated picture of national security and resilience on the domestic front. The army, in particular, had learned from its mistakes in Northern Ireland and greatly improved its provision of military aid to the civil power, and to the community more widely. The post-2001 years, as Omand points out, were marked by a more coherent approach across government, and among the security agencies, police and emergency services, in dealing with domestic contingencies, from natural hazards to the threat of extensive terror attacks on the homeland. The armed forces played a very specific role in this, offering specialist expertise in relation to the prospect of chemical, biological or radiological terrorism and engaging in intelligence co-operation and training missions overseas as part of the government's domestic counter-terrorism strategy, CONTEST.

The analysis of the costs of the UK's foreign operations in the chapter by Malcolm Chalmers indicates that the material costs (excluding spending on veteran care) can be calculated as somewhere between roughly £35 billion and £42 billion (at 2012/13 prices) for all ten operations. The lower figure represents the officially reported net additional costs for the ten operations. Other writers concerned about the true costs of Afghanistan have tried, in addition, to calculate the material cost of deaths and injuries in subsequent compensation payments and the commitment to long-term health care and support, though not all of these costs would be borne by government. On this basis, it is estimated that if these more extensive calculations were applied to all of the cases analysed here the material costs of operations between 1990 and 2013 would amount to the upper figure of £42 billion. This range of costs equates to between 5 and 6 per cent against the total of average annual defence budgets over the period. Some 84 per cent of the net additional cost (£29 billion out of £35 billion) was accounted for by the Iraq and the post-2006 Afghanistan operations alone. If the material costs seem generally low in both absolute and relative terms, other factors should also be considered. Such calculations take no account of opportunity costs – including what else the armed forces might have been doing, how many might have remained in service, and what reorganisations or economies did not take place because of the drumbeat of continuous operations. Levels of veterans' care, historically low in the UK, might also become much higher depending on the public mood, and could add greatly to the eventual net additional cost figures.

The contrast with US levels of military commitment is also notable. The UK's population is just over 20 per cent of the total in the US, but the UK only deploys 14 per cent of the number of regular forces that the US does, and it has spent only 3.5 per cent in hard cash on Iraq and Afghanistan, as compared with US expenditure. It has incurred less than 10 per cent of the number of fatalities suffered by the US in both operations and is liable for only 0.5 per cent of the total of the approximately £600 billion that the US will spend on care, veterans and future liabilities. These discrepancies suggest that what looks like a significant military commitment to the UK may seem, in material terms, relatively trivial in the US. As Malcolm Chalmers notes, 'given this disparity in the resources expended, it is remarkable that the UK has managed to exercise the degree of influence that it has done on the course of events'. By implication, this influence should not be taken for granted and the idea of an unequal but somehow natural military partnership between the US and the UK cannot merely be assumed if UK forces, and levels of political commitment to their use, remain as divergent from US practice. Alternatively, on the basis of the same evidence, it might be argued that the effect of the military partnership on the UK's relations with the US has been overestimated, and perhaps other factors, such as permanent membership of the UN Security Council, or the general standing of the UK in the world could be relatively more significant.

The broad picture since 1990 describes a pretty good record of military success, which has brought some of the attendant advantages of being engaged in constant operations (and at low relative cost, at least in cash terms). It is important also to acknowledge that these smaller, successful operations had the effect of stabilising south eastern Europe at a critical time and played an important part in bolstering the rules and values of international relations in the new Europe. Given the enormity of the shift that the ending of the Cold War represented, the consequences for Europe and for the principles of legitimacy in international relations might have been much worse were it not for such military interventions. And that does not count the very successful preventative action in Macedonia in 2001 which almost certainly forestalled another Balkan conflict at a critical time.

Nevertheless, it should be asked why the two biggest operations – the second phases in Iraq and Afghanistan – cast such a shadow over the UK's record as a whole. The analysis here suggests that this cannot merely be explained by a journalistic concentration on recent events at the expense of perspective, nor by a swing in British public opinion when these operations became difficult. Something more serious than a failure of public relations was involved in the second phases of Iraq and Afghanistan, though certainly the image of these wars has been an interesting factor. Indeed, public opinion was more robust than the politicians about military operations in the Balkans, but less robust than the politicians when it came to post-2004 operations both in Iraq and Afghanistan. By 2009, public opinion had become a dominant constraint on politico-military ambitions.

Nevertheless, the judgement here is that the armed forces were militarily and strategically successful in smaller operations prior to 2001; militarily successful in the first phases of the Iraq and Afghanistan operations; and then only tactically successful in the latter stages of those conflicts, when there was an increasing mismatch with both the essential political objectives, and the US as the key ally and campaign leader.

What had gone wrong? We could point to failures within the armed forces to adapt quickly enough to rapidly changing conditions; to inadequacies in post-Cold War command structures; to some genuinely poor campaign planning, or to the ever-diminishing military resources which meant that UK forces were always doing what they could with relatively small numbers of troops and equipment. These factors are all discussed in this volume. But there are two deeper reasons that cannot be ignored. One is the conspiracy of optimism that produced both a political and a military hubris that gave UK forces too much to do with too few resources. The inherent abilities of the forces, it was assumed, would make a decisive difference in large operational theatres; their sophisticated equipment and their skill in using it would tell; the manoeuvrist principles of the army would show how effective small numbers of warriors could be in large areas; and the legacies of the imperial experience would come into their own in this post-Cold War world of fragmented conflicts. All these implicit assumptions were made by politicians and military commanders alike. And they could prove true in the first flush of operations. The British were, and are still, good at 'kicking the door in' in short, sharp wars. These assumptions could also prove true in more sustained operations in their aftermath, as long as the environment was, or quickly became, more benign as normality returned (as in Bosnia and Kosovo). But they proved not to be true in the aftermath of wars where the operating conditions were not benign, and were deteriorating. In these cases, both in Iraq and Afghanistan, the British proved to have bitten off more than they could sustainably chew over a long, post-conflict period.

As is pointed out in Chapter VIII, the motives behind UK operations in this period were always heavily influenced by a strong desire to stay close to the US politically and to operate with it militarily where appropriate. In Chapter III, Malcolm Chalmers analyses how this took the UK's political objectives from acting as a 'force for good' where possible and operating within an alliance to help maintain 'world order', to the far more ambitious goal of 'state-building' in conditions that were not benign, and with limitations on resources and on the patience of domestic public opinion in the absence of clear results. The UK's most successful interventions were in cases in which the strategic objectives were clear but limited. The least successful were in cases where the strategic objectives were unclear or implied radical aims which became unachievable. Yet there seemed to be no appreciation in political or military circles of how different these various objectives were and how much strain they would put on available military resources. It was as if this was all a continuous trend from the 1990s that progressively built on experience and would show how good the UK's armed forces really were. Politicians asked for too much, without being clear in their own minds of the implications, and the military thought it could deliver this within an envelope of resources that would be unrealistic if anything went seriously wrong. Political leaders are correct when they assert that they never turned down any specific requests from the military for more resources; the military accepted the resource limitations from the start and did not ask for what would have been regarded as unrealistic in that context. Both were complicit in a conspiracy of optimism and hubris over what could be achieved.

This was reinforced by the second major reason these operations have cast such a shadow over the full record. It is easy to underestimate the momentum that multinational frameworks impose on national operations. The UK has long made it clear that, in most circumstances, it expects to act in major operations as part of a multinational coalition, and it certainly does not expect to enter into a major war except as an ally of the US. This is a reasonable position to take, but many observers have not given sufficient weight to the limitations this imposes on the ability of national leaders to adjust or review their strategies. Once a decision to commit to a foreign multinational operation is made, the realistic options for defence planners immediately narrow, and the cost of any strategic reorientation increases greatly. It is not that alliance members cannot change their minds or decide to do things very differently, and there are cases in Iraq and Afghanistan – no less than in the Balkans and North Africa – where this did happen. But the political costs and the implications for other allies of such changes tend to seem prohibitive to a country like the UK, which casts itself as a resolute military power and a staunch and reliable ally. So changes and adjustment become essentially tactical, rather than strategic, in a difficult multinational operation. Where the strategically unrealistic objective of 'state-building' in a less-than-benign environment was endorsed as a multinational NATO operation, UK policy-makers found themselves effectively locked into a commitment. Whereas in previous post-colonial operations the British had a great deal of influence with the political centre of the countries in which they were operating – that is, the government and leaders that they were supporting – and could generally choose to hand over control when they were confident the results would be satisfactory, in Iraq and Afghanistan they were reduced to a 'cope-and-hope' scenario in which the handover of control was neither complete nor predictable.

Allowing for the disappointments involved in the second phases of Iraq and Afghanistan, however, it is unlikely that we have seen the last of UK expeditionary operations in the present era. The source of strategic continuity is still present for the UK: it has a clear interest in defending Western values in a world where they are not universally supported; observance of the rules of the international system continues to be very much in the national interest of the UK as a globalised trading nation; and the UK's relationship with the US will remain its key security relationship for the foreseeable future.

The armed forces are in a phase of cuts and retrenchment, and if they need a break to reorganise they are still far from on their knees. The military is available to be used and is prepared to act. If we have seen the limitations on action in the contemporary world we have also seen the costs of inaction in Rwanda, Darfur and Syria, and we have seen how delayed action in the Balkans prior to 1995 made action, when it came, all the more difficult and expensive. And we see that our own neighbourhood in Europe, the Mediterranean and North Africa is less benign and stable than has long been assumed, and that the ripple effects of major geostrategic changes in the Middle East have yet to be fully felt in Europe. Indeed, the UK may witness a mirror image of the last ten years in the next three or four, with more immediate and direct calls for military deployments around its own region to perform a range of tasks, while both military and political leaders will be more cautious in deciding to commit. They know that the first decision is the most important, and may be more reluctant to take it than was the case a decade ago.

When military power is really required, nothing else will do. But in the last two decades it has been less than clear how the British military instrument should most effectively be used in a disordered world and how this should be tied to essential strategic objectives. If the UK's own region is beginning to feel less benign for a new generation of policy-makers, it is important that the modern utility, as well as the limitations, of hard military power are understood more precisely. In the future, policy-makers may not have as much discretion over whether or not to reach for the military instrument and what resources to put behind it as they have enjoyed since 1991.

NOTES AND REFERENCES

Adrian L Johnson, 'Introduction', pp. 1–12.
1. International Monetary Fund, *World Economic Outlook: Transitions and Tensions* (Washington, DC: IMF, 2013).
2. OECD aid statistics, <http://www.oecd.org/dac/stats/>, accessed 9 February 2014.
3. SIPRI Military Expenditure Databse, <http://www.sipri.org/research/armaments/milex/milex_database>, accessed 27 February 2014. All figures are in 2012 dollars.
4. Gideon Rachman, 'Disarmed Europe will Face the World Alone', *Financial Times*, 18 February 2013.
5. NATO, 'Financial and Economic Data Relating to NATO Defence', press communique, <http://www.nato.int/nato_static/assets/pdf/pdf_topics/20140224_140224-PR2014-028-Defence-exp.pdf>, accessed 24 February 2014.
6. Rory Stewart and Gerald Knaus, *Can Intervention Work?* (London: Amnesty International, 2012), p. xviii.
7. Mats Berdal, *Building Peace after War* (Abingdon: Routledge for IISS, 2009).
8. James Fergusson, *A Million Bullets: The Real Story of the British Army in Afghanistan* (London: Bantam Press, 2008), e.g. pp. 202, 204.
9. Max Benitz, *Six Months without Sundays: The Scots Guards in Afghanistan* (London: Birlinn, 2011).
10. Frank Ledwidge, *Losing Small Wars: British Military Failure in Iraq and Afghanistan* (London: Yale University Press, 2012), p. 259.
11. David Ucko and Robert H Egnell, *Counterinsurgency in Crisis: Britain and the Challenges of Modern Warfare* (New York, NY: Columbia University Press, 2013), p. 109.

12. *Ibid.*, p. 143.
13. Ledwidge, *Losing Small Wars*, p. 11.
14. See for instance Hew Strachan, *The Direction of War: Contemporary Strategy in Historical Perspective* (Cambridge: Cambridge University Press, 2014); Patrick Porter, 'Why Britain Doesn't Do Grand Strategy', *RUSI Journal* (Vol. 155, No. 4, August 2010); Paul Newton, Paul Colley and Andrew Sharpe, 'Reclaiming the Art of British Strategic Thinking', *RUSI Journal* (Vol. 155, No. 1, February/March 2010).
15. Stewart and Knaus, *Can Intervention Work*.
16. Sherard Cowper-Coles, *Cables from Kabul: The Inside Story of the West's Afghanistan Campaign* (London: HarperPress, 2011), p. 277.
17. Sandy Gall, *War Against the Taliban: Why It All Went Wrong in Afghanistan* (London: Bloomsbury, 2013).
18. Jonathan Bailey in Jonathan Bailey, Richard Iron and Hew Strachan (eds), *British Generals in Blair's Wars* (London: Ashgate, 2013), p. 7.
19. Hew Strachan, 'Conclusion', in *British Generals in Blair's Wars*, p. 330.
20. *Ibid*, p. 337.
21. Emile Simpson, *War from the Ground Up: Twenty-first Century Combat as Politics* (London: Hurst, 2012).
22. Michael Clarke (ed.), *The Afghan Papers: Committing Britain to War in Helmand, 2005–06*, RUSI Whitehall Paper 77 (Abingdon: Routledge for RUSI, 2011), pp. 90, 93.
23. Porter, 'Why Britain Doesn't Do Grand Strategy', p. 6.
24. Newton, Colley and Sharpe, 'Reclaiming the Art of British Strategic Thinking', p. 45.
25. James De Waal, *Depending on the Right People: British Political-Military Relations, 2001–10* (London: Chatham House, 2013), p. 30.

Michael Codner, 'I. Fighting for Peace, 1991–2001', pp. 13–48.

1. See University of Ulster, Conflict Archive on the Internet, <http://cain.ulst.ac.uk/index.html>, accessed 23 January 2014.
2. FOFA was an operational concept in which conventional forces would be used to attack Warsaw Pact forces as far to the rear as range would permit, in order to reduce 'to a manageable ratio ... the number of enemy forces arriving at our General Defensive Position'. It was a concept based on the principle of the 'manoeuvrist approach' to warfare, intended to reduce the huge Warsaw Pact advantage in terms of numbers without resort to nuclear weapons. See Bernard W Rogers, 'Follow-On Forces Attack (FOFA): Myths and Realities', *NATO Review* (No. 6, December 1984).

Notes and References 337

3. The term was defined and used, for example, in a classified revision of NATO's maritime strategy, on which the author provided comment whilst serving in the UK Ministry of Defence in 1992.
4. For a considered and authoritative account of the First Gulf War, see Lawrence Freedman and Efraim Karsh, *The Gulf Conflict 1990–1991: Diplomacy and War in the New World Order* (Princeton, NJ: Princeton University Press, 1993).
5. Margaret Thatcher, *The Downing Street Years* (London: HarperCollins, 1993), excerpt available at <http://www.margaretthatcher.org/archive/displaydocument.asp?docid=110709>, accessed 6 March 2014.
6. *Ibid.*, at <http://www.margaretthatcher.org/archive/displaydocument.asp?docid=110710>, accessed 6 March 2014.
7. Freedman and Karsh, *The Gulf Conflict 1990–1991*, p. 114.
8. James A Baker, 'Memorandum for the President', 10 November 1990, <http://www.margaretthatcher.org/document/645CABEDAE9642F18B0126A12EF1AD57.pdf>, accessed 23 January 2014.
9. Freedman and Karsh, *The Gulf Conflict 1990–1991*, p. 111.
10. Douglas Hurd, *Memoirs* (London: Abacus, 2004), p. 431.
11. In this context, 'strategic influence' signifies affecting decisions made by the lead and dominant nation's military leadership with regard to the conduct of the campaign in theatre and the policy outcomes.
12. General Schwarzkopf gave a lecture at the US Naval War College shortly after the war, in which he highlighted the importance of the manoeuvrist approach to the success of the ground campaign.
13. For more on the Bosnian War, see William J Durch and James A Shear, *Fault Lines: UN Operations in the Former Yugoslavia* (New York, NY: St. Martin's Press, 1996), p. 208; UN Department of Public Information, 'Former Yugoslavia – UNPROFOR', 31 August 1996, <http://www.un.org/en/peacekeeping/missions/past/unprof_p.htm>, accessed 22 January 2014.
14. Department of Public Information, 'Former Yugoslavia – UNPROFOR'.
15. Defence Analytical Services Agency, *UK Defence Statistics Compendium 1995* (London: The Stationery Office, 1995), <http://www.dasa.mod.uk/index.php/publications/UK-defence-statistics-compendium/1995>, accessed 22 January 2014.
16. John Major, *The Autobiography* (London: HarperCollins, 1999), p. 535.
17. Author interview with Admiral Sir Ian Forbes, London, 2012. Forbes had been assistant director in the NATO/UK Directorate of the Policy

Department, responsible for policy regarding military commitments in the former Yugoslavia.
18. Major, *The Autobiography*, p. 535.
19. Effective peace-enforcement requires adequate combat power on the part of the intervening forces to dominate escalation and to use combat if necessary against a particular party or parties which will not abide by an imposed peace instruction.
20. In this section, 'Serb' refers to the self-proclaimed Republika Srpska within Bosnia and its armed forces, albeit supported by Serbia. Bosnian Muslims are also referred to as 'Bosniaks'.
21. Interview with Admiral Sir Ian Forbes.
22. Royal Air Force (RAF), 'Return to Expeditionary Warfare', in *A Short History of the Royal Air Force*, p. 297, <http://www.raf.mod.uk/rafcms/mediafiles/F21F8E7A_BD8A_55BA_43FA63F04FC5D6B4.pdf>, accessed 22 January 2014.
23. Ivo H Daalder, *Getting to Dayton: The Making of America's Bosnia Policy* (Washington, DC: Brookings, 2000).
24. RAF, 'Return to Expeditionary Warfare', p. 298.
25. Ministry of Defence (MoD), *The Strategic Defence Review*, Cm 3999 (London: The Stationery Office, 1998).
26. Tony Blair, 'Doctrine of the International Community', speech given to the Chicago Council on Global Affairs, 22 April 1999, <http://www.britishpoliticalspeech.org/speech-archive.htm?speech=279>, accessed 22 January 2014.
27. Michael Codner, 'Is It All About Clout?', *RUSI Journal* (Vol. 143, No. 1, February/March 1998).
28. MoD, 'Supporting Essay Four: Defence Diplomacy', in *The Strategic Defence Review*. See also the chapter by Malcolm Chalmers in this volume, 'VI. On the Offensive'.
29. Michael Codner, 'The Strategic Defence Review: A Good Job', *RUSI Newsbrief* (Vol. 18, No. 8, August 1998).
30. Misha Glenny, *The Balkans: Nationalism, War, and the Great Powers, 1804–1999* (London: Granta Publications, 1999).
31. See Tony Blair, speech in the House of Commons, 23 March 1999, <http://www.publications.parliament.uk/pa/cm199899/cmhansrd/vo990323/debtext/90323-06.htm>, accessed 22 January 2014.
32. RAF, 'Return to Expeditionary Warfare', pp. 301–03.
33. The terminology is significant here. It consciously eliminates any political implications from agreement about military activity on the

ground, which can typically be decisive politically in the late stages of a war. The distinction between 'military-technical' and 'military-political' would have been very significant to Russia. See Irina Isakova, 'The Kosovo Air Campaign's Impact on Russian Military Thinking', *RUSI Journal* (Vol. 145, No. 4, August/September 2000).
34. Articles V and VI of the Washington Treaty define NATO's specific function in collective defence and the geographical area to which it applies.
35. In the language of military doctrine, 'compellence' is a form of coercion whose effect is to compel the leadership of a state, faction or military unit to change a course of action already initiated; in contrast to 'deterrent coercion', which is intended to prevent an antagonist from taking a course of action in the first place.
36. UN Security Council Resolution 1264.
37. Richards was subsequently land-forces commander in Sierra Leone and Chief of the Defence Staff. See Alistair Mack, 'Intervention in East Timor From the Ground', *RUSI Journal* (Vol. 144, No. 6, December 1999), pp. 20–26. This primary source is convincing. In particular, the UK had recent experience in the former Yugoslavia of complex emergencies, and of winning assent and peace-enforcement. Australian command and forces lacked this experience at the force-commander level. British forces were also used to the challenge of working with other actors, such as non-governmental organisations, and to developing civil–military relationships in theatre.
38. Peter Cosgrove, *My Story* (Sydney: HarperCollins, 2010), p. 281.
39. This section draws on Andrew M Dorman, *Blair's Successful War: British Military Intervention in Sierra Leone* (Farnham: Ashgate, 2009) and on David Richards, 'Operation Palliser', *Journal of the Royal Artillery* (Vol. 127, No. 2, Autumn 2000).
40. Dorman, *Blair's Successful War*, p. 41, citing Peter Penfold, then-British high commissioner to Sierra Leone.
41. *Ibid.*, pp. 66–67.
42. David Richards, 'Sierra Leone: "Pregnant with Lessons"', in David Richards and Greg Mills (eds), *Victory Among People: Lessons from Countering Insurgency and Stabilising Fragile States* (London: RUSI, 2011), p. 266.
43. Richards, 'Operation Palliser'.
44. RFA *Fort George* and *Fort Austin*.
45. Richards, 'Operation Palliser'.

46. On 17 May, RUF forces attacked British forces near Lungi airport but were beaten back.
47. Richards, 'Sierra Leone', pp. 267–68. See also Lansana Gberie, *A Dirty War in West Africa: The RUF and the Destruction of Sierra Leone* (Bloomington, IN: Indiana University Press, 2006), p. 172.
48. Richards, 'Sierra Leone', p. 269.
49. Richards, 'Operation Palliser', pp. 14–15.
50. Richards, 'Sierra Leone', pp. 273–75.
51. Including troops from the Parachute Regiment, Royal Signals, Royal Artillery, Military Police, Royal Scots Dragoon Guards, Explosive Ordnance Disposal Regiment and Army Air Corps.
52. It is rather easier to withdraw from a peacekeeping mission, however wide, if it is not succeeding.
53. MoD, *Wider Peacekeeping* (London: The Stationery Office, 1995).

Michael Codner, 'II. The Two Towers, 2001–12', pp. 49–88.

1. *The Economist*, 'Preparing America for Compassionate Conservatism', 27 June 2000.
2. George W Bush, 'President Delivers "State of the Union"', speech given in Washington, DC, 28 January 2003, <http://georgewbush-whitehouse.archives.gov/news/releases/2003/01/print/20030128-19.html>, accessed 27 February 2014.
3. CBC News, 'Bin Laden Claims Responsibility for 9/11', 29 October 2004.
4. George W Bush, 'Address to a Joint Session of Congress and the American People', speech given in Washington, DC, 20 September 2001, <http://georgewbush-whitehouse.archives.gov/news/releases/2001/09/print/20010920-8.html>, accessed 27 February 2014.
5. NATO, 'The North Atlantic Treaty', 4 April 1949, <http://www.nato.int/cps/en/natolive/official_texts_17120.htm>, accessed 7 March 2014.
6. Tony Blair, *A Journey* (London: Arrow Books, 2010), p. 352.
7. *Ibid.*, p. 351.
8. The Northern Alliance – officially the United Islamic Front for the Salvation of Afghanistan – was a resistance force comprising Tajiks and other ethnic groups from the northern provinces, including some Pashtuns.
9. This British contribution was named Operation *Veritas*.
10. Blair, *A Journey*, p. 362.

11. Made up of Foreign Office and Department for International Development (DfID) staff, in addition to 100 troops.
12. These were handed over to Sweden and Norway when the UK's commitment of forces to southern Afghanistan began after 2005.
13. Granted under UN Security Council Resolution 1510.
14. NATO, 'About ISAF: History', <http://www.isaf.nato.int/history.html>, accessed 27 February 2014.
15. Ministry of Defence (MoD), *The Strategic Defence Review: A New Chapter*, Cm 5566 (London: The Stationery Office, July 2002).
16. *Ibid.*, p. 18.
17. *Ibid.*, p. 14.
18. Michael Codner, 'British Military Strategy Home and Away', *RUSI Journal* (Vol. 147, No. 2, April/May 2002).
19. These reserves would volunteer specifically for this role to ensure rapid availability.
20. MoD, *The Strategic Defence Review*, p. 24.
21. Robert Fry, 'End of the Continental Century', *RUSI Journal* (Vol. 143, No. 3, June 1998).
22. MoD, *Delivering Security in a Changing World: Defence White Paper*, Cm 6041-I (London: The Stationery Office, December 2003).
23. Discussed in Chapter I. The term later evolved to become the 'effects-based approach'.
24. House of Commons Defence Committee, *Defence White Paper 2003: Fifth Report of Session 2003–04*, HC 465-1 (London: The Stationery Office, July 2004).
25. Blair, *A Journey*, pp. 373–414.
26. *Ibid.*, p. 425.
27. James de Waal, 'Depending on the Right People: British Political-Military Relations, 2001–10', Chatham House, November 2013, p. 5.
28. *Ibid.*, p. 5.
29. In his evidence to the Chilcot Inquiry, the then-Chief of the General Staff, General Sir Mike Jackson, said that he was surprised that the ground option had not been considered earlier. The necessary troops would have been available notwithstanding domestic commitments due to the firefighter strike at the time.
30. Blair, *A Journey*, p. 411. See also De Waal, 'Depending on the Right People', p. 7, quoting MoD advice provided on 15 October 2002 to Blair, which mentions 'the negative reaction of our military personnel – particularly in the Army – if we do not provide a land contribution'.

31. The statutory minimum notice period was fourteen days. Some reservists received considerably less notice. The National Audit Office report recommended a minimum of twenty-one days' notice. National Audit Office, 'Operation TELIC – United Kingdom Military Operations in Iraq', Report of the Comptroller and Auditor General, 11 December 2003, <http://www.nao.org.uk/wp-content/uploads/2003/12/030460.pdf>, accessed 4 March 2014.
32. Michael Codner, 'High Noon for British Grand Strategy', *RUSI Journal* (Vol. 147, No. 5, 2002).
33. *BBC News*, 'Text of Donald Rumsfeld Remarks', 12 March 2003.
34. Access through Turkey by the forces of both nations had been discussed with the Turkish government. See *BBC News*, 'Turkey Ups Stakes on US Troops', 19 February 2003.
35. This label was used in a 1998 concept paper and other work by Harlan Ullman and James Wade. See Harlan Ullman and James P Wade, 'Rapid Dominance: A Force for All Seasons', *RUSI Whitehall Paper* (No. 43, 2004). Ullman since denied, at a private meeting at RUSI, that this operation had been one of 'shock and awe', in his judgement.
36. See Harlan Ullman, James P Wade et al., 'Shock & Awe: Achieving Rapid Dominance', National Defense University Institute for National Strategic Studies, October 1996, <http://www.dodccrp.org/files/Ullman_Shock.pdf>, accessed 27 February 2014.
37. Michael Codner, 'An Initial Assessment of the Combat Phase', in Jonathan Eyal (ed.), 'War in Iraq: Combat and Consequence', *RUSI Whitehall Paper* (Vol. 59, 2004).
38. *CNN*, 'Bush Makes Historic Speech Aboard Warship', 2 May 2003, <http://www.cnn.com/2003/US/05/01/bush.transcript/>, accessed 27 February 2014.
39. Michael Clarke, 'The British Intervention in Iraq: War, Peace and the Costs', in Terence McNamee (ed.), *War Without Consequences: Iraq's Insurgency and the Spectre of Strategic Defeat* (London: RUSI, 2008).
40. James T Quinlivan, 'Burden of Victory: The Painful Arithmetic of Stability Operations', *RAND Review* (Vol. 27, No. 2, Summer 2003), pp. 28–29.
41. Frank Ledwidge, *Losing Small Wars: British Military Failure in Iraq and Afghanistan* (New Haven, CT: Yale University Press, 2011), p. 41.
42. Justin Maciejewski, '"Best Effort": Operation Sinbad and the Iraq Campaign', in Jonathan Bailey, Richard Iron and Hew Strachan (eds), *British Generals in Blair's Wars* (Farnham: Ashgate, 2013).

43. Richard Iron, 'The Charge of the Knights: The British in Basra, 2008', *RUSI Journal* (Vol. 158, No. 1, February/March 2013).
44. Kilcullen observed that 'it is fair to say that in 2006 the British were defeated in the field in Southern Iraq'. Cited in *The Times*, 'US Accuses Britain over Military Failings in Afghanistan', 16 December 2008; see also Ledwidge, *Losing Small Wars*.
45. Michael Clarke, 'The Helmand Decision', in Michael Clarke (ed.), *The Afghan Papers: Committing Britain to War in Helmand, 2005–06*, RUSI Whitehall Paper 77 (Abingdon: Taylor and Francis, 2011).
46. *BBC News*, 'UK Troops Deployed to Afghanistan "to Avoid Cuts"', 13 January 2011.
47. *Press Association*, 'Afghan Envoy Apologised over Troop Redeployment Claims, Says Dannatt', 20 January 2011.
48. Robert Fry and Desmond Bowen, 'UK National Strategy and Helmand', in Clarke (ed.), *The Afghan Papers*.
49. Clarke (ed.), *The Afghan Papers*.
50. *Ibid.*, p. 17.
51. *Ibid.*, pp. 17–19.
52. *Ibid.*, p. 15.
53. See Joseph Caldwell Wylie, *Military Strategy: A General Theory of Power Control* (New Brunswick, NJ: Rutgers University Press, 1967).
54. *BBC News*, 'Afghanistan Mission Accomplished, Says Cameron', 16 December 2013.
55. MoD and Foreign Office, *The Future of the United Kingdom's Nuclear Deterrent*, Cm 6994 (London: The Stationery Office, December 2006).
56. Claire Mills, 'Update on the Trident Successor Programme – Commons Library Standard Note', House of Commons Library, 13 August 2013, <http://www.parliament.uk/business/publications/research/briefing-papers/SN06526/update-on-the-trident-successor-programme>, accessed 27 February 2014.
57. See the National Archives, MoD, 'Defence Operations: Operation Garron', <http://webarchive.nationalarchives.gov.uk/+/http://www.operations.mod.uk/garron/>, accessed 4 March 2014.
58. These include Anguilla, Bermuda, the British Virgin Islands, the Cayman Islands, Monserrat, and the Turks and Caicos Islands. There is an APT(N) ship in the Caribbean in the hurricane season, from June to November.
59. MoD, *Adaptability and Partnership: Issues for the Strategic Defence Review*, Cm 7794 (London: The Stationery Office, February 2010).

60. HM Government, *Securing Britain in an Age of Uncertainty: The Strategic Defence and Security Review*, Cm 7948 (London: The Stationery Office, October 2010).
61. Prime Minister's Office, 'UK–France Summit 2010 Declaration on Defence and Security Co-operation', 2 November 2010, <https://www.gov.uk/government/news/uk-france-summit-2010-declaration-on-defence-and-security-co-operation>, accessed 27 February 2014.
62. This section draws upon Adrian Johnson and Saqeb Mueen (eds), 'Short War, Long Shadow: The Political and Military Legacies of the 2011 Libyan Campaign', *RUSI Whitehall Report* 1-12, 2012.
63. Jonathan Eyal, 'The Responsibility to Protect: A Chance Missed', in Johnson and Mueen (eds), 'Short War, Long Shadow'.
64. A full list of UK and allied assets is available in Johnson and Mueen (eds), 'Short War, Long Shadow'.
65. Michael Codner, 'The British Military Contribution to Operations in Mali: Is This Mission Creep?', RUSI.org, 30 January 2013.
66. Michael Codner, 'Assessing a Ground Intervention in Syria', in 'Syria Crisis Briefing: A Collision Course for Intervention', RUSI, 25 July 2012; Quinlivan, 'Burden of Victory'.
67. David Kilcullen, *Counterinsurgency* (London: Hurst, 2010).
68. Ledwidge, *Losing Small Wars*.
69. The appropriate levels of 'epuration' or de-Nazification were a major concern for Allied powers in their plans for the occupation of Germany, Italy and Austria during the Second World War. Typically, decisions were taken that more junior levels of government management should be left in office.
70. Alexander Alderson, 'The British Approach to COIN and Stabilisation: A Retrospective on Developments since 2001', *RUSI Journal* (Vol. 157, No. 4, August/September 2012), pp. 62–71.
71. Holbrooke died at the end of 2010. His posting and personality were contentious, but as Cowper-Coles notes, 'He knew that the region's problems were primarily political, not military, and was working to that end. The tragedy is that his hour – the hour of negotiation – was about to dawn, and he will not be there when he is most needed.' See *BBC News*, 'Richard Holbrooke: Your Tributes', 14 December 2010.
72. This is now called the MoD Development, Concepts and Doctrine Centre.
73. Where there is commitment on the ground, the point has been made in many places that a roulement of six-month deployments in theatre is

insufficient time to build experience, and that there must be continuity in middle and senior levels of command and staffing. There is also a discrepancy in the balance between time on operations and time at home (harmony rules) among the services, particularly in the army and naval forces.

Malcolm Chalmers, 'III. The Strategic Scorecard: Six Out of Ten', pp. 89–136.

1. Jack Straw, *Last Man Standing: Memoirs of a Political Survivor* (London: Macmillan, 2012), p. 410.
2. Due to its focus on foreign interventions, this chapter does not examine whether the UK's military operations in Northern Ireland during this period contributed to strategic success, which is covered in Chapter IV.
3. For further analysis, see Jonathan Bailey, Richard Iron and Hew Strachan (eds), *British Generals in Blair's Wars* (Farnham: Ashgate, 2013).
4. Because of the focus on the ten most significant operations, the chapter does not examine separately the Iraq-related operations that took place between the 1991 and 2003 invasions (the initial support for a safe haven in the north, the two subsequent no-fly zones and the 1998 Operation *Desert Fox* air strikes).
5. Figures in 2012/13 prices.
6. This includes both the costs of Operation *Granby*, the operation to expel Iraq from Kuwait (£675 million), and £348 million of net additional spending in the Gulf between 1991 and 2003, the bulk of which was on the UK's contribution to no-fly zones over northern and southern Iraq.
7. £20.6 billion had been spent by March 2013. It is estimated that around a further £3.4 billion will be spent before March 2015.
8. Michael W Doyle and Nicholas Sambanis, *Making War and Building Peace: United Nations Peace Operations* (Princeton, NJ: Princeton University Press, 2006), p. 168.
9. For further detailed examination of this point, and in particular of the role of military advice in this judgement, see James de Waal, 'Depending on the Right People: British Political-Military Relations 2001–10', Chatham House, November 2013, pp. 4–10.
10. For a contrary case, see Alan J Kuperman, 'Lessons from Libya: How Not to Intervene', Belfer Center Policy Brief, September 2013.
11. Adrian Johnson and Saqeb Mueen (eds), 'Short War, Long Shadow: The Political and Military Legacies of the 2011 Libya Campaign', *RUSI Whitehall Report* 1-12, 2012.

12. Kuperman, 'Lessons from Libya'.
13. Nuclear Threat Initiative, 'Country Profiles: Iraq', <http://www.nti.org/country-profiles/iraq/nuclear/>, accessed 10 February 2014.
14. Management Sciences for Health, 'Afghanistan Mortality Survey Reveals Substantial Improvements in Maternal Health', 6 April 2012, <http://www.msh.org/news-events/stories/afghanistan-mortality-survey-reveals-substantial-improvements-in-maternal-health>, accessed 17 February 2014.
15. United Nations Development Programme in Afghanistan, 'Millennium Development Goal 2: Achieve Universal Primary Education', <http://www.af.undp.org/content/afghanistan/en/home/mdgoverview/overview/mdg2/>, accessed 17 February 2014.
16. *PBS Newshour*, 'The Blair Doctrine', transcript of speech by Tony Blair to the Chicago Economic Club, 22 April 1999, <http://www.pbs.org/newshour/bb/international-jan-june99-blair_doctrine4-23/>, accessed 10 February 2014.
17. Karl W Eikenberry, 'The Limits of Counterinsurgency Doctrine in Afghanistan: The Other Side of the COIN', *Foreign Affairs* (September/October 2013), pp. 68–71.
18. UN Office on Drugs and Crime, 'World Drug Report 2013', May 2013, p. x.
19. World Bank, 'Fertility Rate, Total (Births per Woman)', <http://data.worldbank.org/indicator/SP.DYN.TFRT.IN>, accessed 17 February 2014.
20. For example, as of October 2013, Iraq Body Count (<www.iraqbodycount.org>) puts the total figure for civilian deaths from coalition military action as well as criminal and paramilitary activity between 114,566 and 125,577 from March 2003 to June 2013. Its figure for violent civilian deaths in March and April 2003 is 7,413. Likewise, Barry S Levy and Victor W Sidel, 'Adverse Health Consequences of the Iraq War', *Lancet* (Vol. 381, No. 9870, 16 March 2013) conclude that at least 116,903 Iraqi non-combatants died during the eight-year period 2003–11.
21. UN High Commissioner for Refugees (UNHCR), 'UNHCR Statistical Yearbook 2007: Trends in Displacement, Protection and Solutions', December 2008, p. 68.
22. *BBC News*, 'Syria Death Toll Now Above 100,000, Says UN Chief Ban', 25 July 2013.

23. World Bank, 'Afghanistan: World Development Indicators Databank', <http://data.worldbank.org/country/afghanistan#cp_wdi>, accessed 17 February 2014.
24. UNHCR, '2014 UNHCR Country Operations Profile – Afghanistan', <http://www.unhcr.org/cgi-bin/texis/vtx/page?page=49e486eb6>, accessed 17 February 2014.
25. Cited in Thomas Ruttig, 'Some Things Got Better – How Much Got Good? A Review of 12 Years of International Intervention in Afghanistan', Afghanistan Analysts Network, 30 December 2013, <http://www.afghanistan-analysts.org/some-things-got-better-how-much-got-good-a-short-review-of-12-years-of-international-intervention-in-afghanistan>, accessed 17 February 2014.
26. World Bank, 'Afghanistan'.
27. Richard Iron, 'The Charge of the Knights: The British in Basra 2008', *RUSI Journal* (Vol. 158, No. 1, February/March 2013), pp. 54–62.
28. Theo Farrell and Antonio Giustozzi, 'The Taliban at War: Inside the Helmand Insurgency, 2004–2012', *International Affairs* (Vol. 89, No. 4, 2013), pp. 850–52.
29. Richard Norton-Taylor, 'Supreme Court MoD Ruling "Will Have Huge Impact on Military Operations"', *Guardian*, 19 June 2013.
30. IDC (Research and Documentation Centre), *The Bosnian Book of the Dead* (Sarajevo: IDC, 2013).
31. UNHCR, 2005 statistical report.

David Omand, 'IV. The Domestic Balance', pp. 137–60.

1. As former Defence Secretary Denis Healey wrote in his memoirs, 'You do not conduct an appendix operation on a man while he is moving a piano upstairs' – a remark also fitting with regard to the Iraq War, which was fought as the Strategic Defence Review was being implemented, just as the 1981 Nott Review had coincided with the Falklands campaign.
2. Specifically, MACP concerns the provision of military assistance to the civil power in its maintenance of law, order and public safety, using specialist capabilities or equipment in situations beyond the capability of the civil authorities.
3. Prime Minister Gordon Brown in an interview with British Forces Broadcasting Service, 12 July 2009.
4. Prime Minister David Cameron, 'Afghanistan and European Council: Prime Minister's Statement', speech given to the House of Commons, London, 2 July 2013, <https://www.gov.uk/government/speeches/

afghanistan-and-european-council-prime-ministers-statement>, accessed 17 January 2014.
5. HM Government, *Statement on the Defence Estimates 1967*, Cm 3203 (London: The Stationery Office, February 1967).
6. HM Government, *A Strong Britain in an Age of Uncertainty: The National Security Strategy*, Cm 7953 (London: The Stationery Office, October 2010).
7. In 1992, there were three brigades deployed (with six resident battalions deployed for two-and-a-half years and four roulement battalions serving six-month tours).
8. Operation *Demetrius*, conducted by the British Army, involved the arrest and detention on 9–10 August 1971 of 342 individuals suspected of being involved in Republican terrorism. The policy lasted until December 1975.
9. The five techniques employed – hooding, white noise, wall-standing, deprivation of sleep, and deprivation of food and drink – were subsequently prohibited by Prime Minister Edward Heath for use at any time by the British armed forces and agencies.
10. European Commission of Human Rights, 'Ireland versus the United Kingdom, 1976', *Yearbook of the European Convention on Human Rights* (Strasbourg: European Commission of Human Rights, 1976), pp. 512, 748, 788–94.
11. Later Sir Frank Cooper, permanent under-secretary of the Ministry of Defence, 1976–82. Cooper was a spitfire pilot in Italy during the Second World War, and had as his administrative officer Merlyn Rees – his secretary of state in the Northern Ireland Office who announced the 'police primacy' policy in the House of Commons on 25 March 1975.
12. A manoeuvrist approach of 'Find, Fix, Strike and Exploit' was adopted.
13. Chief of the General Staff, 'Operation Banner: An Analysis of Military Operations in Northern Ireland', Army Code 71842, July 2006, released by the Ministry of Defence (MoD) in July 2007.
14. *Ibid.*, paras 802, 805.
15. Command of MACP forces continues to rest with the military chain of command.
16. The defence and security industries, with the support of the Home Office and MoD, formed the Security and Resilience Industries Suppliers Council (RISC), which brought together the relevant trade associations, government and academics.

17. The latest version is HM Government, *CONTEST: The United Kingdom's Strategy for Countering Terrorism*, Cm 8123 (London: The Stationery Office, July 2011), available at <https://www.gov.uk/government/publications/counter-terrorism-strategy-contest>, accessed 19 February 2014. The strategic aim is on page 6.
18. Unlike the US, the use of armed drones by British forces is limited to combat zones.
19. The Peterloo 'massacre' in 1819, when cavalry charged a large crowd demonstrating for parliamentary reform and killed fifteen people, profoundly affected the willingness of magistrates to call on troops, and led to the foundation of the *Manchester Guardian* newspaper.
20. This is in contrast to the goals and methods of the original US War on Terror after 9/11.
21. As observed of the role played by service personnel in the London Olympics, 'the public love them, their efficiency, friendly nature and some of the women coming into the Park often admit there is that man-in-uniform factor'. See Gordon Corera and Claire Heald, 'London Olympics: How Was it For the Troops?', *BBC News*, 12 August 2012.
22. Total annual public expenditure on the function was reduced by around a third by the 1966 defence review to £20 million in 1966 prices (around £300 million in 2012 prices) and fell further by 1992 to around £24 million in 2012 prices.
23. The effort to contain the '3 Fs' (flooding, fuel protests and foot-and-mouth disease) is described by Richard Mottram in 'Protecting the Citizen in the Twenty-First Century: Issues and Challenges', in Peter Hennessy (ed.), *The New Protective State: Government, Intelligence and Terrorism* (London: Continuum Books, 2007).
24. The 2010 UK National Security Strategy continues to identify terrorism as one of the four 'top-tier' risks facing the nation, to be managed through CONTEST.
25. MoD, Development, Concepts and Doctrine Centre (DCDC), 'Operations in the UK: The Defence Contribution to Resilience', Joint Doctrine Publication 02, September 2007, chapter 5.
26. HM Government, *Statement on the Defence Estimates 1967*.
27. Defence doctrine can be found in MoD-DCDC, 'Operations in the UK'.
28. House of Commons Defence Committee, 'A New Chapter to the Strategic Defence Review', HC 93-I, May 2003.

29. Fawaz A Gerges, *The Far Enemy: Why Jihad Went Global* (Cambridge: Cambridge University Press, 2005).
30. As he explained to the Iraq Inquiry. Oral evidence provided by Tony Blair, 21 January 2011, <http://www.iraqinquiry.org.uk/transcripts/oralevidence-bydate/110121.aspx>, accessed 22 January 2014.
31. Oral evidence provided by Baroness Manningham-Buller DCB to the Iraq Inquiry, 20 July 2010, <http://www.iraqinquiry.org.uk/transcripts/oralevidence-bydate/100720.aspx>, accessed 22 January 2014.
32. Prime Minister Gordon Brown, interview with the British Forces Broadcasting Service, 12 July 2009.
33. For example, David Cameron, 'Afghanistan and European Council'.
34. Prime Minister's examination by the Liaison Committee, 21 January 2003, question 125, <http://www.parliament.the-stationery-office.co.uk/pa/cm200203/cmselect/cmliaisn/uc334-i/uc33402.htm>, accessed 21 January 2014.
35. Including, for example, Al-Qa'ida in the Arabian Peninsula (AQAP), Al-Qa'ida in the Islamic Maghreb (AQIM) and Boko Haram.
36. David Omand, *Securing the State* (London: Hurst and New York, NY: Columbia University Press, 2010).

Joel Faulkner Rogers and Jonathan Eyal, 'V. Of Tails and Dogs: Public Support and Elite Opinion', pp. 161–90.

1. Anthony King (ed.), *British Political Opinion 1937–2000: The Gallup Polls*, compiled by Robert J Wybrow (London: Politico's Publishing, 2001), pp. 346–48.
2. *Ibid.*, p. 347.
3. Robert J Wybrow, 'British Attitudes towards the Bosnian Situation', in Richard Sobel and Eric Shiraev (eds), *International Public Opinion and the Bosnia Crisis* (Lanham, MD: Lexington Books, 2003), pp. 46–48.
4. *Ibid.*, p. 74.
5. King (ed.), *British Political Opinion 1937–2000*, p. 356.
6. *The Times*, 9 December 1992.
7. A representative quota sample of 1,002 adults aged 18+ was interviewed for MORI between 16–18 April 1993, at which time Bosnian Serb forces were surrounding the town of Srebrenica. Interviewing was conducted by telephone by On-Line Telephone Surveys. Data are weighted to match the profile of the population. For more information, see Ipsos MORI, 'Attitudes towards Bosnia', 19 April 1993, <http://bit.ly/1mpugwB>, accessed 7 February 2014.

8. MORI interviewed 1,104 adults aged 18+ at fifty-four constituency sampling points throughout Great Britain. Interviews were conducted face-to-face, in the street, on 21 July 1995. Data are weighted to match the profile of the population. For more information, see Ipsos MORI, 'Attitudes towards Bosnia', 23 July 1995, <http://bit.ly/1hJE7gv>, accessed 7 February 2014.
9. MORI interviewed a representative quota sample of 606 adults aged 18+. Interviews were carried out by telephone throughout Great Britain. Interviewing took place between 26–27 March 1999. Data are weighted to match the profile of Great Britain. For more information, see Ipsos MORI, 'Mail on Sunday – Kosovo Poll', 28 March 1999, <http://bit.ly/LCns3k>, accessed 7 February 2014.
10. MORI interviewed a representative quota sample of 604 adults aged 18+. Interviews were carried out by telephone throughout Great Britain. Interviewing took place between 1–2 April 1999. Data are weighted to match the profile of Great Britain. For more information, see Ipsos MORI, 'Mail on Sunday – Kosovo Poll', 2 April 1999, <http://bit.ly/1dN0LW9>, accessed 7 February 2014.
11. MORI interviewed 1,008 adults aged 18+ across Great Britain (627 adults on Qs 8–21). Interviews were conducted by telephone between 30 April–1 May 1999. Based on all respondents unless otherwise stated. Data are weighted to the profile of Great Britain. For more information, see Ipsos MORI, 'Local Elections, Kosovo and the Tory Leadership', 2 May 1999, <http://bit.ly/LCoz2N>, accessed 7 February 2014.
12. King (ed.), *British Political Opinion 1937–2000*, p. 360.
13. Ipsos MORI, 'Mail on Sunday – Kosovo Poll', 28 March 1999.
14. Ipsos MORI, 'Mail on Sunday – Kosovo Poll', 2 April 1999.
15. Ipsos MORI, 'Local Elections, Kosovo and the Tory Leadership'.
16. Ipsos MORI, 'Mail on Sunday – Kosovo Poll', 28 March 1999.
17. ICM interviewed a random sample of 1,001 adults aged 18+ by telephone between 9–10 October 2001. Interviews were conducted across the country and the results have been weighted to the profile of all adults. For more information, see Alan Travis, 'Bombing Gets Support of 74%', *Guardian*, 12 October 2001.
18. For more on this discussion, see Harold D Clarke, David Sanders, Marianne C Stewart and Paul F Whiteley, *Performance Politics and the British Voter* (Cambridge: Cambridge University Press, 2009), p. 103; Ben Clements, 'There is a Gender Gap in Public Opinion towards UK Military Intervention, with Women Less Supportive of British Action

in Iraq, Afghanistan and Libya', LSE British Politics and Policy Blog, 27 December 2011, <http://bit.ly/1jmThvo>, accessed 14 February 2014.
19. For more on this discussion, see Douglas L Kriner and Graham Wilson, 'Elites, Events and British Support for the War in Afghanistan', paper prepared for the annual meeting of the American Political Science Association (APSA), Washington, DC, 2–5 September 2010, <http://bit.ly/1ime6GY>, accessed 14 February 2014; Sarah Kreps, 'Elite Consensus as a Determinant of Alliance Cohesion: Why Public Opinion Hardly Matters for NATO-Led Operations in Afghanistan', *Foreign Policy Analysis* (Vol. 6, No. 3, July 2010), pp. 191–215; Jason Reifler, Harold D Clarke, Thomas J Scotto, David Sanders, Marianne C Stewart and Paul Whiteley, 'Prudence, Principle and Minimal Heuristics: British Public Opinion Toward the Use of Military Force in Afghanistan and Libya', *British Journal of Politics and International Relations* (Vol. 16, No. 1, January 2014), pp. 28–55.
20. Thomas J Scotto, Jason Reifler, Harold D Clarke, Julio Amador Diaz Lopez, David Sanders, Marianne C Stewart and Paul Whiteley, 'Attitudes towards British Involvement in Afghanistan', Institute for Democracy and Conflict Resolution Briefing Paper BP 03/11, <http://bit.ly/KDHQAG>, accessed 14 February 2014.
21. Kriner and Wilson, 'Elites, Events and British Support for the War in Afghanistan', p. 12.
22. YouGov.com, 'YouGov/*Daily Telegraph* Survey Results', October 2006, <http://bit.ly/1fZhvLx>, accessed 14 February 2014. Fieldwork was conducted online between 24–26 October 2006, with a total sample of 1,722 British adults. The data have been weighted and the results are representative of all British adults aged 18+.
23. YouGov Archive, 'Afghanistan Tracker', <http://bit.ly/1jycDLq>, accessed 14 February 2014. Fieldwork was conducted online and sample sizes vary above n=1,000 in each case. The data have been weighted and the results are representative of all British adults aged 18+.
24. Scotto et al., 'Attitudes towards British Involvement in Afghanistan', p. 5.
25. Clarke et al., *Performance Politics and the British Voter*, p. 142.
26. Kishwer Falkner, 'Baroness Falkner on Syria and Intervening Abroad', LibDemVoice.org, 30 August 2013, <http://bit.ly/1aKswsz>, accessed 14 February 2014.
27. YouGov.com, 'YouGov Survey Results: The War in Iraq', prepared for ITN, <http://bit.ly/1bhAnOm>, accessed 14 February 2014. Fieldwork was conducted online between 10–12 January 2003, with a

Notes and References 353

total sample of 1,425 British adults. The data have been weighted and the results are representative of all British adults aged 18+.
28. YouGov.com, 'YouGov Survey Results: Iraq and Terrorism', prepared for the *Mail on Sunday*, <http://bit.ly/1mF5Dit>, accessed 14 February 2014. Fieldwork was conducted online between 16–17 January 2003, with a total sample of 1,884 British adults. The data have been weighted and the results are representative of all British adults aged 18+.
29. YouGov.com, 'YouGov Survey Results: for *The Mail on Sunday*', <http://bit.ly/1fbe2F7>, accessed 25 February 2014. Fieldwork was conducted online between 30–31 January 2003, with a total sample of 1,955 British adults. The data have been weighted and the results are representative of all British adults aged 18+.
30. YouGov.com, 'YouGov Survey Results: A Possible War in Iraq', prepared for Jonathan Dimbleby – *Showdown in Iraq*, <http://bit.ly/1mF6gIM>, accessed 14 February 2014. Fieldwork was conducted online between 14–16 March 2003, with a total sample of 2,343 British adults. The data have been weighted and the results are representative of all British adults aged 18+.
31. YouGov.com, 'YouGov Survey Results: The War in Iraq', prepared for the *Sunday Times*, <http://bit.ly/1kWVyyS>, accessed 14 February 2014. Fieldwork was conducted online between 21–22 March 2003, with a total sample of 2,116 British adults. The data have been weighted and the results are representative of all British adults aged 18+.
32. YouGov Archive, 'Iraq Tracker', <http://bit.ly/1bhAPMz>, accessed 14 February 2014. Fieldwork was conducted online and sample sizes vary above n=1,000 in each case. The data have been weighted and the results are representative of all British adults aged 18+.
33. YouGov.com, 'YouGov/*Sunday Times* Survey Results: The Butler Report and the Iraq War', <http://bit.ly/1cUm6XB>, accessed 14 February 2014. Fieldwork was conducted online between 16–17 July 2003, with a total sample of 1,717 British adults. The data have been weighted and the results are representative of all British adults aged 18+.
34. YouGov Archive, 'Iraq Tracker'.
35. Peter Kellner, 'Libya: Voters Divided on Military Action', YouGov Commentaries, 28 August 2013, <http://bit.ly/1jDqoIN>, accessed 17 February 2014.
36. YouGov.com, 'YouGov/The Sun Survey Results', <http://bit.ly/1dv7HkE>, accessed 17 February 2014. Fieldwork was conducted online between 20–21 March 2011, with a total sample of 2,745 British

adults. The data have been weighted and the results are representative of all British adults aged 18+.
37. YouGov Archive, 'Comparative Survey Results on Iraq and Libya', <http://bit.ly/1ey0jJr>, accessed 17 February 2014. Fieldwork was conducted online and sample sizes vary above n=1,000 in each case. The data have been weighted and the results are representative of all British adults aged 18+.
38. *Ibid.*
39. YouGov.com, 'YouGov/The Sun Survey Results' <http://bit.ly/KGbc0R>, accessed 17 February 2014. Fieldwork was conducted online on 22 January 2013, with a total sample of 738 British adults. The data have been weighted and the results are representative of all British adults aged 18+.
40. YouGov.com, 'YouGov Survey Results', <http://bit.ly/1ee9qMr>, accessed 17 February 2014. Fieldwork was conducted online between 18–19 March 2013 with a total sample of 1,920 British adults, and between 28–29 April 2013 with a total sample of 1,632 British adults. In each case, the data have been weighted and the results are representative of all British adults aged 18+.
41. YouGov.com, 'YouGov Survey Results', <http://bit.ly/1dOIacq>, accessed 17 February 2014. Fieldwork was conducted online between 28–29 April 2013, with a total sample of 1,632 British adults. The data have been weighted and the results are representative of all British adults aged 18+.
42. *Ibid.*
43. Peter Kellner, 'Syria and the Shadow of Iraq', YouGov Commentaries, 28 August 2013, <http://bit.ly/19NoZPc>, accessed 17 February 2014.
44. YouGov.com, 'YouGov-Cambridge Survey Results', <http://bit.ly/1dONAnB>, accessed 17 February 2014. Fieldwork was conducted online between 28–29 August 2013, with a total sample of 1,954 British adults. Data from the whole sample have been weighted and these results are representative of all British adults aged 18+. Subsample 1 (with UN support) included 1,004 respondents. Subsample 2 (without UN support) included 950 respondents.
45. Peter Kellner, 'Voters Tell Cameron: Don't Bomb Syria but Do Help Obama', YouGov Commentaries, 1 September 2013, <http://bit.ly/1aKTxwb>, accessed 17 February 2014.
46. For Survey 2, see YouGov.com, 'YouGov-Cambridge Survey Results', <http://bit.ly/1jzpTiW>, accessed 17 February 2014. Fieldwork for

Survey 2 was conducted online between 9–10 September 2013 with a total sample of 1,579 British adults. The data have been weighted and the results are representative of all British adults aged 18+.
47. For Survey 1, see YouGov.com, 'YouGov-Cambridge Survey Results', <http://bit.ly/KFFx0f>, accessed 17 February 2014. Fieldwork for Survey 1 was conducted online between 21–23 August 2013 with a total sample of 1,948 British adults. For Survey 2, see YouGov.com, 'YouGov-Cambridge Survey Results', <http://bit.ly/1jzpTiW>, accessed 17 February 2014. Fieldwork for Survey 2 was conducted online between 9–10 September 2013 with a total sample of 1,579 British adults. In each case, the data have been weighted and the results are representative of all British adults aged 18+.
48. *Ibid.*
49. Kellner, 'Voters Tell Cameron: Don't Bomb Syria but Do Help Obama'; see also YouGov.com, 'YouGov Survey Results', <http://bit.ly/1dP9zLk>, accessed 17 February 2014. Fieldwork was conducted online between 30–31 August 2013 with a total sample of 1,822 British adults. The data have been weighted and the results are representative of all British adults aged 18+.
50. *Ibid.*
51. *Ibid.*
52. YouGov.com, 'YouGov Survey Results', <http://bit.ly/KFXbRt>, accessed 17 February 2014. Fieldwork was conducted online between 23–24 April 2013, with a total sample of 1,976 British adults. The data have been weighted and the results are representative of all British adults aged 18+.
53. *Ibid.*

Malcolm Chalmers, 'VI. On the Offensive', pp. 191–214.

1. While the UK provided counter-insurgency assistance in Oman until 1975, the scale of this operation (a small number of officers and special forces) was limited. See Walter C Ladwig III, 'Supporting Allies in Counterinsurgency: Britain and the Dhofar Rebellion', *Small Wars and Insurgencies* (Vol. 19, No. 1, March 2008), pp. 62–88.
2. For an excellent summary of recent developments, see Gareth Stansfield and Saul Kelly, 'A Return to East of Suez? UK Military Deployment to the Gulf', RUSI Briefing Paper, April 2013.
3. Ministry of Defence, *The Strategic Defence Review*, Cm 3999 (London: The Stationery Office, 1998), p. 4.

4. For a longer perspective, see Martin Ceadel, *Semi-Detached Idealists: The British Peace Movement and International Relations, 1854–1945* (Oxford: Oxford University Press, 2000).
5. See Chapter V in this volume.
6. International Security Assistance Force (ISAF), 'History', <http://www.isaf.nato.int/history.html>, accessed 12 February 2014; and ISAF, 'ISAF Placemat Archives', <http://www.isaf.nato.int/isaf-placemat-archives.html>, accessed 12 February 2014.
7. ISAF, 'ISAF Placemat Archives'.
8. Bruno Tertrais, 'The Demise of Ares: The End of War as We Know It', *Washington Quarterly* (Vol. 35, No. 3, Summer 2012), p. 10.
9. Nicholas J Wheeler, *Saving Strangers: Humanitarian Intervention in International Society* (Oxford: Oxford University Press, 2002).
10. Human Security Report Project, *Human Security Brief 2006*, 2006, Figure 2.3.
11. The most comprehensive study of war-related deaths in Bosnia is the IDC, *Bosnian Book of the Dead*. For detailed analysis of its methodology, see Patrick Ball, Ewa Tabeau and Philip Verwimp, 'The Bosnian Book of the Dead: An Assessment of the Database', Households in Conflict Network, University of Sussex, June 2007.
12. For a full transcript, see *PBS Newshour*, 'The Blair Doctrine', 22 April 1999, <http://www.pbs.org/newshour/bb/international/jan-june99/blair_doctrine4-23.html>, accessed 12 February 2014.
13. Michael W Doyle, 'Liberalism and World Politics', *American Political Science Review* (Vol. 80, No. 4, 1986), pp. 1,151–69. Liberal democracies still make war, but they tend not to fight each other.
14. Edward D Mansfield and Jack L Snyder, *Electing to Fight: Why Emerging Democracies Go to War* (Boston, MA: MIT Press, 2005).
15. UN Peacekeeping Fact Sheet, <http://www.un.org/en/peacekeeping/resources/statistics/factsheet.shtml>, last accessed 21 July 2013.
16. A recent example of this was the establishment of an Intervention Brigade for the UN mission in the Democratic Republic of the Congo, MONUSCO.
17. Virginia Page Fortna, 'Does Peacekeeping Keep Peace? International Intervention and the Duration of Peace After Civil War', *International Studies Quarterly* (Vol. 48, No. 2, June 2004), pp. 269–92; Human Security Report Project, 'Part I: The Causes of Peace' and 'Part II: The Shrinking Costs of War', in *Human Security Report 2009/2010* (Oxford:

Oxford University Press, 2011), <http://www.hsrgroup.org/human-security-reports/20092010/text.aspx>, accessed 12 February 2014.
18. Christopher M Blanchard and Catherine Marie Dale, 'Iraq: Foreign Contributions to Stabilization and Reconstruction', Congressional Research Service Report for Congress, 26 December 2007, pp. 3–5.
19. See, for example, Richard Lugar, remarks to the Atlantic Council seminar 'Senator Richard Lugar: Congressional Perspective on the Future of NATO', Washington, DC, 28 September 2009, <http://www.atlanticcouncil.org/events/past-events/senator-richard-lugar-congressional-perspective-on-the-future-of-nato>, accessed 13 February 2014.
20. Ben Judah, *Fragile Empire: How Russia Fell in and out of Love with Vladimir Putin* (New Haven, CT: Yale University Press, 2013).
21. Fyodor Lukyanov, 'What Russia Learned From the Iraq War', *Global Affairs*, 19 March 2013.
22. For example, see Robert Kagan, *The Return of History and the End of Dreams* (New York, NY: Knopf-Doubleday, 2008).

Robert Fry, 'VII. Strategy and Operations', pp. 215–36.

1. Eric Hobsbawm, *The Age of Extremes: The Short 20th Century, 1914–1991* (New York, NY: Vintage Books, 1994).
2. Joseph Chamberlain, quoted by Michael Howard, *The Continental Commitment: The Dilemma of British Defence Policy in the Era of Two World Wars* (London: Maurice Temple Smith, 1972), p. 11.
3. The no-fly zones were supported by subsequent UN Security Council resolutions.
4. Lawrence Freedman, *The Transformation of Strategic Affairs,* Adelphi Paper 379 (London: Routledge, 2006), p. 44.
5. Michael Howard, *War and the Liberal Conscience* (London: Maurice Temple Smith, 1977).
6. Freedman, *The Transformation of Strategic Affairs*, p. 9.
7. 'Armies' here is shorthand for the US Army and US Marine Corps force elements deployed on ground operations, and those from other services employed in a supporting function.
8. However, it did deploy on operations to liberate Kuwait in 1991 in what was seen as a vindication of its core assumptions.
9. Named after General Colin Powell and defined during his tenure as chairman of the US Joint Chiefs of Staff, 1989–93.
10. A good example being Brigadier Nigel Aylwin-Foster's 2005 article, 'Changing the Army for Counterinsurgency Operations', *Military*

Review (November/December 2005). This seminal article showed both the British capacity to capture key arguments and the US capacity to act on them.

11. Ministry of Defence (MoD), *The Strategic Defence Review: A New Chapter*, Cm 5566 (London: The Stationery Office, July 2002).
12. Attributed to Richard Armitage. See: Jason Burke, *The 9/11 Wars* (London: Allen Lane, 2011); p. 366.
13. Burke, *The 9/11 Wars*, p. 74.
14. *Ibid.*, p. 78.
15. Most recently described by William Dalrymple, *Return of a King: The Battle for Afghanistan* (London: Bloomsbury, 2013), p. 391.
16. Sandy Gall, *War against the Taliban: Why It All Went Wrong in Afghanistan* (London: Bloomsbury, 2012), p. 341.
17. The curious bedfellows Saudi Arabia and Israel both see the November 2013 agreement between the EU/E3+3 and Iran on nuclear enrichment as a further consolidation of Iranian power.
18. Michael Howard and Peter Paret (eds, trans. by), Carl von Clausewitz, *On War* (Princeton, NJ: Princeton University Press, 1976), book 1. Common usage takes the trinity as the interaction of the people, the armed forces and the state. This is a paraphrase of the interplay of passion, probability or chance, and reason originally cited by Clausewitz.
19. House of Commons Defence Committee, *Operations in Afghanistan: Fourth Report of Session 2010–2012* (London: The Stationery Office, 2011).
20. See 'The Afghan Decisions', special section, *RUSI Journal* (Vol. 157, No. 2, April/May 2012).
21. Jack Fairweather, *A War of Choice: The British in Iraq 2003–9* (London: Jonathan Cape, 2011).
22. Britain outfought Germany in the twentieth century only between 1 July 1916 and 11 November 1918. For the rest of the time, the UK relied on the decisive efforts of allies, mediated through competent grand strategy.
23. Sherard Cowper-Coles, *Cables from Kabul: The Inside Story of the West's Campaign in Afghanistan* (London: Harper Collins, 2011).
24. See Anthony Seldon, *Blair Unbound* (London: Simon and Schuster, 2007), p. 57; *BBC News*, 'UK in "Generational Struggle" against Terror, Says PM', 21 January 2013.

25. The formal responsibilities of occupying powers ended with the assumption of power by an interim Iraqi government in 2004, but this would not have been tenable without continued coalition support.
26. Anatol Lieven, *Pakistan: A Hard Country* (London: Allen Lane, 2011), p. 286.
27. Matt Cavanagh, 'Ministerial Decision-Making in the Run-Up to the Helmand Deployment', *RUSI Journal* (Vol. 157, No. 2, April/May 2012), p. 51.
28. Lieven, *Pakistan*.
29. Theo Farrell, 'Review Essay: A Good War Gone Wrong?', *RUSI Journal* (Vol. 156, No. 5, October/November 2011), pp. 60–65.
30. Frank Ledwidge, *Losing Small Wars: British Military Failure in Iraq and Afghanistan* (New Haven, CT: Yale University Press, 2011).
31. 'America's interests and role in the world require armed forces with unmatched capabilities and a willingness on the part of the nation to employ them in defense of our interests and the common good'. See US Department of Defense, 'Quadrennial Defense Review Report', February 2010, p. iv.
32. Stephen G Brooks et al., 'Lean Forward in Defense of American Engagement', *Foreign Affairs* (January/February 2013).
33. Christopher Layne, 'The End of Pax Americana: How Western Decline Became Inevitable', *Atlantic*, 26 April 2012.
34. The global commons have been defined as 'those areas beyond national jurisdiction that constitute the vital connective tissue of the international system'. US Department of Defense, 'Strategic Guidance: Sustaining US Global Leadership – Priorities for 21st Century Defence', January 2012, p. 3.

Michael Clarke, 'VIII. Brothers in Arms: The British–American Alignment', pp. 237–66.

1. See Walter Russell Mead, *God and Gold: Britain, America and the Making of the Modern World* (London: Atlantic Books, 2007).
2. John Baylis, *Anglo-American Defence Relations 1939–84*, 2nd edition (London: Palgrave Macmillan, 1984).
3. Keith Jeffery, *MI6: The History of the Secret Intelligence Service, 1909–1949* (London: Bloomsbury, 2010), p. 720.
4. *Ibid.*, p. 721.
5. Hew Strachan, 'British Generals in Blair's Wars: Conclusion', in Jonathan Bailey, Richard Iron and Hew Strachan (eds), *British Generals in Blair's Wars* (Farnham: Ashgate, 2013), p. 329.

6. Theo Farrell and Tim Bird, 'Innovating within Cost and Cultural Constraints: The British Approach to Military Transformation', in Terry Terriff, Frans Osinga and Theo Farrell (eds), *A Transformation Gap? American Innovations and European Military Change* (Stanford, CA: Stanford University Press, 2010), p. 40.
7. Emile Simpson, *War From the Ground Up: Twenty-First-Century Combat as Politics* (London: Hurst, 2012), pp. 1, 30.
8. Patrick Porter, 'Last Charge of the Knights? Iraq, Afghanistan and the Special Relationship', *International Affairs* (Vol. 86, No. 2, March 2010), pp. 363–65. See also Frank Ledwidge, *Losing Small Wars: British Military Failure in Iraq and Afghanistan* (New Haven, CT: Yale University Press, 2011), pp. 150–61.
9. See John Mackinlay, *The Insurgent Archipelago* (London: Hurst, 2009), chapter 11.
10. See Gian P Gentile, 'A Strategy of Tactics: Population-Centric COIN and the Army', *Parameters* (Vol. 39, No. 3, Fall 2009), pp. 5–17.
11. James de Waal, 'Depending on the Right People: British Political-Military Relations, 2001–10', Chatham House, November 2013, especially pp. 22–23.
12. On the difficulties of implementing a genuine counter-insurgency strategy, and particularly in Afghanistan, see, for example, Christopher Griffin, 'British and American Military Operations in the Battle of Helmand, 2006–2011', *Cambridge Review of International Affairs* (Vol. 26, No. 2, 2013), pp. 411–29.
13. For example, see Eitan Shamir, *Transforming Command: The Pursuit of Mission Command in the U.S., British, and Israeli Armies* (Stanford, CA: Stanford University Press, 2011); Justin Kelly and Mike Brennen, *Alien: How Operational Art Devoured Strategy* (Carlisle, PA: Strategic Studies Institute, 2009); Alexander Mattelaer, 'The Crisis in Operational Art', paper presented at the European Security and Defence Forum, Chatham House, November 2009, pp. 14–15.
14. This list does not include all armed-service deployments by the US and the UK over this period, since both countries contributed some military contingents to many operations – such as the UK's deployment of 300 Gurkhas to the East Timor stabilisation force led by Australian forces. A judgement has been made over which operations required some unanticipated and significant commitment of forces.
15. General Sir Peter de la Billière, *Storm Command: A Personal Account of the Gulf War* (London: Harper Collins, 1992), pp. 26–27.

16. International Institute of Strategic Studies (IISS), *Strategic Survey 1990* (London: Brassey's for the IISS, 1990), pp. 93–98.
17. The UK's Operation *Granby* deployed some 53,400 troops to the Gulf, which was just under 8 per cent of the 697,000 troops sent by the US under the *Desert Storm* banner, and 5.5 per cent of the 956,000 troops deployed in total on the coalition side.
18. Strachan, 'British Generals in Blair's Wars: Conclusion', p. 329.
19. Mark Laity, 'Preventing War in Macedonia: Pre-Emptive Diplomacy for the 21st Century', *RUSI Whitehall Paper* (No. 68, 2008).
20. Bruce George, 'The House of Commons Defence Committee Report: Lessons of Kosovo', *RUSI Journal* (Vol. 145, No. 6, December 2000), pp. 12–14.
21. On the desperation which prompted the plan, see Tony Blair, *A Journey* (London: Arrow Books, 2011), pp. 239–42. On US reactions, see Dana Priest, 'Kosovo Land Threat May Have Won War', *Washington Post*, 19 September 1999; Steven Erlanger, 'NATO was Closer to Ground War in Kosovo than is Widely Realized', *New York Times*, 7 November 1999.
22. Thomas R Mockaitis, 'Reluctant Partners: Civil-Military Cooperation in Kosovo', *Small Wars and Insurgencies* (Vol. 15, No. 2, 2004), pp. 59–61.
23. Benjamin S Lambeth, *NATO's Air War for Kosovo: A Strategic and Operational Assessment* (Santa Monica, CA: RAND, 2001), pp. 230–42; IISS, 'Air-Power over Kosovo: A Historic Victory?', *Strategic Comments* (Vol. 5, No. 7, 1999), pp. 1–2.
24. David Richards, 'Sierra Leone 2000: Pregnant with Lessons', in Bailey, Iron and Strachan (eds), *British Generals in Blair's Wars*, pp. 55–63.
25. Andrew M Dorman, *Blair's Successful War: British Military Intervention in Sierra Leone* (Farnham: Ashgate, 2009).
26. Blair, *A Journey*, p. 351; see also Alastair Campbell, *The Alastair Campbell Diaries: Volume III, Power and Responsibility, 1999–2001* (London, Hutchinson, 2011), p. 694.
27. In answer to a parliamentary question, then-Secretary of State for Defence Geoff Hoon stated that 'a force drawn from the exercise would be retained in the region ... the deployment to Afghanistan of other units or personnel which took part in Saif Sareea 2 remains under review.' See *Hansard*, House of Commons, Written Answers, vol. 375, col. 901W, 28 November 2001.

28. Gordon Corera, *MI6: Life and Death in the British Secret Service* (London: Hachette, 2011), pp. 312–13, 337–40.
29. See, for example, Richard J Aldrich, *GCHQ: The Uncensored Story of Britain's Most Secret Intelligence Agency* (London: HarperPress, 2010), pp. 448–57.
30. It should be noted that Denmark was prepared to participate from the outset. It already had a submarine deployed in the Gulf and it was joined by a corvette. Poland, too, deployed at the outset a small detachment of special forces of twelve men, joined by seventy-four chemical contamination specialists. Other nations made strictly non-combatant contributions at the commencement of hostilities.
31. Jack Straw, *Last Man Standing: Memoirs of a Political Survivor* (London: Macmillan, 2012), p. xx.
32. Richard Iron, 'Basra 2008: Operation Charge of the Knights', in Bailey, Iron and Strachan (eds), *British Generals in Blair's Wars*, p. 199.
33. Michael E Gordon and Bernard R Trainor, *Cobra II: The Inside Story of the Invasion and Occupation of Iraq* (New York, NY: Pantheon Books, 2006), pp. 145–47.
34. David Betz and Anthony Cormack, 'Iraq, Afghanistan and British Strategy', *Orbis* (Vol. 53, No. 2, Spring 2009), p. 324. See also Hilary Synnott, *Bad Days in Basra: My Turbulent Time as Britain's Man in Southern Iraq* (London: I. B. Taurus, 2008).
35. John Baylis and James J Wirtz, 'The U.S.–UK "Special Military Relationship": Resetting the Partnership', *Comparative Strategy* (Vol. 31, No. 3, 2012), pp. 254–55. See also Warren Chin, 'British Defense Policy and the War in Iraq 2003–2009', *Defense and Security Analysis* (Vol. 27, No. 1, 2011), pp. 65–76; Michael Evans, 'US General Warned the British Commanders that their Afghan Strategy was a Disaster', *Times*, 30 August 2010.
36. Iron, 'Basra 2008', p. 196.
37. See several opinions cited in Ledwidge, *Losing Small Wars*, pp. 53–59.
38. See, for example, Frank Ledwidge, *Investment in Blood: The True Cost of Britain's Afghan War* (London and New Haven, CT: Yale University Press, 2013), pp. 205–07.
39. Michael Clarke (ed.), *The Afghan Papers: Committing Britain to War in Helmand, 2005–06*, RUSI Whitehall Paper 77 (London: Taylor and Francis, 2011).
40. Anthony King, 'Understanding the Helmand Campaign: British Military Operations in Afghanistan', *International Affairs* (Vol. 86,

No. 2, 2010); Betz and Cormack, 'Iraq, Afghanistan and British Strategy', pp. 328–29.
41. Rajiv Chandrasekaran, *Little America: The War Within the War for Afghanistan* (New York, NY: Vintage Books), pp. 223–24.
42. Gov.uk, 'PM Announces UK Troop Withdrawals from Afghanistan', 6 July 2011; Nick Hopkins, 'Afghanistan Withdrawal: 500 Troops to Leave Next Year, Says Cameron', *Guardian*, 6 July 2011.
43. Ivo Daalder and James G Stavridis, 'NATO's Victory in Libya', *Foreign Affairs* (Vol. 91, No. 2, 2012).
44. Dave Sloggett, *A Century of Air Power* (Barnsley: Pen and Sword, 2013), pp. 137–40.
45. Secretary of Defense Robert Gates made a point of criticising NATO's ability to respond over Libya in one of his final speeches in Brussels prior to stepping down. 'The military capabilities simply aren't there,' he said. *CBS News*, 'Gates Criticises NATO: How Much Does the US Pay', 10 June 2011.
46. Baylis and Wirtz, 'The U.S.–UK "Special Military Relationship"'.
47. Department of Defense, 'Air-Sea Battle: Service Collaboration to Address Anti-Access and Area Denial Challenges', May 2013, <http://www.defense.gov/pubs/ASB-ConceptImplementation-Summary-May-2013.pdf>, accessed 21 February 2014.

Malcolm Chalmers, 'IX. The Sinews of War', pp. 267–90.

1. As the reference to 'net' costs suggests, the allocation also takes account of offsetting savings: for example, reductions in training commitments arising from the cancellation of, or reduced participation in, military exercises.
2. HM Treasury, *Public Expenditure Statistical Analyses 2013*, Cm 8663 (London: The Stationery Office, July 2013), Table 4.3.
3. Part of this comprised spending in relation to access and overflight for operations in Afghanistan.
4. For data on Bosnian operations between 1992 and December 1995, see National Audit Office (NAO), 'Ministry of Defence: The Financial Management of the Military Operation in the Former Yugoslavia', Report of the Comptroller and Auditor General, HC 132, 6 December 1996. Bosnian figures for 1995 to 2004 assume that costs of Operation *Oculus* are equally divided between Bosnia and Kosovo.
5. This included £275 million from Germany and £183 million from Japan. See Malcolm Chalmers, *Sharing Security: The Political Economy of Burdensharing* (London: Macmillan, 2000), p. 57.

6. On the basis of current plans, the UK will reach this target in 2013. Lorna Booth, 'The 0.7% Aid Target', House of Commons Library, 10 June 2013.
7. HM Treasury, *Public Expenditure Statistical Analyses 2013*.
8. NATO annual reports on defence expenditure by member states.
9. Calculated on the basis of Treasury figures (total departmental expenditure limits in real terms) and Office for Budget Responsibility projections (GDP at market prices). See HM Treasury, *Public Expenditure Statistical Analyses 2013*, Table 1.11; Office for Budget Responsibility, *Economic and Fiscal Outlook*, Cm 8748 (London: The Stationery Office, December 2013), Table 1.2.
10. Total regular strength, including untrained personnel. House of Commons Library, 'Defence Statistics 2000', Research Paper 00/99, 21 December 2000, Table 2.8.
11. This is calculated on the basis of the average percentage of GDP spent on defence in 2010 by nine other West European NATO member states (namely France, Germany, Italy, Spain, the Netherlands, Belgium, Norway, Denmark and Portugal).
12. Frank Ledwidge, *Investment in Blood: The True Cost of Britain's Afghan War* (New Haven, CT: Yale University Press, 2013), chapter 5.
13. *Ibid*., p. 141.
14. See the Appendix, Table 1 for a table of casualties over the period 1991–2012.
15. The Korean and Vietnam Wars cost the US $341 billion and $738 billion respectively, also in 2011 prices. See Stephen Daggett, 'Costs of Major U.S. Wars', Congressional Research Service, 29 June 2010, p. 2.
16. *Ibid*.
17. Congressional Budget Office, 'Congressional Budget Office Cost Estimate: S.995, National Desert Storm and Desert Shield War Memorial Act', 24 January 2014, <http://www.cbo.gov/publication/45056>, accessed 21 February 2014.
18. In cash (includes spending on Iraq from 2003, total costs of Afghanistan, and costs of the 'wider Gulf').
19. For military personnel, see NATO, 'Financial and Economic Data Relating to NATO Defence', press release, 13 April 2012, <http://www.nato.int/nato_static/assets/pdf/pdf_2012_04/20120413_PR_CP_2012_047_rev1.pdf>, accessed 21 February 2014; for population, see World Bank, 'Population (Total)', <http://data.worldbank.org/indicator/SP.POP.TOTL>, accessed 21 February 2014.

20. Linda J Bilmes, 'The Financial Legacy of Iraq and Afghanistan: How Wartime Spending Decisions Will Constrain Future National Security Budgets', Kennedy School Faculty Research Working Paper RWP13-006, March 2013, p. 8. See also Joseph Stiglitz and Linda J Bilmes, 'No US Peace Dividend after Afghanistan', *Financial Times*, 23 January 2013; Joseph Stiglitz and Linda J Bilmes, *The Three Trillion Dollar War: The True Cost of the Iraq Conflict* (London: Allen Lane, 2008). For a cautionary note on Stiglitz and Bilmes, see Congressional Budget Office, 'The Cost of the War: A Comment on Stiglitz-Bilmes', 8 April 2008, <http://www.cbo.gov/publication/24762>, accessed 24 February 2014.
21. Bilmes, 'The Financial Legacy of Iraq and Afghanistan', p. 2.
22. Ledwidge, *Investment in Blood*, chapter 5.
23. This is half of 9 per cent of £600 billion.
24. In addition to the £25–30 billion of long-term costs as a result of the operations in Iraq and Afghanistan after 2001, this includes an allowance for extra costs incurred as a result of other operations since 1990.
25. UK military involvement in the Gulf conflict in 1990. The cost is net of burden-sharing contributions from other countries, which amounted in total to £2,049 million (£3,183 million at 2012/13 prices).
26. The establishment of a no-fly zone over northern Iraq in 1991 in support of UN Security Council Resolution 688 and to prevent the repression of the civilian population (the Kurds) by the Iraqi regime.
27. The establishment of a no-fly zone over southern Iraq in 1992 in support of UN Security Council Resolution 688 and to prevent the repression of the civilian population (the Marsh Arabs) by the Iraqi regime.
28. The precautionary deployment of UK ground forces to Kuwait in 1994/95. These figures are net of burden-sharing contributions from other countries.
29. The deployment of aircraft carrier and Royal Navy and Royal Air Force (RAF) aircraft to the Gulf in 1997/98.
30. Joint air strikes with the US over Iraq in December 1998.
31. This mainly covers the enforcement of no-fly zones under Operations *Warden* and *Jural*, but no breakdown is available.
32. UK military operations in Iraq.
33. UK military operations in Afghanistan.
34. UK military operations in Bosnia and Kosovo.
35. The UK contribution to coalition operations in Libya in support of UN Security Council Resolution 1973.

36. Deployment and redeployment access and overflight for operations in Afghanistan. UK forces also contribute to energy and trade security and support the government's regional counter-terrorism and counter-piracy policies.
37. UK logistical support to France and contribution to the EU Training Mission in Mali.

Trevor Taylor, John Louth and Henrik Heidenkamp, 'X. Industry and the Military Instrument', pp. 291–320.
1. President of the United States, 'Executive Order – National Defense Resources Preparedness', 16 March 2012, <http://www.whitehouse.gov/the-press-office/2012/03/16/executive-order-national-defense-resources-preparedness>, accessed 19 February 2014.
2. Joint Doctrine and Concepts Centre, 'British Defence Doctrine', Joint Warfare Publication 0-01, 1999.
3. The 2010 Strategic Defence and Security Review specified roles and targets for the armed forces and replaced the evolving but essentially similar outputs that had been specified under the Labour government. See HM Government, *Securing Britain in an Age of Uncertainty: The Strategic Defence and Security Review*, Cm 7948 (London: The Stationery Office, October 2010), pp. 18–19.
4. National Audit Office, *Ministry of Defence: The Rapid Procurement of Capability to Support Operations*, Report by the Comptroller and Auditor General, HC 1161 (London: The Stationery Office, November 2004), p. 1.
5. See National Audit Office, *Support to High Intensity Operations*, HC 508 (London: The Stationery Office, May 2009), p. 8, <http://www.nao.org.uk/wp-content/uploads/2009/05/0809508.pdf>, accessed 20 February 2014.
6. See Ministry of Defence, 'The Smart Acquisition Handbook', Edition 5, January 2004.
7. See Mike Docherty, 'GKN Defence: A History in the Making', *RUSI Journal* (Vol. 137, No. 3, June 1992), pp. 27–32.
8. See Caleb Baker, 'Civilian Contractors are Key to High-Tech Success', *Defense News*, 22 October 1990, p. 25.
9. See House of Commons Defence Committee, *Implementation of Lessons Learned from Operation Granby, 1993–94*, 5th Report, Session 1993–94 (London: The Stationery Office, 1994), p. 68.
10. See Baker, 'Civilian Contractors are Key to High-Tech Success', pp. 25, 46.

11. Tim Lewis, 'Rolls-Royce Spreads the Word on Ellamy Support', *Desider* (No. 44, January 2012), p. 9, <https://www.gov.uk/government/uploads/system/uploads/attachment_data/file/33820/desider_44_Jan2012.pdf>, accessed 19 February 2014.
12. Greg Bagwell, 'Gone ... in 60 Hours', in *MAI Magazine* (No. 2), p. 34.
13. *Ibid.*, p. 35.
14. See Colin Chandler, 'Industry in the Firing Line', *RUSI Journal* (Vol. 137, No. 3, June 1992), pp. 19–21.
15. See Docherty, 'GKN Defence', pp. 27–32.
16. See *Jane's Defence Weekly*, 'Torandos get TIALD', 16 February 1991, p. 206; *Jane's Defence Weekly*, 'Early Success for TIALD in "Storm"', 30 March 1991, p. 501.
17. See Carol Reed, 'After the Storm: Industry Waits for Gulf Fall-Out', *Jane's Defence Weekly*, 4 May 1991, p. 732.
18. See Docherty, 'GKN Defence', p. 30.
19. Author interviews with government officials and corporate staff, July 2013, London.
20. Evidence of the Chief of the Air Staff, Air Chief Marshal Sir Stephen Dalton, cited in House of Commons Defence Committee, *Operations in Libya: Ninth Report of Session 2010–12*, Volume 1, HC 950 (London: The Stationery Office, February 2012), pp. 52–53, <http://www.publications.parliament.uk/pa/cm201012/cmselect/cmdfence/950/950.pdf>, accessed 20 February 2014.
21. Authors' discussions with MBDA staff.
22. House of Commons Defence Committee, *Operations in Libya: Government Response to the Committee's Ninth Report of Session 2010–12*, Eleventh Special Report of Session 2010–12, HC 1952 (London: The Stationery Office, April 2012), pp. 13–14, <http://www.publications.parliament.uk/pa/cm201012/cmselect/cmdfence/1952/1952.pdf>, accessed 20 February 2014.
23. See National Audit Office, 'Performance of the Ministry of Defence 2006–07', Briefing for the Defence Committee, November 2007, p. 12, <http://www.nao.org.uk/wp-content/uploads/2013/01/mod_perf0607.pdf>, accessed 20 February 2014.
24. '[T]he Royal Air Force used so many of its Dual Mode Brimstones it both redeployed some from Afghanistan to the Libya campaign and asked MBDA to surge production in the second urgent operational requirement effort for the weapon.' See Robert Wall, 'Aimpoint

Refinement', *Aviation Week & Space Technology* (Vol. 173, No. 33, 19 September 2011), p. 38.
25. Ian Kemp, 'Challenger ERA Revealed', *Jane's Defence Weekly*, 16 March 1991, p. 374.
26. See Docherty, 'GKN Defence', p. 31.
27. Christopher Foss, 'Warrior MILAN Refit Ordered by UK', *Jane's Defence Weekly*, 7 December 1991, p. 1082.
28. *Jane's Defence Weekly*, 'SUPACATS Rebuilt for Gulf Role', 4 May 1991, p. 745.
29. House of Commons Defence Committee, *Implementation of Lessons Learned from Operation Granby, 1993–94*, p. 68.
30. See House of Commons Defence Committee, 'British Forces in Bosnia', press release, 11 June 1996.
31. See Henry S Kenyon, 'Remotely Operated Communications to Link British Forces in Balkans', *Signal Online*, May 2000, <http://www.afcea.org/content/?q=node/744>, accessed 20 February 2014.
32. National Audit Office, *Support to High Intensity Operations*, p. 5.
33. Ibid.
34. National Audit Office, *Kosovo: The Financial Management of Military Operations*, Report by the Comptroller and Auditor General, HC 530 (London: The Stationery Office, June 2000), p. 24, <http://www.nao.org.uk/wp-content/uploads/2000/06/9900530.pdf>, accessed 20 February 2014.
35. Ibid., p. 23.
36. For a more detailed assessment of the British CSO policy as well as dynamics and challenges in the CSO market, see Henrik Heidenkamp, 'Sustaining the UK's Defence Effort: Contractor Support to Operations Market Dynamics', *RUSI Whitehall Report* 2-12, April 2012; Trevor Taylor, 'Review Article: Private Security Companies in Iraq and Beyond', *International Affairs* (Vol. 87, No. 2, March 2011), pp. 445–56.
37. Ministry of Defence, 'Operations in Iraq: Lessons for the Future', December 2003, p. 6, <http://archive.org/download/OperationsInIraqLessonsForTheFutureByTheBritishMinistryOfDefence/OIF_REVISED_UK_Lessons_Learned1.pdf>, accessed 20 February 2014.
38. Andrew Higginson, 'Contractor Support to Operations (CSO) – Proactive or Reactive Support?', *RUSI Defence Systems* (Vol. 13, No. 2, October 2010), p. 16.
39. See Ministry of Defence, *Annual Report and Accounts 2010–11*, HC 992 (London, The Stationery Office, July 2011), p. 47, <http://

www.mod.uk/NR/rdonlyres/E0440EEF-1A7E-4335-B6CD-1CC394FA0AAD/0/mod_ara1011.pdf>, accessed 20 February 2014.
40. House of Commons, 'Operations in Afghanistan', Defence Select Committee Written Evidence from the MoD, 2011, pp. 90–91. It should be stressed that the author regards these official figures on CSO spending and personnel to be conservative estimates. The authors' interviews with senior CSO experts revealed a general deficit in the government's ability to provide accurate, up-to-date figures on CSO. Although they present a general trend, therefore, the existing official figures on CSO, as well as figures provided by analysts and commentators, should be treated with caution.
41. Office of the US Deputy Assistant Secretary of Defense (Program Support), 'US/UK Force Generation Analysis Sustainment Strategies: Use of Contractors to Support Operations (Collaborative Element 6)', 9 October 2012, <http://www.acq.osd.mil/log/PS/ocs/multi-national/US-UK_CE6_final_9Oct2012.docx>, accessed 20 February 2014.
42. There is substantial literature on private military and security companies providing services in the operational space where military capability is used. See, for example, Foreign and Commonwealth Office, *Private Military Companies: Options for Regulation*, HCP 577 (London: The Stationery Office, February 2002); Sam Perlo-Freeman and Elisabeth Sköns, 'The Private Military Services Industry', *SIPRI Insights on Peace and Security* (No. 2008/1, September 2008); Sarah K Cotton et al., *Hired Guns: Views about Armed Contractors in Operation Iraqi Freedom* (Santa Monica, CA: RAND, 2010); Sabelo Gumedze (ed.), *Merchants of African Conflict: More than Just a Pound of Flesh*, Institute for Security Studies Monograph 176, January 2011.
43. See General Dynamics, 'March 7th 2011 – General Dynamics UK Plays Key Role in Camp Bastion Equipment Sustainability System', 7 March 2011, <http://www.generaldynamics.uk.com/news/camp%20bastion%20equipment%20sustainability%20system>, accessed 20 February 2014.
44. See 'Sustaining the Commitment' in *Defence Management Journal* (No. 59, December 2012), pp. 84–85.
45. See Andrew Chuter, 'U.K. Taps KBR for Deployment Support', *Defense News*, 2 April 2012.
46. See KBR, 'Afghanistan Soft Multi Activity Contract (MAC)', January 2013, <http://www.kbr.com/Projects/Afghanistan-Soft-Multi-Activity-

Contract/Afghanistan-Soft-Multi-Activity-Contract.pdf>, accessed 20 February 2014.
47. This contract included the deployment, construction, operation and maintenance of twenty camps. See KBR, 'Temporary Deployable Accommodation (TDA): UK/Iraq/Afghanistan', <http://www.kbr.com/Projects/Temporary-Deployable-Accommodation/Temporary-Deployable-Accommodation.pdf>, accessed 20 February 2014.
48. See KBR, 'Afghanistan Infrastructure Service Provider (ISP)', <http://www.kbr.com/Projects/Afghanistan-Infrastructure-Service-Provider/Afghanistan-Infrastructure-Service-Provider.pdf>, accessed 20 February 2014.
49. See Seeking Alpha, 'KBR's CEO Discusses Q4 2011 Results – Earnings Call Transcript', 23 February 2012, <http://seekingalpha.com/article/387651-kbr-s-ceo-discusses-q4-2011-results-earnings-call-transcript>, accessed 20 February 2014.
50. See Purple Foodservice Solutions, 'FAQs', <http://www.purplefoodservicesolutions.com/faqs.htm>, accessed 20 February 2014.
51. See Purple Foodservice Solutions, 'Purple Foodservice News', <http://www.purplefoodservicesolutions.com/purple-foodservice-news.htm>, accessed 20 February 2014.
52. Ministry of Defence, 'Contractor Support to Operations (CSO): Policy Overview, Joint Service Publication 567, 5th edition', Defence Council, 2009; Ministry of Defence, 'Contractors on Deployed Operations (CONDO): Processes and Requirements, Defence Standard 05-129, Issue 4', Defence Equipment and Support, 12 March 2010; Ministry of Defence, 'Contractors on Deployed Operations, DEFCON 697, Edition 12/10', 2010.
53. Office of the US Deputy Assistant Secretary of Defense (Program Support), 'Synchronized Predeployment and Operational Tracker – Enterprise Suite', information sheet, <http://www.acq.osd.mil/log/PS/SPOT/TOPSS_About_InfoSheet.pdf>, accessed 15 July 2013.
54. See Office of the US Deputy Assistant Secretary of Defense (Program Support), 'US/UK Force Generation Analysis Sustainment Strategies', p. 7.
55. National Audit Office, 'Performance of the Ministry of Defence 2006–07', p. 17.

56. See RUSI Acquisition Focus Group, 'Acquisition Focus Group and the Defence White Paper', *RUSI Defence Systems* (Vol. 14, No. 3, March 2012).
57. Ministry of Defence, *National Security Through Technology: Technology, Equipment and Support for UK Defence and Security*, Cm 8278 (London: The Stationery Office, February 2012), p. 26.
58. *Ibid.*, p. 23.
59. 'Ellamy – Industry Earns a Pat on the Back', *Desider* (No. 44, January 2012), p. 8, <https://www.gov.uk/government/uploads/system/uploads/attachment_data/file/33820/desider_44_Jan2012.pdf>, accessed 20 February 2014.
60. See, for instance, the statement by Secretary of State for Defence Philip Hammond after the announcement of the chancellor's 2013 spending round: 'The savings that I have agreed will have no impact on military manpower or equipment. Our Armed Forces will continue to be backed by the fourth largest defence budget in the world and a programme of investment in state-of-the-art equipment worth about £160 billion'. The Chief of the Defence Staff, General Sir David Richards, stated on the same occasion: 'Our soldiers, sailors and airmen, backed by state-of-the-art equipment, including new aircraft carriers, hunter-killer submarines, Type 45 destroyers, fifth-generation stealth fighters and a range of armoured vehicles, will provide the UK with a flexible, agile and adaptable force to defend our interests at home and abroad.' See Gov.uk, 'Spending Round 2013 for MOD', 26 June 2013, <https://www.gov.uk/government/news/spending-round-2013>, accessed 20 February 2014.

APPENDIX

Table 1: British Military Fatalities by Service on Selected Operations, 1991–2012.

	Total	Army	RAF	RM	RN
Northern Ireland, 1991–2008[1]	28	27	0	0	1
Iraq, 1991[2]	45	38	7	0	0
Iraq, 1991–2003	5	?	?	?	?
Bosnia and Croatia, 1993–2002[3]	59	58	0	1	0
Kosovo, 1999–2004[4]	11	10	1	0	0
Macedonia, 2001[5]	1	1	0	0	0
Sierra Leone, 2000	1	1	0	0	0
Afghanistan, 2001–05[6]	5	5	0	0	0
Iraq, 2003–09[7]	178	137	22	11	8
Afghanistan, 2006–12[8]	433	360	22	50	1
Libya, 2011	1	0	1	0	0

Notes and Sources

General information may be found at: Ministry of Defence, FOI Request 05-08-2013-120915-007, 5 August 2013, <https://www.gov.uk/government/uploads/system/uploads/attachment_data/file/249544/20131010_PUBLIC_00000001_FOI.pdf>.

1. CAIN Project/Malcolm Sutton, 'An Index of Deaths in Northern Ireland', <http://cain.ulst.ac.uk/sutton/>, accessed 12 February 2014.
2. Ministry of Defence; Britain's Small Wars, 'Roll of Honour', <http://britainssmallwars.com/gulf/Roll.html>, accessed 12 February 2014.
3. Ministry of Defence, 'Operations in the Balkans: British Fatalities', <http://webarchive.nationalarchives.gov.uk/20121026065214/http://www.mod.uk/DefenceInternet/FactSheets/OperationsFactsheets/BalkansBritishFatalities.htm>, accessed 12 February 2014.
4. *Ibid.*
5. *Ibid.*
6. DASA, 'Afghanistan Fatality and Casualty Tables', 31 December 2013, <http://www.dasa.mod.uk/index.php/publications/health/operational-casualties/fatality-and-casualty/2013-12-31>; *BBC News*, 'UK Military Deaths in Afghanistan', <http://www.bbc.co.uk/news/uk-10629358>, accessed 12 February 2014.
7. Ministry of Defence, 'Operations in Iraq: British Fatalities', <https://www.gov.uk/government/fields-of-operation/iraq>, accessed 12 February 2014; *BBC News*, 'British Military Deaths in Iraq', <http://www.bbc.co.uk/news/uk-10637526>, accessed 12 February 2014.
8. The total number of fatalities at the time of going to press was 448.

Table 2: Net Additional Cost of Military Operations, 1991–2013, £ millions, 2012/13 prices.

	Granby[2]	Warden[3]	Jural[4]	Driver[5]	Bolton[6]	Desert Fox[7]
1990/91	1,386.7	0.0	0.0	0.0	0.0	0.0
[1]	-852.9	0.0	0.0	0.0	0.0	0.0
1991/92	1,352.4	4.0	0.0	0.0	0.0	0.0
[1]	-2,330.4	0.0	0.0	0.0	0.0	0.0
1992/93	809.9	6.3	7.9	0.0	0.0	0.0
1993/94	242.1	14.0	9.6	-3.5	0.0	0.0
1994/95	62.1	15.1	6.7	0.2	0.0	0.0
1995/96	4.3	8.3	6.6	0.0	0.0	0.0
1996/97	0.0	3.1	5.6	0.0	0.0	0.0
1997/98	1.0	3.2	4.7	0.0	13.0	0.0
1998/99	0.2	4.3	6.9	0.0	31.6	4.1
1999/2000	0.0	0.0	0.0	0.0	0.0	0.0
2000/01	0.0	0.0	0.0	0.0	0.0	0.0
2001/02	0.0	0.0	0.0	0.0	0.0	0.0
2002/03	0.0	0.0	0.0	0.0	0.0	0.0
2003/04	0.0	0.0	0.0	0.0	0.0	0.0
2004/05	0.0	0.0	0.0	0.0	0.0	0.0
2005/06	0.0	0.0	0.0	0.0	0.0	0.0
2006/07	0.0	0.0	0.0	0.0	0.0	0.0
2007/08	0.0	0.0	0.0	0.0	0.0	0.0
2008/09	0.0	0.0	0.0	0.0	0.0	0.0
2009/10	0.0	0.0	0.0	0.0	0.0	0.0
2010/11	0.0	0.0	0.0	0.0	0.0	0.0
2011/12	0.0	0.0	0.0	0.0	0.0	0.0
2012/13	0.0	0.0	0.0	0.0	0.0	0.0
Net Total	675.5	58.3	47.9	-3.3	44.6	4.1

Continued overleaf

Table 2: Net Additional Cost of Military Operations, 1991–2013, £ millions, 2012/13 prices (ctd).

	Various (Gulf)[8]	Telic[9]	Herrick[10]	Kosovo	Bosnia[11]	Oculus (Balkans)[12]
1990/91	0.0	0.0	0.0	0.0	0.0	0.0
[1]	0.0	0.0	0.0	0.0	0.0	0.0
1991/92	0.0	0.0	0.0	0.0	0.0	0.0
[1]	0.0	0.0	0.0	0.0	0.0	0.0
1992/93	0.0	0.0	0.0	0.0	0.0	0.0
1993/94	0.0	0.0	0.0	0.0	111.3	0.0
1994/95	0.0	0.0	0.0	0.0	111.1	0.0
1995/96	0.0	0.0	0.0	0.0	53.4	0.0
1996/97	0.0	0.0	0.0	0.0	0.0	0.0
1997/98	0.0	0.0	0.0	0.0	537.6	0.0
1998/99	0.0	0.0	0.0	19.0	200.9	0.0
1999/2000	37.5	0.0	0.0	435.8	144.7	0.0
2000/01	33.3	0.0	0.0	292.8	159.7	0.0
2001/02	79.0	0.0	286.8	183.8	120.5	0.0
2002/03	57.0	1,073.9	393.2	132.9	102.5	0.0
2003/04	0.0	1,628.0	57.6	0.0	0.0	128.7
2004/05	0.0	1,099.7	81.0	0.0	0.0	105.1
2005/06	0.0	1,136.6	236.6	0.0	0.0	74.8
2006/07	0.0	1,103.2	851.2	0.0	0.0	64.6
2007/08	0.0	1,640.4	1,692.8	0.0	0.0	0.0
2008/09	0.0	1,511.9	2,871.6	0.0	0.0	0.0
2009/10	0.0	365.4	4,070.7	0.0	0.0	0.0
2010/11	0.0	0.0	3,921.5	0.0	0.0	0.0
2011/12	0.0	0.0	3,510.1	0.0	0.0	0.0
2012/13	0.0	0.0	2,673.2	0.0	0.0	0.0
Net Total	206.8	9,559.1	20,646.4	1,064.3	1,541.6	373.2

Appendix

Table 2: Net Additional Cost of Military Operations, 1991–2013, £ millions, 2012/13 prices (ctd).

	Sierra Leone[13]	Macedonia[14]	DRC[15]	Ellamy[16]	Wider Gulf[17]	Newcombe[18]
1990/91	0.0	0.0	0.0	0.0	0.0	0.0
[1]	0.0	0.0	0.0	0.0	0.0	0.0
1991/92	0.0	0.0	0.0	0.0	0.0	0.0
[1]	0.0	0.0	0.0	0.0	0.0	0.0
1992/93	0.0	0.0	0.0	0.0	0.0	0.0
1993/94	0.0	0.0	0.0	0.0	0.0	0.0
1994/95	0.0	0.0	0.0	0.0	0.0	0.0
1995/96	0.0	0.0	0.0	0.0	0.0	0.0
1996/97	0.0	0.0	0.0	0.0	0.0	0.0
1997/98	0.0	0.0	0.0	0.0	0.0	0.0
1998/99	0.0	0.0	0.0	0.0	0.0	0.0
1999/2000	0.0	0.0	0.0	0.0	0.0	0.0
2000/01	22.5	0.0	0.0	0.0	0.0	0.0
2001/02	51.8	0.0	0.0	0.0	0.0	0.0
2002/03	0.0	0.0	0.0	0.0	0.0	0.0
2003/04	1.2	1.2	1.2	0.0	0.0	0.0
2004/05	0.0	0.0	0.0	0.0	0.0	0.0
2005/06	0.0	0.0	0.0	0.0	0.0	0.0
2006/07	0.0	0.0	0.0	0.0	0.0	0.0
2007/08	0.0	0.0	0.0	0.0	0.0	0.0
2008/09	0.0	0.0	0.0	0.0	0.0	0.0
2009/10	0.0	0.0	0.0	0.0	0.0	0.0
2010/11	0.0	0.0	0.0	21.8	131.9	0.0
2011/12	0.0	0.0	0.0	216.2	37.6	0.0
2012/13	0.0	0.0	0.0	0.0	57.3	17.4
Net Total	**75.6**	**1.2**	**1.2**	**238.0**	**226.8**	**17.4**
GRAND TOTAL						**34,778.8**

Source: *Response to a Freedom of Information request to the Defence Resources Secretariat, MoD, accurate as of 24 September 2013. Data for Bosnia 1993/94–95/96 was not included in this response, and is derived from NAO, 'Ministry of Defence: The Financial Management of the Military Operation in the Former Yugoslavia'.*

Note: *The figures between 1990/91 and 2000/01 have been calculated on a cash basis; the figures from 2001/02 onwards have been calculated on a full cost basis following the introduction of the Resource Accounting and Budgeting regime in that year across government.*

Notes and References to Table 2
1. The credits represent burden-sharing cash contributions from other nations.
2. Operation *Granby*: UK military involvement in the Gulf conflict in 1990/91.
3. Operation *Warden*: establishment of a no-fly zone over northern Iraq in 1991, in support of Security Council Resolution 688, to prevent the repression of the civilian population (the Kurds) by the Iraqi regime.
4. Operation *Jural*: establishment of a no-fly zone over southern Iraq in 1992, in support of Security Council Resolution 688, to prevent the repression of the civilian population (the Marsh Arabs) by the Iraqi regime.
5. Operation *Driver*: precautionary deployment of UK ground forces to Kuwait in 1994/95.
6. Operation *Bolton*: deployment of an aircraft carrier and RN/RAF aircraft to the Gulf in 1997/98.
7. Operation *Desert Fox*: joint air strikes with the US over Iraq in December 1998.
8. Gulf: mainly covers the enforcement of the no-fly zones under Operations *Warden* and *Jural*, but no breakdown is available.
9. Operation *Telic*: UK military operations in Iraq between 2003 and 2011.
10. Operation *Herrick*: UK military operations in Afghanistan since 2001.
11. Spending for 1993/94–95/96 derived from NAO figures. We assume that the high figure in 1997/98 includes peak spending on IFOR in 1995/96 and 1996/97.

12. Operation *Oculus*: UK military operations in Bosnia and Kosovo from 2003/04.
13. The allocation to Sierra Leone in 2003/04 reflects the MoD's contribution to an interdepartmental cost-sharing arrangement (the Conflict Pool). This arrangement is only reflected in NACMO for this year.
14. The allocation for Macedonia in 2003/04 reflects a UK contribution to the common costs of the EU's Operation *Concordia*.
15. The allocation for DRC in 2003/04 reflects a UK contribution to the common costs of the EU's Operation *Artemis*.
16. Operation *Ellamy*: UK contribution to coalition operations in Libya in support of UN Security Council Resolution 1973.
17. Wider Gulf: UK forces are deployed to the Gulf to sustain UK influence in the region, reassure regional allies and support. A rather wider definition of NACMO is clearly being used in this case than is otherwise normal, deployment/redeployment access and overflight for operations in Afghanistan. UK forces also contriubute to energy and trade security and support the government's regional counter-terrorism and counter piracy policies.
18. Operation *Newcombe*: UK logistical support to France and contribution to the EU Training Mission.

ABOUT THE AUTHORS

Professor Michael Clarke has been Director General of the Royal United Services Institute since 2007. Prior to that he was Professor of Defence Studies at King's College London and Deputy Vice Principal responsible for research development. He is now a Visiting Professor at KCL and at the University of Exeter. He has served as Specialist Adviser to the House of Commons Foreign Affairs Committee in 1994–95 and then to the Defence Committee since 1997. He was appointed to the Prime Minister's National Security Forum in 2008 and to the Chief of the Defence Staff's Strategic Advisory Panel in 2010.

Professor Malcolm Chalmers is Research Director and Director (UK Defence Policy) at RUSI. He is a Special Adviser to the UK Parliament's Joint Committee on the National Security Strategy, and was a member of the MoD's Advisory Forum for the 2010 Defence Green Paper. He was previously a Special Adviser to Foreign Secretaries Jack Straw MP and Margaret Beckett MP. His recent publications have included papers on UK defence strategy and priorities, defence economics, nuclear arms control and the Scottish question.

Michael Codner is a Senior Research Fellow in Military Sciences at the Royal United Services Institute. His research includes defence policy, strategic theory, the future security environment, missile defence, military ethics, and multinational military interoperability including the Franco-British relationship. He lectures at British and overseas universities and military staff colleges. As a Royal Navy Seaman Commander he was a Lecturer at the US Naval War College and a Defence Fellow at King's College London. He studied philosophy and psychology at Brasenose College, Oxford University. His written work includes strategic doctrine for the Royal Navy and many papers, articles, and book chapters.

Dr Jonathan Eyal is RUSI's International Director and Editor of the *RUSI Newsbrief*. He was born in Romania, but has lived most of his life in Britain. Educated at Oxford and London Universities, his initial training was in international law and relations. He has written extensively about European defence matters and was a leading commentator on the Yugoslav wars of secession during the 1990s. He has acted as an adviser to the European Union's studies on the process of dividing the assets of the former Yugoslav state, and has published two studies on the errors committed by the West in handling the Balkan conflicts, and the broader security relationship with Russia.

Lieutenant General Sir Robert Fry KCB CBE is a Trustee of the Royal United Services Institute. After a military career that included posts as Commandant General of the Royal Marines and Director of Operations in the Ministry of Defence, Sir Robert is chairman of Albany Associates and an advisor to a number of other companies in the security, communications and banking sectors. He is a visiting professor at the University of Reading and an occasional columnist for *Prospect* magazine; he is also a trustee of Help for Heroes.

Dr Henrik Heidenkamp is a Research Fellow in the RUSI Defence, Industries and Society Programme. His current research interests are the role of the private sector in defence, national and international defence management approaches and contemporary aspects of European and international security and defence policy. Henrik is also a lecturer, consultant and frequent media commentator on European security and defence industrial policy (*Bloomberg*, *Wall Street Journal*, *New York Times*, *Economic Times*, *Reuters* and other outlets). Prior to joining RUSI, Henrik worked as a post-doctoral fellow for the Centre for International Relations at Queen's University, Ontario as well as for the military policy branch of the German Ministry of Defence in Berlin.

Adrian L Johnson is Director of Publications and a Research Fellow at RUSI. He is chair of the RUSI editorial board and is the book reviews editor for the *RUSI Journal*. Adrian is a co-editor of the Whitehall Reports 'Short War, Long Shadow: The Political and Military Legacies of the 2011 Libya Campaign' (2012) and 'Hitting the Target? How New Capabilities are Shaping International Intervention' (2013). His research focuses on international intervention, peace-building and United Nations peace operations. Adrian is also a co-author of *Decade* (Phaidon Press: 2010).

Professor John Louth is a Senior Research Fellow and Director of the Defence, Industries and Society Programme at RUSI. As a young man he was an officer in the RAF and later, as a consultant, audited the governance of the UK strategic deterrent. He spent part of his business career in the Middle East developing defence capabilities across a number of Gulf countries. Professor Louth teaches at the University of Roehampton Business School and is a specialist adviser to the House of Commons Defence Select Committee. He is a non-executive adviser to NDI Ltd.

Professor Sir David Omand GCB is a Visiting Professor at the War Studies Department, King's College London. He was appointed in 2002 the first UK Security and Intelligence Coordinator, responsible to the Prime Minister for the professional health of the intelligence community, national counter-terrorism strategy and 'homeland security'. He was Permanent Secretary of the Home Office from 1997 to 2000, and before that Director of GCHQ, the UK's signals intelligence and cybersecurity organisation. Previously, in the Ministry of Defence he served as Deputy Under Secretary of State for Policy, Principal Private Secretary to the Defence Secretary, and served for three years in Brussels as UK Defence Counsellor to NATO. He is the Senior Independent Director of Babcock International Group Plc, a Non-Executive Director of Finmeccanica UK Ltd, and is a Trustee of the Natural History Museum, London. His book, *Securing the State* (Hurst) is now in paperback.

Dr Joel Faulkner Rogers is the Academic Director at YouGov and an Associate Fellow of the Royal United Services Institute, where his research is focused on foreign policy and public opinion. He was previously a Research Fellow on the Donner Atlantic Studies Programme at Cambridge University and a ghost-writer in Washington, where he produced books, speeches and papers on subjects including US–China relations, the rise of state capitalism and military intervention after Soviet collapse in the Balkans, Afghanistan and Iraq.

Professor Trevor Taylor is Professorial Research Fellow in Defence Management at RUSI, where he co-directs the Defence, Industries and Society Programme. In addition, he is Professor Emeritus at Cranfield University, where he still teaches, and where he was head of the Department of Defence Management and Security Analysis from 1997 to 2009. He also works regularly for the Naval Postgraduate School in Monterey. His career has linked the academic sphere with that of governmental and industrial professionals in defence, and he speaks and writes regularly at conferences on defence acquisition. He has been elected both as Chairman of the British International Studies Association and as a member the Council of the (former) Defence Manufacturers Association.